Real Jews

Real Jews

Secular Versus Ultra-Orthodox

and the Struggle for Jewish

Identity in Israel

NOAH J. EFRON

BASIC
BOOKS

A Member of the Perseus Books Group
New York

Designed by Lisa Kreinbrink
Set in 11-point Minion text

Library of Congress Cataloging-in-Publication Data
Efron, Noah J.
    Real Jews : secular versus ultra-Orthodox and the struggle for Jewish
identity in Israel / Noah Efron.
        p.   cm.
    Includes bibliographical references and index.
    ISBN 0–465–01854–8
    1. Orthodox Judaism—Israel.   2. Ultra-Orthodox Jews—Israel.
3. Orthodox Judaism—Relations—Nontraditional Jews.   4. Secularism—
Israel.   5. Jews—Israel—Identity.   6. Judaism and state—Israel.
7. Israel—Politics and government.   8. Israel—Social conditions.   I. Title.

BM390.E34   2003
305.6'9605694—dc21
                                                                2002156216

        03   04   05 / 10   9   8   7   6   5   4   3   2   1

Contents

To Dvora and Ben Efron, who lived *Yiddishkayt*,

And to Rosalyn and Herman Efron, who live *mentshlekhkayt*.

It must be absolutely clear to us that we have two paths to choose in Palestine. . . . Let each man choose whichever of the two ways he will, but let him know for certain that the choice of one forever excludes the other.
—A. D. Gordon, "Some Observations," 1911

Aeneas: We know each other well.
Diomedes: We do, and long to know
each other worse.
—William Shakespeare, *Troilus and Cressida*, 1609

We praise a man who feels angry on the right grounds and against the right persons and also in the right manner at the right moment and for the right length of time.
—Aristotle, *The Nicomachean Ethics*, ca. 340 B.C.E.

The ability of Jews to internalize any critical and condemnatory remark and castigate themselves is one of the marvels of human nature.
—Aharon Appelfeld, to Philip Roth, 1988

Every country has the Jews that it deserves.
—Karl Emil Franzos, *The Jews of Barnow*, 1877

Preface

The weeks leading up to the January 2003 election in Israel were dreadful. Everything was wrong. On New Year's Day, the twenty-four-hour bodega across the street from my apartment started selling, alongside the pints of Ben & Jerry's and magnums of Moët et Chandon, industry-size rolls of plastic sheeting and six-packs of strapping tape, to seal off windows and doors in case of attack by Iraq. The Ministry of Health instructed citizens to buy and stow eleven liters of bottled water a head. The municipality of Ramat Gan, near Tel Aviv, distributed dozens of tranquilizer guns to police and fire fighters, fearing that wild lions and tigers would take to the streets of the city should the retaining wall of the tourist "animal safari" be breached by incoming missiles. My wife, like all other physicians, was inoculated against smallpox, but a week later someone leaked to the papers a secret report concluding that the vaccine had been poorly prepared and might not work. Ads appeared in the papers offering reserved spaces on flights out of the country, for a nonrefundable reservation fee of $50 to $100. A full-page advertisement for emergency lights ran in a Tel Aviv weekly under the forty-point-type headline, "Did you know that a candle can use up valuable air in a sealed room?" Newspapers published stories about when and when not to administer the intravenous doses of atropine that all citizens had been issued along with gas masks. The army opened distribution centers for new gas masks, keeping some of the centers open all night, but the wait for a new gas mask could still extend for three or four hours.

My growing hysteria about an attack by Iraq complemented nicely my panic about Palestinian suicide bombers. Three weeks before the election, I was buying a shutter release in a camera store in the photography district on a grimy Tel Aviv street called Allenby, when the man behind the counter asked, "What was that sound?" I thought it was a sonic boom, and a moment later there was another. Biking home, I heard radio reports wafting out of sidewalk cafés, describing a dual suicide bombing at the old bus station that left twenty-three dead and a hundred-odd wounded. Israeli etiquette demands a certain stoicism about such bombings, but as time goes on, whatever stoicism I evince is phony. I don't ride public buses anymore, because every scruffy man with a bulky coat has come to look like a suicide bomber to me, and even on the chilliest winter day, by the time I reach my stop, I am damp with anxious sweat.

Fear was not the main thing, though. The weeks leading up to the election were distinguished less by danger than decay. The process hastily organized by Likud in December to select the party's Knesset candidates produced a great number of scandals. Candidates were chosen by the 2,940 members of the party's Central Committee according to a complicated calculus, a system that lent itself to bribery and vote buying. The eleventh slot on the party list was secured by a twenty-seven-year-old waitress, Inbal Gavrielli, whose father and uncle are restaurateurs whose family became wealthy by investing in gambling establishments abroad and who some suspect have Mafia connections. In the weeks leading up to the Central Committee elections, the Gavrielli family hosted hundreds of Likud activists in their restaurants, shmoozing them with merlot and superior cuts of beef. Days after the voting, police questioned the woman who secured the ninth position on the party list, Deputy National Infrastructure Minister Naomi Blumenthal, whom they suspected of renting hotel rooms in the five-star Sheraton City Towers for Central Committee members the night before the vote. Footing expensive hotel bills, investigators were persuaded, is a form of bribery. When Blumenthal refused to cooperate with the police investigators, exercising her right to remain silent, Sharon fired her from the Ministry of Infrastructure, but she remained a top Likud candidate for the next Knesset. Dozens of other Likud activists were also suspected of bribing Central Committee voters with cash and favors. Some set themselves up as "vote contractors," offering candidates blocks of votes on a cash-per-head basis, with volume discounts. The sums that transferred hands were small, but it was widely suspected that even these small sums significantly altered the results of the election. Many also feared that candidates exploited connections with organized crime to raise cash needed for buying votes, working up debts to gangsters that would later be paid in political favors. Newspapers editorialized about the frailty of Israel's democracy, pointing to the Likud scandals as mile markers on the road to banana republic–style corruption.

Two weeks before the election, a state's attorney named Liora Glatt-Berkowitz leaked to *Ha'aretz* newspaper that Sharon himself was under investigation for corruption. A year earlier, Sharon had received a $1.5 million loan from an old friend, South African businessman Cyril Kern. The loan served as collateral for a bank loan taken in order to refund campaign contributions illegally funneled to Sharon by a straw company named Annex Research, after these contributions were discovered by the attorney general. Sharon did not report Kern's loan, contrary to the requirement of the law, and the circuitous routing of the funds transfer, from Africa to Europe to the United States and then on to Israel, raised suspicions that perhaps Sharon (or his sons, who were handling this matter for their father) wished to keep it a secret.

Throughout January, each day brought new accusations and revelations of corruption, and the net impact was like that of being pummeled—pain, then disoriented numbness. It was during this period that the Central Elections Committee, headed by Supreme Court Justice Mishael Heshin and staffed by representatives of all the Knesset political parties, voted to bar representatives from two Arab parties from participating in the election, on the grounds that their leaders and party platforms demonstrated antipathy and ill-will toward the State and expressed sympathy for Israel's enemies. Heshin strongly opposed the bans and disparaged them as politically motivated. Leftist politicians went further, characterizing the vote as racist, and a precursor of the collapse of Israeli democracy. The Supreme Court reversed the ban.

It was a shock to register the fragility of Israel's democracy in the weeks before the election, like seeing a grandfather falter and realizing at once how much he has aged, but it was the economy, really, that seemed to be closest to disintegrating before our eyes. Bank ha-Poalim, one of Israel's two largest banks, welcomed 2003 by laying off 900 workers. Tel Aviv University announced that among its plans for reducing its 150 million shekel deficit were dismantling departments and firing one-fourth of its professoriate, including tenured professors. Municipal workers in Tel Aviv agreed to a voluntary cut in pay, rather than suffer mass layoffs. A report issued a week and a half before the election found that in 2003 the number of unemployed in Israel would exceed 300,000. One of four citizens, roughly 1.5 million, would live at or below the poverty line. Half a million children were said to be hungry. Production was dropping steeply, the shekel was plummeting in value against the dollar and the Euro, exports were diminishing, imports increasing. Every economic indicator was negative. Soup kitchens, flop houses, and other charities providing basic services announced that they were exhausted; they could not meet the growing demand for their services. Through much of the 1990s, Israel's was among the world's fastest expanding economies, and Israel's standard of living had increased by 25 percent. Suddenly it was Weimar.

All these problems together produced a general malaise in the month leading up to the election. Pollster Mina Tzemach found in early January that of secular Jews, aged twenty-two to thirty-three, fewer than 60 percent believed that they would be living in Israel in ten years. Of the 40 percent who didn't, many doubted that Israel would exist in another decade.

Which is why it is significant that, amid all this despair, the most successful political campaign of the season was that of the Shinui (Change) party. Shinui won fifteen seats in the Knesset, two and a half times its showing in the 1999 election, making it both the fastest-growing party in Israeli politics and the third-biggest party in the Knesset, just behind the Labor Party, which received nineteen seats. This achievement is still more impressive when one considers that Shinui offered voters no real political platform. The party did not take a clear stand on negotiating (or not) with Arafat, enhancing or dismantling settlements in the occupied territories, or initiating or scrapping welfare programs. Campaign pamphlets offered bromides about the party situating itself "between the destructiveness of the Right and the defeatism of the Left," but such statements were not translated into position papers and policy initiatives. Down my block, the party hung from the roof of the apartment building that houses a storefront BMW dealership (a showroom big enough to hold two sedans and a desk) a two-story-high banner reading, "Shinui: The Party of the Secular and Middle Class." The allusion to the middle class refers to the party's vague commitment to laissez-faire economics that would lower the tax burden of salaried workers. The crucial term on the banner (and the key to Shinui's electoral success) was "secular." Shinui is a one-issue party, dedicated to fighting, as their bumper stickers put it, "against religious coercion." One sure sign that Shinui is a one-issue party is the fact that its leader, Joseph (Tommy) Lapid, emphasized at every campaign stop that Shinui is *not* a one-issue party, but never seemed to persuade any of his constituents of this. It hardly mattered, because Shinui's issue—"putting an end to the usurious exploitation of the State's coffers for religious purposes" by the ultra-Orthodox, as the party's statement of principles had it—resonated with voters. I accompanied Lapid on a midnight barnstorm of Tel Aviv bars and dance clubs a week and a half before the election. In one smoky room after another, drunken Gen-Xers rose to clap Lapid on the back and scream over pounding techno music, "Kol ha-kavod, Tommy" (Way to go, Tommy). These were Lapid's hard-core constituents, secular young men and women who serve in the army while saving to buy a plasma screen high-density television. "Zayen otam, Tommy" (Fuck them, Tommy), one of them yelled, encouraging Lapid to give the ultra-Orthodox hell. To many secular Israelis, especially the young,

Lapid is a hero, their Martin Luther King, Jr., and his dream is their dream, that someday on the arid hills of Judaea, the sons of former rabbis and the sons of former radicals will cruise bars together on Shabbes.

That the ultra-Orthodox should emerge as the most potent electoral issue of the campaign, amid war, corruption, and poverty, may be puzzling to those who do not follow the minutia of Israeli politics. It is hard to see, at first, why this issue matters more than so many other pressing issues. It is like waking to find the house is on fire, rushing about to save what's most important, and finally fleeing to safety clutching the waffle iron. Can *that* really be what matters?

For many, it is. Everyone knows that Israel is engaged in a brutish war with the Palestinians, one that Ariel Sharon once characterized as "the final chapter of Israel's long war of independence." Within Israel, another battle has been declared. It is sometimes called a Kulturkampf, a culture war, sometimes a civil war, sometimes a war over the character of the State, sometimes, as one activist described it to me, the war of light against darkness. It is the battle between secular Israelis and very religious, or ultra-Orthodox, Israelis. Incredibly, almost one of every three voters casts a ballot in support of either a religious party or a party devoted to fighting the religious. Shinui is so popular because its leaders understand that this battle concerns Israelis just as much as the battle against the Palestinians does. Shinui hoists the secular standard with brio. And Tommy Lapid is to his war what Arik Sharon is to his—an uncompromising old warhorse, a tough let-'em-eat-hot-lead sort of leader in a crisis.

Of course, there are many other reasons for Shinui's extraordinary success in the January election. The political scandals in the Likud left voters searching for alternatives, and Lapid's straight-talking demeanor suggested appealing integrity. Likud's early lock on the election—from the start of the campaign there was never a moment when Sharon's reelection was not certain—also allowed voters to stray from their traditional party affiliations. And discomfort with the choice between a Likud that might compromise too little and a Labor that might compromise too much led some people to prefer a party whose positions on the subject were vague and fungible. Still, the greatest part of Shinui's success must be attributed to the power of their simple message: It's us or the ultra-Orthodox, and we will defeat them before they defeat us.

In fact, the simplicity of the message obscures the complexity of religious observance in Israel. On close examination, it turns out that Shinui's binary typology is too rigid; there is no monolithic "us" or "them." Most obviously, as Lapid himself recognizes, there are hundreds of thousands of observant Orthodox Jews who view themselves as modern, productive citizens. (The campaign slogan of their political party, the National Religious Party, was "Army *and* Faith," emphasizing that in contrast to the ultra-Orthodox, their ilk serve enthusiastically in the Israel Defense Forces, the IDF.) Then there are thousands of Reform and Conservative Jews, who tend to despise the ultra-Orthodox with a passion that matches Lapid's, but who are themselves not exactly secular. And then there are hundreds of thousands, perhaps millions, of Israelis who call themselves *traditional*, meaning that they are not quite secular, but also that they are not quite religious.

And among the ultra-Orthodox, the "them," there are also important distinctions that Shinui's schema overlooks. Some ultra-Orthodox are anti-Zionist, some are non-Zionist, and some are Zionist. Some proselytize and some don't. Some embrace tokens of modernity, computers and televisions and the like, and some reject them. Scholars of ultra-Orthodoxy describe in learned monographs fractured, decentralized, highly heterogeneous subcultures among the very religious in Israel. All of this nuance is lost in the us-versus-them of the religious war and in the rhetoric of its popular shock troops, like Shinui.

In writing this book I have not tried to describe this nuance (others have already written of ultra-Orthodox society with wisdom and authority), but I have instead tried to learn why this nuance is so utterly invisible. The book was written before the 2003 election, and though as a result of that election, the number of ultra-Orthodox Knesset members has declined somewhat and the number of anti-ultra-Orthodox Knesset members has grown, the basic questions have remained unchanged. Why do the ultra-Orthodox seem like an undifferentiated horde to so many of the rest of us here in Israel? And why—beset by bombs, hunger, and hopelessness—do so many of us see as our primary enemy, as the *real* cause of all our problems, the great mass of men in black?

I am writing only hours after the results of the election were tallied. Coalition negotiations will soon begin. Shinui may or may not persuade Sharon to mount, as it hopes, the first "secular government of national unity" in Israel's history, blocking the ultra-Orthodox parties from power and radically reducing their funding and influence. However the politics play out this time, Israel's *other* war is now irrevocably, probably tragically, under way.

NOAH J. EFRON
TEL AVIV
JANUARY 29, 2003

Acknowledgments

Many people helped me write this book, in many different ways. I have the excellent fortune to work shoulder to shoulder with extraordinary scholars, whose insight is outdone only by their generosity. Professor Menachem Friedman is the world's leading authority on the ultra-Orthodox, and he managed to save me months of floundering research in short happenstance conversations on the sidewalk outside the library or in the cafeteria. As usual, Professor Avi Sagi understood what I was trying to do well before I did myself, and he sent me scurrying to the library to make up the difference. Professor Eva Etzioni-Halevy, who has written beautifully about tensions between religious and secular Jews in Israel, also gave me a short course on the subject at a crucial stage in my own work. Professors Dafna Yisraeli and Dov Schwartz have also influenced me perhaps more than they could realize, in small ways and large.

Several people read some or all of this book while I was writing or editing it, and then corrected, challenged, and cajoled. Criticism of this sort is a high form of charity, especially when alchemized, as it was, with kindness and encouragement. The book is certainly better for the battering. For this I thank Amy Brinn, Herman Efron, Rosalyn Efron, Rachel Efron, Miriam Erez, Don Futterman, Audrey Kasten, Helen Plotkin, Michael Schacter, Rich Schuldenfrei, Emily Silverman, Hillel Wachs, and

Charlie Yawitz. Bill Slott, Michael Field, and Marshall Brinn were particularly dedicated and discerning readers, and traces of their urbane wisdom vein the book. The sensitive responses of Rabbi Michael Lerner, editor of *Tikkun*, and Leo Haber, editor of *Midstream*, to earlier essays about the ultra-Orthodox I wrote for their magazine led me to think about things with greater clarity and sophistication. I also am grateful to them for allowing me to reproduce sections of those essays.

Many more people helped me gather information for this book and make sense of what I learned. Among them are Jay Abramoff, Rabbi Yitzhak Adlerstein, Uri Avneri, Harvey Blume, Aaron Beck, Rabbi Ehud Bandel, Lihi Belfer, Itai Ben-Horin, Jeremy Benstein, Eran Binyamini, Tamara Coffman-Wittes, Vered Dar, Marav Datan, Rebecca Doctors, Ruth Ebenstein, Adam Efron, Betty Fehr, Marilyn Feit, Rachel Feit, Jonathan Ferziger, Adam Ferziger, Ofer Feirstein, Gal Fisher, Yakov Garb, Yizhak Gertel, Yizhak Ginzburg, Tal Golan, William Grassie, Mattis Greenblatt, Richard Gussow, Moshe Halevi, Rabbi David Hartman, Miriam Herschlag, Shai Horowitz, Shahar Ilan, Nahum Karlinsky, Merav Katz, Ofira Krakova, Gordon Lafer, MK Joseph Lapid, Meir Lapid, Reuven Lerner, Adam Lefstein, Shimon Levy, Tal Littman, Yaron London, Dina Mardell, Don Mahler, Sofia Mahler, David Mirchin, Leslie Mirchin, Naftali Moses, Boaz Nul, Stella Padeh, the late Yair Parag, MK Yosef Paritzky, Dan Perry, Gili Pliskin, Naomi Ragen, Rabbi Einat Ramon, Vardit Ravitsky, Rabbi Uri Regev, Yisrael Rosenfield, Yifat Rosenman, Becky Rowe, David Sandberg, Abby Schacter, Moshe Schecter, Becky Schlisselberg, Eilon Schwartz, Leo Schwartz, Rob Schwartz, Hananel Serri, Tom Sgouros, Anita Shapira, Yair Sheleg, Emily Silverman, Mark Silverman, Evelyn Simha, Mark Steiner, MK Yuval Steinitz, David Strassman, Alon Tal, Dorit Tanay, Debbie Taylor-Zimelman, Theo Theoharis, Gil Troy, Dan Urian, Andrea Warchaizer, Shalom Wasserman, Osnat Weider, Debra Weismann, Daniel Weitzner, Rabbi Eric Wittstein, Oshrit Yikneh, Anat Yisrael, Victor Zachut, Ariel Zimmerman, Tsvi Zohar, Noam Zohar, and Dalia Zomer. Phyllis and Stanley Warchaizer offered abundant encouragement, even when they thought that, as with a renaissance cathedral, none of us would live to see the completion of this book. I am grateful for this and much more. My students helped me in many ways, from e-mailing torrents of relevant newspaper articles, caricatures, and photographs that might otherwise have escaped my attention, to challenging pretty much every conclusion I reached. I am grateful for the constant, smart disputation, and the lovely desire to lend a hand. I am also in debt to (and some awe of) the librarians of Widener, Houghton, Hayden, Butler, Sorasky, and Wurzweiler Libraries, the Jewish National and University Library in Jerusalem, and the Central Zionist Archives. I would also like to thank Reuven Kupler, the photo curator of the Zionist Archive, who helped search for photographs to illustrate my story, and Bernard Fisher, who kept me up to my chin in ultra-Orthodox newspapers. I am also grateful to the Israel Cartoonists Union, and the editors of its magazine, *Shpitz*, for graciously allowing me to reproduce political cartoons and caricatures. I am grateful too to Moshe Halevi (Halemo), Dan Mahler, and photographer David Rubinger, for allowing me to use their illustrations and photos.

In the front row center of my pantheon, you will find a likeness of Rick Balkin. He skillfully did everything one hopes a literary agent will do, and then did much more that I never dreamed of. He patiently explained (and inevitably explained *again* and *again*) the technicalities of writing a book. Then he sparked a discussion about the content of the book, displaying great wisdom and often leading me to new insight. Discussing his reactions and suggestions to what I wrote and what I was planning to write was one of my greatest pleasures, all the greater for being so unexpected. He is one part big brother, one part mentor, one part oracle, and I know how lucky I am to call him a friend.

Just over from Rick in my pantheon is Sarah McNally, my editor at Basic Books. There is barely a paragraph here that she didn't improve, and if there is anyone who can convey criticism with greater charm and gentility, I haven't met her. Though the historical record says nothing about it, I imagine that Plato's editor was like Sarah, though probably less winning. Again, I recognize my good fortune, knock wood. The others at Basic Books who have helped me—Don Fehr, who was my editor until he moved to the Smithsonian Institutions Press (and suggested the title of the book), John Hughes, Elizabeth Tzetzo, John Sherer, Jamie Brickhouse, Kay Mariea, and Joanna Pinsker—also beguiled me with their competence, wit, and intelligence. Marian Safran, my copy editor, used her extraordinary erudition to save me from my excesses and sporadic illiteracy. It's as though the whole damn publishing house was written by Aaron Sorkin.

This book owes a great deal to two men who may not immediately see how much they contributed. Rich Schuldenfrei, a mentor at Swarthmore and a friend since, taught me how to worry, but constructively. The anxieties I acquired from him—my nervous wish to make some sense out of my life, and my dispirited certainty that this is no easy task—are what sparked this book (and most everything else I've done). In writing this book, I was trying to answer questions that he taught me to ask twenty years ago. Menachem Fisch, a mentor at Tel Aviv University and a friend since, taught me by example how to make sense of groups by taking seriously, and striving to understand, the questions and problems that move individuals. Each man's genius is inseparable from his extraordinary decency; in fact both are geniuses at *being* decent. As it happens, I don't think a thought crosses my mind that does not carry their imprint. The way I experience the world was in large part fashioned by them, and there are no words to thank someone for a gift as great as that.

That praise is not to say that I was an unformed lump of clay when my formal philosophical education began. My earliest memories are of books and convictions. My father, Herman Efron, is a contrarian with moral passion of biblical dimensions, and I think it was because of him that I grew up believing that snapping a newspaper shut in disgust is just the way you are *supposed* to read it. When I write or speak, I do so in a voice that my mother, Rosalyn Efron, nurtured through her patience, encouragement, and example. As a kid, when I visited the school where she taught, teachers and children would tell me how lucky I was to have her for a mother. They didn't know the half of it. So it is a biological fact that I owe my mother and father everything, but it is just as much a simple emotional and ethical fact as well.

Finally, I'd like to thank two women and two children. Rachel Efron, my sister, taught me most of what I know about how to listen and how to appreciate people who are different from me. Compared to her I remain autistic, but the best moments in the interviews behind this book were those in which, for a short spell, I came closest to being like her. It is disappointing that I am not more like her all the time, but at least I have the great good fortune that *she* is so much like her, and she's *my* sister.

It was Susan Warchaizer, my wife, who gently jostled me in the first place into writing this book. Because nothing I see or do seems entirely real to me until she knows about it, she was part of the writing well before I wrote a word. When I finally did write, she read each word, handing back drafts hacked and hatch-marked with her brilliant, micrographic, physician's scrawl. But her unpaid labor is a small part of her contribution. The greater part has been making our home into a place of joy, laughter, love, passion, debate, surprise, and creativity.

Dara and Micha, my children, also contribute a great share to this. By being who they are, they make me at once more contented with my lot than I thought possible, and more dejected about what goes on beyond the walls of our little apartment. I wish that I could improve their world a small fraction of how much they've improved mine. That's a vain hope, but the sheer pleasure of them offers ample compensation.

Introduction

A fixation led me to write this book. It originated at a precise moment: 3 P.M. on Tuesday, January 29, 1991, while I was waiting in line for coffee at the cafeteria of the Tel Aviv University humanities building. I jotted a note to myself at the time, but even if I hadn't, I'd still remember the date, time, and place. It was a poignant moment at an overwrought time, and it made an impression.

It had been a strange autumn. I had not yet abandoned the lunatic hope of finishing two doctorates in two fields of study at two universities. This arrangement created economies of scale in procrastination: Having two dissertations to complete freed me to write nothing at all. I threw myself into teaching a course on Zionist philosophy and swung between a manic sort of depression and a depressed sort of mania, drinking cup after cup of coffee and staying up nights reading Max Nordau and Friedrich Nietzsche.

Beyond my own study, things were happening. Iraqi soldiers had invaded Kuwait the summer before, and throughout the fall American and European negotiators failed and failed again to persuade Saddam Hussein to withdraw his troops. Israeli analysts were quick to predict war, and as the weeks passed, this prediction grew first more plausible, then more inevitable. By the end of November, the UN Security Council had issued an ultimatum: Either Iraq would quit Kuwait by January 15, 1992, or a consortium of armies would attack and force the Iraqis out.

Deadlines passed and negotiations failed. In December, Saddam Hussein threatened for the first time to launch Scud missiles with chemical warheads on Tel Aviv. The army distributed gas masks. All around, it seemed, an atmosphere of anticipation prevailed. Half an hour was added to the nightly news, the extra time given to pundits hypothesizing and prognosticating. Newspapers added pull-out sections, describing pedantically the chain of command in Iraq's Revolutionary Guard, the architecture of Saddam's bunkers, and the clockwork technology of American smart bombs.

It was lovely.

In normal times, life in Israel has a quotidian brutality. People tend to be excitable. Salesmen, waiters, clerks, and cab drivers are as likely as not to harass you when you seek their services: Here, the customer is *not* always right. Strangers give advice—insistently, infuriatingly—about every imaginable thing: Your child isn't dressed warmly, your hair is mussed, the book you're reading isn't worth the effort, anything. (A popular joke: Why won't Israelis have sex in public? Because a crowd would gather to tell them what they're doing wrong.) The overall feeling is that people are constantly in your face, and the guff and gruffness wear you down.

In the months leading up to the Gulf War, things were different. Sociologists report that employees in offices on high floors are more likely to have affairs; they hypothesize that the altitude and the atavistic sense of danger that goes with it keeps these workers always in an excited state. That fall, Israel was slightly giddy. Strangers spoke affably on street corners, exchanging predictions and good wishes. Politicians of all ideologies conspicuously supported Prime Minister Yizhak Shamir's policy of restraint, keeping a low profile, and not scuttling the efforts of George Bush and Jim Baker to forge a coalition that included Saudi Arabia, Egypt, and other Arab countries. For once, the entire world seemed to be on the same side as the Jews.

On the night of January 16, when Marlin Fitzwater memorably announced that "the liberation of Kuwait has begun," the esprit de corps in Israel was beautiful. Just after the bombing started, I forgot to bring my wallet when I went to the corner market for provisions, and the tiny, ancient woman behind the counter said, "Oh, that's alright. You don't need to pay." We were a tribe.

The missiles brought their own rituals. Each of us had to seal off a room in our homes by taping plastic sheeting over the windows. When the sirens went off, warning that missiles would land in three or four minutes, we were instructed to go into the sealed room, tape the door shut behind us, put on our gas masks, and tune in the radio or turn on television. Ten minutes later, we'd receive the all-clear signal from the genial army spokesman, Nahman Shai. The sirens made a million hearts skip at once, and the all-clear was met with a million sighs of relief. More than a religious ritual ever could, Saddam's Scuds had unified a country. On the third day of the war, I was in a department store when the sirens went off. I crowded into the store manager's office with the saleswomen and the other customers, all of us in gas masks. When the all-clear signal came, the manager produced bottles of single malt, and we passed them around in cheery relief.

The controversy that shattered this odd solidarity concerned the gas masks. Army ordinance supplied several sorts. Infants received collapsible polyurethane boxes fitted with air filters; when the missiles were fired, parents stuffed their babies into these boxes and sealed them. Young children and adults with breathing problems received masks with motorized fans that propelled air through a filter. Older children and adults received standard "passive" masks, in which air is drawn through a filter by the suction created by inhalation itself.

In order to work, a passive mask has to sit flush on the chin, cheeks, temple, and forehead. If the rubber doesn't fit snugly enough against the skin to make a seal, then one draws air in through the sides of the mask instead of through the filter, defeating the purpose of the mask. Passive masks do not work for men with beards, and the army advised them to shave their faces clean.

This was fine for most Israeli men,* but it posed a dilemma for many ultra-Orthodox men who—based on an interpretation of a biblical injunction to grow the hair "on the corners of your face"—believe that shaving is proscribed. Though the official rabbinate quickly published a religious opinion permitting shaving in case of attack (on the principle that saving lives overrules ritual obligations), many Haredi (ultra-Orthodox) rabbis were more hesitant. They lobbied hard for the army to distribute masks with fans, the kind given to children and asthmatics, which would work for bearded men as well.

There were two difficulties with this proposal. First, masks with pumps are more than twice as expensive as passive masks. Providing every ultra-Orthodox male with a motorized mask would cost hundreds of thousands of dollars. Second, there were apparently too few motorized masks to go around. Not all the children or sick adults had received them yet. To distribute these masks to healthy men who refused to shave was to delay or deny giving them to people who quite simply could not breathe without them.

---

*That's what we thought at the time. After the war, we learned that most of the masks distributed would have been ineffective against the gas attack that Saddam had threatened.

On January 28, an army spokesman announced that the ultra-Orthodox would receive the expensive masks. The public outcry was quick and vicious. Member of Knesset (MK) Avraham Burg of the Labor Party (later the speaker of the Knesset) demanded that Defense Minister Moshe Arens intervene, preventing distribution to the ultra-Orthodox. "Malingerers—who are willing to rob the sick and the young of gas masks just so they won't have to shave their beards—should be put at the end of the queue," Burg said. Israel's self-styled intellectual newspaper, *Ha'aretz* ("the paper for people who think," according to its ads), surveyed people in the streets about why the ultra-Orthodox wanted the masks in the first place. Some attributed it to greed: "Anything that's valuable in this country, they want it." Others to immaturity: "They are just like children, so they want the masks that children get."

Waiting in line for espresso in the university cafeteria that Tuesday afternoon, I overheard two students discussing the "scandal," as they called it, of the gas masks. One offered: "The best thing for the country would be if there was a chemical attack in [the ultra-Orthodox city of] Bnei Brak now, before they get new masks. That would get rid of them all at once." The other said that it would be "amusing" to forcibly shave the beards off all the "little Jews."

This snapped me to attention. Held down and shaved against their will? Gassed? I didn't know these women, but students at Tel Aviv University tend to be an urbane, cultured bunch. Most are proud of their liberal-left politics. When Noam Chomsky (whose leftist credentials are about as unassailable as V. I. Lenin's) came to lecture some years later, he filled the largest room on the campus, and during the question period was flummoxed to find himself attacked from the Left, as a dupe of Zionist propaganda. ("You claimed that Israel was a pawn of Western, especially American, imperialism—perhaps you have been fooled by Zionist misinformation to underestimate the extent of Israel's own expansionist aims.") Tel Aviv University is ground zero for what right-wingers here call *yefei nefesh*, literally "the beautiful of soul," which is the local way of saying "bleeding hearts." Held and shaved? Gassed? One would never hear such casual malevolence toward the Palestinians in the cafeteria line.

Once I had noticed this ill-will toward Haredim (ultra-Orthodox Jews), other examples of it cropped up everywhere. Soon after the war, I flew El Al to the United States. I was squeezing back from the bathroom through a crowd of ultra-Orthodox Jews noisily praying in front of the emergency exit, when a flight attendant caught my eye and, smiling slyly, whispered in Hebrew, "You open the door, I'll push." I smiled back and found my seat.

In October 1994, a Palestinian with a briefcase of explosives detonated himself on the Number 5 bus on Tel Aviv's main drag, Dizengoff Street. The explosion sounded loud in my apartment three blocks away, and the percussion shook our building. The charge ripped the roof off the bus, and the shrapnel and the flames killed ten people. Storefronts within a city block shattered. Bits of seared flesh were heaved hundreds of feet. When I passed several hours later, the charred skeleton of the bus rested on the sidewalk. A knot of onlookers shuffled in the street, some quietly sobbing. A makeshift memorial of candles and flowers was already in place at the foot of a tree trunk that the explosion had stripped of all its branches. The wounded were in emergency rooms across the city, and the dead were already being prepared for burial. A handful of ultra-Orthodox Jews, each holding a plastic bag, pushed through the crowd. They had come to collect shreds of human remains from the street, trees, gutters, stores, and rooftops, so that these fragments too could receive a proper burial according to Jewish law. They worked for many hours, collecting lumps of flesh, later analyzing them to determine whose flesh they were.

These men belong to a loosely affiliated organization called "Chesed shel Emet" (True Righteousness), which provides a training course, including hours of videos of mutilated bodies in order to desensitize the volunteers and exercises with practice dummies. For Rabbi Elazar Gelbstein, the director of Chesed shel Emet, terrorist attacks like the one in Tel Aviv, and the gruesome work left in their wake, are "what makes us a Jewish nation, this type of experience that doesn't differentiate between us" religious and secular Jews. He was perhaps naïve. As I watched from the charred sidewalk on Dizengoff, secular Jews raged at the religious ones, shouting that they should be ashamed of themselves, and that the ultra-Orthodox had no right to participate in this national tragedy. They accused the religious of enjoying bagging dead secular Jews. They said that the ultra-Orthodox (Haredim) were no better than terrorists themselves. All the while, the men with the bags quietly continued their grim work.

Six months later, I pulled reserve duty that included guarding Beitar, an ultra-Orthodox city hastily erected five years earlier in the Judaean Desert. ("A City of Torah in the Hills of Judaea" is its municipal slogan, emblazoned on flags that fly from every lamppost.) On the first night of Passover, the night of the seder, I found myself riding around the perimeter of the town in the back of a jeep with a gun and night-vision binoculars on my lap, scanning the neighboring hills for infiltrators. About midnight we parked in the town for a break, and before ten minutes had passed, two boys approached, one burdened with a platter of meat, the other with a plate of desserts. They said that their mother had seen us from the window and felt sorry for us. We were welcome to come up and join their seder, one by one, if we were allowed. We took the food greedily, but turned down the invitation. The children lingered, asking us about our guns and whether we also carried knives. Had we ever killed an Arab? When they finally walked away, our driver hissed after them in a stage whisper, "ultra-Orthodox sons of whores."

Once alerted to its existence, I observed enmity toward very religious Jews everywhere in Israel, and it seemed to me that it was growing. Newspapers and magazines print political cartoons and caricatures depicting ultra-Orthodox Jews as vampires, leeches, and apes, sometimes with horrible hooked noses, warts, and stooped backs. Others show them controlling the strings of government from above like a puppeteer, or perched on the backs of secular Jews, who bow under the weight. A letter printed in a Jerusalem weekly called *Kol Ha-Ir,* which comes free with the weekend *Ha'aretz,* caught my eye some years back, and I clipped it:

ISN'T IT ENOUGH?

As a researcher who has worked for many years on the scientific aspects of the symbiotic relations between parasites and their hosts in infectious diseases, it is hard for me not to see a similarity between [that and] what has transpired recently in the halls of the Knesset and in its committees. I will try to explain.

A parasite is generally a living creature which has lost its ability to produce its own food, and therefore it goes to great efforts to procure it, almost at any price, parasitically from its host, be it a plant or an animal. In principle, the parasite, which contributes nothing to the sustenance, well-being or protection of the host, is not at all interested in destroying the host, because, as the saying goes, one oughtn't saw off a branch one is sitting on. Sometimes, though, in the heat of parasitism, the parasite goes too far, and can drive the host to extinction. . . .

This is a call for all who are frightened for the welfare of our country (viz., the host) to protest against not just the various parasites, but especially against those who, for short-sighted opportunistic reasons, cooperate with the parasitic system, those who are sucking the juices out of the country, and may push it to the edge of the abyss. Isn't it enough that we must deal with the enemy forces from the outside, that we let parasites from within dictate to us how we are to be in our own country?

PROF. YIZHAK GINSBURG

Not long after this letter appeared, Yigal Tumarkin, a painter and sculptor of some renown, was indicted for defamation for writing in another local newspaper that "when you see them, you understand why there was a Holocaust, why people don't like Jews." The popular poet, lyricist, and sometime journalist Yonatan Geffen (I sing my three-year-old to sleep each night with songs that he wrote) remarked in an interview at about the same time that soon secular Jews would set forth "with a song on their lips, toward the inevitable battle" with the ultra-Orthodox. Artists, professors, poets—the influential class known here as "men of the spirit"—seemed fixed in an arms race of invective, all aimed at the ultra-Orthodox. But not just them. A study carried out in the summer of 2000 found that 49 percent of Israeli high school students, when asked, said that they "hate the ultra-Orthodox," the same percentage that admitted to hating Arabs.

I cannot help, to a degree, taking this hatred personally. My grandparents—my Bubby and Zaidy—moved to the ultra-Orthodox city of Bnei Brak when I was nine, and lived there until they died. They themselves were very observant Jews, but not ultra-Orthodox. At least I never thought of them as such. However zealous their families may have been in Russia at the start of the century, their fifty years in America had softened their religiosity without diminishing it. My grandmother had left Minkowitz as a child and had grown up in Detroit, where her father worked as a janitor for Ford. His job called for a regular six-day workweek, but he refused to work on Saturday, and eventually he was fired for truancy. Ford was big and disorganized, and he was soon hired by another department, where he worked until he was fired for truancy, only to be hired by another department.

With time, the family moved to Brooklyn, where observance of the Sabbath was less exotic. It was there, eventually, that my grandmother met my grandfather, who some years before had sailed from Slutzk. My grandfather had grown up in Harlem, where his father was a *melamed*, a traditional teacher, who was named after his great uncle, the famous rabbi of Brisk, Joseph Baer Soloveichik, the patriarch of one of the greatest rabbinic dynasties of modern times. In 1889, Soloveichik had damned the Zionists of his day: "They are a new sect like that of [the false messiah] Shabbetai Zevi, may the names of the evil-doers rot." Near the turn of the century, his son, Rabbi Hayyim Soloveichik, found the Zionists an even greater abomination: "Regarding the 'Zionist cult,' . . . is it not their goal to overturn the bases of our religion, and in order to achieve this, to take control of all the Jewish communities? . . . Jews should be careful not to join a venture that threatens their souls and destroys religion." A zealous pedigree.

After my grandparents married, however, they settled into a two-family house on 91st street in Brooklyn—a Jewish neighborhood, but not a religious one. My grandfather became a door-to-door dry goods peddler. It was my grandmother who maintained the standard of religious commitment, spending most of her energy running the "mother's club" of Yeshiva Chaim Berlin, an academy so admired (to this day, in fact) in religious circles that it might be considered the ultra-Orthodox Andover.

To me they were old-world greenhorns, with their Yiddish accents, and "is it good for the Jews?" parochialism, but my grandparents were in their way very American. Though they went for days without laying eyes on a gentile, most of the Jews they lived and worked with were not religious. Even within their Orthodox shul, there was an early-morning Shabbes minyan for men who worked Saturdays. They read the socialist Yiddish daily, the *Forverts,* ignoring its relentless rejection of religion. They were dismayed by the drift away from tradition that they saw all around them, but they never much let on. Live and let live. Theirs was a kinder, gentler religion.

Still, when they retired, and with their Social Security payments finally had the money to move to Israel, my grandparents chose to live among strictly religious Jews in Bnei Brak. As I was a child when they moved, it was in Bnei Brak that I came to know them. And it was because of them that I was a frequent visitor for much of a decade in that ultra-Orthodox city.

To many Israelis, Bnei Brak is fanaticism's heartland. According to an often-repeated rumor, in the late 1970s a motorcyclist was decapitated here when he rode into the wire strung at neck height across Rabbi Akiva Street to keep people from "desecrating the Sabbath" by driving, and that many of the citizens of the city felt he got what he deserved. I have searched years of back issues of newspapers and found no mention of this beheading, but people talk about it still. Whether or not it is historically accurate, for some this anecdote is powerfully symbolic of a callous cruelty born of the zealotry that many Israelis associate with ultra-Orthodoxy. Ultra-Orthodoxy signified a population united in a persuasion that God's law was more important that human life, and that they alone understood God's law.

The Bnei Brak that I knew was different. The city I saw from my grandmother's window was not of a single mind. In her modest apartment building alone, there were people of many different backgrounds and beliefs. The Weinstocks, one flight down, were gentle and open-minded working-class Holocaust survivors; their greatest pride was their daughter and her young children, who were no longer observant. One door over were the Itzkavitzes, a piously observant couple who believed, among other things, that television was an abomination, yet who never criticized the large set prominent in my grandparents' living room. There was Shinansky, an ultra-Orthodox real estate mogul, who in his retirement amassed a huge library of "Torah Tapes"—cassettes of Talmud lessons and the like—which he spent his days trying to lend to whoever would listen. There was Nathanson, whose small apartment was filled with used clothes and other goods he collected to distribute to the needy, taking a small commission himself. There was the *Americaner*, a woman who visited several times a week and complained about the bad treatment she received at the health services clinic. My grandmother, until she became sick, was rarely without a visitor, and if the visitors were as quirky a bunch of Jews as any imagined by Isaac Bashevis Singer, they were also of widely varying casts of mind. And when the conversation came around to secular Jews—as it often did—these characters sighed, heartbroken that so many had abandoned God and *Yiddishkayt*, "Jewishness" ("and so soon after Hitler!" Shinansky despaired), but I never heard a hateful word.

Bnei Brak has *Yiddishkayt* in abundance. When I visited for the Sabbath, as I often did, after Friday night dinner I would stroll down Rabbi Akiva Street. For six days a week the tightly packed pocket storefronts of Rabbi Akiva are the site of frenetic commerce. On a weekday morning it resembles Canal Street in New York: dirty, loud, and choked with exhaust. The architecture is the same Bauhaus style that dominates Tel Aviv, but decay and disregard have been unkind to facades, which hemorrhage cracked stucco and rotted fiberglass. After the start of the Sabbath, however, the street is transformed. It remains crowded, but now with husbands and wives walking, young children leading younger children by the hand, and *yeshive bukhers* leaning on lampposts, vigorously disputing. On a cool spring Friday evening, Rabbi Akiva summons nostalgia for a time and place that may never have existed, an Anatevka without Cossacks, a life-is-with-people Lower East Side.

Bnei Brak has an awkward grace during the working week as well. Just off the main roads, there is everywhere a constant din of study and prayer, with a distinctive swallowed rhythm. One can walk from one edge of the city to the distant border, accompanied the entire way by the sound of Talmud chanting through open windows.

When I was in the Israeli army and would come for weekends in uniform and with a gun, I was stopped in the street by children, enraptured by my rifle, which they asked me to take apart, to let them hold, to demonstrate without bullets. When I offered, they held my bullet cartridges as though they were made of porcelain. At such moments, I felt as foreign as Gulliver, but never unwelcome.

I *was* foreign. If my grandparents' place in Israel was Bnei Brak, mine was Tel Aviv. My grandparents were not quite ultra-Orthodox, but they fit in among the ultra-Orthodox. I was not quite secular, but I fit in among the secular. I grew up a *yeshive bukher*. I still insist on kosher food and observe the various prohibitions associated with the Sabbath. But my people are secular. If it was some religious devotion that brought my grandparents to the Holy Land, it was political ideology that brought me, and political ideology that had little to do with the dry formalisms I had been taught by the clueless East European rabbis who had *shtupped* me with Gemara as a kid. As a religious child, I loved Israel for the achievements of its no-apologies *apikorsim* (heretics), the ones who won wars against impossible odds (for so those victories were described to me), and as people often said in those days, "made the desert bloom." The way a boy growing up in America today might feel about Shaquille O'Neal, I felt about Moshe Dayan.

That is why I cannot get out of my head the jokes about gassing ultra-Orthodox or pushing them out of planes. Growing up in the United States, I was innocent of anti-Semitism. I never experienced it: I was never insulted; I was denied nothing because of my religion. Anti-Semitism existed as a grand abstraction, like communism, an unseen threat to all that I loved, an organizing principle of my worldview, but it was utterly absent from my life in any practical way. My first encounter with anti-Semitism was in Israel, and the anti-Semites were my people, my heroes, the people I'd moved halfway around the world to join. After many years, I had finally seen the face of anti-Semitism, and it looked surprisingly like my own.

It was a startling realization, but not a sophisticated one. The most ugly stereotypes about Jews—stereotypes that never find expression in polite company in the United States—received daily, credulous airing in Israel: Ergo, many Israelis are anti-Semites. The evidence for this simple hypothesis was everywhere, and it was easy to identify the worst offenders: secular politicians like the leader of the anti-Haredi Shinui (Change) Party, Tommy Lapid, secular writers like Amos Oz, and secular journalists like the *Ha'aretz* man on the Haredi beat during most of the 1990s, Shahar Ilan. I thought that these people, for whatever mysterious alchemy of poisoned psychology and tainted politics, were Louis Farrakhan–style anti-Semites, at least as far as Haredim went, and that's all there was to it.

But I was wrong. Of course that *isn't* all there is to it. Not long ago, I read an article in the newspaper about a nonprofit group named Da'at Emet (True Knowledge), whose members produce counterfeit Haredi pamphlets that look remarkably like the sort of educational material yeshivot (Talmudic academies) produce for their students, but that instead debunk the Torah, the Talmud, and the rest of the rabbinic tradition. Using stolen mailing lists, they send these pamphlets to yeshiva students, hoping to stimulate some, a few, to abandon their belief. Bolder still, they sneak into yeshivot at night, carefully placing the heretical material between the pages of the Talmud, so that students will find them the next morning when they return to their studies.

I was appalled. These are Dada vigilantes and intellectual vandals, with breathtaking disdain for Judaism, I thought; they are poster children for the sort of anti-Semitism that I had set out to study. The article listed a P.O. box, and I sent a short note asking if I might meet a representative of the organization. Two days later an e-mail message arrived, explaining that members of their group frequently receive death threats, which they prudently treat seriously, and would I please provide further information about myself so I could be vetted. I did, and we arranged to meet later in the week—on my fortieth birthday, as it turned out—in a café in an affluent suburb north of Tel Aviv.

A man was waiting for me when I arrived, and another man and two women joined us just as we were ordering coffee. Raffi (I have changed the names, as I promised I would), a fiftyish, white-haired man, with a broad face and penetrating gaze, shook my hand and asked me why I wanted to meet him and what I

בס״ד

קונטרס

דעת אמת

ובו תמצא

התומך יתדותיו
באמיתות שלושה:
סקרנות, למדנות,
מחשבה ישרה
יבין כי אמת,
מן המציאות שורשה
זה סוד החכמה
וזה מקורה

גליון מספר 3

נא לשמור על קדושת הגליון

מהדורא תנינא

ניסן ה׳תשנ״ט

Pamphlet intended to lead ultra-Orthodox students to question their faith, example of material smuggled into yeshivot by Da'at Emet activists.

hoped to learn. I told him who I was, about my religious grandparents, about my ambivalent reactions to the newspaper piece about Da'at Emet.

My ambivalence didn't surprise him, he allowed, as most people don't understand the spiritual and physical threat posed by the ultra-Orthodox. He had seen the changes in the ultra-Orthodox over the past two generations, and the little guerrilla actions of Da'at Emet were by no means disproportionate. Raffi was born to a Haredi family in Tel Aviv, "at a time when everything about ultra-Orthodoxy was different." He studied in Haredi schools, and when the time came, a marriage was arranged, and he wed an ultra-Orthodox woman who was a stranger to him. In those days, most ultra-Orthodox boys served in the army, typically in the military rabbinate, and Raffi enlisted as well, and he was sent by the army to study at the university and allowed by the army to keep up his Talmud studies at night. He studied economics and political science, but soon drifted to philosophy, and it was philosophical questions that first led him to doubt his piety. He read constantly, and it was not long before—"with all sorts of trials and familial troubles"—he removed his hat, his yarmulke, his black coat, and became a secular Israeli. "The switch was total. I went from being entirely religious to entirely secular. But I continued to learn. I was never without a book, though now instead of the Mishnah, it was a book of philosophy or Israeli history or politics." He went into business and was successful enough to retire comfortably at fifty and devote himself to reading and politics. And looking around Israel, he concluded that the two most important political issues of the day were (1) water, which was being badly mismanaged by bureaucratic hacks, and (2) the ultra-Orthodox, who were stealthily taking over the country.

Raffi's partner in his anti-Haredi activism, whom I'll call Yossi, had a very different background. He grew up in a secular family, his father opposed to religion as a matter of socialist principle. When he was seventeen, Yossi concluded that secularism was vacuous and started searching for an alternative. He started attending free lectures by rabbis, and it was not long before he renounced his family and his previous life and set up in a yeshiva. He was a quick study and advanced swiftly through yeshiva ranks; after ten years, he was viewed by his rabbis as something of an adept. It was then that his problems began, because he noticed internal contradictions and plain errors in the holy texts that betrayed basic misunderstandings of physics, biology, and psychology. Some months later, he removed his yarmulke. And it was several years after that that he began his anti-Haredi activities.

Yossi and Raffi surprised me. As we spoke, my 120-minute tape ran out, and then so did the 90-minute tape I had brought as a spare. I finished four cups of coffee. By the time I left, I was late for the birthday party my wife had been arranging for me for months.

Maybe my birthday—which put me in a reflective state of mind—affected my reactions. I had approached the interview the way a scholar reads a book by an inferior colleague—expecting to be scandalized by the mindless inadequacy of it and, in an odd way, looking forward to being scandalized. These Da'at Emet fanatics would be prime evidence—hard proof of what I anyway already knew—of the clueless bigotry of secular Israelis.

But they confounded me. Yossi and Raffi are, it turns out, decent people, *mentshn*. They embody the traits I admire most. They live *examined* lives. They read voraciously. They care about others. Their politics are heartfelt and human. They speak beautifully, violently gesticulating as they do. They have passion. They are anything but clueless bigots.

Raffi and Yossi resent the ultra-Orthodox greatly, but they have good reasons. Anyone who has spent three years of exhaustion, boredom, and constant, low-level fear in the army, and then another month and a half every year in the reserves until he turns fifty can be excused for holding a grudge against a group that refuses en bloc to serve. Parents who send their children to understaffed schools with no computers and too few books can't be blamed for fuming when they read in the papers of millions of shekels being diverted to yeshivot, as part of a sleazy coalition-politics deal. (However, whether the fiscal reality matches what is written in the newspapers is not certain.)

Still, I couldn't help feeling that the rage that Yossi and Raffi (and most secular and "modern" religious Israelis) feel toward Haredim goes beyond the objective circumstances. Some animosity makes sense, I suppose, but there is also a measure of surplus hatred, antipathy that goes beyond that justified by the facts of Israeli politics and society at the beginning of the twenty-first century. The enormity of the passions that the ultra-Orthodox inspire is not explained (or it is at least *under*-explained) by the impact that this small segment of society (roughly 10 percent) has on the country as a whole. The outrage and panic, the certainty that it's us or them ("we are at war with them and all they stand for," a respected writer told journalists a few years back, a war that must be won "if we are to be able to live here at all") with which many seculars regard Haredim are *immoderate*, if not outright misplaced. Why are the ultra-Orthodox so disturbing?

The political and economic battles between secular and ultra-Orthodox Jews in Israel are invariably technical: What should be the precise criteria for military exemption, how much money per student ought the government contribute to the ultra-Orthodox school system, how many rabbis ought to be kept on the government payroll to perform weddings, divorces, and so forth?

Member of Knesset and journalist Joseph "Tommy" Lapid, head of the anti-Haredi Shinui Party. © Reuters.

Such matters are crucially important, but they are not the entire story. Behind these sorts of political skirmishes, I suspect, a great shadow battle is taking place in Israel over what it means to be a Jew. Tommy Lapid, the avuncular journalist who took over the moribund Shinui Party six weeks before the 1999 election and, amazingly, steered the party to win six Knesset seats by running a single-issue, "beat back the Haredim" campaign,* thumped his fleshy fist on the table as he told me, "They say that *they* are the real Jews. *I* am the real Jew! If Moses were around today, or Maimonides, they would recognize *me* as the true Jew, not the ultra-Orthodox." The surprising thing is not that he thinks that; he has good arguments and—as one must say about such hypotheticals—he could be right. What's surprising is that it matters so much to a very secular member of very secular parliament just what Moses and Maimonides might think of him.

So the story of Israel's ultra-Orthodox is really more than one story. Ask an Israeli why he hates the ultra-Orthodox, and he'll talk to you about draft quotas and government budgets and the number of people living off the dole. This political tale is important. But it fails to explain the passion behind the hatred itself. That is a different tale, and it is more complicated. For most Israelis, Haredim are our collective obsession, the monster under our beds, the thought that we cannot banish. It is this obsession that I set out to investigate. As such, this book is not really a book about the ultra-Orthodox, though much of it concerns them. It is a book about how the rest of us see them, and why, which is not at all the same thing. There is a gap between the cold, hard facts of ultra-Orthodoxy here in Israel and the way we take in those facts, understand them, exaggerate them, fret over them.

---

*As a result of the 2003 election, Shinui representation increased to fifteen.

This gap—the surplus hatred, the underjustified tie-them-down-and-shave-off-their-beards rage—is the subject of this book.

Yossi says that fighting Haredim is a vocation, a calling, and I think he is right. It has taken the cast of a religious rite, and it is undertaken with the fervor of piety. For those who heed this calling, something greater is at stake than budgets and military roles. Perhaps that is what Raffi and Yossi had in mind when they chose the name Da'at Emet (True Knowledge), for their group. For what they seem to be engaged in (along with many of the rest of non-Haredi Israelis) is a struggle for the true knowledge about what it means to be a Jew in the Jewish state. It is a struggle that is fought over practical issues, but concerns something more abstract, ineffable, something like the "soul" of a people.

It is this tale that explains why Israelis are so obsessed with their ultra-Orthodox. And no less, why I am obsessed with the obsession.

1

History

Who are Israel's ultra-Orthodox, and where did they come from? It is tempting to assume that they were always here. This is how they view themselves. The term they most commonly use to refer to themselves is *Yidn*, Yiddish for "Jews." The name reflects a profound truth about Haredi self-image. In their view, they are not a *sort* of Jew, they are simply Jews: real Jews, true Jews, good Jews, gold-standard Jews, platonic Jews, the ideal from which all other Jews deviate. Along with this view goes a persuasion that they represent the only authentic heirs of past Jews, of the mantle of Jewish history. The Jews who stood at the foot of Mount Sinai to receive the Torah were like them. For as long as there have been Jews, there have been Haredim. All the rest—Reform, Conservative, modern-Orthodox, secular, Reconstructionist, Jews for Jesus, whatever—are recent corruptions of the true practice of Judaism, which Haredim alone carry on.

This view captures a fact of history. There have always been Jews in the Holy Land, and these Jews have for the most part been pious, with a fervor matched in our day only by ultra-Orthodox Jews (though perhaps also by the more ecstatic varieties of New Age Jews). Like today's Haredim, Jews who lived in the Holy Land in past epochs isolated themselves from their neighbors, often finding spiritual inspiration from faraway places and long-ago times. Like today's Haredim, these bygone Jews considered themselves chosen, God's best and brightest.

In the sixteenth century, there were bustling communities of pious Jews in the Holy Land who lived a great deal like today's ultra-Orthodox Jews, at least at first glance. Like those today, most of the pious Jews then had recently quit Europe or were the children of Jews who had quit Europe under dire circumstances. In 1492, Spain's many Jews were given a choice of converting or leaving. Five years later, the Jews of Portugal were given a similar choice. Many of these Jews kicked around Central and Eastern Europe, which hardly proved safe havens. Towns in Germany, Bohemia, and Poland, one after another, expelled Jews, and the beginning of the sixteenth century saw waves of forced migration for Jews of all backgrounds. Jews wandered, and it was not uncommon for a single family, with time, to become refugees a half dozen times over. It was against this background that the Turks' stunning victory over the Mamluks in the Battle of Marj Dabiq, near Aleppo, Syria, in August 1516, took on special significance for Jews. This was the turning point in Sultan Salim's campaign to capture the Fertile Crescent.

The Holy Land came under Ottoman rule, where it would remain for four centuries, until the British Mandate took hold in 1917. At first, Turkish administration brought prosperity. Industry, trade, and farming all grew quickly, and to shore up these gains, Ottoman functionaries took steps to draw new residents from near and far. Among those who came were a great number of Jews. By the middle of the sixteenth century, there were 10,000 Jews in the Holy Land by some estimates, and more were arriving from Europe each month. Most of these Jews set up in Jerusalem and Safed, which ever since have remained, along with Bnei Brak, the hometowns of most ultra-Orthodox Jews in Israel. It is with these pioneers in mind that Haredim today maintain that it was they who led the Jewish return to the Holy Land, not the secular Zionists.

This point is debatable. Modern historians insist that those pious Jews who settled in Palestine almost half a millennium ago were hardly direct forebears of today's ultra-Orthodox. Like Heraclites, the Greek philosopher who observed that one never steps into the same river twice, these scholars hold as an axiom that the pious Jews of 500 years past are not, cannot be, the same as those of today. But today's ultra-Orthodox, who have scant respect for the principles of academic historians, point to many similarities. Like us, they point out, the Jews who made their way to Palestine from Europe soon after Columbus discovered America settled into an austere life dominated by prayer, study, and work. As we do today, these

Jews considered study the best of all possible pursuits. Two rabbinical academies competed in Jerusalem at the beginning of the sixteenth century, and by the middle of the century there were many more. Just as today, these schools were meant not only for children; grown men too studied rather than worked, relying on gifts from abroad (and a special tax exemption for scholars) to provide meager sustenance for themselves and their families. Just how they spent their days would also be familiar to their Haredi counterparts today. In 1521, some Jerusalem *yeshive bukhers* sent home to Italy a letter describing their routine, and an identical description could just as easily be e-mailed from Jerusalem to New York today:

> We study the entire Talmud in consecutive order with [the commentary of] Rashi of blessed memory and the glosses of our French rabbis. In the morning, we also learn Halakhot [legal rulings] in the Talmud, two or one and a half pages daily, however it works out. And in the evening one chapter of the Mishnah with the commentary of Maimonides of blessed memory.

This immersion in Talmud and legal studies in school ought not obscure an even more passionate interest in Jewish mysticism. In Jerusalem and Safed 500 years ago, much as in Jerusalem and Safed today, Jewish mystics gathered in small circles to pursue the occult arts and spiritual disciplines of the *kabbalah*, conversing with angels and demons, performing miracles, seeking union with God. Like today, students and rabbis were certain that theirs was an apocalyptic age, and that the Messiah perhaps already walked on earth among them. Like today, they took rumors of exotic Jewish tribes in Ethiopia (then, as now, recently rediscovered) as intriguing proof that the ingathering of the exiles, a process foreshadowing the Messiah's return, was already under way.

All that is why today's ultra-Orthodox—who have no truck with Heraclites in the best of circumstances—see themselves as the natural heirs of the Jews of Palestine of five centuries ago. From their point of view, it is the Zionists who are the interlopers, the imposters in the Holy Land.

The circumstances surrounding the arrival of Zionist Jews in Palestine, including secular Zionists, are complicated. Though they began to come late in the nineteenth century, the story of their arrival properly begins in the eighteenth century, not in the Holy Land, but in Europe, with what is called the *haskalah*, or "Jewish Enlightenment."

The Jewish Enlightenment owed everything to the European Enlightenment. It was, after all, philosophes like Voltaire who advanced the progressive notion that Jews ought to be treated like all other people. Sure, Jews are distasteful, this line of thought went, but that is no justification for excluding them from society. In fact, they are distasteful because they are excluded, and not the opposite. Eighteenth-century intellectuals in France, Germany, and even England wondered whether, if freed from the crushing disdain of polite European culture, the Jew might once and for all prove himself *salonfähig*, "fit for the salon." This question came to be known as the "Jewish question," and in order to answer it, Enlightenment intellectuals hesitantly sought ways to extend greater rights and opportunities to Jews. Treated as humans rather than Jews, would Jews *act* like humans rather than Jews?

Those Jews who came to call themselves *maskilim*, "enlightened," were only too happy to demonstrate that Jews could be just as human as Christians. None was more influential than Moses Mendelssohn, the grandfather of the composer Felix Mendelssohn. Mendelssohn was still a youth with a swelling reputation for brilliance and imperiousness when he quit Dessau, where his father was a Torah scribe, for Berlin, a cultural center of *Mitteleuropa*. There he dedicated himself to mastering German literature, picking up Latin and a handful of European languages as he went. He was still in his twenties when he met the renowned writer Gotthold Ephraim Lessing, and little time passed before Lessing started publishing the philosophical treatises Mendelssohn had begun to draft in German. In his mature philosophical writings, including his most famous book, *Jerusalem*, Mendelssohn argued that the laws of Judaism were closer to natural, rational religion than the dogmas of Christianity or any other religion. Torah and reason were not strangers. Jews were never far from being human; rabbis were never far from philosophes.

Such views were unconventional, but not heretical, and they were not in themselves enough to raise concerns about Mendelssohn among pious Jews. When visiting Hamburg in 1761, Mendelssohn met one of the famed rabbis of the age, Jonathan Eibeschütz, and carried away a letter from the great man attesting to his erudition in Talmud. Were he married, the letter stated, the rabbi would have felt bound to offer him rabbinic ordination on the spot. Mendelssohn earned the approbation of other leading rabbis as well. With the years, however, suspicion grew that he was straying from the righteous path. In 1778 he set out to publish his own German translation of the Bible, pointedly refusing to solicit rabbinic approval for what was destined to be a controversial project. Many feared that the volume would more effectively teach Jewish children how to speak German than it would teach them the Bible itself (which is precisely what happened). Mendelssohn, for the first time, was considered dangerous, his writings condemned.

But Mendelssohn's waywardness was soon outdone by the more alarming departures of his students and disciples. Soon after Joseph II issued his

Toleranzpatent (Edict of Tolerance) in 1782, one Hartwig Wessely published a Hebrew polemic, the title of which may be translated as "Words of Peace and Truth," in which he argued for broad reform of Jewish education, including more time spent on secular subjects and less on Talmud. This sounds tame enough from today's remove, but at the time it was pure napalm. Rabbis attacked Wessely and the new "free-thinking" trend he represented. They demanded that he and his ilk be muzzled or excommunicated. Wessely and his supporters replied by founding a new "Society of Friends of the Hebrew Language" with its own journal, *The Gatherer,* to promulgate their ideas. The new divide in European Jewry—between the "Enlightened" and the "traditional"—was now institutionalized.

Over the next four decades this divide grew wider, harder to traverse, and the ideas and schemes floated by *maskilim* became more radical and their expression more vehement. When a disciple of Mendelssohn, Herz Homberg, was appointed chief inspector of schools in Galicia late in the 1780s, he commissioned special textbooks for studying the tenets of Judaism, and petitioned the Austrian authorities to censor traditional Hebrew books. When the rabbis refused to cooperate, he threatened to have them arrested and punished. Other *maskilim* petitioned civil authorities to prohibit Jewish innkeeping, leasing of land, moneylending, and other debauched occupations, hoping instead to train Jews for more productive work in agriculture or crafts. Another prominent *maskil,* Zalkind Hourwitz, suggested that the use of Yiddish and Hebrew be banned in business contracts, even between Jews, so that all transactions would be transparent to all, Jew and gentile alike. Yiddish, in particular, took a beating, and was denounced regularly in the pages of *haskalah* journals as "repulsive to the reader in style and content." Most incendiary were the efforts of *maskilim* to reform Judaism's religious rites. Prayers were changed and deleted. Vernacular was added. The marriage ceremony was tinkered with, and the bar mitzvah was replaced in some areas by confirmation. Israel Jacobson, who served as chief of the Central Consistory of Westphalian Jews at the beginning of the nineteenth century, offered that Jewish prayer ought to resemble the more cultured Protestant ceremonies of his day. His friend, David Friedlaender, demanded that the "dead Hebrew language" be replaced by German in prayer books, and that all reference to Zion or Jerusalem be expunged. In 1799 Friedlaender published an anonymous pamphlet in Berlin, offering in the name of "several Jewish households" to join a Protestant church and undergo baptism, so long as they were not asked to embrace the whole of Christian dogma. Friedlaender's identity was discovered, and his scheme came to naught. Friedlaender deflected his energies and in time became known as the forefather of the Reform Movement.

A backlash was inevitable. *Maskilim* offended almost everyone. Workaday Jews understood that Enlightened ideals of "productive labor," even if nice on paper, could destroy their livelihoods. It's all very well to think that Jews should till soil, but just getting by was hard enough, and *banning* lending and trading would only make it harder. Educational reforms championed by *maskilim* were seen by most Jews as equally clueless. It also took little time to observe that Enlightened schools produced not just well-cultivated Jews but also many Jews who, upon reaching majority, converted and lived out their lives as well-cultivated Protestants and sometimes Catholics. Perhaps this was secretly what *maskilim* wanted, many wondered. Worse still than the reforms in the economy and in education were those in the religion itself. For those of a traditional leaning, it seemed that, for the first time in their history, Judaism was being devastated by Jews themselves. "We have met the enemy, and he is us." Something had to be done, as one leader of the countercharge insisted, "to restore the glories of the past."

That leader was Moses Sofer. Sofer was a refugee from Frankfurt, who knocked about Central Europe a bit before accepting the position of municipal rabbi in Pressburg, Hungary, where he remained from 1806 until he died in 1839. There he founded a Talmudic academy that was soon the biggest in the world. Sofer's reputation grew apace with his school, in part owing to his superior scholarship, and in part to his zealous opposition to the reforms of the *maskilim*. ("There are no conflicts without wounds," he wrote as a *cri de coeur*.) Sofer's campaign to restore past glories had two thrusts. He sought to buttress the institutions of traditional Judaism. He agitated to strengthen pious schools and community organizations, the weakness of which had left Jews dangerously vulnerable to the schemes of the *maskilim*. Along with this, he sought to strengthen traditional Judaism itself, which in his view had proven unduly susceptible to corruption. This he achieved by *fixing* Jewish law. He ended two and a half centuries of debate about the authority of a Jewish code of law called the *Shulhan Arukh* by insisting that all Jews submit fully to each of its dictates. He raised an old Talmudic dictum—"innovation is forbidden by the Torah"—to high and inviolable principle. Nothing could be done differently than previous generations had done it. Even folk customs, once accepted by Jews, could never be forsaken, not for all eternity. Innovation was innovation, and there was no distinction to be drawn between the most insignificant traditional folkway and a divine edict recorded in the Bible. Change was forbidden.

There was sense in Sofer's reaction to Enlightenment. The *maskilim* had demonstrated all too well that change is hard to contain. Once any part of the tradition is modernized or rationalized, others parts are immediately exposed to criticism. If the laws of the Sabbath are bent, why not those of kashrut? And if those, why not the rituals surrounding Passover? The slope is not only slippery, it's steep. Sofer determined that if Judaism were to survive with any integrity, it had to survive intact, in its totality. And if doing so meant isolating traditional Jews not just from their Christian neighbors, but also from wayward Jews, all the better.

Moses Sofer was, in short, the first ultra-Orthodox Jew, just as Moses Mendelssohn had been the first "Enlightenment Jew." This is an important turning point because it illustrates that only when "modern" Jews came into being, ultra-Orthodox Jews came into being too. The conjunction seems odd at first. In ways most evident to the eye, pious Jews had simply remained pious Jews. In comparison with *maskilim*, who refashioned themselves in many ways and found themselves dressing differently from their parents, speaking different languages, observing different religious rites, reading different books and papers and magazines, in short, living lives altered beyond recognition, the trappings of piety for more traditional Jews had hardly changed. They dressed as their great-grandparents had, spoke the same languages, read the same books, observed the same rites, and so forth. But something important had changed in their attitudes toward themselves, toward other Jews, and toward Judaism itself. They now viewed themselves as different: purebred Jews, not like all those other mutts. They viewed other Jews as sellouts, imposters, and—most important—as a constant danger. And they viewed their Judaism as fixed, frozen, unchangeable by virtue of being perfect. Outside of history.

Zeno would have admired the paradox. Sofer introduced to Judaism an innovation perhaps as radical as any the religion had absorbed during its long history: the idea that innovation *itself* was forbidden and had always been forbidden. The irony grows. Sofer's innovation gave rise to a new sort of Jew, one who accepts as an axiom that the very notion of a new sort of Jew is nonsense. Such new Jews would reject anyone altering the tradition— *a maskil*, a Reform Jew, whoever—as a sinner, a heretic, and as a danger to Judaism itself. At the same time, such new Jews *defined* themselves largely in terms of those they rejected. They were the Jews at the ramparts, and their station was defined in no small part by those they struggled to keep at bay.

Therefore, the lines were drawn, and if one reads the sermons of the early nineteenth century or, for that matter, the polemics in *haskalah* quarterlies, one sees just how much bad blood there was between the traditionalists and the *maskilim* and reformers. It was with cold satisfaction that traditionalists recounted the story of how Mendelssohn's own daughter, Dorothea, had abandoned her Jewish husband for an affair with the Romantic philosopher

Friedrich Schlegel. Small wonder, some said, as Mendelssohn's views were an invitation to conversion and licentiousness. *Maskilim* replied that the views of the traditionalists were superstitious, primitive, unpatriotic, un-couth, and uncultured—in sum, un-*European*.

The antagonism between the traditionalists and the *maskilim* and reform-ers was a leitmotif of nineteenth-century Jewish life in Europe. It split com-munities—sometimes families—down the middle. The differences between the groups quickly metastasized, and as there was little in common between them (not language, not literature, not clothing, not profession, not man-ners, and barely religion itself), it is not overreaching to conclude that the groups became unique species of Jews. Separate cultures. Warring cultures.

These cultural wars did not reach the Holy Land until late in the nine-teenth century, and then in an unusual form. There was a simple reason for Palestine's immunity to this conflict. While the conflict was heating to a boil in Europe, there were few if any *maskilim* or reformers in the Holy Land. This, in fact, is one of the reasons why Moses Sofer himself and his sons, who were also famous rabbis, encouraged their students and congregants to settle in Palestine. The Holy Land, in Sofer's view, had remained pure, safe from the contamination of European culture, and free from Jews willing to sacrifice God and their heritage on the altar of that culture. The lack of in-terest in the Holy Land evinced by *maskilim* and reformers galled Sofer, who took it as yet another sign of their debauchery.

Maskilim saw things differently. Enlightenment and reform, in their first incarnations, were all about finding a modus vivendi that would allow Jews to assimilate into the cultured European societies in which they found themselves. For most of Judaism's modernizers, the notion of a special tie to the Holy Land conflicted with everything they stood for. If they were trying to demonstrate that they could be good Germans or Frenchmen, a longing for Zion of the sort that the traditionalists expressed could only make them seem like unrepentant orientals, like foreigners, the very opposite of true citizens. Gabriel Riesser, one of the greatest boosters of Jewish moderniza-tion in the middle decades of the nineteenth century, put it this way: Any Jews who preferred a state that did not exist, Israel, over Germany ought be put under lock and key, not because they were criminal, but because they were insane. The whole point was that Jews could, should, and would fit in just where they were, and that their loyalties to hearth and homeland were no weaker than that of any Christian citizen. They strove to be, as the slogan went, "Jews at home and *Menschen* [human beings] in the street," and that meant no special attachments to foreign lands, including the Holy Land. It was in this way that Palestine was spared the conflict between traditionalists and modernizers that wracked Europe at the beginning of the nineteenth century. Palestine had its share of intramural tensions, but the Jewish factions that existed were all traditionalist.

It is just as well that the Holy Land was saved from this struggle, because life proved hard enough as it was. At the beginning of the nineteenth century, the total number of Jews in Palestine was only several thousand, and though this number grew steadily over the century, it grew slowly. Critical mass was the least of the problems. The Jews of the Galilee, Jerusalem, and Hebron suffered plague, earthquake, drought, marauding Bedouin, and other disasters of biblical scale. In 1831, Egypt's Mohammed Ali dispatched his son Ibrahim Pasha with an army to conquer Palestine and Syria, and the campaign succeeded. Nine years of skirmishes followed, Jews finding themselves in the crossfire, until Constantinople once again conquered the land.

In the generation that followed the Turkish reconquest, the Jewish community finally stabilized, owing in part to the efforts of European Jewish philanthropists, especially Moses Montefiore and, later, Baron Edmond de Rothschild. From 1840 to 1880, the Jewish population of Palestine more than doubled, growing from ten to twenty-five thousand. Most of these Jews lived off the *halukah* (distribution), an elaborate network that collected money from Jews in Europe and dispensed it in the Holy Land. Jews in the ancestral homeland, so went the thinking, should give themselves over to study alone. But the money was never enough, and with time, agricultural settlements and trade schools were established to provide skills for earning a livelihood.

Jewish society in Palestine was fissured, and life there was hard, but compared to the tumultuousness of Jewish life in Europe, the Holy Land was remarkably stable from the return of the Turk until the last two decades of the century. When things finally began to change, though, they changed radically and in ways that could not be foreseen.

The force behind the change was Zionism. Just why Zionism sprang into being is complicated and again draws us back to Europe. The Enlightenment ideals that gave impetus to *haskalah* and reform largely exhausted themselves in the first half of the nineteenth century. Mirabeau had beamed to the French National Assembly soon after the revolution that France had "reduced the art of living to the simple notions of liberty and equality" and would soon "conquer the whole of Europe for Truth, Moderation, and Justice," but matters unfolded in unexpected ways. Leaders of the revolution had championed these ideals, at least in their endless oratory, and the reckoning of the German philosopher Immanuel Kant that the French Revolution was "the enthronement of reason in public affairs" was shared by many

contemporaries. Still, what happened in France in the twenty-five years after the revolution illustrates that reason and truth were not the only forces
at work. The Rationalist *liberté* and *égalité* found themselves muscled aside
by their junior partner, the Romantic *fraternité*. If the revolution was two
parts Voltaire, it soon proved three parts Rousseau. The Jacobin party,
Robespierre, and soon Bonaparte—these men melded the universalist, liberal principles of the Enlightenment with chauvinist zealotry. The Terror—
in which the revolutionary tribunal sentenced 2,000 heads to roll in just
seventeen months—was supposed to protect "the fatherland in danger." Jig-
gers of reason had been chased by strong shots of nationalism.

This new sort of nationalism soon spread across the continent (in large
part owing to Bonaparte's European campaigns), and with it came new
attitudes and changed culture, which together might be called *Romantic*.
These new attitudes and this new culture had sweeping effects—literature
changed (compare *Young Werther* to *Candide*, for instance), science
changed (compare Goethe to Voltaire), music changed (compare the famous offspring, Felix Mendelssohn and Johann Christian Bach, to each
other). Politics changed too. A German philosopher named Johann Gott-
fried von Herder reflected his times, and powerfully influenced them, when
he wrote that good citizenship demanded more than faithful adherence to
laws of state. To be part of a nation was to partake of the spirit, *geist*, of the
people, a *geist* molded by a million intangibles—the air, the terrain, the
flora and fauna, the folk music and tales.

If *maskilim* and reformers had been confident that they could master
the formalities of citizenship to become law-abiding, respectable citizens,
these new Romantic intangibles proved much harder to learn. These Jews
were cosmopolitans, but effete when compared with the ruddy-cheeked
rustics who now replaced pasty bespectacled intellectuals as model citizens. Enlightenment had promised that Jews could become French or German simply by excelling at being *human*, by embracing a universalist
rationality. Romanticism greatly changed the rules of the game, insisting
that becoming French or German required, well, becoming *very* French or
German. Since the cultures of Europe were still profoundly Christian—the
agrarian, folk cultures far more than the cultures of the cities to which
maskilim were mostly exposed—assimilating into these cultures in their
Romantic versions was an enormous, often impossible, challenge.

More crucial than Romanticism's impact on Europe's Jewish minority was
its effect on the Christian majority, for whom Romanticism marginalized,
sometimes also subverting and discrediting, Enlightenment ideals. "Energy is
the only life, and it is from the body," William Blake wrote, "and Reason is the

bound or outward circumference of Energy." The problem, at least as many
Jews saw it, was that Reason was also the cement into which European tolerance was anchored. When Reason was denied ample weight, tolerance
teetered. And that was indeed what began to happen in the middle decades
of the nineteenth century. Romantic nationalists of various commitments
came to doubt the place of the Jews in their countries. Jews might be no less
rational than anyone else—this almost anyone would warrant. But could
Jews really be authentically German or French? They could partake of the
European mind no less than other cosmopolitan intellectuals. But could they
really partake of this or that body politic? The answer was far less obvious.
"The new patriotism," historian Walter Laqueur summarized, "was a reaction to the humanitarian-cosmopolitan movement of the century before; it
stressed national exclusivity and was soon to insist on the inferiority of other
races." This was the crux of the problem for Jews, who, try as they might,
never managed to become part of the German, French, or Italian race.

That is one of the multitude of reasons why many Jews came to despair of
the possibility of full assimilation, as equals, into nineteenth-century European society. One of the many results of this despair is that by the 1840s
some reform-minded Jews looked for new answers to what was universally
referred to as "the Jewish problem," and one of these new answers was a new
sort of Jewish nationalism (that would later be called "Zionism"). The editor
of the leading Jewish paper in Germany, *Allgemeine Zeitung des Judentums*,
wrote in 1840 that he was not surprised that young Jews recoiled from the
anti-Semitism in Europe and sought to escape to their own patch of earth in
Palestine (though the Holy Land would hardly prove hospitable, he added).
These early rumblings led to nothing, and with the revolutions of 1848, the
hopes of many Jews to successfully assimilate into European society were
boosted. The new German constitution barred all discrimination along religious lines, and if this principle was only sporadically implemented, that was
not enough to dampen the enthusiasm of Germany's Jews. Or indeed of Jews
elsewhere in Europe, who saw their own complete emancipation as only a
matter of time. Two Jews (Adolphe Crémieux and Michel Goudchaux)
served in the French Republican government in 1848, and another—Achille
Fould—soon served as Louis Napoleon's finance minister. Benjamin Dis-
raeli, in Britain, had been baptized, of course, but to many he still served as a
sign of just how far a Jew could go in mid-nineteenth-century Europe.

The optimism among Jews inspired by these achievements continued to
rise and fall, inevitably adjusting itself to the bursts of anti-Semitism that
have punctuated modern European history. By 1862 a prominent socialist
(and onetime collaborator of Marx and Engels), Moses Hess, had written a

book, *Rome and Jerusalem,* explaining why even Jews who were willing to give up their religion would need to move to Palestine:

> Even an act of conversion cannot relieve the Jew of the enormous pressure of German anti-Semitism. The Germans hate the religion of the Jews less than they hate their race—they hate the peculiar faith of the Jews less than their peculiar noses. Reform, conversion, education and emancipation—none of these opens the gates of society to the German Jew; hence his desire to deny his racial origin.

Rome and Jerusalem was much discussed, but its immediate influence was slight. The idea it expressed, however—that Palestine could be home to irreligious European Jews or to those for whom European ideals were as dear as Jewish ones—remained in the air. It found sympathetic audiences in Western Europe (where Chaim Lurie established, for instance, the Frankfurt-an-der-Oder Society for the Settlement of Palestine), but audiences were even more enthusiastic in the East, where the position of Jews had improved little over the course of the century. When the murder of Alexander II in Russia, in 1881, set off a wave of pogroms, for the first time groups of Jews who considered themselves "modern" and "Enlightened" organized to emigrate to Palestine. They constituted what Zionist historiography calls the "First Aliyah," or the first *ascension* or wave of immigration. They counted only several hundred souls.

The arrival of these Europeans in Palestine was a shock for themselves and also for the Jews they met there. The land was inhospitable, especially for immigrants from Russia and Romania, who had an intellectual bent and no real experience in agriculture, much less in the punishing agriculture of the Levant. Illness struck immediately, mercilessly. Only months after these new settlers established the agricultural settlements of Rishon le-Zion, Zikhron Yaakov, and Rosh Pina (today three lush bedroom communities), the settlements stood at the brink of disintegration. Were it not for money that the philanthropist Edmond de Rothschild began to send in 1882 (and which came to more than £1.5 million over the next decade and a half), they would not have survived their first year.

Relations between these new settlements and existing Jewish settlements were tense from the start. Though many of the new settlers were religiously observant—some more, some less—they didn't admire the Jews they found in Palestine. The new settlers were not live-and-let-live types. They had come to the Holy Land with reform on their mind and critique on their tongue, and they found much to disparage in the traditionalist communities. They were embarrassed that their fellow Jews lived like paupers from the *halukah*, or the handouts gathered for them in Europe (an ironic emotion, in light of the fact that the new settlers were sustained only through the largesse of a Rothschild). And they made light of the primitive ways of Jews who—to their eyes—were now far more levantine than European.

The antipathy was mutual. Jews already living in Palestine found little to esteem in the new settlers, who knew nothing and were too arrogant to learn. In the best of times, money and food were tight in Palestine, and those were not the best of times. Money sent to these new settlers might well in the long run come at the expense of money sent to the established communities. Further, the religious observance of the neophytes was always suspect (it was, indeed, often lax by traditionalist standards). An anonymous broadsheet called "Voice from the Sanctuary" made the rounds in 1885, reviling the settlers and condemning the very notion of new settlement from Europe. Tensions grew until a crisis arose in 1889. This was a "sabbatical year," a yearlong biblically ordained respite for the earth, during which time agriculture is forbidden. The new settlers cited recent rabbinical interpretations and concluded that farming (which they in any instance needed to survive) was permissible. The rabbis of the established communities were furious, preaching week after week about the heresy of the newcomers. It was forbidden henceforth to buy their produce. They were to be avoided whenever possible.

This friction between Zionists and traditionalists would never go away; it has only gotten steadily worse in the hundred and twenty years since the first Zionists arrived. By the last decade of the nineteenth century, the traditionalist rejection of Zionism was nearly complete, not just in Palestine, but for traditionalist Jews the world over. When it had become clear that the Zionists intended to till soil during the sabbatical year, Europe's most esteemed traditionalist rabbi, Joseph Baer Soloveichik, called the Zionists "a new sect like that of [the seventeenth-century false messiah] Shabbetai Zevi, may the names of the evildoers rot." (As I've mentioned, in the spirit of full disclosure, Soloveichik was my great-uncle, several times removed. My grandfather was named for him.) In the same year, the Lubavitcher rebbe, Rabbi Shalom Dov Baer Schneerson, also attacked the Zionists: "In order to implement their idea, the Zionists must distort the essence [of Jewishness] in order to get [the Jews] to assume a different identity." The Bialer rebbe, Yitzhak Ya'akov Rabinowitz, was still more piqued about Zionism, which represented in his eyes:

> The struggle of the Evil Urge and its assistants, who wish to bring us down, heaven forbid, by false and harmful opinions, claiming that, if Jews will not perform some concrete action to settle in the Holy Land and to actually work

Gates of Torah Yeshiva, Jaffa. Photographed in 1895, the yeshiva was part of the well-established religious Jewish community in Palestine before the Zionist immigrations. Photograph from Central Zionist Archives, Jerusalem.

the land, then they will be unable to leave this bitter exile, heaven forbid. . . . In fact, Jews have no greater foe and enemy, who wish to deprive them of their pure faith.

This is a powerful condemnation: In a world where Jews did not lack for enemies, their worst adversaries were the Zionist heretics. The analogy to Shabbetai Zevi was a precise one in the minds of rabbis condemning Zionism. Shabbetai Zevi had promised utopia and had led to the disillusionment, disaffection, and even conversion of trusting Jews, sometimes whole communities at once. Zionism was doing the same, right before their eyes. And along with such condemnations came political action. During Hanukkah of 1893, traditionalists reported to the Turkish authorities that the Zionist journalist and linguist Eliezer Ben-Yehuda, was recklessly inciting rebellion in his radical Hebrew newspaper. The credulous Turks imprisoned him, and the chasm between the two Jewish communities yawned wider.

Ben-Yehuda's case illustrates how difficult, perhaps impossible, it was for the old settlers and the new to achieve some workable détente. His father was a Lubavitch Hasid, who died when Eliezer was only five. By and by the boy was sent to a traditional Talmudic academy, or yeshiva, in Lithuania, where the headmaster, secretly a *maskil*, covertly introduced him to secular literature. The yeshiva became oppressive, and Ben-Yehuda studied for matriculation, taught himself Russian, and soon entered the Dvinsk Gymnasium. It was there that he found Zionism: "It was as if the heavens had suddenly opened and a clear, incandescent light flashed before my eyes, and a mighty inner voice sounded in my ears: the renascence of Israel on its ancestral soil." Ben-Yehuda graduated and traveled across Europe to Paris where he studied medicine so that he would have a productive profession when he moved to Palestine. At the same time, he began to write for Zionist periodicals, arguing with gusto that the new Zionist settlers could not afford to alienate the religious: "Desist gentlemen! . . . We need unity, total and absolute!" This unity could be achieved only through respect for traditional observance: "Our desire is not to transgress the commandments of the Torah and Talmud. We want to make Halakha [Jewish ritual law] the cornerstone of all our efforts."

When Ben-Yehuda moved to Israel (after a bout of tuberculosis had made finishing medical school impossible), he already viewed himself as "a national Jew without religion." But that did not keep him from not only fastidiously observing Jewish customs, but also dressing the part of a traditionalist Jew, growing a beard and *peyes*, "earlocks," and wearing robes favored by the traditionalists. He insisted that his wife wear a *sheytl*, or wig, as is customary among traditionalist women.

Ben-Yehuda had two goals. Soon after arriving in Palestine he had determined his calling: sparking the revival of Hebrew as an everyday spoken language. He eventually compiled the first comprehensive etymological Hebrew dictionary (the seventeen volumes of which were completed by his son, some thirty-seven years after the elder Ben-Yehuda died), which included hundreds of his own coinages. Ben-Yehuda sought the goodwill of the traditionalists because it was they, far more than the new settlers from Europe, who had the greatest mastery of the language. His other goal was to try to repair the rift in relations between the traditionalists and the Zionists. Ben-Yehuda failed to achieve this goal; it may simply have been unachievable.

There were many reasons for Ben-Yehuda's failure. First, traditionalist Jews were wary of reviving Hebrew as a spoken language. Hebrew was holy, the language of the Bible, the language of God, and Ben-Yehuda and the other Zionists were trying to make it profane, in the etymologically correct sense of the word—"outside the Temple." Ben-Yehuda and his compatriots wanted to make Hebrew the language of the train station and the brothel, no less than the synagogue, and that in itself infuriated traditionalists. It became an emblem of the more general concern that the old settlers had about the new. Even when the newcomers embraced tradition, they seemed always to somehow warp it, damage it, cheapen it. Add to this the suspicion of some traditionalists that Ben-Yehuda and his lot were disingenuous in their religious observance, and more than a little hypocritical, not an idle suspicion in light of the fact that the bearded, yarmulke-wearing, three-times-a-day-praying Ben-Yehuda considered himself a Jew without religion.

And so when Ben-Yehuda wrote an article arguing against the alms that the traditionalists received from Europe and used a Hebrew idiom meaning "let us gather strength and go forward," ultra-Orthodox Jews reported to the Turks that he had called on his fellow Zionists to "gather an army and rise up" against the Ottoman Empire. The police took him away in irons. Although Ben-Yehuda did not serve out the year's imprisonment to which he was sentenced, any sympathy he had for the traditionalists was forever gone. In print and from the lectern, Ben-Yehuda remained an uncompromising critic of the traditionalists until his death in 1922, untiringly devoted to doing away with the *halukah*, despite, or perhaps because of, the fact that it was the major source of income of the traditionalists.

Ben-Yehuda was not alone, and it must be said that the Zionists gave as good as they got. "The distinguishing trait of the rabbinate is standing still and shrinking back into one's own small corner," wrote journalist Samuel Rosenfeld in 1900. "The distinguishing trait of Zionism is precisely the opposite, forging ahead, evolving." He added, "Let people know that the age of rabbinic monarchy has ended forever." Zionists in both Europe and Palestine lambasted the ultra-Orthodox as backward thinking, parasitic primitives.

The Zionist attacks were not just intellectual. The first Zionist settlers, those who came in the 1880s, were few, ill prepared, and hapless. Their practical impact on the country was small and easily ignored. But the second wave of settlers was different: They immediately altered the countryside they found, and in so doing they forever shifted the balance of power between Jews in Palestine. This second wave, or Second Aliyah, as it is known, began to arrive in 1904 (the year that Theodor Herzl died), and over ten years brought 80,000 Jews to Palestine (though many left again, in time, for the United States and, tragically, Germany and Russia). Like those of the First Aliyah, these second-wave settlers set up new agricultural villages. Unlike during the First Aliyah, these villages thrived. Among them were the first kibbutzim, or socialist communal settlements, just one token of the ideological creativity and militancy that characterized the young, fervent population. Also unlike the settlers of the First Aliyah, these newer settlers set up political parties, trade and labor groups, fraternal organizations, professional associations, school systems, and much of the rest of what would eventually become the infrastructure of the state. These new settlers *institutionalized* Zionism in Palestine.

In 1908, for instance, the Palestine Office was established in Jaffa to coordinate the colonizing efforts of the Zionists and to purchase lands for settlement. The Palestine Land Development Company trained newcomers to be farmers and also bought the land that it could. Large tracts that would eventually become modern Haifa and Tel Aviv were acquired and haltingly developed. Several labor unions were established. Two Hebrew-language daily papers appeared, a national library was established, several publishing houses, an art school, a national theater company, a teachers' association, and much more. Groups arose whose aim it was to gather weapons, legally when possible, covertly when not, and to train informal militias in their use.

It is difficult to take proper measure of all these activities without unwittingly bringing hindsight to bear. In retrospect, it is clear that the institutions founded in the first decades of the twentieth century were the backbone of Israel when it was finally established at midcentury. But this retrospection makes these institutions seem stronger, more inevitable, than they must have seemed at the time. The Zionist settlement at the beginning of the century was small, vulnerable, fractious, and utterly dependant upon rich Jews living abroad. The traditionalists at this time could still reasonably believe that secular Zionism was a fad that would fade until eventually forgotten by history, like so many other Jewish cults of epochs past.

At the same time, something of significance had happened. The Zionists had created a Jewish infrastructure in Palestine in which there was no place for the traditionalists, one that was secular, modern, and Europhilic, if not Eurocentric. The rift between the largely secular Zionists and the ultra-Orthodox traditionalists had transcended simple bad blood and ideological and religious differences. The rift was now institutionalized.

It is no surprise, then, that around this time, in 1912, the ultra-Orthodox concluded that it was time to establish their own institutions. Various rabbis and Orthodox lay leaders in Europe and Palestine had for years contemplated starting an international fellowship but never managed to agree among themselves about how to start it or what it should look like. There was a fundamental breach between the Orthodox communities in Germany, Hungary, and Poland, and between emigrants from these communities in the United States, Palestine, and elsewhere. To this breach were added dozens of smaller conflicts between various religious groups—between enthusiasts of different Hasidic rabbis, between Hasidim and *mitnagdim*, or the "opponents" of the Hasidim, and so forth. It took Zionism, as a common enemy, to bring together these splintered groups. When the Tenth Zionist Congress met, in 1911, all sorts of secular "cultural activities" were added to what had until then been dry speeches-from-the-lectern affairs. This angered Orthodox Jews, who took it as an attempt to legitimate secular Jewish culture ("secular Jewish" being an oxymoron, an impossibility, and a monstrosity, in their view) by fiat. Differences were laid aside, and Orthodox groups vowed to find a way to work with one another to battle their common enemy, the Zionists. In May 1912, the first assembly of Agudat Yisrael (the "Israel Union," the Agudah) was held in Kattowitz (Katowice), in Upper Silesia.

At this assembly, branches of Agudat Yisrael were chartered throughout Europe, in the United States, and in Palestine. The Palestine branch languished for seven years, issuing ineffectual protests against the increasingly powerful secular Zionist organizations, but accomplishing little. It did not come into its own until 1919, and only then after its members despaired of releasing Palestine from what they saw as the stranglehold of the Zionists. Its leader was by this time a young rabbi named Moshe Blau, who had concluded that the only way to protect "Torah Judaism," as he called it, was to separate it entirely, in its politics and culture, from the Zionists' community in Palestine. He agitated to keep Agudah Jews from being included in any of the political frameworks the Zionists organized. He established Agudah rabbinic institutions, Agudah schools, Agudah courts, Agudah civil authorities, and so forth. He even went so far as to negotiate independent Agudah peace agreements with Arab nationalists. The goal was to sever all ties with the Zionists, and this goal was largely achieved during the 1920s.

There were mishaps along the way. In 1920, a man named Jacob Israel de Haan was elected to serve on the Agudah's executive board and set to work with extraordinary vigor. De Haan was a colorful figure, whose life was short and tragic. He was born in Holland, and in his youth he was a socialist and freethinker, his commitment to Judaism attenuated enough that he fell in love with and married a Christian. After he embraced Orthodoxy, his past tortured him, and he couldn't shake the fear that he would inevitably revert to libertine ways. De Haan was a poet of some talent, his verse ambivalent and tortured, for example: "For whom am I waiting in this night, sitting at the wall of the temple—for God or for Muhammad the stable boy?" Though de Haan refused to divorce his wife (who refrained from converting to Judaism), his animus toward secularism—especially Zionism—had a convert's zeal. He cabled letters to English papers condemning Zionism, and he attacked the British government for its allegedly pro-Zionist leanings. His message was stern: Secular Jews everywhere stirred dissent and revolution.

At right, Agudat Yisrael leader Rabbi Moshe Blau, who advocated separation between "Torah Judaism" and Zionist institutions, conversing with Judah Magnes, Zionist and founder of the Hebrew University. Photograph from Central Zionist Archives, Jerusalem.

They had toppled the Czar in Russia and the Kaiser in Germany. Palestine had no place for such Jews, who would bring instability to an already shaky region. De Haan found other ways to make his point. He refused to speak to Jews in Hebrew, for instance, using Arabic even with people who had not mastered the rudiments of the language. He became the symbol of the ultra-Orthodox rejection of Zionism, and for that he paid a price. While walking the cobbled streets of Jerusalem, on June 30, 1924, de Haan was gunned down by a sniper. Years later was it discovered that he was murdered by members of the Haganah, the left-leaning Zionist paramilitary organization that became the nucleus of the Israel Defense Forces (IDF) after the state was established.

De Haan's assassination confirmed the feeling shared by many traditionalists that the Zionists were "evil men and ruffians," as an ultra-Orthodox rabbi and charismatic leader named Joseph Hayyim Sonnenfeld liked to call them. De Haan was seen as a martyr, who had died "to sanctify God's name," just like Jews who had been killed by Cossacks or burned by the Inquisition, an evaluation that cast the Zionists in the role of the rough-hewn goyish anti-Semites.

But attitudes toward the Zionists were never static. In 1929, riots broke out among Palestinian Arabs, in the course of which Orthodox, anti-Zionist Jews were murdered in Hebron, Safed, and Jerusalem. The deaths stunned many traditionalists: Some concluded that they ought to distance themselves still more from the Zionists, and others concluded the opposite, that there was reason to band together with the Zionists, at least for the sake of mutual protection.

As waves of refugees from the Nazis arrived in Palestine in the mid-1930s, the attitudes of the traditionalists toward the Zionists changed more. Among the new immigrants were ultra-Orthodox Jews who could not muster the same antipathy toward the Zionists as their compatriots who had arrived earlier. Perhaps witnessing the rise to power of the Nazis was a chastening experience and knocked the fight out of them for the intramural battles between Jews in the Holy Land. In any case, in the mid-1930s, there were calls within the Agudah for détente with the Zionists. Within the Agudah there were those who wanted greater economic integration with the Zionists, and those who advocated greater political cooperation as well.

Bnei Brak, summer 1928. The village synagogue is the first building on the right. Photograph from Central Zionist Archives, Jerusalem.

Reactions among the ultra-Orthodox to the spread of fascism in Europe were varied and invariably complicated. Rabbi Isaac Breuer implored Agudah members in a 1934 speech: "Do not leave Jewish history to the Zionists," by which he meant that the ultra-Orthodox themselves ought to take part in "rebuilding" a homeland for the Jews. This charge reflected an important and controversial theological innovation. Until then, ultra-Orthodox Jews were nearly unanimous in their belief that it was sinful to try to hurry the Messiah along by rebuilding the Holy Land through mundane means. But in light of what was happening in Europe, the price of this quietist attitude seemed to be increasing by the day. Breuer turned the conventional, ultra-Orthodox wisdom on its head. Working to "gather the exiles" was not contravening God's will; rather, it was God's will, as the nearly miraculous successes of even the heretical Zionists illustrated. Breuer did not believe that the traditionalists should join forces with the Zionists, who still represented a mortal danger to Judaism. But they ought to do what the Zionists claimed to be doing, only this time with proper respect for God and his commandments. Breuer's analysis found little overt support among Agudah members, but it is noteworthy that a prominent rabbi could even voice such views.

Some saw Breuer's attitudes as a weakening of ideological resolve and reacted to the politics of their day in a very different way. In 1935, a group of ardent followers of Rabbi Sonnenfeld (whose death three years earlier had only increased the devotion with which his disciples regarded him) split from the Agudah, which they thought had grown too chummy with the Zionists. Their goal was to establish "a circle free from the influence of the contemporary spirit and its fallacious opinions." At first this group called itself Hevrat ha-Hayyim, but they soon changed their name to one in Aramaic, by which they are known to this day: Neturei Karta. Neturei Karta literally means "guardians of the city," and it is taken from a passage in the Jerusalem Talmud that teaches that the religiously scholarly and pious are the true defenders of Jerusalem (and not the brawny bearers of arms; the Talmudic passage almost seemed to have been *written* with Zionists in mind). Neturei Karta was led by Amram Blau, the brother of the erstwhile head of the Agudah, Moshe Blau, from its founding until his death in 1974.

Blau approved of his followers' calling him a zealot, because in his view, zealotry was all that prevented Judaism from deteriorating entirely. Just as the Hellenists (the spineless Jews who had embraced Greco-Roman ways) had done more damage to the Jews than the Romans themselves ever did, so too the secular Zionists were doing more damage than the Europeans. Dur-

Boys studying in a Neturei Karta school, or ultra-Orthodox heder, circa 1940.
Photograph from Central Zionist Archives, Jerusalem.

ing World War II, Blau and his followers attacked the Agudah mercilessly for choosing to cooperate more closely with the Zionists. The tragedy unfolding in Europe could not justify such an alliance with heretics. After the war, as the founding of a Jewish state in Palestine became increasingly inevitable, Neturei Karta sent ambassadors around the world, lobbying hard against it. They traveled to the new United Nations, demanding that Jerusalem be internationalized, and in any case that it under no circumstances be left solely in the hands of the Zionists. They negotiated with Jordanian diplomats, in quixotic hope of fashioning their own accord that would allow them to live under Jordanian sovereignty. When David Ben-Gurion declared the establishment of the State of Israel, Blau rejected the state, denied its legitimacy under international law, and ordered that Neturei Karta functionaries issue their own monetary notes, so they would not have to use the unkosher currency of the unkosher country.

When, by and by, Israel's War of Independence broke out, Blau was appalled by the recklessness of the Zionists, which might well result in the slaughter of the Jews of Palestine, including the pious ones, and for what?

Their defamation and conniving against our holy Torah have placed the whole
Jewish population in mortal danger . . . plunging the surviving remnant of the
people of Israel in the Holy Land into a war against powerful forces both
within and without. . . . We shall not be drawn into exposing ourselves, our
wives, and our children to them, heaven forbid, to die for the sake of the Zionist idolatry. It is inconceivable that wicked, unbelieving, ignorant, utterly irre-
sponsible heretics should come along and drag the entire population, several
hundred thousand Jews, like sheep to the slaughter, God forbid, because of
their false, insane ideas, and that the entire population, like an innocent dove,
should allow them to lead it away to be killed, God forbid.

Blau's holocaust never occurred, but the Zionists' successful defense of
their new state still produced vexing dilemmas. There was nothing novel
about pious Jews living under the administration, often oppressive, of heathens and heretics. But *Jewish* heathens and heretics, and in the Holy Land,
that was something else altogether. In Israel's first years, Blau experimented,
seeking ways to express his outrage. First he organized what came to be
called the "Sabbath Riots." In the hot summer of 1950, Blau publicized a demand that traffic around the ultra-Orthodox Jerusalem neighborhood of
Meah Shearim—home to most of the members of Neturei Karta—be curtailed from sundown, Friday, to sundown, Saturday, out of "respect for the
Sabbath." When his demand went unheeded, Blau organized protests. At
first, young ultra-Orthodox Jews gathered at roadside on the Sabbath,
chanting, "Shabbes! Shabbes!" at motorists driving past. Matters escalated,
and what followed was an ultra-Orthodox intifada. Stones were thrown,
windshields shattered. Motorists registered complaints, outraged articles
appeared in the secular press, and soon the police were called in to neutral-
ize the protests. Teens with earlocks were clubbed with nightsticks and
dragged into police vans, which naturally encouraged many more teens,
who were joined by sympathetic adults, to gather to protest in following
weeks. A cycle was established, quite literally vicious, in which violence bred
violence, which of course led to only more violence. The protests continued
for most of five years, occasionally diminishing, but overall increasing in intensity with time. They ended only after they succeeded. People stopped
driving where they were shouted down and pelted with stones, and in time
the Jerusalem municipality outlawed motorized transportation in the con-
tested areas.

Success encouraged Blau, and from then until his death in 1974, rare
were the times when Neturei Karta was not involved in a public struggle
against Israeli authorities. In 1954, Blau and his followers again took to the

streets to scuttle plans to establish a community center in Meah Shearim
that would host activities for boys and girls together. In addition to chanting, knotting traffic, and occasionally hurling rocks, Blau and his people
wore thick yellow armbands with the letter "J" for *Jude,* implying that the
members of the left-wing Zionist Labor Union that was funding the center
were no better than Nazis. Barely ten years after the Holocaust had ended,
in a city bustling with concentration camp alumni, this bit of street theater
had a chilling effect. Ultimately, the Haredim prevailed, and plans for the
center were changed. In 1958, Blau and his followers rioted in a failed effort to prevent the city from building swimming pools open to both sexes.
Dozens of Haredim and police officers spent nights in the hospital, having
bones set and scrapes tended. Eyewitnesses on both sides of the dispute
agreed that Blau himself approached the public disruption with as much
exuberance as rage. He enjoyed the fight. The rabbi soon found himself
doing time—four months for multiple infractions against public health,
safety, and order.

Protest against building of public swimming pools that would be open to boys and
girls at the same time, Jerusalem, 1958. Photo by David Rubinger. © *Yediot
Aharonot.*

Blau's career ended in controversy, some say shame. His wife died, and in 1965, Blau decided to marry again, this time to a woman named Ruth Ben-David, who was lovely, young, blond, and a convert. A rabbinic court forbade the marriage on the grounds that it was unseemly, but Blau, as combative in private life as in public, went ahead with the wedding anyway. Neturei Karta split into factions, defined by their attitudes toward Blau and his new bride. The combined influence of all the factions never matched that of Neturei Karta in its heyday under Blau and remains reduced today, although when Yassir Arafat sought a "minister of Jewish affairs" for the Palestinian National Council (the provisional government of the Palestinian Authority) he chose Rabbi Moshe Hirsh, a member of Neturei Karta.

Neturei Karta, which never counted more than some dozens of families (though thousands attended Blau's funeral), was in any case always more important as a symbol than as a political force. Although it had its share of successes, its greatest accomplishment may have been legitimating militant, rejectionist activism among the very religious. Before Blau, such activism was unthinkable, but it is now so familiar at the margins of Israeli politics that it seems natural, inevitable. Any number of things have precipitated protests over the years. For much of the 1980s, Haredim took to the streets to block the construction of a Mormon university—Brigham Young's Jerusalem campus—on the Mount of Olives. For many of the same years, groups of ultra-Orthodox Jews demonstrated against archaeological excavations near the site of Jerusalem's ancient Temple. More recently, in 1996, Haredim mounted months of violent rallies protesting the refusal of the Jerusalem municipality to shut a road named "Bar Ilan" to traffic on the Sabbath. These protests are only a few among many.

So many, in fact, that together the protests have engendered a new genre of book, coffee-table religious-protest albums, hagiographies glorifying battles waged by the fearless God-fearing against cowardly secular thugs. *The Cry of Pain: Vandalism Under Cover of Science* records an ultra-Orthodox struggle against (according to the book jacket) "the scandal of the desecration of ancient graves in the land of Israel by the Department of Antiquities and the State of Israel." A photograph on the cover depicts two policemen dragging forward an ultra-Orthodox Jew. The arms of one officer are clamped in a headlock around the Jew's neck, his teeth gritted hard from exertion. The other officer seems to be holding his captive from behind while kneeing him in the leg or groin. Following the frontispiece, the book's editor, one Y. Schiff, includes a page carrying another photograph and an epigraph—"From one Jewish cemetery in the Lvov region, we appropriated two thousand square meters of raw materials for building roads"—attributed to an S.S. general named Katzman. The photograph shows happy Nazis defiling Jewish graves. Beneath the photograph, Schiff added, "There is nothing new under the sun. . . . In the 'Jewish State,' archaeologists, with the aid of the authorities, are doing the same things by destroying ancient Jewish cemeteries for commercial purposes and with the excuse of 'science.'" The remaining 402 pages of the book include letters, government papers, photographs, personal accounts, and newspaper articles documenting the Nazi heartlessness of Zionist grave robbers. The book is one of many. Another on my shelf is subtitled *The Battle for the Holiness of the Sabbath in [the Tel Aviv suburb of] Petach Tikvah.* Still another is called *Pogrom: Kristalnacht in Meah Shearim;* it begins:

> With bitter hearts and broken spirits we make known to the world, the terrible acts that were committed in Jerusalem on March 7, [1981,] this past week. The police of the Zionist state carried out a cruel and horrible pogrom in the Toldos Aharon Synagogue. During religious services, the police threw tear gas bombs into the synagogue, and proceeded to beat mercilessly the people who were praying there, including old men and children. Then they desecrated and destroyed everything they could, including many Holy Books.

Photos show Israeli soldiers in formation like storm troopers, dragging Haredim through Jerusalem's streets. The events described concerned a protest over whether a road to a secular suburb of Jerusalem that ran beneath an ultra-Orthodox neighborhood ought to be open to traffic on the Sabbath. But the subtext concerned the unspeakable brutality to which Haredim are subjected. These books are testaments to a new sort of ultra-Orthodox heroism, one that is activist, one that is combative, one that owes everything to Amram Blau and his Neturei Karta.

One can admire this new heroism or abhor it, but one must admit that Blau and the other separatists had a point when they complained that the accepted ultra-Orthodox leadership, Agudat Yisrael, had lost its fighting edge and become chummy with the Zionists. Though images of the confrontations valorized in *The Cry of Pain* (and the many others like it) are powerful, they reflect the actions and attitudes of only a small portion of the ultra-Orthodox. When Neturei Karta split from the Agudah in 1935, the eagerness of the established organization for accommodation with the Zionists was growing as quickly as the enthusiasm of the upstart group for dispute.

Some ultra-Orthodox leaders also sensed a similar change on the part of the Zionists, who became less doctrinaire about their heresy. There were signs that the secular zealotry of the Zionists was abating. One sign was the increasing influence of religious Zionists in the governance of Palestine. To be sure, ultra-Orthodox Jews were ambivalent about religious Zionists, who were in some ways worse than their secular compatriots, because they offered religious sanction to a dangerously heterodox movement. But there was no denying that they brought some *Yiddishkayt* into the otherwise barren (according to the ultra-Orthodox) Zionist culture. In 1936, religious Zionists managed to persuade the Jewish Agency, the body charged with "the purpose of advising and cooperating with the [British Mandatory] administration of Palestine in such economic, social, and other matters as may affect . . . the Jewish population in Palestine," to establish religious councils throughout Israel, and to appoint chief rabbis to oversee their operation. What is more, these councils and rabbis were left on their own to a larger degree than ultra-Orthodox leaders expected, enjoying remarkable autonomy to interpret matters of Jewish law without interference from Zionists. These new positions were attractive to ultra-Orthodox rabbis because they provided a salary and job security without much actual work, and because they provided a platform from which these rabbis might persuade godless Zionists to return to the religious fold. In taking these jobs, ultra-Orthodox rabbis found themselves for the first time on the Zionist payroll, a state of affairs that made it less convivial to criticize the Zionists en masse.

The Nazis also drove the Agudah and the Zionists closer together. As alarming information about persecution of Jews in Germany, and in Poland after the occupation, filtered into Palestine, ultra-Orthodox leaders scrambled to find ways to save relatives and other victims. What few legal entry visas the British allowed Jews, they funneled through the Zionist Jewish Agency, so Haredi rabbis found themselves posting beseeching, ingratiating letters to godless Jews, or keeping appointments to meet ignorant, Zionist functionaries, the most learned scholars of their generation coming as supplicants to mere bureaucrats. It was humiliating, and it demonstrated the importance that circumstance had conferred on the secular Jewish authorities in Palestine. They might be scorned, but they could no longer be ignored.

In the aftermath of the Holocaust, ties between mainstream ultra-Orthodox and mainstream Zionists grew stronger still. In practical terms, the ultra-Orthodox needed the Zionists more than ever. The great centers of European Jewish Orthodoxy had been decimated in the war: It is now an almost forgotten fact that, although the Holocaust afforded such great suffering to such great numbers that comparison is almost obscene, the most religious of Jewish communities suffered disproportionately great misfortunes. The ultra-Orthodox communities of Palestine had until the 1930s been a small backwater in the ultra-Orthodox world, as had the ultra-

Orthodox community in the United States. These two communities—having escaped the ravages of Nazism, owing to dumb luck—were now the largest and healthiest Orthodox communities in the world. Leaders in both places were aware that the mantle of history had been forced upon them, and that to assume this mantle successfully they would need to shore up relations with the "authorities" in their respective homes. For leaders of the Agudah in the Holy Land, that meant finding some way of living side by side with the Zionists.

This task wasn't easy, especially at first. Friction was constant, and the next crisis in relations was always near at hand, even if it was impossible to predict what would precipitate it. Conflicts flared suddenly, sometimes far from Palestine itself. In June 1942, Soviet and Polish diplomats signed a pact in London that included a clause calling for the release of Poles who had slipped across the Russian border after the Nazi invasion, and who found themselves doing hard time in Soviet work camps. The agreement also called for the repatriation of Polish orphans who had found their way into the Soviet Union, and among them were 700 Jewish children. These children were shipped from country to country until, at the end of 1942, they arrived in Iran. The Jewish Agency got wind of this and began to lobby intensively for permission to transport these children to Palestine, rather than Poland, where no one believed they would long survive. While diplomacy continued, the children lived in displaced persons (DP) camps at the edge of Tehran (where they would remain for over a year). Optimistically, the Jewish Agency sent "counselors" to the DP camps, to prepare the children for life in Palestine.

Eyewitness accounts of life in the DP camps survive, but they conflict with one another; precisely just what went on there will probably never be accurately reconstructed. Still, some basic facts are well established. Among these counselors, most not much older than kids themselves, were several affiliated with a youth group named Ha-Shomer ha-Tzair (Young Guard), which was Marxist and vigorous in its rejection of religion. These counselors, and perhaps others with a less ideological pedigree, employed standard-issue tools of teens to persuade the refugees, many of whom came from pious backgrounds, to forsake religion: ridicule, peer pressure, and appeal to lascivious impulses. They had an effect. Orphans whose Judaism had survived Hitler and Stalin were rendered atheists by a small handful of Zionist teens. That was what had transpired, at least according to ultra-Orthodox Jews, when news from Tehran arrived in Palestine. When the children themselves finally made it to the Holy Land, in 1943, most of them were sent to secular kibbutzim, with 278 shipped to kibbutzim and schools run by religious Zionists, and only 32 were allowed to join the ultra-Orthodox community.

Such occurrences illustrated the irksomeness of the Zionists, but no less the importance of establishing ways to influence the Zionists. After the war, it seemed ever more likely that the Zionists would someday declare their own state, and it no longer seemed wise for ultra-Orthodox Jews to maintain pristine rejectionism. It was not too soon to contemplate, and negotiate, the rights, freedoms, and powers that ultra-Orthodox Jews would be granted in a Zionist country, as well as the responsibilities that they would be expected to fulfill.

And they did contemplate and negotiate their position in Palestine, obsessively, over the next years. A consensus finally emerged, one that both ultra-Orthodox and secular Zionists seemed willing to live with. On June 19, 1947, David Ben-Gurion (who less than one year later would become Israel's first prime minister) and two other Zionist functionaries sent a two-page letter, in the name of the Jewish Agency, to the leaders of the Agudah. It began: "The leadership of the Jewish Agency has heard . . . about your desire for assurances about matters of matrimony and divorce, the Sabbath, education, and kashrut in the Jewish State when it is established in our time." The new country would not be a "theocratic state," the letter went on, and its citizens would include Christians and Moslems. Still, the Jewish Agency pledged that the Jewish Sabbath would be the official day of rest in the country, that kitchens in schools, museums, and other public buildings would be kosher, that all efforts would be made to ensure that traditional Jewish matrimony laws were enacted ("to prevent, heaven forbid, any schism within the Jewish people"), and that the ultra-Orthodox would have full autonomy in educating their children. The letter represented the modus vivendi that the ultra-Orthodox had sought with the Zionists, and it quickly attained the mythical status of a Magna Carta for the religious in Israel.

Ben-Gurion was by all accounts a savvy politician, and he had good reasons to send this letter. Three days before he wrote it, a delegation from UNSCOP, the United Nations Special Committee on Palestine, had arrived in Jerusalem to continue its study of the plausibility and desirability of establishing a Jewish state. Ben-Gurion figured that a forceful plea by a group of religious Jews like the Agudah to forestall such a state might affect the committee's recommendation, either by actually swaying its opinion toward opposition or by legitimizing the opposition the committee had already registered. He sent his letter in hope of buying the silence of the ultra-Orthodox and making it possible for them to lend political support (or at least withdraw their political opposition) to the Zionist program.

For more than half a century, this letter has served as a constitution of sorts for the uneasy union of Zionist and anti-Zionist Jews in Israel. And it represents the Faustian bargain that has been at the foundation of this union since even before Israel was established: Secular Zionists accede to the ultra-Orthodox on religious matters, in exchange for ultra-Orthodox support in those other political matters that don't directly impinge upon religion. Ben-Gurion's letter established a double status quo: in religion per se and in the politics of the religious. Status quo in the etymologically correct sense—this is the condition in which relations between secular and ultra-Orthodox Jews remained for some time, and in many ways remain until today.

Mainstream Zionists and mainstream ultra-Orthodox had come a long way since the 1920s. Just how far is illustrated by the fact that, on Friday afternoon, May 14, 1948, after David Ben-Gurion declared the establishment of the State of Israel, a representative of the Agudah, a Rabbi Levenstein, signed the Declaration of Independence. Over the next seven months, the Agudah joined with religious Zionists in founding the United Religious Front, a political party that garnered 52,982 votes, 12 percent of all voters, entitling it to 16 seats in the new 120-seat Knesset (parliament) elected in January 1949. An ultra-Orthodox rabbi, Yizhak Meir Levine, was chosen to serve as minister of welfare. In just twenty years, the Agudah had gone from rejecting all cooperation with the Zionists to forming a political party with religious Zionists, assuming seats in the Zionist parliament, and sending a minister to the first Zionist cabinet.

The change was significant, but it meant less than it might seem to at first. It meant that the ultra-Orthodox had accepted Zionist rule as a fact of life and decided to cooperate with the Zionists rather than oppose them. But it did not mean that most ultra-Orthodox had adopted a positive view of the secular Jews who ran the new Israel. Matters of the heart are more complicated than this, and within the Agudah there was gut-ripping ambivalence. Some members maintained a view of the Zionists that was just as jaundiced as ever, in some ways even more. Around this time, the Agudah translated into Hebrew and printed (and then reprinted several times, for interest was high) a pamphlet by Elchanan Wasserman, the headmaster of the Talmudic academy in Baranowicze, killed by the Nazis in 1941. It was Wasserman's view that, theologically, the Zionists were to blame for the Nazis, for they embraced "two idolatries," socialism and nationalism. The rest was inevitable, Wasserman wrote: "In Heaven the two idolatries were fashioned into one—national-socialism. A terrible rod of fury was forged from them that strikes at Jews in every corner of the earth. The same abominations that

we worshiped are now hammering us." This view, which became something
of a commonplace among ultra-Orthodox Jews in the 1950s, both likened
Zionists to Nazis and implicitly blamed them for the deaths of the 6 million.
It reflected a potent contempt for the goals and sensibilities of secular Zionists, uncontaminated by even trace amounts of sympathy.

Other Haredim, however, began to look at Zionism in a new light. The
day after the United Nations voted in favor of the creation of "a Jewish state
in Palestine" (on November 29, 1947), the executive committee of the Agudah gathered for a meeting that had been scheduled before the historic vote
in New York. Naturally, the meeting was dominated by discussion of current
events, and the minutes report that in the course of the meeting a committee member named Raphael Katzenellenbogen declared:

> The declaration of a Jewish state is an historical phenomenon, that after two
> thousand years of dispersion and oppression, they give us a piece of the Land
> of Israel in which to establish a Jewish state with the agreement of all the na-
> tions of the world. There is no doubt that this is divine provenance. Certainly
> this is not the hoped-for redemption, but it does seem to be the start of the re-
> demption. And we must appeal to the Jewish people, taking advantage of this
> historic moment, for spiritual change and a return to the ways of the Torah,
> and to prepare ourselves for the full redemption.

This view—which took the Zionists as a harbinger of divine intervention—was adopted by some ultra-Orthodox Jews in the first years of the
state, and it proved particularly convivial for those who found themselves
working shoulder to shoulder with the Zionists, whom not long before they
had condemned as evil. Perhaps the Zionists were part of a great divine
plan, and perhaps their role in this plan was positive. At best they were
pawns, but perhaps they too were doing God's work, if largely unawares.

Such rationalizations made cooperation with the Zionists more palatable
for some ultra-Orthodox. For most, however, the reason they accepted the
cooperation had much more to do with fear of the Zionists than with true
reconciliation with them. Right-thinking Haredim could disagree about
whether Zionism represented a theological disaster, but most agreed that
there was real danger that Zionist rule might be a practical disaster. Some
elders remembered with bitterness the Yevsektsiya, the Jewish division of the
Soviet Communist Party, whose members after the Russian Revolution set
out to eliminate all traces of Jewish observance with ruthlessness and vigor
that their non-Jewish comrades could only envy. In the late 1940s, as the establishment of Israel grew more inevitable, ultra-Orthodox Jews worried

Haredi youth participating in civil defense, Tel Aviv, 1949. Photograph from
Central Zionist Archives, Jerusalem.

that Jewish socialist Zionists would apply similar energy to uprooting Jewish
observance. The Sabbath might be ignored, *treyf* (nonkosher) food promoted, all sorts of improper marriages sanctioned and given force of law.
The authority of rabbis might be officially nullified. Religious boys might be
dragged into a secular army, as they had been in Russia, never to return, at
least not with piety intact. Ultra-Orthodox children might be herded into
secular schools, brainwashed, and lured to the fleshpots of Zionism.

The only safeguard against this plausible dystopia, leaders of the Agudah
came to believe, was cooperating with the Zionists, in what amounted to
mutual co-optation. For Zionists, like everyone else, a vote is a vote, and by
choosing to participate in Israeli politics, instead of boycotting them (as had
been the Agudah's first impulse and earlier wont), the ultra-Orthodox established for themselves some political influence. One practical result of
this influence was an agreement on the part of the army, in 1948, to exempt
a limited number of yeshiva students each year from the army. Trading support for government policies for this sort of concession seemed to serve the

Voters standing in front of a religious party office in Meah Shearim during Israel's first parliamentary election, in 1949. Photograph from Central Zionist Archives, Jerusalem.

interests both of the Haredim and of the ruling Labor Party. This was the logic of ultra-Orthodox participation in a government for which they clearly had no affection, and it remains the logic for such participation to this day.

Given its nature, this participation was always a tenuous thing, and in 1952 the uneasy alliance between the Zionists and the ultra-Orthodox had its first real test. The flash point was whether women should serve in the new country's army. Ben-Gurion was persuaded that they should or, at the very least, that they ought to be drafted into some sort of national service. In April 1951, Ben-Gurion tried to pass a law to that affect. Before the vote, he was visited by two leading Agudah rabbis: Zvi Pesah Frank and Isser Zalman Melzer, who opposed the law with great vehemence. They objected for several reasons: Drafting religious women would bring them into illicit contact with men, it would expose them to the heretical lifestyle of the Zionists, and it would doubtless demand that they compromise their own fastidious observance in all sorts of ways—and all this at a still-impressionable age. So serious were these objections, the rabbis told Ben-Gurion, that they classified women serving in the army among those rare sins—like worshiping idols under duress—that one ought to die rather than commit. And this classification made compromise on the issue a religious impossibility. Around this time, Ben-Gurion arranged a meeting with the highest Haredi spiritual authority of his day, Rabbi Avraham Yeshayahu Karelitz, most often known as the "Hazon Ish." The prime minister appealed to the rabbi to soften the views of his constituents, and the rabbi responded with a parable. When two carts meet on a narrow bridge, each heading its own way, surely the empty cart ought make way for the full one. Zionists, empty of spirit, ought not ask for concessions from the pious, full of spirit. Discouraged, Ben-Gurion delayed putting forth his law in the Knesset. But in August of the next year he presented the law to parliament. On the eve of Rosh Hashanah of that year, the ultra-Orthodox representatives announced that they were quitting the government. For the first time in twenty years, the Agudah was going head-to-head against the Zionists.

But by now, the balance of power between the Zionists and the ultra-Orthodox was no longer uncertain. In December, Ben-Gurion persuaded opposition parties to join his coalition, and he no longer needed the ultra-Orthodox vote to govern. By the middle of the next year, draft of women—with an option of national service for religious women—had become law, and the Agudah remained outside the government. It turned out that this was a more satisfactory state of affairs than anyone had expected. Politicos from the Agudah no longer found themselves in the embarrassing position of explaining to their constituents why they had linked their

fortunes to those of godless Zionists. And the ruling Labor Party discovered that the Agudah could be counted on to support their policies, provided the government provide funding for Agudah schools and other such fiscal benefits. Unofficial coalition proved much more fruitful than formal coalition had, and it continued with near-perfect reliability for the long, twenty-nine year reign of the Labor Party, from Israel's independence to the election of the perennial opposition party, the Likud, in 1977.

Rabbi Avraham Yeshayahu Karelitz, the "Hazon Ish." Photograph from Central Zionist Archives, Jerusalem.

During the 1950s and 1960s, with the exception of the guerrilla theater of the Neturei Karta, relations between the Zionists and the ultra-Orthodox were less embattled and more convivial than they had been before (and than they have been ever since). There are many reasons for this, but they all boil down to one: It was a time when the ultra-Orthodox, for the most part, kept a low profile, a time when they "knew their place." And for the most part, their place was in Meah Shearim, Bnei Brak, and other small enclaves, far from the gaze of most secular Jews.

Beginning in the 1950s, the Agudah withdrew from more than just parliamentary politics. Quitting the coalition was part of a more general phenomenon, a turn inward on the part of the ultra-Orthodox. This turn can be seen in the changing demographics of the time. Mixed neighborhoods—those in which secular Zionists and ultra-Orthodox lived side-by-side—lost their equilibrium, and one after another became one or the other: either secular or ultra-Orthodox, but not both. In Jerusalem, the ultra-Orthodox population concentrated increasingly in Meah Shearim. The ultra-Orthodox in and around Tel Aviv moved in great numbers to Bnei Brak. Life among nonbelievers was fraught with "constant spiritual danger," as perhaps the most powerful Haredi rabbi of the postwar period, Eliezer Menachem Shach, once wrote. Rabbi Yizhak Zev Soloveichik, an eminent great-grandchild of Josef Dov Soloveichik, recalled:

> A great scholar and dear scholar who lived for many years in Tel Aviv told me that he was greatly taxed by protecting his children from any ties to the "street." He lived in a single-family house, with no neighbors, and he put a fence around the yard, with a locked gate. When the children went out, he would accompany them himself to make sure that they didn't befriend any of the children on the street. And of course this was an enormous imposition on him, not to mention how much of his attention it diverted from studying Torah, until finally he came to the conclusion that it was impossible to raise children [devoted] to Torah and true Judaism in Tel Aviv, and he decided to move to Bnei Brak, a city of Torah and God-fearing [people].

Along with the growing concentration of ultra-Orthodox Jews in just a few places—some scholars call them ghettos—came other changes. Ben-Gurion had promised the ultra-Orthodox their own school system, and he kept his promise. In 1949, the government created four "streams" of education—essentially four independent school systems—of which the ultra-Orthodox controlled one. In 1953, this arrangement was changed, the streams were disbanded, and the ultra-Orthodox set up their own school system (which they call "independent education"), not under government supervision. From the start, 70 percent of their budget was paid with government funds, so in the view of many Haredim, they enjoyed the best of both worlds: Zionist money without Zionist interference. (Testimony to this noninterference: Chumming with two ten-year-olds I met at a bodega in Beitar, a Haredi town built ex nihilo in the Judaean desert, I asked what they learned in school about math and geography. They'd stopped studying both subjects two years earlier. Neither knew long division, and both believed that America was part of Europe.)

The ultra-Orthodox also diverged from the Zionists in matters of traditional religion. Rabbis who worked for the Zionists, as part of the official state rabbinate, were no longer viewed by Haredim to have the authority to determine what is and is not kosher. The ultra-Orthodox community established its own alternative system of rabbinic authorities, circumventing and ignoring those of the Zionists. At the same time, the Haredim set up their own networks of social services. These networks were in addition to, not instead of, those provided by the government, but they established an ideal—rarely met—of Haredim caring for their own, without the interference of the Zionists. Ultra-Orthodox distanced themselves from Zionist culture, which was, as Rabbi Eliezer Shach put it memorably, "poisoned by the secular press, full of heresy and alienation, which incites and demeans all that is holy to us." In Bnei Brak when I was a child, only one newsstand sold the "Zionist" newspapers that everyone reads. An arsonist burnt the small wooden structure to the ground. Rabbi Shach also forbade television. On the shores of Tel Aviv, Herzlia, and Holon, beaches—cordoned off by high concrete walls—were set aside for the ultra-Orthodox. The ultra-Orthodox established for themselves a life apart.

There is something paradoxical in this. The life apart of the ultra-Orthodox was made possible by the Zionist state itself. Many of the institutions that facilitated Haredi separatism were funded by the Zionists. "Independent education" was true to its name, inasmuch as it allowed the ultra-Orthodox to determine their own curriculum. But economically, it owed its existence to Zionist taxpayers. The ultra-Orthodox social service network could maintain a high profile in large part because basic social services—medical care, money for retirement, unemployment benefits, food stamps—were provided by the government. In a sense, it was the state that made it possible for the ultra-Orthodox to ignore the state.

This state of affairs hardly bothered most secular Israelis in the first decades after Israel's independence. At that time, ultra-Orthodox Jews were regarded primarily with nostalgia, as one might today regard a Norman Rockwell scene. In 1972, when I was twelve years old, my parents took me on a two-week tour of Israel. Among the sights, our tour bus stopped in Meah Shearim, where the guide told us about the customs of what he called "old-fashioned" Jews. His tone had the same condescension as when, the next day, he took us to see "liberated Jericho," and pointing to a woman urinating in the street, he explained that Arabs are closer to nature than Jews, more like animals or pygmies. Palestinians were seen as part of the landscape, and perhaps Haredim were seen as part of the Jewish "history-scape." Both were viewed as primitives, quaint, and generally harmless.

After October 1973—the Yom Kippur War—Palestinians stopped seeming quaint, and after May 1977—and the election that brought Menachem Begin and the Likud into power—Israel's ultra-Orthodox also stopped seeming quaint. The two phenomena are linked. The Yom Kippur War severely damaged the confidence of many Israelis in their government, which had been blindsided by Egypt and Syria. This ought not have happened. Israeli intelligence knew that hostile troops had been concentrated to the south and to the north, but had mistakenly concluded that both Egypt and Syria lacked the air power they would need to undertake an offensive war. It was not until hours before the war began that this evaluation changed, and by then it was too late to mount an adequate defense. During the first days of the war, the armies of both Egypt and Syria fought their way miles into Israeli territory, and though Israel regrouped and ultimately won impressive victories on both fronts, by then many Israelis had entertained in earnest their worst nightmare, being overrun by Arab armies. During the eighteen days of fighting, 2,552 Israelis died, and more than 3,000 were wounded; it is hardly an exaggeration to say that no one escaped the tragedy of a relation or friend dying before his time.

The aftermath of the war brought more hardship. The cost of matériel lost during the short war had been $7 billion, which roughly equaled Israel's entire GNP for 1973. The cost in manpower—funding the standing army and especially the reservists who remained mobilized for long months after the war—would surpass $1 billion before the end of 1974. To cover these costs, the government levied new taxes according to complicated formulas that gave Israelis the distinction of being the most highly taxed citizens in history. All this at a time when government-appointed committees issued report after report damning the army and the government for not having anticipated, and prepared for, the Yom Kippur War.

One result of all this was widespread dissatisfaction with the Labor Party, which had ruled Israel since its establishment (and through the stewardship of the Jewish Agency, for two generations before the state came into being as well). It was not long after this period that the Labor Party lost its grip on Israel's government: In May 1977 voters went to the polls and reduced the Labor Alignment's share in the Knesset from fifty-one seats to thirty-two, a loss of nearly 40 percent in its electoral power. The Likud Party's representation increased from thirty-nine to forty-three seats. This gain was enough to give Menachem Begin the opportunity to form a coalition. Begin was a man who personified the extremes of the early-twentieth-century Europe in which he had come of age, fusing cultured gentility with fire-spitting ideology, an odd mixture made odder by Begin's coke-bottle-thick glasses and gnome-like stature. His forty-three seats, together with two won by Ariel Sharon's boutique right-wing party and twelve controlled by the Zionist National Religious Party (which had become ever more firmly associated with Gush Emunim, the West Bank settlers' movement) brought him to fifty-seven of the sixty-one seats he needed to form a government. The hero of the 1967 war, Moshe Dayan, abandoned the Labor Alignment in exchange for the post of defense minister, which brought Begin to fifty-eight. A centrist party—the Democratic Movement for Change—run by famed archaeologist and acclaimed general Yigal Yadin balked at the notion of joining Begin's government (though it did eventually join, with Yadin becoming vice-premier). It was necessary for Begin to persuade the Agudah to join his coalition. After twenty-five years of refusing to take active part in Zionist government, Haredim once again found themselves around a highly polished table in the Knesset, discussing budgets, ministry appointments, diplomacy, and all other matters of state.

This was a crucial change. Sociologists give many complicated explanations for it, but one simple explanation stands out. Begin made an offer the ultra-Orthodox couldn't refuse. Actually, many offers. Of the eighty-odd clauses in the coalition agreement that formalized the new government, over fifty concerned religious matters, and each one contained concessions to the ultra-Orthodox. Of these concessions, two are conspicuous. Begin promised to greatly increase government funding for Agudah schools. And he promised to remove the upper limit of 800 on the number of exemptions that would be made available to ultra-Orthodox youth studying in yeshivot. This limit had been established by a ministerial committee in 1968, when the numbers of Haredi students had been far smaller. The two concessions catalyzed a remarkable metamorphosis in Haredi culture.

The result of increased funding for yeshivot and effectively canceling the requirement that men leave the yeshiva to serve in the army was a huge increase in the number of students learning in Agudah schools. This increase was a blessing, but a mixed blessing. Just as the Agudah benefited from Begin's patronage, so too people and places associated with Agudah benefited from Agudah patronage. But the Agudah represented only a portion of the ultra-Orthodox world. As long as government funding had been limited, all Haredi factions lived in relative deprivation, and the gaps in wealth between them, if they existed at all, were relatively easy to ignore. In the late 1970s, Agudah schools got richer, and that made all the rest feel poorer and, increasingly, unfairly discriminated against. Among those who felt ill-treated were ultra-Orthodox Jews of Sephardi, or North African and Middle Eastern, extraction. These Jews had good reason to feel resentful. For years they had been treated as second-rate citizens, and what is worse, their religious and intellectual traditions were seen as inferior. When Begin clanged the bell on the government gravy train, Sephardi Haredim decided that they wanted to serve themselves, instead of settling for the Agudah's leftovers. By the 1984 election, they had organized their own political party, Shas, which received a respectable three seats in its first contest. In 1988, Shas captured 4.7 percent of the vote, for six seats. In each successive election the party registered steady gains, until in the 1999 election it received seventeen seats, making it the third-largest party in Israel, only two seats smaller than the Likud Party, which had first made substantial concessions to the ultra-Orthodox twenty-two years earlier.*

Shas is the most remarkable electoral success story in Israel's history. It owes its success to many things, but the most important factor in Shas's success is certainly luck. Since 1977, the ultra-Orthodox have held the deciding votes in every election. They are perfect candidates to be kingmakers because of their basic antipathy toward, or alienation from, the issues of mainstream Israeli politics. About most things that parliamentarians lose sleep over—budgets, tariffs, social programs, diplomacy, the environment, and so forth—the Haredi parties don't give a damn. Their active interests are so highly circumscribed—money for religious education, the upholding of Halakha where possible—that their votes are more fungible than those of anyone else. They amount to a big special-interest group, and outside the realm of their special interests, they're easy. They can govern with the Right or with the Left. As the chairman of Shas, Eli Yishai, said to reporters recently, "We are a coalition party, not an opposition party," which translates roughly to, we can support any program, as long as the check is in the mail.

Haredim have been in government for twenty-six years, almost as long as they avoided it before. The past quarter century has been a sort of golden age for Israel's Haredim. During this time they have registered some remarkable achievements. Their political clout has doubled and redoubled. They are wealthier, more sophisticated, better educated, and more combative. Owing to the high birthrate in the Haredi community, they are more numerous than they have ever been.

---

*In the 2003 election, Shas received eleven seats.

But all these successes have come at a cost. The golden age of Haredim has also become the golden age of "the Haredi problem," and—to be blunt—hatred of Haredim. Beginning in the 1980s, anti-Haredism became a winning political platform, and party after party (Ratz, Meretz, Tzomet, Shinui) powered its way to the Knesset by enflaming secular fear of the ultra-Orthodox. In every parliamentary election since 1984, a different secular party printed election posters showing an angry mob of Haredim, and promising that that secular party, only that one, will beat the Haredi back. Dozens of anti-Haredi organizations now operate with tax-exempt status. Hunger strikes protest Haredi exemptions from the army.

But the most extreme new opposition to Haredim is not organized. It turns up in graffiti: "Kill them while they're young" was sprayed some years ago on the side of a Haredi day-care center (the same sentiment was expressed on a crude handbill as well), or the carefully hand-lettered poster I saw one morning on Tel Aviv's main street: "You die so 30,000 of them can stay home." It turns up in letters to the editor comparing Haredim to parasites. It turns up in our dreams—like the recurrent nightmare of a professor friend of mine who sees her ten-year-old daughter being gang raped repeatedly by Jews in *shtraymls,* their strange, furry hats.

Tensions between Haredim and Zionists have existed for as long as there have been Haredim and Zionists. In one way of looking at it, the tensions have existed for even longer, ever since Mendelssohn's followers first tangled with the traditionalist rabbis. But these tensions ought to have slackened by now. Two hundred and fifty years after Mendelssohn, it seems that both the traditionalists and the reformers have succeeded beyond

Anonymous handbill protesting the establishment of a religious day-care center in a secular neighborhood. It reads, "The New Enemies!!! They must be *liquidated* while they are still *young!!!*"

all expectations. Haredi culture is enjoying an astonishing renaissance, only a generation after reasonable people lamented its utter destruction. Today there are more people studying in yeshivot than ever before in history. At the same time, secular Israel is strong and secure. If Theodor Herzl rose from his grave in Jerusalem today, he could only admit that things had turned out better than his greatest hopes. But Herzl, who loathed the ultra-Orthodox for their primitive parochialism, foresaw a Jewish state that would embrace them with gentle understanding. Today, we greet them with fear and raw hostility.

I discussed this problem recently with my friend Yuval Steinitz, a philosopher who quit Haifa University to become a Likud Knesset member. In his view, the history of the relationship between the ultra-Orthodox and the Zionists in Israel is a history of ever-increasing integration, and that explains the hatred with which the ultra-Orthodox are regarded today. "There's a paradox here," he began, with a philosopher's relish for identifying and resolving apparently logical inconsistencies.

> Because integration is increasing, the threat posed by Haredim *seems* more immediate and concrete. As long as the Haredim are off in their ghettos and secular Israelis are in their ghettos, the issue does not come up. . . . Today, we see them more, we hear them more, they appear on secular media, they don't cordon themselves off in their ghettos, they go to city council meetings, which in the past didn't interest them, they are mayors and vice-mayors, and it suddenly becomes clear that they have some influence. . . . So if there is today more anger and hatred between Haredim and secular Jews in Israel, this is really sign that the two camps are growing closer, not further.

If Steinitz is right, then "kill them while they're young" graffiti is, after all, a sign that after many years of alienation and anger, the relationship between ultra-Orthodox and secular Jews in Israel is on the mend.

But I have my doubts.

2

A Society of Slackers?

Some years ago, in 1985, a now-defunct leftist daily, *Al ha-Mishmar*, printed a political cartoon depicting a greasy Haredi, his gut hanging in rolls over the dinner table, clutching in one chubby fist a goblet of wine, while the other hand holds to his mouth a miniature secular Jew, whose blood he is sucking daintily, pinky extended. The paper's editors may have expected to startle readers with the cartoon, but I don't think they did; the image is hackneyed, too stock to shock. Around the same time, the leader of Israel's ACLU-ish Citizens' Rights Party, Shulamit Aloni, referred to ultra-Orthodox from the dais of the Knesset as "leeches" who "suck our blood." Uri Avneri, then editor of the weekly politics magazine *Koteret Rashit,* wrote that yeshiva students were "parasites sucking the blood of the nation," and Hayyim Hefer, a journalist with a weekly column of light verse, complained in rhyming couplets that "no one dares to raise their voice against the leeches who are sucking our blood." When students went on strike in 1998, they marched with a gargantuan effigy of an ultra-Orthodox black hat, on the side of which was painted, "the march of the leeches."* In a speech to the local bar, an appeals court

---

*In Hebrew, this is a pun. *"Masa Alunkot"* means a "stretcher march," which is a standard army training exercise in which soldiers practice traveling long distances while carrying a soldier in a stretcher. *"Masa Alukot,"* which was on the side of the stretcher, means "march of leeches." The pun emphasizes Haredi avoidance of the army. In the context of the students' rally, the slogan emphasized the injustice of Haredim who don't serve in the army receiving greater financial support than university students. Whether this is true is debatable; university tuition in Israel is highly subsidized.

judge in Beer Sheva, Oded Aligon, compared the ultra-Orthodox to lice and parasites, a widely reported bit of candor that
did not dampen the resolve of the chief justice of the Supreme Court, Aharon Barak,
to lobby hard for Aligon's advancement to a
national judicial post.

Leeches are only one metaphor; other
imagery is used to make the same point. A
few years ago, small round stickers depicting a secular Israeli with a Haredi on his
back started turning up on bus stops and
lampposts. Dozens of cartoons employ the
same motif, with Haredim sitting piggy-
back, riding horseback with spurs, holding
on as to a bucking bronco, and more. But
blood-sucking remains the gold standard,
easily the image most often used to de-

Ultra-Orthodox man drinking
blood of secular Israeli. From
Al ha-Mishmar, 1985.

scribe the ultra-Orthodox in Israel. It is an ugly picture, and it recalls centuries of anti-Semitic iconography, from sixteenth-century woodblocks of
Jews draining the blood of Christian innocents to Nazi portrayals of Jews as
vermin. Why is this image so common, so popular, in Israel today?

According to Yizhak Ginsburg, a bacteriologist and former dean at the
Hebrew University of Jerusalem, the image is constantly invoked because it so
perfectly captures the nature of Haredim. Ginsburg created a stir with a piece
he wrote in the early 1990s (see Introduction), about how we ought not "let

parasites from within dictate to us how we are to
be in our own country," and warning that these
parasites "are sucking the juices out of the country,
and may push it to the edge of the abyss." I wondered whether his views had changed over the past
decade, and I phoned him to ask. In the interven-
ing years, Ginsburg retired from teaching, but he
still maintains an active lab and advises doctoral
students studying parasite-host relations.

Ginsburg, who accents his conversation with
biblical quotations and poetic verse, and who

"March of the Leeches" student protest, 1998.
Photograph from Central Zionist Archives, Jerusalem.

lapses into English when the search for the mot juste takes him there, told me that what he wrote then is more topical than ever now, and truer:

> What I claimed then, and I still claim today, is that there is a vested interest which is cynically camouflaged by religious and ideological sentiments, and the political part, which is all about money, control.
>
> Now I am very aware of the mechanism of parasitism, which is an evolutionary mechanism that began long ago. At the start it was perhaps symbiosis or synergism between two parasites; today, for example, we believe that the normal flora of the gastrointestinal tract has value to the host; they provide vitamins, they protect from certain bacteria and virulent organisms. With time, parasitism developed to very high levels of sophistication. And one of the things is mimicking. The parasite surrounds itself in a capsule that includes a substance that is very similar to the substances in the human body, and hence the body doesn't recognize it as foreign, and it doesn't develop antibodies. . . . What happens in parasitic societies? The society that, for the sake of heaven, quote-unquote, and in complete surrender, owing to ignorance and poverty, blindly obeys a leader who promises them all sorts of things, and heaven forbid, what will happen if one day this setup collapses, and thousands of people without professions, without knowledge, will wander about and will fall onto the shoulders of the state as welfare cases. This is what is happening today.

I asked Ginsburg if he felt awkward describing Haredim in terms that the Nazis had used to describe Jews, and he told me that parasitism was, in fact, a traditional Jewish trait in Europe.

> But then and there it was not the Jews' fault, because they weren't given a chance. They weren't allowed to work land, to buy property, they forced them to become money changers, and to lend at interest. . . . Jews were pressured by their "hosts"—once again I'm translating it into scientific terms—to trick and outfox, which were ways of surviving. All these modes of surviving, the more Jews were pressed, the more they used them, and this is how they survived. But I don't think that this is appropriate for us today, in our society.
>
> Let's assume that the Haredi parties continue in their cynical, brutal way, to diminish the resources of the state. In the end, this will have a boomerang effect. As soon as they kill off their host, they too will die. This much is clear.

If you set out to find an emblem for Israel's intellectual elite, which is as close as one comes here to aristocracy, you couldn't do any better than

Ginsburg. He and his wife are in their seventies, and both were born in Jerusalem. Ginsburg's grandfather, after whom he was named, was a leader of the early Zionist Hovevai Zion Movement, who moved to Palestine in 1890. During the course of an enormously productive life he founded the first orphanages in Jerusalem and opened the first hospital in the Old City. The Jerusalem in which Ginsburg grew was small and *heymish*. His family, which was religious, knew and entertained writers, professors, and politicians. Ginsburg continued this tradition, while building a sterling scientific reputation and an outstanding career at the Hebrew University.

But the Jerusalem that produced Ginsburg is gone. To celebrate his wife's seventieth birthday, Ginsburg took her and several friends on a walking tour of the Jerusalem of her youth. When they went to visit her old school, a Haredi vandal doused them with a bucket of water from the rooftop, because one of the women wore a sleeveless shirt. A couple in their seventies. They cannot even walk around what used to be their city. It's ruined. Ginsburg sighed, "This is what Haredim do to whatever they touch."

It is debatable whether Ginsburg's expertise with microorganisms affords him any unique insights into the nature of Haredim in Israel. He feels that it does, because the logic of natural selection operates just as surely at the level of the complex organism (in this case, Haredi and secular organisms) as it does at the level of the microorganism. Ginsburg is not alone in making such assumptions. Sociobiologists and evolutionary psychologists argue that the behavior of populations and species can be explained in the language of evolution. A recent book explained in evolutionary terms why some men are rapists, and it's not much of a leap from this to an explanation like Ginsburg's about why some men are shiftless parasites.

Because of his education and profession, Ginsburg takes a more technical view of parasitism than most Israelis, who do not link the ultra-Orthodox directly to the mechanisms of microbiology and evolution. For most, the image of the ultra-Orthodox parasite simply captures better than any other the perception that Haredim consume more than they produce, that they take more from the country than they give back. This simple idea doesn't require any fancy metaphors to be explained. As the head of the Shinui Party, Tommy Lapid, told me, "When I was young, I supported a Haredi family. My son Yair supports two. His children will need to support three."

Broadly speaking, two complaints stand behind the view that Haredim are parasites: that they don't serve in the army, and that they are a drain on the economy. Both complaints have a hard factual basis, and both have come about because of an anomalous development in ultra-Orthodox society over the past two generations.

More boys and men study in yeshivot and *kollelim* (yeshivot for adults) today than ever before in Jewish history. Some say that more are studying today than in all past epochs combined (which is plausible, though I don't know how one could know whether it's true). These are potent statistics. They offer some satisfaction if taken as a sign—as they reasonably can be—of how utterly Hitler failed to wipe out traditional Judaism. In fact, it is in light of Hitler that the statistics are especially startling. The majority of yeshiva types of Jews in Europe (where almost all of them lived in the first place) were killed by the Nazis, hundreds of thousands of them. Ultra-Orthodox families have lots of children, on average, but the demographic hole that Hitler punched in the Jewish people has not yet been filled. Despite their third-worldish birthrate, there are fewer ultra-Orthodox Jews alive today than there were seventy-five years ago. Why then are there many more ultra-Orthodox students? Because a far greater percentage of today's ultra-Orthodox men study, and they do so for a far greater percentage of their lives.

According to sociologist Menachem Friedman, who has made a brilliant career of studying Haredi society, this change is now the defining characteristic of Israeli ultra-Orthodoxy. Haredim have fashioned for themselves "a society of learners." At least since the days of the Talmud, outstanding students of holy texts have been lionized, and *talmidei hakhamim* (literally, students of wise men; figuratively, those who handily master the religious corpus and offer innovative interpretations thereof) have been among the most respected members of the community. What has changed recently, Friedman told me, is that this ideal is no longer thought to be attainable by a small and especially talented minority. It is now considered an ideal for the masses, the norm for all men. To put it into a secular frame of reference, it is as if suddenly every father expected his child to become a high-energy physicist, and mandatory education ended not with high school, but with a Ph.D. program. A well-known Bnei Brak rabbi, Moshe Sheinfeld, commented on the change as early as 1954:

> Everyone who observes with open eyes will see an extraordinary phenomenon. Sons today are better than their fathers. . . . The faithful young man is today completely unmoved by the false charms that once entrapped him. He believes that the Torah is more important than everything. One finds today, like hundreds of years ago, women who devote their souls to winning husbands for whom the Torah is their vocation, and these women happily assume the responsibility of the bread-winner. This fact is a sort of miracle and wonder, in our crass materialist reality.

The phrase "Torah is their vocation" *(toratam omanutam)* is crucial. It describes *the* ideal of the contemporary ultra-Orthodox: Learning is seen as a calling to be pursued singlemindedly by all (males, that is). Friedman emphasized that this ideal is new (gaining wide acceptance only since the 1960s), and that it is unique to Israel's ultra-Orthodox Jews. Amiram Gonen, a geographer at Hebrew University, spent last year on sabbatical in New York, where he surveyed America's ultra-Orthodox community in the hope that he might learn something of use to policy makers in Israel. He found that in America Haredim work. "The vast majority of ultra-Orthodox men are in the workforce by the age of thirty." In America there is no ideal of cradle-to-grave study, except for the most talented. Rabbis encourage their students to gain vocational skills. The American Agudat Yisrael runs vocational-training programs to teach Haredim programming and accounting. Rabbis even approve of their students studying in universities. None of this is true in Israel. When a Haredi yeshiva named Maarava was established in the 1980s with the goal of teaching Torah and work skills, the influential Rabbi Eliezer Shach attacked it with gusto. Shach argued that secular studies would serve as a bridge from piety to heresy. For the same reason, university study is unthinkable for most ultra-Orthodox. In contrast to the norm in America, Israeli Haredim are expected to study all their lives—vocational skills are a waste of time and, far worse, a vehicle for abandoning Torah. Employability is nothing but a gratuitous temptation.

Toratam omanutam (Torah is their vocation) is behind the two principal complaints of Haredi parasitism. The army exempts those Haredim for whom Torah is their vocation. And the reason why Haredim receive disproportionately greater government benefits (such as unemployment compensation) and why they pay disproportionately few taxes is that many Haredi men pass their entire lives without working, because Torah is their vocation. It is this concept, more than any other, that angers secular Israelis.

Army

On a sweltering day last July, I drove from Tel Aviv to Jerusalem to watch four men share an apple. It was the first food that any of them had eaten since eight days earlier, when they had declared a hunger strike to protest Haredi draft dodging. Months before, the four had founded an organization named Hitorrerut, "Awakening,"* which aimed to compel the government

---

*This is a pun of sorts, as in religious circles, a *hitorrerut* is a gathering intended to increase religious fervor.

to force the ultra-Orthodox into the army. The organization's first action was a petition ("Enough exploitation, enough discrimination, enough extortion!" reads part of the text), which, according to sources in the organization, now contains several hundred thousand signatures. They are shooting for a million signatures, an ambitious goal, but not an impossible one. Activists also set up card tables in malls and on city streets, from which they explained their cause to passersby, handing out leaflets and bumper stickers reading, "One Nation, One Draft." I first encountered Hitorrerut at the Tel Aviv Book Fair, when a white-haired man called me over and asked, "Do you believe in equality?" I supposed I did. "Good. The greatest inequality in Israel today is that some eighteen-year-olds are asked to risk their lives for the sake of the country, while others are paid to do nothing." We chatted about this for a while, and as I walked away I heard him call to another passerby, "Do you believe in equality?"

During the summer of 2000, Hitorrerut adopted a more radical line and launched its hunger strike. The precipitating event was a debate in the Knesset about the recommendations of a government-appointed commission for "an appropriate arrangement" that would solve the problem of Haredim and the army. The founders of Hitorrerut, Boaz Nul and Itai Ben-Horin, along with a handful of similarly earnest twenty-somethings, launched their hunger strike to coincide with the debate, and they set up their "protest tent" across the road from the prime minister's office, not far from the Knesset. "Today, thanks to the enormous groundswell of support for us, everyone in the country knows about the importance of our struggle," a wan Boaz Nul told me. The setting gave this claim an air of unreality—under the nylon shade of the "protest tent" stood perhaps twenty supporters in a motley assembly. Among them were several high school kids looking for a way to pass a hot summer's day, a sixty-year-old man with a handlebar moustache wearing a highly decorated, lime green dress uniform of some Eastern European army, a paraplegic, some worried mothers of the strikers, and about a dozen journalists. All told, there were more placards than there were people, placards with droll slogans like, "Our Dicks are Broken," which is army slang for, "We're fed up." When a team arrived from the early evening news, the sparse group, including the journalists, gathered around the strikers so that on television it would look as if we were a thick crowd.

But Nul was not exaggerating when he spoke of a groundswell of support for his position. The commission findings that Hitorrerut protested had few supporters among secular Israelis. Even the chairman of the commission—an ex–chief justice of the Supreme Court, Tzvi Tal—prudently announced that he too was dissatisfied with the commission's findings, but he insisted they represented the best possible beginning of a solution to a problem that had festered for over fifty years.

Israelis tend to refer to any contemporary problem as though it was age-old and hence intractable, but Justice Tal had a point. The commission he chaired was established when the Supreme Court ruled in December 1998 that the "administrative deferral" from the army that the ultra-Orthodox had been granted year after year by the minister of defense was illegal. "Our conclusions are that in the present circumstances, the Minister of Defense exercises his authority . . . in a matter for which the [proper] authority is vested in the hands of the Knesset. This exercise of authority is . . . therefore unlawful." The Supreme Court charged the government to craft within a year legislation that would clarify the military status of the ultra-Orthodox.

The massive two-volume report ultimately issued by the Tal Commission (hoisting it while standing on my bathroom scale moves the needle by more than seven pounds) begins by noting that the system of deferrals was "as old as the State of Israel itself." It began with an edict issued during the War of Independence, on March 3, 1948, stating that "a decision has been reached that yeshiva students . . . are exempt from military service. Able-bodied students will receive training in self-defense in the place where they study, by order of the Knesset. This decision will remain in force until the end of the year." In 1949, David Ben-Gurion, in his capacity as minister of defense (a post he held alongside that of prime minister), extended the exemption. It was not until 1951 that he formalized this policy with a letter to the army chief of staff that somehow managed to be both telegraphically short and sluggishly wordy: "I have released yeshiva boys from mandatory service. This exemption applies only to yeshiva boys who are actively studying Torah in yeshivot, and only for as long as they are studying Torah in yeshivot."

Just why Ben-Gurion offered the exemption is a matter of much speculation and considerable disagreement. Understanding his motives is akin to trying to figure out the intentions of the framers of the U.S. Constitution: It's not clear whether and why it ought to matter, but somehow it does. Realpolitik is not in itself a sufficient explanation. Although the support of Orthodox parties made governing the young state that much easier, Ben-Gurion would have maintained power without this support. Sociologist Menachem Friedman insists that Ben-Gurion granted the exemption as a matter of principle: "After the Holocaust [Ben-Gurion felt it was] the responsibility of the State of Israel to ensure the continuation of the values of religion and tradition, as they were reflected in the yeshivot. . . . The yeshivot in Israel must provide spiritual leaders for the Jewish people." Ben-

Gurion himself wrote in a letter to then Defense Minister Pinhas Lavon, "The exemption that I gave to the *yeshive bukhers* is not the result of a coalition agreement—I did it freely and voluntarily"; but then Ben-Gurion was a political genius who was not above spinning his own policy decisions. I asked Uri Avneri, a left-leaning journalist and politician who knew Ben-Gurion well and served in the Knesset with him, about this, and he had a different explanation. "This was actually the only thing that Ben-Gurion and I agreed on. We both felt that it was acceptable to give the religious what they wanted because they were in any case dying off. It never occurred to either of us that this primitivism would survive for another generation."

Whatever the initial motive, a durable precedent was set, though it was subject to small changes over the years. In 1954, Minister of Defense Pinhas Lavon announced his decision to change Ben-Gurion's order from a blanket exemption to a deferral. After four years of deferrals, *yeshive bukhers* would be drafted. Rabbis from Haredi yeshivot demanded a meeting with the prime minister, Moshe Sharett, at which they accused the government of stifling Torah in the Holy Land. Sharett pressured Lavon to revoke his decision and promised to establish a government commission to study the problem. Lavon acceded, but there is no evidence that such a commission ever met. In 1957 Shimon Peres became minister of defense, and after meeting with the secretary-general of the Council of Yeshivot in the Land of Israel, a Rabbi Tannenbaum, he agreed to extend the deferral agreement. In 1968, after the Six-Day War, Minister of Defense Moshe Dayan organized a ministerial committee to reconsider the deferral, and this committee too decided to leave well enough alone. They did, however, add that the maximum number of new deferrals to be added each year could not exceed 800. This number was acceptable to Haredi representatives, because it handsomely surpassed the number of applicants who had applied in any single year up to that point.

But matters would soon change. In 1977, when Menachem Begin set out to persuade ultra-Orthodox parties to support a Likud-led coalition, he brought the army deferrals to the negotiating table. Begin offered three changes in the long-standing rules. First, he offered to apply the deferral not just to students of full-time yeshivot, but also to students in a variety of hybrid, vocational schools, who had previously not been eligible for a deferral. Second, he offered deferrals to *hozrim be-teshuvah*, penitents who had abandoned their secular backgrounds and embraced ultra-Orthodoxy. These two changes promised to double and perhaps quadruple the population who could attain army deferrals by enrolling in recognized yeshivot. This was a desirable state of affairs from the point of view of the rabbis, but one that created a serious problem: The new, lesser students would compete with the more serious students for the 800 annual deferrals. Begin's third change was meant to solve this problem: he proposed removing the cap on deferrals.

Taken together, these changes held powerful appeal for ultra-Orthodox rabbis, especially those who ran yeshivot. They served to shepherd to the classroom many students who would otherwise have found themselves in the army. No single act—not anytime, not anywhere—was singularly responsible for as swift and as great a rise in Torah study as Begin's changes to the rules governing ultra-Orthodox army deferrals.

Since that time, several government commissions have come and gone—the Yisraeli Commission in 1981, the Cohen Commission in 1988, and another Yisraeli Commission in 1992—and all of them either essentially endorsed the existing agreement (while finding ways to improve its implementation) or made recommendations for changes that went unheeded.

In the twenty-odd years since Begin's reforms, the deferment arrangement has grown increasingly problematic and powerfully unpopular. According to statistics gathered by the army manpower division, in the summer of 1999, over 28,000 *yeshive bukhers* were enjoying army deferments. Of this number, almost half (48.8 percent) were between the ages of seventeen and twenty-one, roughly a quarter between the ages of twenty-two and twenty-five, with most of the remaining under thirty-five. In other words, the army was missing 14,000 boys who could be in compulsory service, and another 14,000 who—in other circumstances—might reasonably be expected to give six productive weeks a year to reserve service. The change over time has been dramatic. In 1978, when the cap was formally removed, 800 *yeshive bukhers* were granted exemptions; a decade later, 20,000 were freed from the obligation to serve in the army. Today, the number is over 30,000 a year. In less than twenty-five years, the number of exemptions has grown by 3,750 percent. This accounts for almost 10 percent of all available recruits.

These are alarming statistics, especially if one pays close attention to the trends. In its investigations, the Personnel Division of the army found even more unnerving numbers. In the past five years, it performed random reviews of the files of army-age Haredim with deferments, and found that of the 248 files examined, 66 of the Haredim did not meet the deferment criteria. In some cases, they had stopped studying altogether; in others, they studied part-time and worked part-time. In other words, 27 percent of those *not* drafted ought to have been drafted even under the current arrangement. Worse still, in 1998 and 1999 the percentage of fraud was high; of the 64 deferment files studied for those two years, 32 proved ineligible. In addition, Defense Ministry statistics showed that in 1998, 16 percent of all *yeshive bukhers* were evaluated as "profile 21," a designation of poor physical or psychological health that renders the candidate ineligible for service. In the same year, only 4.2 percent of other recruits received this designation. Yehudit Naot, an MK representing the anti-Haredi Shinui Party, voiced the popular *J'accuse* when she wondered, "Is it possible that the Haredi population is more exposed than the rest of the population to . . . physical and mental diseases? . . . The high percentages reflect a Haredi dodge, in a desperate effort to evade army service." Add to this the calculation of Major-General Yehuda Segev, who heads the IDF Personnel Division, that cancellation of the deferment would allow the army to reduce mandatory service of all soldiers by four months, and you can understand why Haredi deferment from the army is seen by many as a great injustice.

After Ehud Barak was elected prime minister in 1999, a commission was created to study the problem and to recommend ways to ameliorate it. As often happens with such commissions, it was engulfed in controversy before it ever met. There was great debate about who ought to serve on the commission and, especially, who ought to head it. Barak personally chose Justice Tzvi Tal to head the commission because he is both Orthodox and Zionist, in the hope that Tal's religious observance would make him more acceptable to the ultra-Orthodox. It may have, though at the same time it made him suspect in the eyes of some secular Jews. The remainder of the commission was made up of Defense Ministry lawyers and bureaucrats, the mayor of Hadera, a retired general, and two prominent Haredim, the mayor of Bnei Brak and the head of the Israel Council of Yeshivot. Glaringly absent were any representatives of the secular parties and organizations working to draft the ultra-Orthodox.

Many secular Israelis concluded that they had been sold out even before the Tal Commission ever met. In a sense, they were right. The bull's-eye that the commission was meant to hit was drawn before it ever convened. The nature of the commission had been deliberated during the painstaking coalition negotiations that followed Barak's election, and the new prime minister more or less promised that the body he appointed would do little more than memorialize the status quo. Barak's coalition contract with the Haredi Yahadut ha-Torah (Torah Judaism) Party, included the following clause: "Since it is no one's intention to prevent yeshiva boys from continuing their studies, it will be necessary to revise the 'Defense Services Law' in such a way that . . . the minister of defense can, in accordance with his own judgment, . . . exempt or defer service, including for the reason 'Torah is his vocation'. . . . The deferment or exemption can apply to any number of yeshiva boys," the coalition agreement further stipulated. This was a long way from Barak's campaign promise of forcing all but 700 yeshiva students into the army, but he signed his assent only weeks after he was elected.

The commission's mandate was to present a report within ninety days of its formation, but it was soon obvious that this timetable could not be met. The delay was caused by the commission members' admirable desire to hear the testimony of people from many different backgrounds and views. During sixteen exhausting days of hearings, the commission heard the testimony of forty-seven experts. At first the commission members spoke with army experts in manpower, finance, and logistics. They spoke to lawyers from the government, the army, and universities. They invited moral philosophers, Haredi and secular journalists, heads of yeshivot, sociologists, economists, politicians, leaders of pro- and anti-Haredi organizations, religious and secular kibbutzniks. Almost no view of the issue was left unheard. Commission members then convened alone for two "study days" to review the testimony and thrash out recommendations.

Early on, the Tal Commission report informs us, "it became clear . . . that the problem with the 'Torah as Vocation' arrangement was not fundamentally military, but rather social." Behind this careful statement was the simple fact that the generals who testified before the commission were not enthusiastic about drafting the ultra-Orthodox. In general, the Israel Defense Forces have been finding ways of thinning their ranks in response to continuous budget cuts. When Ehud Barak was army chief of staff, he set out to create a "smaller, smarter army," which is to say, a *cheaper* army. Still, in their testimony, the generals emphasized that there was more to the army than security. In PowerPoint presentations to the commission, General Yehuda Segev and Lieutenant-General Avinoam Laufer explained army policy: "The IDF as a people's army encourages the induction of all parts of the population." Although "the principle purpose of the IDF is providing security, the IDF is a people's army in a democratic state, and the unity of the people is a crucial element of its security." In other words, even if the army doesn't need Haredim, even if it doesn't want them, it is important that they be drafted to preserve the "unity" provided by universal conscription.

The Tal Commission took seriously the desideratum of social cohesion, and it was this goal more than any other that determined its recommendations. Strictly speaking, it was an impossible goal. There is no way to finesse the fact that the question of Haredim and the army is a zero-sum one. For the hunger-striking members of Hitorrerut, justice could be achieved only through the induction of the ultra-Orthodox on equal terms. For the hard-studying *yeshive bukhers*, only recognition that learning Torah is a social good on a par with driving a tank could diminish their alienation. There is no common ground between these positions and no way to compromise that would increase rather than diminish social cohesion.

In the end, inevitably, the Tal Commission proposed changes that satisfied no one. "There are some among those who learn Torah who devote themselves to their studies as they ought to," the report concluded, "and for them the [present] arrangement will continue. But there are students who are not well-suited for intensive study, and for them a different way is appropriate." For this latter group, "alternative ways of serving, appropriate to their way of life, need to be initiated." The law drafted by the commission provides that Haredim may defer their army service while studying until they turn twenty-four. They would then be given a choice of remaining in the yeshiva, where their deferral would be automatically renewed, or getting a job for a year. If at the end of this "decision year," as the commission called it, they were to decide to return to the yeshiva, their deferral would be reinstated. If working suited them better, then they would be sent to three months of military service for training or to nonmilitary national service, working in hospitals, schools, or poor neighborhoods. Those who received military training would then serve in the reserves, at least until they had five children, at which point they would be released.

Reactions among the ultra-Orthodox to the proposed law were mixed. One Haredi commission member—Rabbi Asher Tannenbaum, the secretary-general of the Israel Council of Yeshivot—refused to sign the report. The leaders of the major ultra-Orthodox political parties were relieved by the proposal, which they feared would be much worse. The present proposal would likely cause a small exodus from the yeshivot at age twenty-four, especially among those who had enough children by that age to ensure that they would never be inducted. But the proposal had clear advantages too, from an ultra-Orthodox perspective. It did not limit the number of Haredi deferrals. It did not force anyone who objected into the army. And if ratified, it would be anchored in law, and not subject to the whims of the minister of defense as the present arrangement was, at least in principle.

Even before the commission's findings were released, *Ha'aretz* columnist Nehemia Strasler dismissed them for their "heavy bias toward the Haredim," for "rewarding draft dodgers" and "discriminating between two types of Jewish blood." General Shaul Mofaz, who was then the army chief of staff and later, under Sharon, minister of defense, attacked the proposed law, not so much because he thought the army would miss the Haredim themselves, but because the law would disgruntle everyone else. Speaking to a bunch of reservists during a break from military exercises in the Negev Desert, he said, "I'm not pleased by the recommendations. They don't enhance social solidarity or the strength of the army. People are willing to serve, but they don't want to be suckers." Dan Shomron, who himself had served as chief of staff in the 1980s, was even less politic: "This is an absurdity and a very dire law, because it is discriminatory. The proposal clearly discriminates against . . . regular soldiers and reservists." The poet Yehuda Amichai, himself a veteran of the 1948 war, wrote that "the battle against implementation of the conclusions of the Tal Commission is equal in importance to the battle for the independence of Israel." Boaz Nul, of Hitorrerut, said, "It is simply clear to everyone, from the simple citizen to general public to the prime minister himself, that the Tal Law is an awful piece of legislation, and in its present form, it cannot pass." Awful legislation, Nul explained, for several reasons: because it fixed into law the unfair ad hoc concession wrenched from Ben-Gurion half a century ago, because it made a hash of the principle of equality, because the IDF opposed it, because the Ministry of the Treasury opposed it, because it would lead to a wave of secular draft dodging, and because it completely ignored the question of army service for ultra-Orthodox women, just as if they didn't exist, which in a way for the ultra-Orthodox, they don't.

Most appalled of all, perhaps, were Orthodox Zionists, who felt that the Tal Commission had endorsed the mistaken notion that army service somehow conflicts with religion. If one rejects this notion, then the Tal Commission seems to create a gratuitous double standard. MK Nahum Langertal, of the Zionist, modern-Orthodox National Religious Party, insisted that "the moral implications of accepting the [commission's] conclusions is the creation of two classes of citizens: those who bear the burden of security and in so doing endanger themselves, and those who are exempt from this responsibility." Morality demands, religion itself demands, that Haredim be drafted.

To Shai Horowitz, the spokesman for an ultra-Orthodox anti-defamation league, Manof, such reactions are hysterical. I met with Horowitz on the last day of the Hitorrerut hunger strike, and it was his opinion that it was all much ado about nothing, and that the question of whether Haredim serve in the army is of no interest. It is crucial, Horowitz said, that even the army itself admits that we aren't needed. If we needed to serve in order to save lives, we would, but that is hardly the case. Horowitz handed me a pamphlet he had prepared, filled with quotes of generals and secular politicians and journalists about the superfluousness of inducting Haredim. He quoted Yizhak Rabin, who found as prime minister that within the army "there is hidden unemployment of soldiers, and a surplus of manpower." He quoted General Yoram Yair, once head of the Army Personnel Division, complaining that "the problem of the IDF isn't a shortage of people, but rather what to do with all the extra manpower." He reminded me of a government commission that Rabin appointed that had recommended thinning the ranks of the army and reducing the number of reservists. Anyone with the least intellectual honesty, Horowitz said, would have to admit that Haredim aren't hurting anyone by staying in the yeshiva. They're not needed in the army.

Also, Horowitz told me, before critics accuse the ultra-Orthodox of freeloading, they ought to check the statistics about secular induction. If they did, they would find that fewer and fewer secular eighteen-year-olds are going to the army, and not because they have something better to do, as the Haredim do. Here, too, it seems that Horowitz is right. Yoram Yair made headlines several years back when he told the Knesset security and foreign affairs committee that "one in every three citizens who are obliged to serve in the IDF receives a full exemption for medical or other reasons." Only a quarter of those who did not serve were yeshiva students, a statistic that suggests that secular Jews are almost as adept at avoiding the army as the ultra-Orthodox. It is difficult to unpack this statistic. Of the secular three-quarters, the great majority were either abroad or medically ill suited to serve. But how many secular eighteen-year-olds make their way abroad, and how many fake physical and psychological disabilities, in order to avoid army service? No one knows.

Horowitz said that he understands the feelings of secular Jews because he used to be one. This is an understatement. Horowitz grew up with eight brothers and sisters in a Haredi family in Meah Shearim and studied in yeshiva. But while still a teen, he rejected it all, stopped studying and praying, and a few years later enrolled to study philosophy at the Hebrew University. He became an activist in an organization to help Haredim who want to leave Orthodox circles—a sort of underground railroad that provided the information, inspiration, contacts, advice, and sometimes even the cash needed to make a break from Bnei Brak. He knows that there is a great difference between how the world looks through secular eyes and how it looks through religious eyes. And he understands that through secular eyes, it looks as if the ultra-Orthodox are selfishly, spinelessly avoiding the dangerous and disagreeable responsibility of serving in the army.

What secular Jews don't understand, Horowitz continued, is that there is more to defending the country than shooting a gun. The Hazon Ish, Rabbi Avraham Karelitz, put it well two generations ago when he said, "It is because *we* study the Torah that *they* [secular Israelis] can exist at all. It is the Torah that is protecting us." This is a theological point of the first importance, Horowitz continued, but it is absent from the secular view of the issue.

Horowitz paused for a moment, relishing the prospect of illuminating a theological point. Leaning back in his chair, he held his forefingers together in front of his mouth, looked up to the ceiling, and smiled. Then he looked me deep in the eyes.

I'll tell you why the army is not a problem. It's very simple. The Jewish nation has two missions. One mission is to survive, so you need the army. The second mission is to bring a message to this world. . . . God gave us some kind of way that we could both survive and deliver our message. Now not everyone can deliver the message. It's very complicated. So that is why all of us, from when we are youngsters we try to learn Torah and to know it. That is the theory behind *elef nikhnasim la-Torah, ahad yotzeh*—A thousand go in to Torah, and only one comes out—so why the hell do a thousand go in? Why not just pick the most talented ones to deliver the message?

Shai Horowitz paused to let his words register. It occurred to me that he looked a lot like John Lennon.

It's because we don't know who they are. The point is, it's not just intellect. You cannot just choose the ones with high IQ. It may be EQ, emotional intelligence, too, and strength of will, maybe these determine who is fit to learn and teach God's message. So what do you do? How do you find the talented ones? Does everyone go to yeshiva? It's like what Ben-Gurion told the Hazon Ish, "So everyone will go to war with a Talmud instead of a gun? Who'll carry arms?" No. If you have a pilot-training course, and you want the best to come, you may need a thousand applicants to fill ten places. You put ads in the papers, but no one comes. You put more ads in the papers, and only five come. So you take them. So this one isn't so smart, and this one maybe isn't in the best shape. We take them. That's our situation today. There is a very small group who will all go to the battle to learn torah. From all the youth today, we are only maybe 10 percent, and that's the reason why we need everyone who wants to give his life to Torah. We have to take the people that we have to deliver God's message. Now there is another point. The fact is that every place where you don't have the people trying to go to this battle, the Jewish community fades away. And when you have centers of Torah, even people far from Torah stay part of the community. That's the power that we have. That's what we bring to the battle.

I asked him if he literally believes that studying Torah is as important to Israel's security as, say, my job in the reserves, firing wire-guided antitank missiles.

"Absolutely. They're both important, and one can only do what one is able to do [meaning, I suppose, that if all I'm good for is firing those missiles, then I ought to do that] but Torah is more important. If everyone studied Torah and no one fought, Israel would be invincible."

I pressed him further, asking if he means that as a metaphor or as a hard objective fact, and he insisted that Haredi Torah study really keeps Israel's enemies at bay, no less than the IDF. This is a difficult point for me to grasp; it seems crazy to me. But if you believe in providence, that God watches out for his own, then it is not crazy at all. A lieutenant-general named Noah Hertz, a pilot who was shot down over Syria, lost his leg in the POW jails, and found God on his return to Israel, put it this way: "The yeshiva students are the IDF's weapon systems, by virtue of which the IDF wins and will win whatever wars arise or, God willing, don't arise. Without Torah, there is no future." For Hertz and Horowitz, the claim that the ultra-Orthodox protect the security of Israel is not a flight of poetic fancy or a metaphor. They mean that *yeshive bukhers* are as effective militarily as tanks and planes. In the balance of arms between Israel and enemies like Syria, they believe, the clear Israeli advantage in Talmud students is of greater strategic importance than an advantage in advanced weapons systems.

This is a formidable theological point, and for many Haredim it is an obvious one, but it is not the complete explanation why the ultra-Orthodox avoid the army. Another important reason is the fear that after a few good years, a Haredi youth will emerge from the army, if not secular, then at least different from when he went in. This fear has a history that may be traced back to Czarist Russia, where Orthodox Jews were forcibly conscripted, sometimes for mandatory service that lasted a decade or more. Children whose parents could not buy their way out, and who failed to flee, would enter as studious, pious *Yidn* (Jews), but when they returned, if they ever returned, they often displayed the ruddy ignorance of crass Cossacks. Russian rabbis did everything in their power to keep Jewish children out of the military, including sanctioning bribing, lying, whatever it took.

At first glance, this history impeaches the validity of Haredi fears of Israel's army. Israel, after all, is hardly Czarist Russia. The food in the IDF is kosher, the Sabbath and holidays are celebrated, and Judaism is admired. Soldiers are in constant contact with their families; they return home on most weekends, and many speak to their parents on cellular phones every day. In the worst instance, conscription is three years long—a long hiatus to be sure, but not long enough to prevent a successful return to studies. And the army offers a program called *hesder,* a unit in which young men alternate periods of soldiering with periods of yeshiva study, so that they needn't be away from the Talmud for more than several months at a time, a year tops.

Haredim are right, though, to worry that the army might lead youth astray. Religious observance inevitably slackens in the field. For example, it is IDF policy for all its units to maintain a kosher kitchen, but this is an ideal that is met only in the most general way, which is to say, an ideal that is rarely met at all. Cooks have little familiarity with the rules of kashrut, and the soldiers who are sent to help in the kitchen on a rotating basis often have none at all. Milk and meat pots and utensils and plates are jumbled. Usually it is the result of inattention and laziness, but sometimes it is purposeful. I've seen soldiers laughing as they pour milk into vats of chicken, making it all *treyf,* so that the religious would unwittingly eat forbidden food. Sabbath observance also goes on holiday in the army, where religious soldiers have to decide either to screw their friends by not pulling their weight, or to do things that are religiously proscribed, like riding in jeeps, writing in logs, turning on flashlights, answering phones, and so forth. The same is true for fasting on fast days, praying three times a day, and practically every other aspect of a religious regimen. There is a certain "zero-summitude" in army life, and when one soldier exempts himself from army drudgery in favor of religious rites, another finds himself doing that much more of the dirty work.

But the main problem is not so much the obstacles to observance in the army as the intangible *culture* of the army. When you're in it, the army is what the sociologist Ervin Goffman called a "total institution," like a prison or a psychiatric hospital. It has its own slang, its own humor, its own codes of dress, honor, behavior. All of them are, if not exactly secular, at least profoundly *this-worldly.* Sex is a constant topic of discussion (though not as pervasive a topic as money, and in a tight contest with high-tech start-ups, cars, refrigerators and other household appliances, and large durable goods). Though no one actually discourages study or contemplation, these and other aspects of the life of the spirit are well out of step with the atmosphere of the army. I have a friend in the reserves named Zippori (we are friends, but I never learned his first name), who rejected his secular upbringing and embraced ultra-Orthodoxy, but as a matter of honor insisted on continuing to serve in our unit. Zippori is soft-spoken and thoughtful, and sitting on a rooftop in Hebron, he would patiently try to teach the rest of us a little Talmud. He never succeeded, but we did manage to draw him into conversations far more vulgar, he once told me, than anything he ever heard outside the army. Zippori is in his early thirties, has five children, and studies throughout the year in a *kollel*. Our crassness probably causes him no permanent damage. But what about a more impressionable eighteen-year-old Haredi boy, with no experience of secular culture, who might easily be dazzled by worldliness, even in its cruder aspects? I sympathize with ultra-Orthodox parents who hesitate to pack their son off to spend three years with people like me.

In Czarist Russia, promoting assimilation was policy, and the army was a means of implementing this policy. This is true in Israel as well. Ben-Gurion described the army as Israel's greatest melting pot, as the only institution capable of taking young Russians and Germans and Moroccans and stamping them all into Israelis. When Raful Eitan was army chief of staff (he would later be a member of Knesset for many years), he instituted a program for drafting hard-bitten, semiliterate, poor kids mixed up with drugs and crime. The army taught them to read, gave them vocational skills, sobered them up, and generally beat them into shape. It made *citizens* of them. It made *Zionists* of them. Behind the program—known to this day as *yaldei Raful,* "Raful's kids"—was the notion that the army is a tool for socializing.

There are two ways to look at it. One is as manipulative Big Brotherism that strips people of their heritage. The notion of "making Israelis" out of immigrant riffraff is condescending, and at odds with today's more multicultural sensibilities. The other way to look at it is as using the army not just to protect, but also to serve: by teaching citizens to be comfortable and productive in a culture that is otherwise foreign and uninviting. Both ways of seeing it are right. Acculturation is a gift and an assault, an alchemy of philanthropy and violence.

In contrast to immigrants or kids from the wrong side of the tracks, though, for most Haredim, acculturation bears no gift. For Haredim, comfort and productivity in the Zionist sense of the words are at odds with their most cherished beliefs. Comfort and productivity (within the larger secular culture) are themselves an assault. When Haredim fear that the army will gut their kids of their culture, will alter them, will make it hard for them to return to the *yeshiva* from which they came, that is not paranoia. The fact is, if the army works the way that many of us think it ought to, that is precisely what will happen. The army makes Israelis of Russian immigrants, the army made an Israeli of me, and if given the chance, the army will make an Israeli of young Yankel from Bnei Brak. And Israeli, in this sense at least, is the last thing that Yankel wants to be (and how much less so his parents).

Even if this weren't so, even if Haredim did not *want* to feel foreign, they are different from secular Israelis, and this difference itself feeds a certain alienation from the army. Though most Zionist Israelis go to the army, it remains in many ways a "Skull and Bones" secret society. The army does not come with a users' manual, and when I landed in the infantry a brightly scrubbed twenty-two-year-old with a degree in philosophy and psychology, I understood only a fraction of what went on around me. People, places, and things are all named by acronyms. Rules are never spelled out. Soldiers who grew up in Israel, who had older brothers who'd been through the army, whose high school buddies were with them or in a similar unit somewhere else, somehow naturally came by the occult knowledge of how the army works and how to work the army. But I suffered through years of green-horned cluelessness, never really knowing what had just happened or what would happen next. This cluelessness has continued through all my years of reserves. It's been fifteen years of missing the joke, of being a wallflower at a freshman mixer, of being the new kid on the first day of sleepaway camp. As I was, Haredim are largely innocent of the army, and just as for me, this innocence makes the IDF that much harder to embrace.

For all this, it must be said that some Haredim do serve in the army, in a variety of ways. Some are drafted into the IDF rabbinate, which spotchecks kitchens to ensure that they're kosher, distributes *Haggadot* on Passover and *siddurim*, tefillin, and other articles of religious observance, organizes prayer services, and provides the occasional sermon at memorials, celebrations, and other military affairs. Two other units draft Haredim. The first is *Hesder*, which drafts soldiers for a five-year tour of duty, of which all but one and a half years are spent studying in a yeshiva. Haredim are a tiny minority of the soldiers in this unit; the great majority are modern-Orthodox Zionists, most of them West Bank settlers. The second unit is named, or rather misnamed, the Nahal Haredi. "Nahal" is an acronym standing for Noar Halutzi Lohem, "Fighting Pioneering Youth." If the name recalls the earnest institutions of postrevolutionary Russia or China, this is not a coincidence. Nahal was founded as a tool of socialism. Its early goals were to defend Israel by establishing pioneering communes in border hinterlands. Many of Israel's kibbutzim started out as Nahal settlements. *Nahlawim*, as soldiers in the infantry unit are still called, were taught to kill and to farm, and they split their army service almost evenly between soldiering and pioneering. After army service, *Nahlawim* were expected to remain on the settlement that they helped establish, to build it, to raise families on it, and ultimately to be buried on it. *Nahlawim*, most of whom began attending meetings of a Communist youth movement when they were in grade school, tended to view themselves as a "revolutionary vanguard."

Over the years, Nahal's revolutionary fervor waned, and by the time I enlisted in the unit in 1984, only a handful of recruits planned to spend their lives on a kibbutz. By then, most of Israel's pioneering was done by settlers building villas in West Bank fortress villages with ready funds provided by the Likud-led government. Nahal, whose bread-and-butter recruits were leftists hostile to building in "occupied territories," experienced a crisis of identity. By the 1990s, the settlement and pioneering aspects of the unit were quietly replaced by a "year of service," during which soldiers worked in poor city neighborhoods, teaching in schools, building parks, or doing other good works.

Several years ago Yehudah Duvdavani, a now-retired brigadier-general, had the brainstorm of adapting the Nahal to Haredim. The match made some sense. The Nahal had always inducted not just individuals but, most often, large, homogeneous groups (called *garinim*), usually kids who had banded together after years in the same youth groups. Nahal organized companies comprising only members of the Communist movement Ha-Shomer ha-Tzair, for example. Why couldn't Nahal organize companies comprising only Haredim? These companies could be fitted to the special needs of ultra-Orthodox soldiers; they could provide extra religious services, serve food that meets more stringent kashrut requirements, quarantine the men away from female soldiers, offer extra training, and bring in a rabbi to give Talmud classes if that's what it takes to keep the soldiers happy.

In January 1999, the first thirty-one soldiers were inducted into the Nahal Haredi, which was given the additional name of Netzah Yehudah. "Netzah" is an acronym, standing for Noar Zioni Haredi, "Zionist Haredi youth." This may be wishful thinking; critics of the program insist its soldiers are neither Zionist nor Haredi. Everyone refers to the unit as the Nahal Haredi. The unit's first-year "work plan" called for four months of basic training, followed by four months of "operations duty," which usually means guarding the border or patrolling the occupied territories, and then four months of advanced military exercises and maneuvers. The remainder of their service includes another six months of "operations," a year of nonmilitary community service, and a final six months of guarding and patrolling.

I caught up with the first group of soldiers near the end of their middle six months of border duty on the Jordanian border. A few years ago, I had spent a month in the same place as a reservist, and I knew that the work has pluses and minuses. In its favor, for a combat soldier, it's about as safe a place as you can be. Israel's relations with Jordan are better than those with any other neighboring country, and it's been a generation since there was any real threat of hostile fire between Jordan's soldiers and our own. As a result, the job of

One of the first group of Nahal Haredi soldiers, after completing basic training, receiving his beret in 1999 in a ceremony at the Western Wall. © Reuters.

border patrols is to keep a wary eye out for terrorists and, much more common, smugglers, and although such undesirables cross the border frequently enough to justify the army's efforts, they are infrequent enough to pose only a wisp of a threat to soldiers on the beat. I haven't seen the statistics, but it must be safer to patrol the Jordanian border than to drive Israel's highways, which have the highest per capita death rate in the world. This relative safety is good, of course, but it also accounts for the hardship of the station. It is boring. It is *very* boring, watching-paint-peel boring. Soldiers drive, four to a jeep, up and down the soft sand near the border fence looking for unexplained footprints in the sand. The fence itself is fitted with computer-coordinated pressure sensors, so usually infiltrators are identified automatically, back at a permanent observation station. The soldiers are the belt to the computerized fence's suspenders—should a terrorist somehow manage to outsmart the sensors, the hope is that the patrol would come upon them or at least their tracks. This is an exceedingly rare occurrence. Most of the time, soldiers drive up and back several kilometers over and over, either baking in the desert sun or bundled against the chill of the cloudless desert night. Time passes slowly.

I don't know what I expected Haredi soldiers to look like, but when I saw them I was surprised that—save *peyes* curled discreetly around their ears under their olive-drab hats—they didn't look any different from any other soldiers. One kid with closely cropped hair in a uniform looks pretty much like the next. These Haredim also look like soldiers in the less tangible ways that transcend their mere physical appearance. Institutions have cultures, and like the attenuated, glassy-eyed shuffle of long-term psychiatric patients, who cannot leave the institutions in which they are confined, soldiers have their own characteristic disposition. I walked past a clutch of soldiers kicked back, their feet up on a rusty table covered with crushed empty coke cans, discussing what they were going to do on their weekend leave. No one paid much attention to what anyone else said, and the conversation, which I stopped to listen to, loped aimlessly. A soldier noticed me and called out to ask if I had the morning's sports section. I gave it to him, and another soldier asked for the whole paper, which was efficiently divided among the soldiers. The ambience was slow and desultory, just another anesthetized army afternoon. I asked the kid standing sentinel at the gate of the fence that circled the camp whether being a soldier was what he expected. "I don't know. Didn't really expect anything." I asked him if people at home were angry at him for enlisting. "I don't know. Some, I guess, but some aren't." I asked him if being in the army made him any more Zionist or less Haredi, "I don't know. No. Maybe. I don't know." Then he asked for my lighter.

Later, I asked the base commander (whom I'll call simply David, because the IDF understandably objects to revealing the full names of their soldiers) if Haredi soldiers were any different from the other soldiers he'd commanded, and he said that he wished they were. "They're like all soldiers. They want food, they want to sleep, and they want weekend leave. . . . I haven't noticed anyone here arguing ideology, whether Haredi or not Haredi. If only there was such a thing, but there is not. These are soldiers like any other soldiers."

In fact, David continued, this is just about the only accurate generalization you can make about the soldiers, who were a surprisingly heterogeneous group. Most of them came from a Haredi background, but this group included all sorts. Some were exemplary yeshiva students, who decided for one reason or another that they wanted to leave Talmud study, at least for a few years. Some were from broken families, kids who had no place to live, no place to go. Some were expelled from yeshivot, and found themselves spending their days on the streets, not managing to resist the temptations of the streets—basically sex, drugs, and rock and roll. Some of the soldiers stopped being religious before they ever enlisted. Some were never Haredi, David continued, but were religious Zionists looking for an army unit that would know how to take their religious needs seriously. "There is no average soldier here," David concluded.

I asked if the heterogeneity didn't cause tensions. I imagined fist fights in the showers over religious observance.

David sighed, "If only there were such tensions, that would be a sign that something good was happening, but there aren't. These guys are as mindless and apathetic as any soldiers anywhere else in the army."

I mentioned that several Haredim had told me that they would never send their kids to the army, not just because it's heartbreaking to think of them outside the walls of the yeshiva, but because they fear the army will *ruin* the kids, making them Zionists or causing them to doubt their religion.

David disagreed:

This can happen in my opinion only if the Haredim themselves decide to reject kids who have been in the army, and not allow them to marry, or to live in their neighborhoods, and generally treat them like second-class citizens. But if they accept these kids, they'll only be doing themselves a favor, and they'll be rewarded with better citizens, who know how to work, who are selfless, who understand commitment to their society.

David paused. "Parents all over the country send their kids, knowing that they might be *killed*. Let's say that one or two Haredim are 'ruined' and reject the culture they came from. Is this any worse than being killed? It's a risk that they ought to be very willing to take."

David's point has a certain logic, but for Haredi critics of the program, the risk of spiritual ruin is graver than the risk of death, and not one to which they wish to expose their children. In September 2000, posters appeared throughout Meah Shearim and Bnei Brak comparing service in the Nahal Haredi to a concentration camp. Under the bold heading "Gas Chambers," the posters warn "Yeshiva heads and parents" that "Nahal agitators have managed to tempt" their kids to come to an induction weekend sponsored by the Nahal Haredi and to lie to their parents about it. Around the same time, a *yeshive bukher* who inquired about enlisting in Jerusalem was attacked and beaten. Some Haredim continue to see the Nahal Haredi as a road to spiritual ruin. In September 2000, several hundred Haredim gathered in Bnei Brak for a rally against the army program, which rabbi after rabbi likened to a "spiritual holocaust."

This attitude accounts for a fundamental tension in the Nahal Haredi, as Brigadier-General Eitan Usseri, the Nahal's second in command explained to me in a spare Tel Aviv office belonging to the IDF spokesman. "If the Nahal

Haredi fails, well, it fails. But if it succeeds, at least if it succeeds too much, it also fails. The moment we begin to attract the sorts of youth who might otherwise stay in yeshivas is the moment they'll shut us down."

"In fact," Usseri continued:

the biggest fear Haredim have of the Nahal Haredi is that it will succeed. Because if it succeeds, there will be many yeshiva students who'll choose to go to the army. The army is appealing to teenagers. It offers action, weapons, adventure, and teens are naturally drawn to these sorts of things. The percentage of Haredi kids who really want to learn for all their lives isn't very high. . . . So the Rabbis' big fear is that suddenly the yeshivot will empty, and our unit will fill up. That's why the army decided from the beginning not to draft anyone learning in a yeshiva.

Anonymous poster in Bnei Brak, warning youth of the spiritual danger of joining the Nahal Haredi. It reads, "Suicide! Your Place Is in the Nahal."

But many Haredim are still worried about us. In some quarters, there is a very vigorous objection to the Nahal; they've essentially declared war on us. Opponents phone those planning to enlist to talk them out of it, and sometimes they attack the rabbis who support the program. All of this stems from the major fear that it will succeed.

I asked why, then, any of the rabbis support the unit.

They do because this program is a lifesaver for a certain sort of Haredi youth, who if they didn't come to us, would end up secular in the best case, and criminal in the worst. Therefore, the Haredim have a genuine interest in keeping this program going. . . . Many parents see the program as the last, best hope for their children. Because until they enlisted, the kids slept until noon, then spent all day around town, doing God knows what, and now they're in a Haredi structure, and parents see their children maturing through their service.

And we do provide a crucial service. To us it was clear that to make these boys into good soldiers, and even into good human beings, wasn't enough, and that we had to do more, both to attract them, and that those who come won't feel like they are suckers for coming to the army, but rather with the feeling that they got something useful for their civilian life after the army. We figure that in this way we are also contributing to Israeli society, creating not just a combat soldier, but also a useful citizen. Therefore, we provide them with remedial education, and also a useful profession.

These soldiers come to us with a very weak general education. In their yeshivot, they learn math, science, geography Hebrew only until fifth or sixth grade. During the first year, we bring them up to at least ninth-grade level in all these subjects. These educational and ultimately social objectives, we decided, are more important than our military objectives. So they'll do fewer long marches, fewer military exercises. But there'll be more soldiers who are educated.

Secular Jews also complain that Haredim don't serve in the army. I think that there are many people in the army and the Defense Ministry who understand that it is not enough to talk about how we should draft Haredim, or to pass laws about it, and that we need to do something practical. The Nahal Haredi is an opportunity not just to complain but to create the conditions in which it would actually be possible for Haredim to serve. It is a service, to Haredi parents, to Haredi society, to the Haredi recruits themselves, but ultimately to the whole of Israeli society.

Usseri has an exhilarating earnestness, for which I have a particular weakness—he's the sort of adult parents hope for when they enroll their kids in the Boy Scouts—and by the end of the interview, I found myself inspired. When I listened to the tape of the interview, I was embarrassed to hear myself gushing to Usseri that "this program reminds me of what I love about this country and especially about the army. What we're talking about here really boils down to good works. One could say that, from a strictly military point of view, there are countless better ways for the army to spend this money, but the army spends it on the Nahal Haredi because it is a social good, a service to the country." In fact, I feel ambivalence toward the army that has grown during the violence of the recent years. It may or may not be right to distinguish between the impact that the IDF has upon those who serve in it and those whom it battles and polices. I am also mindful that even the impact upon those who serve is of mixed value—arguably the army is the petri dish in which a viral sort of sexism is nurtured and from which it spreads to other parts of Israeli society. At the same time, there is something moving about the degree to which the army views itself as fostering and furthering ideals of justice and equality, at least among those who serve in it. This self-image, I think, is not without justification. In any case, Usseri smiled indulgently in response to my naïve enthusiasm, and added, "Yes, and in a period when the army's budget is being cut every year, it means something that we keep getting more money, essentially everything we ask for."

This largesse can be seen in different ways. MK Tommy Lapid called it a charade and a public relations stunt that serviced the propaganda interests both of the army and of the ultra-Orthodox. "You could fit the entire Nahal Haredi in this room," he said, indicating his modest office with the sweep of his arm, "It's nothing." He said that he could think of hundreds of ways in which the money could be otherwise better spent. I take a less jaded view, and believe that the IDF does see the Nahal Haredi as a service to the country. Whichever view one takes, it is a simple fact that the program is expensive, and in strictly military terms probably not worth the money, and this fact points to a fundamental truth about Haredim in the army. In the strictest sense, the army doesn't need them and doesn't want them. This is true of both the standing army and the reserves. Many Haredim apply for the short basic training, called *Shelav Bet,* or "Stage B," which readies older citizens for reserve duty. On Rabbi Akiva Street in Bnei Brak I met a young man who was bitter over having been turned down, who insisted that you have to have connections to get in. "Contrary to popular belief," ex-MK Ron Cohen said in a lecture, "it is the leadership of the army that refuses to draft yeshiva boys into the army, and this for economic reasons. Many of those yeshiva students do try to enlist, but the army rejects them because the IDF has no shortage of personnel, and because the army would rather use the budget for drafting them for greater goals, like weapons purchases." The Nahal Haredi may be a boutique, pilot project that no one—neither the rabbis nor the generals—would like to institute on a large scale.

To many, probably most, Israelis, the fact is obvious but also beside the point. Of course the army doesn't want Haredim. The point is not what's necessary; the point is what's fair. The point is blood.

Blood is a powerful image and it comes up over and over again. It is doubly evocative, calling to mind the secular boys who have died defending Israel, and also the Nazi dogma that Jewish blood was inferior and infected. Blood carries two messages. We are dying for *you.* And, *you* think that our blood is cheap.

Understanding this imagery is important because it explains why the practical question of whether

Veteran giving blood and *yeshive bukher* receiving blood. Cartoon originally appeared in *Ma'ariv.* Reprinted with permission of *Shpitz,* journal of the Israel Cartoonists Union.

the army needs or even wants Haredim is irrelevant to many people who strongly advocate drafting the ultra-Orthodox. What's at stake is not exigency—what the army or the country needs—but rather fairness and decency. Fairness in dividing the risks of defending the country among everyone. And decency in treating everyone as equals and as valuable. One of my graduate students, a refined man with a quick smile and affable nature, told me:

> What really gets me about Haredim is this. On the night of the "Helicopter Disaster" [dozens of soldiers were killed when two Israeli helicopters collided during maneuvers], there was a sense of mourning in every neighborhood in every city in Israel, except in Bnei Brak and Meah Shearim, where it was like nothing happened. It's like they didn't even *care* that so many people died defending them. It's like they totally take it for granted. For them, nothing at all happened. Seventy soldiers meant nothing to them. It's as if we are an inferior race, not entirely human, bred to defend them."

Ehud Barak captured the issue in his most famous campaign promise of 1999: "A situation in which the Haredi public is exempt from serving in the army, but receives substantial benefits from the state, is unfair and must be changed." So did thirty-three reserve officers who sent an open letter to Barak in September 2000, in which they wrote: "Can you look us in the eyes and tell us that our blood is less red than the blood of other citizens in our society? [The Tal recommendations] discriminated between different sorts of blood and is creating a schism that will never heal. Prime Minister Barak, heed our call. We are sick of being suckers!" This attitude is hard to fault. Who can blame the rest of us for resenting that Haredim not only don't do their part, but feel as if they *deserve* not to do their part?

The problem is the double standard. Haredim are not alone in avoiding the draft. Avoiding the army, escaping the army, conning the army—these are things that plenty of Zionist Israelis do. Shai Horowitz, the Haredi anti-defamation watchdog, is right that the statistics are impressive. A social services department in Jerusalem estimated some years back that roughly a quarter of secular Jews in the city are not inducted into the IDF for a variety of reasons—ailing health, psychological instability, or "incompatibility" with the army. The numbers seem to be rising. In absolute terms, non-Haredi Israelis who manage to avoid the army greatly outnumber Haredi Israelis who do the same.

There is something misleading about this line of reasoning. Absolute numbers are not the best way to calculate which segments of the population do their share, and surely there is an important difference between secular Israelis, of whom 75 percent are conscripted,* and ultra-Orthodox Israelis, of whom, according to one army estimate, only 29 percent ever serve, and many of these for far less than the standard three-year stint.

In another way, though, the declining participation among Zionist Jews is significant. This trend both reflects and contributes to the fact that service in the IDF is no longer viewed by many Israelis as the sole measure of good citizenship. This fact is especially evident in the reserves. Several years ago, the police uncovered a "factory" for medical exemptions from military service, based in the army's central hospital, Tel ha-Shomer (Sheba Medical Center). For a fee running from hundreds to thousands of dollars (depending, among other things, on the length and permanence of the exemption), military doctors signed forms releasing reservists from their service. The list of clients included some of Israel's wealthiest and most successful men, some of whom, when interviewed, explained that they could no longer fit military service into their busy schedules. The episode launched brief paroxysms of oy-oy-oy-ing and breast-beating in the media—what has happened to us?—but for most Israelis it simply confirmed what we already knew. By the time I turned thirty, I was already one of the old men of my reserve infantry unit, more savvy soldiers my age having found a way to be released from active duty. (On paper, combat soldiers remain in the reserves until they are forty-five, but recently the army released soldiers earlier; I was retired from the reserves at thirty-nine. Since the second intifada began, the retirement age has reverted to forty-five.)

In some circles, especially among the very secular, left-leaning intelligentsia who fill the coffee houses of Dizengoff and Sheinkin in Tel Aviv, avoiding reserves is de rigueur. Among the dozens of young men in graduate school with me, none were combat reservists. One—now a respected "historian of ideas"—told me that he had convinced army psychologists he was not up to the pressure of reserves service, and instructed me in detail about how to do the same. "If you were serious about your dissertation, you wouldn't waste six weeks a year playing soldier," he chided me. In an interview about the same time, a teen glam-rock idol, Aviv Geffen, called on kids to leave the country rather than serve in the army, a remark that earned him a lot of flak from graying editorialists and politicians, and some enthusiastic approbation from the alienated kids he spoke to and for.

---

*And, it ought to be said, there is no consensus about the numbers themselves. Lapid told me that the head of Army Personnel, Avinoam Laufer, told him that "from within the secular public, the percentage that avoids army service is 1.5 percent." This is very different from the statistics available from other sources, including sources published by the Division of Army Personnel itself.

Recently, at a memorial service for a friend's mother, I met the twenty-something successful manager of a thriving Tel Aviv dot-com start-up who told me that in high-tech companies, avoiding the reserves is almost an economic necessity. "I would never hire anyone who hadn't found a way to get out of the army—I don't think that many companies would. I don't know anyone at work, or in any other Internet company, who does the reserves." This is all the more impressive, because most Internet employees are in their twenties, the prime of their army life. In October 2002, a survey was published finding that 70 percent of those eligible for army service (including in the reserves) avoid conscription, lending a statistical imprimatur to what was already obvious to most Israelis: The army is no longer an object of absolute fealty here.

New immigrants are disproportionately represented among the 70 percent who do not serve. Since the Soviet Union disbanded, over a million Jews have immigrated to Israel from the former empire, of whom well over a hundred thousand were men of army age, far more than the comparable population among the ultra-Orthodox. Of these men, only a slender fraction have been conscripted. It is important to recall that those who arrived as children, and are physically fit, *are* drafted in the same percentages as the general population—this distinguishes the Russians and Ukrainians from Haredim. But it is equally important to recognize that very few of those who were older than eighteen when they arrived ended up serving in the army. By the mid-1990s it was official army policy *not* to draft them.

Russians, historians, and computer entrepreneurs skipping out of the army does not justify Haredim doing the same, any more than the Haredim justify the others. The comparison doesn't exculpate Haredim who avoid the army. But it does raise a curious question. Why do so many Israelis rage at Haredim for not serving in the IDF and so few object to the rest who don't serve? Why are there hunger strikes to get the ultra-Orthodox to uniform up, but no interest at all in having twenty-year-old immigrants from Kazakhstan do the same? Why are we certain that Haredim value their blood over our own, while it never crosses our mind that computer programmers do the same?

I put this question to Yizhak Ginsburg, and he said that it was crucial to understand the entire context. Avoiding the army is just one way the ultra-Orthodox are parasites, but it is part of a larger pattern. If it were just that, probably we would ignore it, just as we ignore the Russians, or the yuppies, or anyone else. But the army is just the beginning. The more important story is the way that they are economic parasites. And of course, the two forms of parasitism—military and economic—are closely related, so the anger spills over from one to the next.

Economy

Ginsburg is right. The question of whether Haredim serve in the IDF is a matter of fairness, and it is a matter of decency, but it is also a matter of money. The deferral that ultra-Orthodox men receive from the army because "Torah is their vocation" remains in effect only so long as they are full-time students. If, say, a twenty-two-year-old Haredi decides to get a job, even a part-time job, on paper he is required to serve three years in the IDF before receiving his first paycheck. This is a powerful disincentive to work, and a powerful incentive to stay in the yeshiva. (It is also a powerful incentive to lie about it if you do go to work.) Many analysts believe that the military exemption is the reason why so many Israeli ultra-Orthodox (in contrast to Haredim in America and Europe) study for their entire adult lives and never work. Haredim who don't work are a quintuple hit on the Israeli economy. They fail to produce government revenue through taxes. They receive government support through student stipends. They enjoy the indirect benefits of government support for the religious academies they attend. Because they are poor, they receive cash every month from *Bituah leumi*, a government welfare program. And because they tend to have many children, they receive cash every month in "child allowances."

I called Vered Dar, the assistant director of the Economy and State Revenues Department of the Israeli Department of Treasury, to help me try to figure out how much the Haredi army deferral costs the country. She reeled off some astonishing figures, and when I expressed skepticism, she offered to e-mail me a copy of the report she presented to the Tal Commission. In it, she estimated that the "present arrangement, in which yeshiva students can postpone their entry into the work market until age thirty-one and beyond, costs the Israeli economy between 1 and 1.2 billion shekels a year," then roughly $250 to $300 million. And this, Dar makes a point of adding, is only part of the story; it is lost income to the economy, but it does not include the many additional costs to the economy incurred by Haredi poverty.

The numbers are impressive. By some estimates, over 60 percent of ultra-Orthodox men between the ages of twenty-five and fifty-four do not work because they study full-time. This number is up from 40 percent two decades ago, so the trend is clearly toward lower, not higher, employment rates. Owing to this trend, the percentage of working-age Israelis who hold down a job is lower than in every other country in the developed world. In 1995, the reported monthly income (which was most likely the *under-reported* monthly income) of a Haredi family was $1,150 a month, which was only 42 percent of the income of an average two-parent Israeli family. And Haredim have to stretch that 42 percent farther, because their families average five children, while the overall average is just over two children per couple. It is not surprising that that average Haredi family with a father who studies lives on a monthly budget beneath the poverty line by more than $100, or almost 10 percent.

Of this modest livelihood, the great majority comes from the government. Under 20 percent of the total income is earned (almost all of this from the woman's work). Just under 40 percent of the family income comes from the yeshiva and other institutions, which itself comes from government allocations. Another 30-odd percent comes from child allowances. Boston University economist Eli Berman, who collected most of these data, summed it up this way:

> The combination of increased yeshiva attendance and natural population increase has created a rapid increase in the absolute number and proportion of ultra-Orthodox families dependent on government support to maintain even very modest living standards. In order to maintain this standard of living at current levels of yeshiva attendance and ultra-Orthodox fertility, outside support of the community would have to continue to increase at 4–5 percent annually, or double each 16–18 years, a growth rate much higher than Israel's rate of per capita output growth.

It gets worse. Those Haredim who do leave their yeshivot and take a job earn almost 25 percent less than their non-Haredi counterparts. There are many reasons for this, and economists argue about which are most important. Ultra-Orthodox men entering the workforce are typically unskilled, often profoundly so. Not only do they not have a trade (which secular men can receive in a vocational high school), but they lack many basic skills. Few can use a computer, which is no surprise, and many cannot do more than grade-school mathematics. Language skills are poor, and general knowledge is limited. One of Berman's most surprising statistics is that whereas the longer a student stays in secular schools, the greater the ultimate payoff in salary is for each year of education, the opposite is true for study in a yeshiva. Another reason why working Haredim earn less is that they typically enter the job market later in life. Even those who leave yeshivot do so on average when they are in their late twenties or early thirties, after most non-Haredim have been working for a decade. They never catch up, their wages always reflecting this relative lack of seniority. Yet another reason is that many of those Haredim who do enter the job market still continue to study Talmud part-time, never becoming full-time workers. There are doubtless other reasons. The irreducible fact is that most Haredi men don't earn anything, save government handouts, and those that do, don't earn much.

This irreducible fact is the unmoved mover of Haredi politics, and its power is felt everywhere. Each morning I ride my bicycle from a well-heeled neighborhood in north Tel Aviv, through Bnei Brak, to Bar Ilan University in Ramat Gan, where I work. The trip is not much more than five miles, much of it through a highly tended Tel Aviv park, but it is harrowing because the roads in Bnei Brak are creviced and cracked, with potholes a half-foot deep and two feet around. I've biked in Addis Ababa, Alexandria, and Algiers, but these are the worst roads I've ridden. The half-life of my tires is measured in days, and if I'm careful, weeks. I asked Charles Yawitz, an architect friend who works on development projects in Bnei Brak, why the city has third world asphalt, and he explained that road repairs, like local parks and similar things, were funded by local property taxes. Most citizens of Bnei Brak are exempt from these taxes because they are too poor to pay them, and as a result, the city has almost no budget for public works. Roads are not repaired. A government-sponsored study in late 1999 confirmed that Bnei Brak is the poorest city in Israel by a significant margin, and that Jerusalem is not far behind it. The average earned income in these and other Haredi enclaves is closer to that of Israel's third world neighbors than it is to the European standards (well, at least *Central* European standards) enjoyed by the rest of the country.

Many secular Israelis are galled by the simple fact that Israel's ultra-Orthodox apparently choose to live in poverty, but most would take a live-and-let-live attitude toward this if they didn't believe that, in the end, they are served the bill for Haredi sloth. It's the *demand* side, not just the supply side of Haredi economics that troubles most Israelis. I have already mentioned the welfare-type payments that unemployed Haredim receive, like all other unemployed adults in Israel, even if the former never seek employment. And I have already mentioned the child allowances, which are structured to compensate families with many children more *per child* than families with few. For each of the first three children, parents receive a stipend of roughly $50 a month, but beginning with the fourth, this number jumps to the neighborhood of $150 a child. A family with ten children—common in Haredi society and almost unheard of outside it—can pull in over $1,350 a month, untaxed, just in child allowances. This is more than the average Israeli salary.

A Haredi family. Father says,
"And they say that I don't work!"
Cartoon by Yakov Shiloh,
originally appeared in *Ma'ariv*.
Reprinted with permission of
Shpitz, journal of the Israel
Cartoonists Union.

What seems to bother people most, however, is the government money given over to ultra-Orthodox institutions, especially schools. When people talk about "Haredi blackmail," it is this money that they most often have in mind, and for good reason. After each election between 1977 and 2003, ultra-Orthodox parties have made joining the government coalition conditional upon receiving massive increases in funding to their schools. Both the Labor Party and the Likud have always agreed to the increases, and the Haredim have always supported the government. To many Israelis, this recurrent spectacle seems a lot like a corruption of the political process, like buying votes, like blackmail, and the resentment that many harbor toward it is keen.

In principle, it should be easy to figure out just how much money ultra-Orthodox institutions—schools and others—receive from the government, but it's not. Israel's budget is public information, available in any library or on the Internet. I downloaded a copy of the 2000 "Budget Book," which stacks up larger than the white pages of the five New York boroughs combined. In the tables describing education outlays, one finds that just under 109 million shekels (or a bit over $27 million at the time) are allocated to Haredi education, while 1 billion, 915 million shekels (or a bit over $477 million) are spent on secular education, excluding special education. Using these figures, it seems that Haredi schools receive roughly 5.5 percent of the Education Department allotments, while secular schools receive roughly 94.5 percent. Haredim represent approximately 7 percent of the population, so it seems that ultra-Orthodox schools are slightly underfunded.

Here the analysis gets fuzzy. Both allocation figures were drawn out of a larger education budget, one that (excluding higher education, which has its own budget heading) totals 2 billion, 892 million shekels (or $721 million). Almost a third of this budget does not go directly to the standard schools, but rather to kindergartens, special education, teacher training, absorbing new immigrants, youth centers, and more. In all of these cases, one must study the precise allocations to determine whether this money goes to ultra-Orthodox or not. The vast majority does not, and this lowers the percentage of the budget allocated to Haredim, perhaps by as much as

25 percent. Add to this the fact that ultra-Orthodox demographics differ from secular demographics, displaying a pyramid structure typical of third world countries. Thus, while 7 percent of the country is Haredim, far more than 7 percent of the country's *children* are Haredim. In light of these statistics, Shai Horowitz may not have been far off the mark when he told me that if you run the numbers properly, you'll find that the state pays only half as much to educate Haredi kids as it does to educate secular kids.

But matters are still more complicated. Many Haredi kids are quite young when they begin their studies in yeshiva, and yeshivot are funded through the Ministry of Religions, not the Ministry of Education. In fact, almost two-thirds of the ministry's budget, over a billion shekels ($250 million), is allocated to "Halakha, research, and Torah study." If one were to add this sum to the sums handed out by the Ministry of Education, one would conclude that Haredim receive a total of roughly $277 million from the government for education, while non-Haredim receive $477 million, which would give Haredim 37 percent of the pie, and everyone else 63 percent. This is a handsome payout to 7 percent of the population.

But this allocation won't work, either. For one thing, most of the Ministry of Religions' budget goes to Haredi schools, but not all of it. The budget includes millions of shekels for religious Zionist schools and youth movements. What is more significant is that this budget supports, not just yeshivot for children, but *kollelim* for adult scholars as well. If this is going to be credited against Haredi education, isn't it only fair to charge the cost to the universities, which are government-supported, to the Zionists? The percentage of university students and university lecturers who are ultra-Orthodox is very small—Haredim have essentially boycotted the universities for as long as they've existed—and many Haredim consider the universities to be the smithy of secular ideology and the bastion of secular privilege. In 2000, higher education was budgeted 5.25 billion shekels (roughly $1.3 billion). Add that to our running tab, and Haredim now stand at $277 million, while everyone else stands at $1,777 billion. With these figures, Haredim now receive 13.5 percent of the education budget, while everyone else receives 86.5 percent of the budget. This cut is twice what you'd expect from 7 percent of the population, but it is perhaps fair in light of the facts that there are more Haredi kids *and* a far greater percentage of Haredi adults study for many years more on average than everyone else.

More than anything else, what all of this manipulation of statistics shows is how very difficult it is to establish how much Israel really spends on Haredim, even when the numbers are right in front of you. And there are formidable difficulties that I haven't even mentioned yet. One is that some government money that goes to Haredim is virtually untrackable, because it is allocated to line items that one would normally never associate with Haredim. No one has done the painstaking detective work to figure out how much money travels to the ultra-Orthodox through unorthodox paths. Tommy Lapid told me that the sums are huge, because money is at every moment passing through hundreds of these paths simultaneously:

> I'm a chess player, and I was once elected President of the Israeli Chess Federation. What I discovered was that tens of yeshivot receive government money through the Chess Federation. Now keep in mind that this is a poor, little association that barely has any money at all, but it receives an annual government grant to support chess clubs in high schools and youth clubs. I asked the Federation chairman, "Do these Haredim play chess?" So the chairman tells me, "No, they don't play." What happened was, they discovered that if they register twenty yeshiva kids as chess players, then they get government support. It's an absurd sum: 370 shekel a month. But to me, this is a microcosm of the system. This is an example of how they get moneys out of the government. I'm sure that if they find out that they'll get money for macramé, then tomorrow they'll register ten yeshiva students for macramé. And I'm sure that the same thing is happening in countless programs where the government gives grants.

Lapid was on a roll. This sort of corruption adds up to a lot of money, he said (though no one has any idea how much, he adds), but it is small potatoes compared to the other techniques Haredim have developed for funneling government cash to themselves. He claimed that if you check closely the expenditures of any government ministry headed by a Haredi, you'll find sophisticated techniques in use. "Here's a case I just heard of," he told me:

> [Rabbi] Shlomo Benizri is now minister of health, and as you know, there are very serious problems in our health care system. But when he took control of the ministry, the first thing he said is, there aren't enough *mashgihim** in the hospitals. The head of a department in Abarbanel [Psychiatric Hospital] told me that he begged for years for money to hire another psychiatrist, which he desperately needs, and he didn't receive it. But they do send him a *mashgiah*. So he tells them, "But I don't even have a kitchen!" And they said, "Yes, but they bring meals onto your ward, so the *mashgiah* will make sure that no one mixes the milk and meat dishes."

---

*Plural of *mashgiah*—literally, an overseer—a man well versed in the rules of kashrut, paid to ensure that food prepared for public consumption, in a factory or restaurant or hotel, is in fact kosher.

This is just a small example, Lapid told me, and unless you knew what you were looking for, you'd never find in the government budget that this money went to Haredim. But the public is not stupid. "This sort of thing trickles through to the secular public, who see it and understand it, and who feel they are being exploited and extorted."

This sort of corruption is endemic in government, Lapid continued, but it has an equal impact, perhaps greater, in the private sector, where it dampens productivity, drives up prices, and generally stifles the economy. Let's stay with the example of kashrut, Lapid said:

Consider how the system of *mashgihim* works in hotels. It's a system based on extortion. . . . Here is a complaint that we received from the manager of a prominent Jerusalem hotel, who refuses to let us act on it, because he is scared of what the rabbis will do to him. Two things happened in his hotel. The first was that one day the *mashgiah* came to him and said, "I'm afraid that non-Jewish tourists might go to the Arab sectors of the Old City of Jerusalem on Shabbat, buy bread, and bring it back to the hotel to make [unkosher] sandwiches. We need to check this, because if it's true, I cannot say that the hotel is kosher. Here's what we'll need to do. Every night, we'll go from room to room and check for bread."

Lapid chortled:

Imagine a Christian couple from Michigan sleeping in their room late at night, and suddenly three Jews with beards knock on their door—"knock, knock, we need to search your room for bread!" The *mashgiah* didn't really mean it, of course. All that he wanted was for the manager of the hotel to offer him another 2,000 shekel *not* to wake up his guests.

The second complaint was this. The *mashgiah* comes to the hotel manager and says, "Your steel pots aren't kosher, and they're contaminating everything else, because they're peeling." So the manager says, "But everything has already been koshered for Passover; what should we do?" So the *mashgiah* says, "If you buy pots made in such-and-such factory in Bnei Brak, they'll be kosher forever, and you'll never have this problem again."

Lapid sighed:

So the manager tells me, "It cost me 5,000 shekels to buy new pots, but this is cheap compared to the cost of losing my certification as kosher."

This is a small part of a much bigger extortion operation. Haredim have an agreement for providing vegetables from *Gush Katif*, where ostensibly they found a way to keep insects off the salad vegetables. So they force restaurants to buy all their vegetables from there, at prices that range between five and ten times normal prices. This is simply an apparatus of blackmail. That every *mashgiah* is forced to stay in the hotel every weekend, and receive a room and food, that's one thing, but then you can't expect that the *mashgiah* will stay alone in the hotel for Shabbat. He needs to bring his wife and nine children. Go to the restaurant of any hotel on a Saturday, and you'll see the *mashgiah* there with his wife and nine children, eating on the house.

The costs add up. A deluxe hotel in Israel spends over 50,000 shekels a month on *mashgihim*. Every restaurant, every farmer, every processed food plant, pays too. And all this, again, is only one small example among many.

The chairmen of a processed food plant told me that every one of their products costs [at least] 10 percent more because of kashrut. This has three parts. (A) He pays for the certificate of approval itself, (B) he pays the *mashgihim*, and if it's a meat product, this includes *mashgihim* who live at his expense in Argentina [where much of Israel's beef comes from], and (C) they force him to buy products that he wouldn't buy if he wasn't kosher. So it turns out that the secular public pays 10–15 percent more than what it would otherwise pay.

Lapid's point is that Haredim have discovered ways of extracting economic benefit from the government and the principally secular economy that are difficult to quantify. He is right. At the same time, many Haredim believe that the opposite is true as well, that there are huge government expenditures and great portions of the economy from which Haredim are locked out. As Shai Horowitz told me, everyone talks about the government support for Haredi schools, as though it were wrong for the government to give large sums to a single sector of the society, to the exclusion of the others. But what they don't realize is that the vast majority of government funds goes to sectors of society that exclude Haredim. I have already mentioned that government support for universities is vast, and that universities are for the most part anathema to Haredim. This is one example among many. "Go look at the budgets for theaters, opera houses, dance companies, and a thousand other 'cultural institutions' that we would never dream of using," Horowitz told me. "No one insists that these expenditures are funneled to 'secular special interests,' though in a way they are." Horowitz hands me a pamphlet that explains that in 1997, Israel subsidized the theater thirty-five times as much, per capita, as the United States did. In Horowitz's view, the government ought not be in the business of subsidizing controversial art at all. Let private contributors do this, as in the States.

And the performing arts are really the least of it. The government spends huge sums of public moneys on state television, which Haredim do not watch, and on state radio, to which Haredim don't listen. Every Haredi who buys a car is forced to pay an additional radio tax, despite the fact that he finds most of the programming crass and objectionable. Public money is used to build museums and then to buy art that offends Haredi sensibilities. Public money subsidizes directors making violent and lascivious movies. All of these outlays are no less excluding of Haredim than yeshivot are of secular Jews. And totaled up, these things—what secular Israelis call "culture"— cost far more than all the Torah education combined.

But it goes beyond public support for culture, Horowitz told me. Haredim live simpler lives than secular Jews, and this fact has economic implications. In percentage terms, Haredim use far fewer prison cells than the general population of Israel, far fewer of them are junkies, far fewer are thieves, bank robbers, and other criminals. Bnei Brak does not have a police force, Horowitz told me, because it does not need one. (After I spoke with Horowitz, the city decided to open a small station with several officers, but crime statistics remain only a fraction of what they are in neighboring Tel Aviv.) Haredim do not contribute to Israel's foreign trade deficit, as they buy fewer imported appliances and cars than the general population and spend a far greater percentage of their disposable income on products made or grown in Israel. What is more, Haredim are responsible for large sums of hard currency entering the country as donations to their yeshivot, a fact that gives the Haredi sector a positive trade balance. In general, they consume less than the general population—less gas and less electricity, for example— and they produce less waste per capita.

The language for discussing how the ultra-Orthodox affect Israel's economy is statistics. This is reasonable, perhaps the only reasonable way of considering the question: First establish the facts of the matter—how much do Haredim contribute to the country, and how much do they cost?—and only then apply moral judgments—are they freeloaders? Do they pull their weight?

But it turns out that there is a problem with this approach, and accurate statistics are difficult to establish. There are a variety of reasons for this. Some are generic and account for the notorious ease with which, in most situations, statistics can be manipulated (remember the old quip, "There are three kinds of lies: lies, damn lies, and statistics"). Data can be grouped and regrouped until their presentation makes the desired point. Graphs can be calibrated to make large differences seem small or small differences large. Absolute numbers can be cited ("My God, over one hundred million shekels to yeshivot!") when the more significant figures are relative. ("Gee, only 5.5 percent of the education budget to yeshivot.")

In the case at hand, there are additional difficulties. Lapid and others believe that the way government funds are allocated and distributed allows for massive, undetected fraud. Small-scale investigations have shown that such fraud exists, but no one knows its true extent. This introduces uncertainty into any accounting and ensures that Lapid's analysis, when he factors in his own estimate of the cost of deceit, will be different from that of, say, Shai Horowitz when he runs the same numbers with his much smaller estimate of the cost of deception. Also, since government money reaches the Haredi community through many different conduits, often without being reported as money intended for the community, it is difficult and perhaps impossible to track how much actually reaches the ultra-Orthodox. Also, it may be impossible to estimate how much of general outlays—on health, defense, culture, and so on—ought to be accounted as a service to the ultra-Orthodox.

These technical barriers to accurate accounting are formidable. There is also another barrier. There is no agreement among the statistics, partly because the way we tabulate them is affected by our assumptions. For Shai Horowitz, it is obvious that government money to study semiotics at the university is just as much a sectarian expenditure as money to study Talmud at a Lubavitch yeshiva. For Tommy Lapid, the university is not a secular endeavor, but a national one, no different in principle from the army. For Horowitz, funding the Bat Sheva Dance Troupe when it choreographs and performs modern dance that incorporates nudity is not a contribution to Israeli (and certainly not *Jewish*) culture, while offering night courses in Bible in poor neighborhoods is. When people read the statistics differently, it's not because they are liars and it's not because they're morons. It's because they see the world differently. That is another way of saying that disagreements about how much Haredim benefit from government support are perhaps as much a result of Haredi-secular tensions as they are the cause of them.

This fact does not mean that there is nothing to say about the place of the ultra-Orthodox in the Israeli economy. Some facts *are* clear. Haredim work less, on average, than the rest of Israelis, and therefore they produce less and earn less. As a result, Haredim receive more government cash per head than the general population. Ultra-Orthodox families are larger than secular families, and owing to "child allowances" that ultra-Orthodox parties helped shepherd into law, this translates to still more government handouts. For decades, ultra-Orthodox schools were underfunded. Now, it is difficult to say with certainty whether they receive less or more per student than the other school systems in the country, but the trend is in their favor, and if it continues, ultra-Orthodox schools will enjoy a clear advantage over the rest.

It is easy to understand why Knesset members, deans of universities, artists, writers, journalists, and many others conclude that the ultra-Orthodox are a drain on the economy, and that, shekel for shekel, they consume more than they contribute. The data can be read in different ways, but the irreducible facts remain that Haredim hardly ever go to the army, that they choose to be poor, that they would rather study than work, and that they eagerly subsidize their unproductive lives with tax money earned by other people. This is a strong brief.

But there are other ways to look at the same facts, equally irreducible. The ultra-Orthodox in Israel make extraordinary sacrifices to study Torah. In contrast to the rest of us, for whom driving an Isuzu Trooper that costs four times the average annual salary is a token of success, in Haredi culture status follows learning. At least for Haredi men. Haredim live modestly, with relatively few possessions. They believe that everyone (again, at least every male) should have equal access to that which is most valuable, study. And although Haredi society is rigidly hierarchical—the rabbi's word is law—the equal access to Torah study creates a certain egalitarianism that has no parallel in Tel Aviv. Haredi society suffers from fewer violent crimes than the rest of Israel. It has a network of charities and good-works societies vastly larger than any other segment of Israeli society. Haredim have not become wealthy by draining funds from the rest of the country. Pick any measure—square footage of apartment space per capita, automobiles per family, food expenditures per capita, trips abroad, savings—and the ultra-Orthodox come out less affluent than the rest of us. And perhaps most important of all, Haredim do not see what they do—studying Torah, teaching Torah, raising Jewish children in wholesale quantities—as unproductive.

On my first visit to Israel, my Bubby led me on a walking tour of Bnei Brak, pointing out yeshiva after yeshiva, *kollel* after *kollel*, *shtibl* (small house of prayer) after *shtibl*. "Look, *mayn kind*," she told me, "everywhere, you can feel the Torah here." And regardless of who's footing the bill, that much is true.

It cannot continue, of course. Demographic trends are stark; in the future the numbers of Haredim will grow, and they will be an even larger portion of Israel's total population. In the long run, something will have to give; there is a limit to how low the "labor force–participation rates" can drop before the country experiences poverty so dire that no one here would be willing to accept it. As economist Eli Berman put it, within the present circumstances are sown "the seeds of economic collapse." The present situation, in which such a large percentage of the ultra-Orthodox are free to devote themselves to study, cannot last indefinitely, at least if they continue to have such large families. This state of affairs, as my Bubby would have thought of it, is simply too good to be true, at least to remain true forever.

It was this fact, Yizhak Ginsburg told me, that first led him to see the analogy between Haredim in Israel and parasitic microorganisms within animal hosts. Parasites weaken their hosts, so much in some cases that they ultimately kill off their hosts. Haredim seem to be doing precisely the same thing in Israel. But that is not the only way to see matters.

The ideal of a society devoted to study and learning is achievable in the long run only on a very small scale, and even then, it relies on the goodwill of others to support it. As Haredi society grows, this ideal must be compromised, perhaps sacrificed altogether. But it is a lovely ideal. As a group, Haredim have made great sacrifices for the sake of this ideal, in comfort and in wealth. They have gracelessly insisted that other Israelis—who do not themselves share the ideal—also make sacrifices so that they, Haredim, can live by this ideal. One can admire that or resent it. But one has to admit that Haredim are up to something altogether different from Ginsburg's microorganisms. This is so obvious, it seemed to me, that I wondered why Ginsburg himself doesn't see it, or the many others who share his view.

I asked this question of Dan Mahler, who together with his wife, Sophia (then a member of the Tel Aviv city council), had founded the Organization for the Prevention of Ultra-Orthodox Domination, known by the Hebrew acronym "Aleh." He was appalled: "Because they're right and *you* are an idiot. You've been duped. You're wrong. You're missing the point. The point is, they are taking over in every way imaginable. We are their slaves, and they have us working for them. You've bought into their romantic crap, which makes you stupid and dangerous."

3

Drowning in
a Sea of Black

The most primal fear of many secular Israelis is that Haredim are taking over our cities and neighborhoods. They are overrunning the rest of us. A political cartoon published several years ago shows a hand reaching out of a great black mass of ultra-Orthodox men, the message being that the rest of us are drowning in a sea of Haredim. A great expanse of black hats and black coats is a stock image among Israeli photojournalists. The image has two modes. When photographed from above, say from a rooftop, a gathering of a thousand ultra-Orthodox men can spill over the frame of a photograph and seem like a great vista of dark conformity. When photographed from below, say kneeling on one knee, a gathering of two dozen ultra-Orthodox men can seem like shock forces of an attacking army. This latter image gave force to election posters used by the left-leaning Ratz Party (which later became part of Meretz) in the 1980s, on which an angry mob of Haredim, photographed from below, was marching menacingly forward. "Only we can stop them," read the caption.

But one need not practice arcane semiotics to register secular fears about being overrun; many openly describe these fears. Hayyim Applebaum, the pen name of an anti-Haredi writer who asked that I not reveal his real

Drowning in a sea of Haredim. Cartoon by Adi Mattas, reprinted with permission of *Shpitz,* journal of the Israel Cartoonists Union.

Standard-issue photograph of a crowd of ultra-Orthodox Jews at a rally and prayer vigil in Jerusalem. They are protesting against archaeological excavations at an ancient Jewish burial site. © Reuters.

name, described on the flyleaf of his book *Black on White: A Glimpse into the Intimate World of Haredim* a new series of books he is writing that "will discuss the political and social implications of a state with a Haredi majority." Working from the assumption that according to present trends in population growth, Ashkenazi Haredim will be a majority in Israel by 2020, the books will explore the "many important questions" that will come up in "a country whose constitution is the Ten Commandments and whose laws are the *Shulhan Arukh* [a sixteenth-century religious legal codex]."

Such dystopic fears about an eventual Haredi putsch affect the way many see events today, long before anyone has been overrun. When, this past summer, the municipal planner of Tel Aviv invited activists, artists, and academics (including me, for some reason) to participate in a series of open discussions about the future of the city, this heterogeneous group arrived at consensus that the most immediate danger facing Israel's most secular enclave is "Haredization," the creeping influx and growing influence of the ultra-Orthodox. One of the participants was Emily Silverman, who was then leaving her job as the Tel Aviv director of the Israel Society for the Protection of Nature in order to study at the London School of Economics. As director, she had organized citizen groups to protest the city's thoughtless development of its waterfront and cannibalization of the small surviving parks. Recently, Haredim had begun to move into Silverman's neighborhood, and not long before the meeting, conflicts had arisen at the swimming pool.

Kiryat Shalom is a small square of neighborhood, an island at the south of Tel Aviv bordered by four ugly highways. There are only two entrances to the neighborhood, and once inside, the roads snake around like a Mandelbrot set, a curled spine with numerous radials. The neighborhood was built fifty years ago, just after Israel was established, for members of Israel's byzantine labor union, the Histadrut. By twenty years later, these workers and ex-workers, almost all of European heritage, had traded up to the fancier neighborhoods further north in the city, and were replaced in Kiryat Shalom by Bukharans, immigrants from what is today Uzbekistan. Bukharans have an astonishing heritage, being descendants of Jewish traders who settled on the Great Silk Route in Central Asia after the Babylonian exile, but like most Jews from the east, in Israel they drifted toward cultural invisibility and working-class hardship. Still, while most neighborhoods in Tel Aviv slid up or down the status ladder, Kiryat Shalom remained for forty years suspended in place, neither wealthy nor poor, neither upwardly nor downwardly mobile—in fact, hardly mobile at all. Nestled in its small crosshair of highways, it remained remarkably stable.

The greatest improvement to the neighborhood came in 1985 when the city council, using money raised from foreign donors, built a sprawling complex that is referred to in Kiryat Shalom as "the country club." The complex is less grand than that name suggests, with its associations of martinis near thick rolling golf greens in Greenwich, Connecticut. Still, by local standards, the country club is magnificent—two half-Olympic-sized pools and a smaller third pool, a weight room filled with new Cybex and Stairmasters, and a recreation center with a plush 400-seat auditorium. It was because of the country club that Silverman bought into Kiryat Shalom in the first place, and like many residents, she spends languid summer afternoons lying near the pool as her three-year-old splashes happily with friends. She also swims laps several times a week and has for years.

Beginning in 1996, Haredi summer camps from around the city began to use the pool at the country club. At first, they received permission to use it on Sundays, when it would otherwise be closed (ostensibly for maintenance), and on Tuesday mornings, through the month of July. The groups that summer were girls' camps, so Silverman was allowed to swim her laps while the kids splashed around the other pools. Men, like Silverman's husband, were prohibited, as Haredim do not allow what they call "mixed swimming," for fear of sexual impropriety. In 2001, more camps came, this time for boys, and for two days each week the municipal pool was closed to women, including Silverman, who was forced to swim her laps elsewhere. Silverman complained to the city administrator who handled pools, and he told her that her pool had been chosen by the Haredim because it was one of only two pools in the city situated far away from high-rise buildings. The problem with high-rises, he explained, is that in the opinion of the rabbis, occupants of these tall buildings can (with binoculars, I suppose) indulge their voyeuristic urges to see religious kids dressed only in immodest bathing suits. The city, which aimed to share its resources fairly, took such considerations seriously.

This explanation seems implausible, especially because a more plausible explanation is so close at hand. Five years ago, a man most people call Reb Asher moved into Kiryat Shalom with ambitious plans for transforming it into a center of ultra-Orthodox piety. The Tel Aviv rabbinate granted Reb Asher the regional sinecure, so he gets paid to coordinate the activities of the many pocket synagogues in Kiryat Shalom, but his main profession by inclination is that of *mahzir be-teshuvah*, or one who causes others to repent. Reb Asher bought a large stucco house on the perimeter of Kiryat Shalom, opposite a stand of pines the size of several football fields laid side to side and slated to become a neighborhood park one day. The city gave him permission to use a large bomb shelter in the trees, which he converted to a small *beit midrash*, or study hall. Using donations he collected, Reb Asher installed a holy ark, bought several Torahs, built floor-to-ceiling bookshelves, and filled them with several sets of the Talmud and several hundred other books, including most of the corpus of basic Judaica. Slowly he began to find people to come and pray before the ark and study the freshly purchased copies of the Talmud. He had his greatest success among the down and out—mostly recovering drug addicts, alcoholics, and ex-convicts—and he soon began to attract a small group of people of such backgrounds who had now found religion. His congregation grew with the years, and now, one of his sons told me, over a hundred souls come each Sabbath to pray with him, and dozens come at various times during the week to study.

Soon after he arrived, Reb Asher petitioned the city to grant him land in the pine grove on which he would build a four-story religious center, including schools for all ages, a *kollel* for adults, a synagogue, an auditorium, dining room, and so forth. Such a center, he maintained, would serve the neighborhood itself, and would also attract followers from all over, attracting new residents to the neighborhood.

It is against this background that the prohibition of women at the neighborhood country club came to seem to Silverman and others as a small part of a larger trend toward transforming a secular neighborhood into an ultra-Orthodox one. The demands in the second year were more intrusive than the demands had been in the first year, and there was no reason to think that these demands wouldn't likewise increase year by year. You do not need a paranoid disposition to suspect that with each additional municipal service the Haredim earmark for their exclusive use in the neighborhood, the cultural balance shifts toward them. Since Reb Asher arrived, a Haredi kindergarten opened its doors, and perhaps because it provides free lunches and free after-school programs, it filled up immediately. The pool was one more thing, and a critical mass of Haredi infrastructure was close to being established.

This is a heartbreaking development for many of Kiryat Shalom's long-time, secular residents. Omri, a spindly tenth-grader with his hair bunched into a thick black mop, babysits for Silverman and lives three doors down from Reb Asher. He took Silverman and me up to the makeshift observation deck his family had tiled on the roof of his apartment building to point out the geography of the conflict. From the deck, just above tree line, the pine stand looks like a lush pocket of forest. Omri is resolutely against handing over this land to the ultra-Orthodox. "I dislike having Haredim here tremendously. They bother us in all sorts of ways. On holidays, they close the road," he said, indicating his street with a sweep of his hand. He continued:

> Actually, the police put up barriers so that no one can drive on the street. The road becomes for Haredim only. It bothers me a lot. I don't like the atmosphere, the whole neighborhood becomes religious. It bothers me to hear their songs, and to see their kids running all over the place, and to hear their praying. They make a mess, throwing trash on the ground. I'm afraid that more and more of them will come. . . . There's already a feeling in the neighborhood that things are becoming religious, and you drive by on Friday night in your car, and they look at you strange and they yell and they curse. They once tried to get me to pray with them to make their minyan, but I told them that I didn't want to, I'm busy, I have no time. They kept on bugging me, but there was nothing they could do. On Shabbat they purposely stand in the middle of the road and don't move when a car needs to pass, then eventually they lethargically move out of the way, slowly. They go out on the streets and always make a ruckus, screaming, and yelling at the neighborhood kids, cursing them out. . . . I don't like religion in general, and I don't like Haredim, and I'm scared that they're going take over the neighborhood.

Omri's fear is shared by many people in Kiryat Shalom. His mother organized a petition against the land grant to Reb Asher, and everyone she asked to sign it did. "Nearly every family in this neighborhood has a close relative who became ultra-Orthodox," Silverman told me, "and it's a lousy situation. One day a kid comes home and won't eat with the family because they're not kosher enough, and tells them that they're not religious enough, and it makes the families resentful and angry. I think the anxiety about ultra-Orthodox snatching children is highest in these working-class neighborhoods; my neighbors are completely terrified of it." Silverman and many others believe that this is a crucial crossroad for the neighborhood, and if they don't fight, or if they fight and lose, their neighborhood will be lost. They have turned to the city council, which agreed to seek ways to preserve the secular character of the neighborhood. Residents of Kiryat Shalom, for instance, were released from having to pay for municipal secular nursery schools, as a way of discouraging parents from seeking highly subsidized ultra-Orthodox alternatives. But many feel that such efforts may be too little and too late. As the neighborhood becomes more obviously Haredi—with closed roads on Shabbat and ultra-Orthodox-only swim days—a dilemma unfolds. As long as secular Jews stay, the neighborhood will remain secular.

However, once a critical mass of secular Jews have sold to Haredim, apartment prices will plummet. Residents wonder if the best time to leave isn't now, before that happens, but in so doing, they help to bring about exactly what they fear. If Kiryat Shalom goes ultra-Orthodox, as Reb Asher hopes and Silverman fears, two generations of secular residents will lose money, and lose long-standing friendships with their neighbors, as many will be forced to move to cheaper cities. They will, in short, lose their homes.

Kiryat Shalom is a small example, close to home, of a sort of struggle that is taking place in dozens of neighborhoods and towns throughout Israel. Some months ago, I received an invitation to attend an "emergency action" at the mall in a posh, northern suburb of Tel Aviv named Ramat Aviv. The invitation came from Dan Mahler, from the Organization for the Prevention of Ultra-Orthodox Domination. In 1999, ultra-Orthodox Jews had leased space in Ramat Aviv, not far from Tel Aviv University. The real estate was a 250-square-meter complex, located above a sparsely attended synagogue, which was zoned as a dormitory, but which its owners—the Jewish Agency—found it could not put to good use. A group associated with Lubavitch—the international ultra-Orthodox organization based in Brooklyn that proselytizes ritual observance, effectively trying to convert Jews to Jewish observance—agreed to pay above-market rates, $15 per square meter, to turn the place into a small Talmudic academy. The term of the lease was five years. As news of the lease spread, residents of the neighborhood organized protest cells (the most vocal of which called itself the "Voice of the Silent Majority.") Yossi Paritsky, a member of Knesset and newly appointed minister representing Shinui, showed up at the proposed site to tell journalists: "If this goes through, there won't be a moment's peace. This is a 'strange [idolatrous] fire' for this secular neighborhood. Many school-age kids hang around here, and Lubavitch has wanted to gets its foot in the door of this absolutely secular neighborhood for some time." Before the visit was over, Paritsky and angry Lubavitchers traded shoves and fisticuffs, as the atmosphere turned school playground.

Paritsky (who, I was told, gave better than he got) was right about the neighborhood. Ramat Aviv is among the wealthiest neighborhoods in Israel, a stronghold of the old secular elite of Israeli culture. Prime Minister Golda Meir lived in Ramat Aviv, and former prime minister and Nobel laureate Shimon Peres lives there now. Any given apartment block might include a number of university professors, owners of Internet start-ups, judges, named partners in Tel Aviv law firms, chairmen of hospital departments, and bank executives. Per capita ownership of sports utility vehicles in Ramat Aviv is the highest in the country. And in the Isuzu Trooper set, there is broad consensus that a yeshiva will harm the neighborhood, lowering property values and attracting undesirables. The "Voice of the Silent Majority" printed a leaflet reflecting the prevailing view, which read:

WARNING

Lately we have witnessed a growing number of cases of apartment purchases and rentals by Haredi families and groups in the neighborhood. Such apartments are located on Brodetsky, Noah, and Brazil Streets, and lately to that have been added apartments on Daliner Street and one on Frankel Street. This document is not a declaration that our Haredi neighbors intend to alter the character of our neighborhood and to force from the neighborhood the secular public that lives here. We residents of the neighborhood who are members of the "Voice of the Silent Majority" believe in the value of mutual respect and pluralism, and therefore we welcome with open arms anyone who intends to be a good and tolerant neighbor. However, past experience teaches that sometimes the best of intentions are not mutual. Beyond this, we are persuaded that Ramat Aviv Alef has been "marked" lately by some Haredi body as the focal point of potential domination. It seems that Haredi efforts to receive permission to start a kollel *on the roof of the Brodetsky Street Synagogue, which was scuttled by pressure by neighborhood representatives, and the "tefillin stand" that Lubavitchers set up at the mall every Friday are part of this trend. . . .*

In the past years we have witnessed attempts by Haredi groups to wrest control of different neighborhoods and towns throughout the country. . . . The system by which these groups come to dominate includes several stages:

A. "Establishing a beachhead" in the neighborhood, which is to say, inhabiting a limited number of houses (at relatively high prices).

B. In this stage, they submit requests to establish "appropriate" institutions for the Haredi population that has moved to the neighborhood, including: Haredi kindergartens, Haredi elementary schools, a kollel, *additional Orthodox synagogues, and more. The establishment of such institutions encourages the entry of more Haredi population to the neighborhood.*

C. The Haredi population, which has established itself in the neighborhood, begins to demand "sensitivity to its feelings" from the secular neighbors. Examples that we have run into of such demands

WARNING (*continued*)

were: Not to listen to music on Shabbat, (for women) to dress "modestly," and at a later stage, even to close off roads and to vandalize vehicles that drive on Shabbat. At the same time, they begin to carry out mass "kabbalot Shabbat" ceremonies, Haredi rallies, demonstrations in front of stores that sell unkosher food, posting offensive and threatening announcements, and spray-painting antisecular graffiti.

D. In the final stage, as a result of the aggression, generally two processes take place: First, secular people who are fed up with the mistreatment begin to leave. Second, as a result of this and in parallel, the value of apartments drops, which allows more Haredi families to buy the empty apartments.

As we said above, this document does not argue that this is the intent of our Haredi neighbors. But past experience demands of us, as a secular public, that we maintain our vigilance.

Therefore, if you have run into any sort of problem related to secular-Haredi relations in the neighborhood, know that you are not alone! You have someone to turn to, and you have someone who will protect your rights!

We call upon the secular public to remain vigilant and preserve its rights, and we call upon our Haredi neighbors to remain neighborly, in the spirit of mutual respect.

Remember—Everywhere we have banded together and fought Haredi coercion, we have won!!!

The "Silent Majority" was taking a systemic view of the issue, and they could make a good case that the founding of the yeshiva was only one part of a larger phenomenon. As the leaflet says, when they investigated, they discovered that apartments in secular neighborhoods had recently been rented to ultra-Orthodox families, including three new rentals at about the time the space was leased for the Talmudic academy. Reports also surfaced of a sophisticated campaign to close a store run by the Kibbutz Mizra, the country's largest pig-breeding enterprise and, in general, Israel's biggest producer of unkosher meats. The store had operated in the same location for thirty years and is something of a Ramat Aviv landmark. The owners of the building Mizra rented began to receive offers to lease the place at a rent well above what the kibbutz paid. Alongside these good-cop efforts were uglier attempts at persuasion. The store's lighted sign was broken one night, and graffiti predicted that it would soon be forced to close. In the same period, several female students from Tel Aviv University reported being urged by ultra-Orthodox men to cover their midriffs. Residents were alarmed and confused. Sofia Doron, who lives across the street from the proposed academy, said: "There's great uncertainty. There's a lack of comprehension and all of this seems very strange to people. We're still trying to figure out what is behind all this. I wouldn't start up a discotheque in [the Haredi] Kfar Habad or an unkosher deli in Bnei Brak. I still don't know what needs to be done."

It was against this backdrop that Haredim started showing up at the mall. Missionary activity at the mall was particularly distressing to many local residents because it was well known that the mall's principal owner is an acolyte of the Lubavitcher rebbe. Like four of the fanciest other malls in Israel—the Savionim Mall, serving many of the bedroom suburbs of Tel Aviv, the Panorama Center and City Center, in Haifa, and the Power Center in Jerusalem (as well as the Flora Plaza opening in downtown Prague), the Ramat Aviv Mall was built by a development and holding company named Africa-Israel Investments, a vigorous concern that raked in almost $150 million in profits in 2000. The company owns roughly 75 percent of the Ramat Aviv Mall. Since 1997, the chairman of Africa-Israel has been Lev Leviev, who holds just over 50 percent of the company's shares and controls just under 55 percent of its votes. Leviev was born in 1956 in Tashkent, Uzbekistan, the son of Rabbi Avner Leviev, and the latest of a dynasty of rabbis issuing from one of Bukharan Jewry's most distinguished families (Rabbi Avner Leviev now lives in Israel; his son built him a large, gated compound in Kiryat Shalom, which has added to the feeling of residents there that Haredim are encroaching on their neighborhood).

Lev Leviev, who made his first millions in international diamond trade (experts estimate that today he owns one of every five raw diamonds on earth), had an audience with the Lubavitcher rebbe, Menachem Schneerson, soon after the collapse of communism, and the Rebbe advised him to expand his business into Eastern Europe and within Israel. The Rebbe encouraged him to accompany his business activities with philanthropy, and Leviev founded the Or Avner Foundation (named for his father), which has established Jewish cultural centers throughout the former Soviet Union, many of them Lubavitch in spirit, and staffed by Lubavitch Hasidim. These activities distinguished Leviev from the other capitalists who trade and purchase large companies in Israel. The distinction became clearer still, and a matter of worry to some, when Leviev announced soon after acquiring Africa-Israel that he would insist that businesses in his malls close on Saturdays, as the law ostensibly required, and that his sales representatives would no longer be allowed to show real estate to prospective buyers on Saturday either. He signaled his resolve by firing corporate senior managers whom he suspected of signing agreements in Africa-Israel's name that permitted business on Saturday. The directors of the mall's minority owners—corporations named Migdal and Shikun u-Pituah, which together owned about a quarter of the mall—wrote outraged letters to Leviev, and Dan Darin, the excitable director of planning of Tel Aviv, announced that he would veto all future Africa-Israel development projects in the city. Leviev did not change his position, and his mall remains closed on Shabbat, to the consternation of most of those who shop there during the other six days a week, making its multiplex the only one in the Tel Aviv area that does not screen movies on Friday night and Saturday. It was for this reason that many local residents justly saw the Ramat Aviv Mall as "soft on Haredim." And it was for this reason that ultra-Orthodox missionizing at the mall was publicized almost the moment it began. One activist described the scene on an anti-Haredi website called www.hofesh.org.il (*hofesh* means freedom):

On July 6 of this year [2001], at about 8 P.M., I walked innocently toward the entrance of the luxurious Ramat Aviv Mall, which is owned by the Haredi businessman Lev Leviev. In open view, on the marble sidewalk leading to the entrance, a young Haredi (in his twenties) with a red beard, was talking with a kid about thirteen to fifteen (by my estimate, but he was certainly a minor). I stood about twenty feet away and overheard the last stages of the discussion. The Haredi offered to have the kid visit him, and accompany him, and so forth. The kid refused time and again, and the Haredi insisted and insisted. In the end, the Haredi went. I called the kid over and checked that he understood what happened to him just then—a Haredi tried to lure him down the slippery slope of coerced "Haredization" and of medieval-style brainwashing. Moments like these are the beginning of children being torn from their families. The kid understood perfectly. I praised his stalwartness, and we parted.

It's unnecessary to point out that all of this happened thirty to sixty feet from more than a hundred secular people sitting in the luxurious Café Arcaffe (which despite the fact that its customers are secular, coerces them to accept the Haredi norms of keeping kosher and rigid Sabbath observance). The Haredi and the kid stood talking on the sidewalk leading to the main entrance of the mall. And it didn't take a well-developed imagination or any inside information to understand what was going on, yet no one disturbed the Haredi.

Almost immediately after this chance encounter, the watchdog groups (whose memberships seem to overlap, which engenders agile coordination and genuine fraternity between the groups) joined forces to stop the missionizing at the mall. When they met to plan strategy, it was soon obvious that they faced a problem of principle, one endemic to protest actions of the sort they proposed. Being basically libertarian in outlook (what they object to about Haredim often boils down to their dogmatic faith and willingness to coerce others to act according to the dictates of this faith), they struggled to find the philosophical grounds on which to ban Haredi proselytizing. Some argued that Haredim preyed on innocent youth, brainwashing the intellectually innocent, an endeavor that might be banned just as selling alcohol or pornography to the young is banned. Others maintained that the Haredim should not be banned from hawking their wares at all, on the grounds that their free expression was as valid as anyone else's. What the people who held this view advocated was a Newtonian approach. For each Haredi action, there should be an equal but opposite secular reaction. This was the strategy that was adopted, as I learned when I visited on a hot August Friday.

Ramat Aviv Mall is posh; you can go home with Godiva and Isaac Mizrahi, and if you find yourself in the Middle East in need of Manolo Blahnik shoes, it is the place to go. The mall attracts a clientele better dressed (and, it seems to me, better looking) than other cross sections of Israeli society. That is why I was already self-conscious as I pedaled my way across the thin strip of park that divides Tel Aviv from Ramat Aviv, my stained Gap button-down oxford sweaty and disheveled.

I locked my bike in front of a knot of twenty protesters, behind banners demanding the end of ultra-Orthodox domination. I found Dan Mahler, and he introduced me to a half dozen other activists. Among them was a young, spiky-haired man I had met some months earlier at a meeting of historians of science. David, as I'll call him, was completing his master's thesis and well along in planning his doctoral dissertation. We chatted about this, and then he offered to show me what he called the modus operandi of the protestors.

I hadn't noticed when I first arrived that not far from Mahler and the others, two bearded men in their twenties, wearing black blazers over white shirts and felt hats, stood behind a TV tray table, upon which lay two tangles of tefillin, and a small pile of plastic bags containing tea lights and a small brochure. David pointed them out, explaining that the Haredim cajole men who pass by into putting on the tefillin and saying a blessing, and accost women who pass, giving them a plastic bag and ask them to light the candles when the Sabbath begins later that day. The women and men often agree, to be polite or because it's easier than arguing with fanatics, but often this is the

Ultra-Orthodox man trying to persuade a secular youth to try tefillin, outside the up-scale Ramat Aviv Mall. Photograph from Central Zionist Archives, Jerusalem.

first step in their eventual conversion, so it's important to stop the process before it starts. The strategy of the protesters is to warn pedestrians that they are about to be missionized, encouraging them to ignore the entreaties of the Haredim and just walk by. For those pedestrians who stop to talk, the protesters "debrief" them immediately afterward, warning them that if the Haredim seemed harmless or even nice, that was simply because they had found this an effective way to brainwash the unsuspecting. Women who took the tea lights are instructed to give them back. Under no circumstances were the protesters supposed to confront the missionaries themselves.

After intercepting three or four passersby and persuading them to ignore the missionaries, David grew impatient and bored. He smiled and told me to watch, while he had some fun. He walked to the tray table, where one of the Haredim stood idly.

"Nice jacket. Where do you get clothes like that? Very stylish." The man behind the tray said nothing.

"And what a nice, long beard. Makes you look very nice. I bet the women really like that beard." Again the man said nothing.

"What I would really like to do is hold you down and shave off that beard. That would be really fun. Would you mind if I shaved off your beard?" The man sighed. David, still bored, sighed too and walked away.

The afternoon wore on, and the relationship between the proselytizers and the protesters settled into a rut of stylized skirmishes, like cartoon cats and mice. The exchanges were tightly scripted—between the protesters and the pedestrians they warned away, between the proselytizers and the pedestrians they somehow reached despite the efforts of the protesters, and between the proselytizers and the protesters. After ninety minutes in the hot sun, I walked into the mall to buy an iced espresso.

Twenty minutes later, I left the mall through the back exit, avoiding the sad choreography of conflict I had left behind. As I walked the path leading to the parking lot, however, a man with a bright red beard stopped me and asked if I had candles for Shabbat. I told him I did, but he put a baggie in my hand and said, "Just in case." I asked him why he bothered to come to Ramat Aviv, where the people he meets must often be inhospitable, resentful, and outright hostile.

"They are hostile, they hate us, they're rarely polite, but what you have to realize is, that's a good sign." Why? "The Rebbe said that true repentance is difficult, painful. It's like giving birth. Horrible pains. If these people weren't ready, at some metaphysical level, to rekindle their Judaism, they wouldn't be hostile. They're hostile because the process is taking place within them, they're being drawn closer, and they feel labor pains. Do you have children?" Yes. "Maybe your wife screamed at you when she was in the throes of labor pains, and if she did, it didn't make you feel angry and it didn't hurt your feelings. It made you happy, because it made you realize that your child is on the way. That's how I feel when the people here attack me."

When I walked away holding my baggie of tea candles, a woman in a tee shirt that read "Enough Haredi Domination!" jogged over to tell me to give the candles back. I said I wanted them.

"It's immoral to keep them." I asked why. "Because they use them to brainwash people." I told her I wasn't brainwashed.

Then because the millions of shekels they use each week for these candles and the other things they give away are paid for by money that was supposed to be used to buy books for poor secular children. Did you know that hundreds of children in the [poor Tel Aviv] Ha-Tikvah neighborhood drop out of school each year because their parents cannot afford to buy books for them? They are supposed to get books for free, but Haredim use the money to pay for proselytizers. Did you know that the man you were just talking to gets 10,000 shekels in cash for every person he manages to brainwash?

I told her that I had studied the government budget figures, and I hadn't noticed money earmarked for candles and proselytizing. "Still, it's a fact." I went back to the man with the red beard and asked him if he got paid for what he was doing. "No money, no, but it's a mitzvah—I'm paid in mitzvot." I asked who funded the candles, and he ripped open one of his baggies, and showed me in the accompanying brochure that they were purchased with money raised by Lubavitch in the United States for this purpose. I asked if they received any money from the Israeli government for this purpose and he laughed, "If only, my son, if only . . . "

I shuttled back to the woman in the tee shirt and told her what the man with the red beard said, and she laughed too. "What did you expect? They're not the most honest people in the world, you know."

The meeting at the mall is tiresome. Each side entrenched in its own view, and the behavior of the other side only serves to lock in the views more fully. The Haredim in Ramat Aviv act the way the secular expect them to, and the secular, the way the Haredim expect, and each side continues to find prooftexts for its own presuppositions. The interaction takes on a seamless inevitability, where there is constant escalation but no real surprises.

In contrast to Ramat Aviv, what I found in the town of Modiin surprised me. In Modiin, the fight against Haredim was organized, vigorously executed, and successful. Parties that ran in Modiin's recent municipal election on an anti-Haredi platform gained seven of fourteen seats on the city council, thereby controlling the municipal agenda and securing the city's key political appointments. This victory would be impressive anywhere, and in fact it was the greatest electoral showing for anti-Haredi parties ever, in any municipality. But the victory was especially impressive in a city without a single ultra-Orthodox resident.

Modiin is the newest city built inside Israel's pre-1967 borders, and the fastest growing. Its origins were one part utilitarian, one part utopian. Its utilitarian goal was to provide affordable housing for professionals priced out of Tel Aviv and Jerusalem. Israel's economy, after tanking at the start of the incursion into Lebanon, recovered in the mid-1980s and grew smartly. So did housing prices in the big cities, roughly doubling between 1985 and 1990, and then again in the next five years. The economic boon—which gained momentum with time—depended on the efforts of the educated middle class, foot soldiers in Israel's growing high-tech army. These white-collar workers created a dilemma in housing policy. They demanded comfortable homes, yet they were unable to afford apartments in Tel Aviv or Jerusalem, or even, increasingly, in the inner suburbs of each city.

Modiin was a solution to this dilemma. It lies midway between Tel Aviv and Jerusalem, convenient to the highway connecting the two metropolises and close enough for residents to commute to either. It is minutes from Ben Gurion International Airport. The government land was vacant and could be priced low enough to allow developers to build handsome neighborhoods of apartments, townhouses, semidetached and single-family homes, and sell them at half the cost of comparable housing in the large cities, while still making a considerable profit.

The decision to build Modiin was a practical one, then, guided by economic need, but once the decision was made, planners and politicians saw in Modiin an opportunity to build a city that was more than blandly utilitarian. One mark of this ambition was the decision of the Israel Ministry of Construction and Housing to hire Moshe Safdie to design the city's master plan. Safdie's sensibilities matched the project's most elevated goals. An Israeli by birth (he has lived in North America for forty years), Safdie has made a career of designing totemic buildings that combine the comforts of suburbia with the rougher pleasures of city life. As a student at McGill University, he designed a building assembled out of identical prefabricated modules laid out in different ways—Lego style—to create different floor plans. It was designed, as Safdie said at the time, to give "privacy, fresh air, sunlight, and suburban amenities in an urban location." The crisscrossing layout of the modules gave each apartment its own terrace and rooftop garden. After apprenticing for Louis I. Kahn in Philadelphia, Safdie was invited back to Montreal to build his school project—now called Habitat '67—in preparation for Canada's centennial and the 1967 World's Fair, Expo '67. When I was seven, my parents drove ten hours in a hot station wagon from New Jersey to bring me and my sister and brother to Expo and to Habitat. They captured for me the hip elegance of adulthood without the tenement rigidity that led me to pity my relatives living in New York apartments, which seemed to me more like prison cells than homes. More than thirty years after it was premiered, Habitat was voted (by a group of Japanese architects) one of the 200 best places to live in the world. Though Safdie hoped that it would be a prototype for similar "environments" elsewhere, it was so expensive to construct (each module, or cube, costing $100,000 in 1967 dollars) that it was never replicated.

Safdie has remained true to the sensibilities of his earliest work: affection for cities and the community one might find there, gentle appreciation for the private luxuries of the suburbs, attraction to the terraced geometry of stacked boxes, and innocent faith in the gestalt by which decent people both make and are made by their environments. These sensibilities found their ways into the plans for Modiin. The rolling landscape is covered with recessed cubes, one owner's roof being the next owner's porch. The center of town is a latticework of bricked streets that serve as driveways and walkways. Building is dense, but everywhere there is a feeling of space. The right-angle severity of the buildings is offset by the irregularly arcing roads, with a web of Judy Chicago streets joining the Mondrian architecture.

Modiin has the amenities of a carefully planned city. Its streetscape is uncluttered, with cables, wires, and pipes all buried. No neighborhood is far from a park, or from shopping, or from schools. Any given area has a certain architectural unity—common facings, for instance, or similar arched windows—which creates a sense of integrity. All of these features were the results of building a city from nothing, at once, and from doing so thoughtfully. They are what distinguish Modiin from other cities in Israel and explain much of its attraction.

Planning a city ex nihilo is an awesome undertaking, but it is easier to build roads, homes, and schools than to create the ineffable feeling of community one finds in the best towns. Even the commonplace task of establishing local government and holding elections is tricky in planned cities. Crucial decisions must be made years before the first residents arrive. That means that the rudiments of democratic life must be put in place autocratically, by developers and government ministry bureaucrats. Even once the first group of residents arrives, it takes time before they sort themselves out, get to know each other, form community service groups and eventually political parties. All the while, the business of government continues of necessity. City planners are often ambivalent about transferring authority to residents who, from a planner's point of view, will muck up the meticulously designed surroundings.

Modiin's new residents were assured that elections would be held within several years of their moving into the city, but they agreed to be governed at first by a government-appointed mayor and city council, until the city was "mature enough" to support its own municipal elections. Between the moment that Yizhak Rabin laid the cornerstone of the city in 1993 and November 1998, when the first election took place, the city was run by technocratic appointees. When the first residents arrived in 1996, an affable manager from the Tel Aviv suburb of Givatayim named Moshe Schechter was appointed mayor. For two years, he oversaw the city during a period of growth unlike any other Israeli city had ever experienced. In the first year, 8,000 residents arrived, and in the second year the number of residents more than doubled. The sound of bulldozers and cement mixers could be heard sixteen hours a day (as indeed they can today), and special care was taken to coordinate the dozens of moving vans that arrived on an average day. When the first elections were scheduled, residents took it as a first sign that normalcy was on its way, after months and months of dizzying change.

Like that of most Israeli cities, the system established by the founders of Modiin called for dual elections. The mayor was to be elected by popular majority, with a runoff if no candidate drew 50 percent of the vote on the first ballot. And members of the city council of thirteen were selected from political party lists, in proportion to the number of votes each party polled.

The campaigns started as one might expect. Moshe Schechter announced that he would seek a second term and organized a party of loyalists to compete for council seats to back him. Local proxies for the big national parties—Labor and Likud—were hastily organized. A branch of the National Religious Party (NRP) founded its own local proxy, and set about to join under its aegis all the religious residents of the city. That proved difficult, as Ashkenazim and Sephardim tussled for control of the three seats they expected the party to carry, leading eventually to the schismatic settlement that two parties—one principally Ashkenazi and the other principally Sephardi—would run, effectively splitting the religious vote. The Sephardi party forged links with Shas, and the Ashkenazi party ran with the support of the NRP. A party named Telem, funded by the leftist Meretz Party, also took shape. By the dog days of the summer before the election, it looked as if Modiin would elect a centrist government consisting primarily of the mayor's ad hoc party, representatives of Labor and Likud, perhaps two or three representatives of national parties further to the left and right, and several religious representatives.

In August, barely three months before the election, a new political party emerged, as its leaders explained, to fill a crucial void in municipal politics. Through the summer the campaigns had focused primarily on grunt practical politics, with candidates emphasizing their civic experience elsewhere, where they lived before Modiin, and presenting menus of "parve" promises about school improvements, neighborhood pools, and such. The new party complained that such politics were shortsighted, effectively ignoring the greatest threat to the lifestyle for which most people had moved to Modiin in the first place. The source of this threat was Haredim. Choosing the name Ir Hofshit Modiin (Free City of Modiin), with its echoes of Radio Free Europe, leaders of the party launched an advertising campaign to publicize the Haredi threat, which, as they saw it, was that city council would split evenly between the Left and the Right, and ultra-Orthodox parties would gain crucial swing votes that they would use to blackmail the city for money, building variances, and disproportionate allocations of city resources. In this way, they argued, Haredim would turn Modiin politics into a microcosm of Knesset politics. Ir Hofshit's ads, which ran in the four local weeklies, repeated this theme, each time with minor variations.

"Do you need a crystal ball to know what will happen to the city if the Haredi parties end up as swing votes in the city council? Look what happened in Jerusalem!"

"The Haredi parties 'divide and conquer,' a method that is a trap for any mayor. This time we cannot be fooled!"

"This time we need to vote smart! So that your joy in victory will not turn to mourning, when the mayor you voted for signs a coalition agreement with the Haredim in the city, take out insurance against coercion!"

This last phrase—"take out insurance against coercion"—became the cri de coeur of the party for the crucial weeks before the election. It captured an odd state of affairs in the city and also accounted for the unexpected potency of Ir Hofshit's message. Insurance, by its nature, does not ameliorate existing problems, but rather safeguards against *future* calamity. In its ads, Ir Hofshit implicitly acknowledged that Haredim did not present an immediate threat to Modiin, because no one had ever seen an ultra-Orthodox Jew in Modiin, with a few exceptions that took on great significance, and there were no ultra-Orthodox candidates contending in the elections. The party, however, implied that such a threat would become real in the future.

These few exceptions, which were skillfully exploited by a remarkable novice politician named Michal Gadot, were enough to fuel the campaign in through its first weeks. Gadot began her political career as spokeswoman for Ir Hofshit, a job she executed effectively enough that when the party's founder and head took a short vacation to New York during the campaign, a palace putsch installed her as the party's undisputed leader. In an early campaign appearance, she said: "I have seen Haredim in our shopping centers, trying to persuade secular Jews to put on tefillin. I understood that if no one stops this process in its early stages, it will continue like it did in perfectly secular cities like Raanana and Petach Tikva that became Haredi cities."

It is hard to gauge how often such proselytizing took place in the compact shopping centers of Modiin. None of the dozens of residents I spoke with remembered it. What is certain is that, though for some people it had symbolic importance, proselytizing was not widespread enough to draw many voters to the party. It was necessary to describe the direct impact Haredim stood to have on Modiin. Several weeks into the campaign, every resident of Modiin found in their mailbox an Ir Hofshit pamphlet itemizing the threat. "Did You Know?" read the banner headline.

**A NUMBER OF HAREDI *KOLLELIM* HAVE
OPENED IN DIFFERENT PLACES IN THE CITY**
    *Each day Haredim arrive from Kiryat Sefer to pray in them. None
of them are residents of Modiin. What are they doing here?*
    *Nurit Kindergarten, in which thirty-five children from Modiin reg-
istered, was handed over to [the Haredi party] Shas.*
    *About eight children were imported, who were brought on buses
from Kiryat Sefer. With the intervention of the Supreme Court, this
was partially prevented. The kindergarten was not closed, and it is in
operation now near City Hall.*

**THERE IS A MASTER PLAN TO BUILD ABOUT
SEVEN HUNDRED HOUSING UNITS FOR ORTHODOX
AND HAREDIM ON TITORAH HILL IN MODIIN**
    Are we going to allow this to happen?
    *Already there are discussions about closing off roads on Shabbat in
the C Hill region of Modiin.*
    And what will happen in the future??

**THIS IS THE ONLY TIME TO
STOP THE DOMINATION OF OUR LIVES**
    *The Free City Movement is working for freedom of lifestyle for all
the residents of Modiin, one alongside the other, secular and religious
of various points of view, in mutual respect, with tolerance and respect for human rights.*

Now, several years after the elections, it is difficult to find a factual basis
for most of the claims in the pamphlet. The municipal and state planners I
asked all felt certain that no plan to build Haredi housing in Modiin had
ever been raised or discussed. Neither the mayor nor his staff members that
I interviewed remembered any discussion of closing any roads in the city on
Saturday. One small *kollel* was operated in a synagogue not far from City
Hall, and a handful of youngish men came to it by bus from the nearby
Haredi town of Kiryat Sefer, as a favor to the city rabbi in an effort to reach
the critical mass needed to conduct six hours a day of serious Talmud study.
On each of the three days I visited, I found only two students, quietly

quizzing each other on intricate minutia. The most credible complaint on the list was that a kindergarten had been handed over to a group of parents associated with the Sephardi religious political party, which was itself associated with Shas. But according to Mayor Schechter, this situation was made to look worse than it was. City policy is to provide facilities for any group of parents who join together enough kids to fill a kindergarten. The religious, Sephardi parents had come up with a kindergarten full of kids, so they were given a kindergarten building. Schechter may have been smoothing over a real problem. Anat Israel, who was eventually elected to the city council on the Telem ticket, pointed out at the time that for a city without Haredi adults, Modiin seemed to have an unusual number of Haredi five-year-olds, which made her suspect corruption. She hypothesized that the lists submitted to the city education committee were padded.

Gadot maintained that the accusations contained in the pamphlet were all strictly true, and that each had been confirmed by credible sources within the city government, who would lose their jobs if they went public with what they knew. She told a rally before the election that "we receive anonymous information from administrators, teachers, and workers but they are frightened to identify themselves, for fear of their livelihood and position," a proposition she made more explicit still in a column in a local paper: "In the atmosphere of terror and fear that rules today certain government offices, our sources prefer to remain secret for fear of being fired." In essence, the lack of explicit corroboration for the pamphlets' claim itself became another component of the brief against ultra-Orthodox influence in Modiin. Not only had the ultra-Orthodox carefully laid the groundwork for the eventual domination of Modiin, but they exercised enough power to silence those city employees who might oppose them.

So it is that the validity of what the pamphlet said remains disputed to this day, and so it is that just what *is* the hard truth turns out to be largely irrelevant. The pamphlet affected the politics of Modiin, and in a way it continues to. What was important was not so much whether Haredim were actually moving in, taking over, closing roads, and stealing schools. What was important was that many Modiin voters could easily believe that even if these things were not happening already, they might happen soon. Dozens volunteered to help Ir Hofshit's campaign. Hundreds showed up to the new party's rallies. As her constituency grew, Gadot became more combative, and as Gadot became more combative, her constituency grew still more. On a Saturday several weeks before the election, Ir Hofshit invited supporters to a deli in the city center to eat pizza and ice cream. Speeches at the luncheon portrayed the gathering as a radical act, and a vigorous demonstration that whatever the flack, Ir Hofshit would fight to allow commerce on the Sabbath. Anyone who came for a slice might infer from this that someone—the ultra-Orthodox or their political lackeys and stooges, presumably—was hankering to close those businesses that stayed open. (Since the elections, only one store has opted to remain open on Saturdays—one restaurant owner told me that too few people eat out on the Sabbath to justify coming to work on his only day off.) Whether or not the threats itemized by Ir Hofshit were real, they had come to seem real to many. And as these threats were repeated in newspaper ads, posters, and stump speeches, they calcified in the minds of voters not just into hard facts, but hard facts of greater importance than any others facing the community.

It was in this way that the first municipal election of Modiin, a city in which *every* issue that usually exercises a local community was at stake, issues like taxes and building restrictions and public lands allocation and recycling, became little more than a plebiscite about Haredim, even though few of the voters had ever seen an ultra-Orthodox Jew within city limits. And the anti-Haredi parties, Ir Hofshit first among them, won it in a walk. Ir Hofshit took four seats, Telem took three, giving the two parties an absolute majority in the council of thirteen. An Ir Hofshit founder and activist named Ayal Maoz described the meaning of the victory after the votes were counted:

> What the residents of Modiin did today is an investment for the generations. The status quo of a city is determined only once, and the residents of Modiin knew this and determined it in the first elections in the city. What was created here is a situation in which the lifestyle and relations in the city will be determined according to secular criteria and by secular groups, and this is an important step toward a better future.

Gadot herself was quoted saying that the importance of the victory lay in the clear message it sent to the ultra-Orthodox, that they are personae non gratae in Modiin. Giora Snapir, one of the founders of Ir Hofshit, stated this view even more forcefully in an essay he wrote for a local weekly, in which he stated that the election results ought to make religious Jews realize that they are not wanted in Modiin. (Not long after this, Giora Snapir died suddenly, an event wryly characterized by one Modiin resident as "the clearest case of divine intervention I'm ever likely to see.") According to Yair Pereg, a militantly secular biology professor at Hebrew University who lived in the nearby town of Maccabim (he died in 2002), one leader of Ir Hofshit announced that the election made plain that "if Haredim dared move to Modiin, there would be blood."

Gadot and Maoz were right that the elections broadcast the message that Modiin did not welcome Haredim, but that in itself does not explain the election results. Even as Ir Hofshit celebrated its victory, the antireligious sentiment in Modiin that swept the party into power remained a riddle. When it came time to place the white slip in the cardboard box, why did more than half the residents of Modiin choose anti-Haredi parties? How did fear of Haredim come to loom so large in a city where there are none?

I put these questions to dozens of Modiin residents, who had several answers. Mayor Schechter, a politician who tends to see such matters from a political perspective, believes that Ir Hofshit simply manufactured the fear. "False propaganda sometimes has far greater impact than true fact," he told me when I visited him in his office at City Hall. Schechter has avuncular, Burl Ives appeal, and I half expected him to reach over his desk and pinch my cheek as we spoke. The shelves behind his desk are cluttered with trophies marking every sporting event from which a Modiin school emerged victorious, and on his walls are dozens of banners and certificates expressing appreciation for his support of this event or that club. The screen-saver on his oversized monitor is a video of a helicopter whooshing through Modiin in great arcs at low altitude, and when Schechter sits in front of it he seems constantly to be monitoring his dominion. But if Schechter is aware that his poppin' fresh huggability is a political asset at local track meets, he also knows that his softer side provides a foil with which to highlight, when the occasion demands, his implacability.

Speaking of Ir Hofshit, he said, "You might not think it to look at me, but I can be tough when I have to be, and I know how to deal with their sort. I don't back down. To this day, I do not take account of them or their views at all in setting municipal policy, and they cannot make me do so." Schechter recognized that his ability to ignore the biggest party in the city council was aided by the implosion of Ir Hofshit soon after the election. Snapir died. Gadot, according to Schechter, realized that her political activities, ironically, were getting in the way of her greater political goals. "When Gadot finished law school," Schechter told me, "she decided that her real ambition is to be a judge. She realized that to achieve this she shouldn't taint herself too much in divisive local politics, so we don't hear from her anymore. Which is why the entire party essentially disappeared." And according to Schechter, since Ir Hofshit's disinformation and "campaign of fear," as he put it, were the only reasons why Modiinites worried about Haredim, when the party was thwarted and collapsed, the worries simply disappeared.

The notion that the Haredi issue in Modiin was cynically manufactured to elect Ir Hofshit's slate was expressed by many residents I spoke with. An

American expatriate named David Strassberg e-mailed me that "Ir Hofshit fought the 'Haredi threat' much the same way that Senator McCarthy fought the Communist threat," suggesting that advancing their careers was more of a goal than protecting Modiin, and no matter if innocent people got hurt along the way. The analogy to McCarthyism was not the most inflammatory analogy I heard. Another resident, Shalom Wasserman, told me that "Ir Hofshit took a page out of the Goebbels's how-to manual and repeated the same lie enough times that people began to believe it." The suggestion of a parallel between Ir Hofshit's legislative agenda and the Nuremberg Laws, and more generally between Ir Hofshit and Nazis, was the analogy I heard most often during my weeks in Modiin.

The putative Haredi threat was the sort of election issue that every campaign manager dreams of discovering and exploiting. It was easy to articulate, and it mattered to many voters in a deep, highly emotional way. It *resonated*. It was an issue that people cared enough about to walk through the rain to the local high school to cast their ballot. It is not utterly cynical to believe that novice politicians might exaggerate this threat because they believed doing so would win them votes. The enthusiastic response that Ir Hofshit registered in the first weeks of its brief campaign undoubtedly set in motion a feedback loop: Portraying Haredim as a threat to Modiin attracted a voluble constituency alert to this danger, and the enthusiasm of this constituency probably pushed party leaders to emphasize the danger still more. The electoral payoff of Haredi-bashing must partially explain the verve with which Ir Hofshit engaged in it.

But this cannot be the whole story. First of all, Ir Hofshit may have stretched the truth, but—like true believers everywhere—when it lied, it often did so ingenuously. Though Ganot and her colleagues seem to have enjoyed the attention and support that came with denouncing the ultra-Orthodox, and though Ganot herself reveled in the role of the enfant terrible, I believe that the leaders of Ir Hofshit were sincere in their denunciations. Bashing Haredim was good electioneering, but it wasn't merely good electioneering. The leaders of Ir Hofshit probably did not believe all their own allegations; it is hard to imagine, for instance, that they believed a secret plan existed to build huge Haredi neighborhoods in Modiin, when no evidence of such a plan has ever been uncovered. But I think that they did believe in the deeper truth behind even fabricated accusations. Whether or not Haredim were actually building hundreds of villas overlooking the town, Ir Hofshit and its supporters were convinced that Haredim, given half a chance, would take over whatever they could. Whether or not anyone had already recommended banning traffic on certain city streets on Shabbat, Haredim would finagle such a ban as soon as they had political clout. Any particular claim might be a poetic excess, but each was intended to illustrate a real threat. In its own way then, Ir Hofshit was a sincere grassroots movement. Haredim were not simply the means to get elected; for most party members, Haredim were really the only reason why it was important to be elected.

And even if Ir Hofshit cynically manipulated the fears of their voters, these voters were not dupes. If the threat of Haredim resonated among the residents of Modiin, it did so for real reasons. Mayor Schechter's explanation of Ir Hofshit's success assumes a certain naïve credulity on the part of voters, who were whipped into a frenzy of fear by a party of demagogues. "You have to understand," he told me, "that it was the city's first election, and the electorate was not yet *mature*."

This reasoning sounds patronizing, but there may be something to it. Scholarly studies of planned cities have found that the first years are marked by a high level of anxiety about municipal identity. Herbert J. Gans, who, in a classic of twentieth-century sociology, *The Levittowners*, described the years he spent in Levittown, New Jersey, as the city took shape, concluded that many of the conflicts of the city's first years were about the social identity of the town. These conflicts took place at different levels. Gans described what he called "definitional struggles" within clubs and associations—groups like the Rotary Club and Bnai Brith—in which early joiners anxiously tried to fashion the group as they thought it ought to be and hoped it would be. The same thing happened at the municipal level, and in the first years there were many conflicts about such matters as zoning restrictions and the placement of houses of worship. In time, these conflicts diminished, as the character of clubs and of the town itself came to seem fixed. People dropped out of associations that did not turn out the way they hoped, and some families left Levittown altogether in disappointment, but the feeling that these groups and the city itself was still plastic in character, and that one must fight to influence them, eventually all but disappeared.

More recently, Andrew Ross described a similar series of developments in Disney's planned city, Celebration, Florida, which began to operate only months before Modiin. Disney's managers were more aggressive than Levitt had ever been, more sanguinely totalitarian in appropriating control, and arriving residents were contractually bound to relinquish most of their rights to influence the city, at least in its first years. But one realm in which a "definitional struggle" took place was the schools. On paper, schools too were beyond the control of parents. The Disney people had hired educational consultants with the fanciest credentials to plan a curriculum, which was then jealously protected from the meddlesome influences of the students who were to use it and their parents. The philosophical approach adopted was far from the mainstream of United States pedagogy, deemphasizing grades, promoting cooperative work in small groups, on the one hand, and independent study beyond the school campus, on the other. This approach appealed to many parents, some of whom moved to Celebration in order to send their kids to such schools. But other parents worried that the untraditional approach and absence of grades would compromise their children's chances of attending the same Ivy League schools where the educational consultants taught.

Ross witnessed a vicious and polarizing war among parents, many of whom soon refused even to speak to their neighbors of the opposing camp. Schooling is the sort of issue that invites division and hostility everywhere—it doesn't take the assassination of an archduke to degenerate a school board meeting to fisticuffs. But in the case of Celebration, much of the sound and fury resulted not only from the issues themselves, which, though they were important, were amenable to compromise. The issue heated up quickly largely because many parents believed that they would have only one chance to influence the schools, and that this was it. Once precedents were set, books bought, tenure granted, traditions established, it would be too late to change matters.

This same feeling undoubtedly existed in Modiin, as Ganot and many others acknowledged. The inaugural elections in Modiin were seen as being particularly important, because they were expected to inaugurate the civic culture of the city. The same anxiety that ionized the atmosphere of Levittown and Celebration contributed to the highly charged elections in Modiin. And there was arguably more at play in Modiin than in other planned cities. Mayor Schechter boasted to me that the students in Modiin's several schools came from over 150 different schools around the country. Schechter prided the city on smoothly assimilating the tired-poor-hungry-wretched-refuse of practically every major municipality in Israel—he admiringly referred to the city schools as a "melting pot."

But Schechter may have overestimated the ease with which so many kids from so many backgrounds were assimilated. I spoke with a psychologist working in Modiin (he prefers to remain anonymous and I will call him Tal), who told me that city children have a very high rate of adjustment disorders. Some of these, Tal said, could be attributed to the stresses of moving, stresses that were perhaps amplified by the fact of moving to a place where everyone else was new too, and social support networks were partial or fluid or altogether absent. For other children, the disorder was not really new. Though it was impossible to estimate how many, there were children in Modiin who had experienced difficulties in their old schools in their old towns. In fact, Tal said, the promise of new and better schools for their floundering children may have been precisely what motivated certain parents to move to Modiin in the first place. A portion of the population moved to Modiin to get a fresh start, after they had failed to thrive in another city. This fact too may have heightened the anxiety of Modiin residents about the character of their new home in its first years. Just what sort of place Modiin would become was an emotionally fraught question at the time of the first election, and this partly explains the appeal of parties like Ir Hofshit. There was a psychological back-story to the anti-Haredi vote in Modiin's first election.

A backstory, however, is only a backstory. Anat Israel rejected such analy-sis as patronizing. In her view, the anti-Haredi vote in Modiin was strong because the anti-Haredi parties represented a crucial agenda. There were good, practical reasons why decent people voted for them.

This rationale is not to say that Israel admired Ir Hofshit's campaign. She didn't. "I could never belong to Ir Hofshit," she told me. "I didn't like their election propaganda. I often had the feeling that the source of their opposi-tion to Haredim was somehow tainted. They sometimes seemed simply to oppose the 'Other,' anyone who is different. This, I can't support."

But her feeling about the propaganda did not mean that Ir Hofshit was not right about many of the issues, in Israel's view, issues that were also at the heart of Telem's campaign. One way to gauge the importance of these issues, Israel said, is by considering the anti-Haredi parties' greatest accom-plishment to date, the establishment of a secular subdivision of the munic-ipal cemetery:

> Our biggest success was creating an atmosphere in which it was simply taken
> for granted that there need to be two cemeteries, one religious and one secu-
> lar. There was no argument about this. It was taken for granted! To get to the
> point where something like this, which exists almost nowhere else, is taken
> for granted, well, that takes work and struggle. If we hadn't campaigned for
> this sort of thing from the start, would it be taken for granted today? Of
> course not!

As Israel sees it, this atmosphere would never have existed were it not for the forceful anti-Haredi vote, and now that it does, it affects the daily functioning of the city in countless ways. "We divvied up city grants last week," Israel told

me, "and one of the synagogues that received money was the Reform Temple.*
No one dared to raise any question about it, which is an extraordinary state of
affairs. Why was this? Because we made a fuss, from the start, and we demonstrated that people with our point of view have power."

Israel continued: "They tell me that young couples who register their
marriage here in Modiin have an easier time than anywhere else. Can you
imagine? Even the Ministry of Religions' offices here are more accommodating than in other places. We created a place where secular sensibilities are
taken seriously."

Another measure of the importance of anti-Haredi politics in a city without Haredim, according to Israel, are the struggles that to date these parties
have lost. Many of these concern education. For instance, Israel sees in-
equities in the distribution of resources in Modiin:

> There are no Haredim in Modiin, right, and there are basically no Shas sup-
> porters. Why then are there so many Shas kindergartens in Modiin?** The an-
> swer is, kids go to these kindergartens because they have no choice—they are
> much cheaper than any of the alternatives. But why is this? Because Shas extorts
> money from the national government and funnels it to local schools to build
> political support for the party. This is an intractable problem at the national
> level. But why do I need to let it happen here in Modiin? Why can't we find
> some way to make secular kindergartens cheaper and accessible to everyone?

Even secular kids in secular schools in Modiin get a large dose of Haredi
propaganda, Israel continued:

> Why should our children's schools take field trips to [the Lubavitch town of]
> Kfar Habad? What is that about, anyway? Why should religious woman doing
> national service teach Talmud to secular girls in middle school?—I don't want
> my kids taught Talmud from a believer's perspective. And do I have to sit qui-
> etly and accept it when I see ultra-Orthodox men teaching classes on the grass
> for secular high school kids? They hand out invitations with candy at the gates
> of the school, and once these kids come, they tell them stories that are really
> terrifying. I've eavesdropped and heard them, about how terrible the lives of
> secular Jews are. And all of this is in Modiin, a city without any Haredim. I
> have a big problem with this.

---

*Orthodox synagogues as a matter of course receive significant financial support from the state govern-
ment. Conservative, Reform, and Reconstructionist congregations do not.

**There are at present two such kindergartens, with about forty kids between them.

Israel also believes that even though Modiin has no Haredim, the city is still bled for money. "Why should I have to pay the electric bill for their *kollel?*" she wonders. "Why should the city pay two large salaries to two chief rabbis, who are both Haredi—why should my tax money go to this?" Behind all of Israel's complaints lies the insight that a city can have a "Haredi problem" without having Haredim. And this, in Israel's view, is largely because municipal policy is greatly influenced by state policy. If a city like Modiin wants to safeguard what Israel calls "its freedom *from* religion, in all its forms, including the freedom from paying for other people's religious needs," then it needs to campaign vigorously against Haredi influence. The question of whether Haredim actually live within city limits is, in this sense, secondary. It is for this reason that Israel concludes that "to come and to say that because there is no Haredi population in Modiin, there's no problem here, everything is fine, and that we're inventing problems ex nihilo (which is what I'm sure people have said about Ir Hofshit)—well that's not accurate."

Israel is right that Modiin politics can be understood only in the context of national politics, a point that I hadn't fully understood before I spoke with her. (Israel's analysis is sophisticated, the result of much reflection; her day job is coordinating a national nonprofit called Am Hofshi, or "A Free Nation," which fights Haredi political influence at the national level. This, her job, and the city council, her hobby, both involve mulling over Haredim, a pastime that occupies almost all her waking hours.) Ir Hofshit was one of many local anti-Haredi parties modeled on Tommy Lapid's Shinui Party that won six Knesset seats in 1999, and every one of these parties succeeded to one degree or another. Israel did not conceal her astonishment that I considered Modiin a unique political phenomenon: "Don't you remember what the atmosphere was throughout the country during those elections? Throughout the country, every party that called itself 'Free Whatever' won several seats. In Ramat HaSharon, in Pardes Hannah, all over. Dozens of parties whose only issue was the ultra-Orthodox sprang up because the issue was very hot nationally. This was after a very difficult year with Netanyahu, in which the ultra-Orthodox parties had enormous influence, greater than they ever had in the past. There was a feeling among the Haredi establishment of, 'Look, we're winning this battle,' a sort of arrogance that angered many people. All these things together created a situation in which in many cities, the anti-Haredim parties received a large mandate. Admittedly, Modiin was the only city in which we became the majority, but still we were part of a national trend."

According to Israel, some people voted for anti-Haredi parties in Modiin because they saw that Haredim did have an impact on local politics. Others voted anti-Haredi in Modiin because they were disgusted with Haredi impact on national politics. Of course, some voted anti-Haredi for both reasons at once. Both of these motives were rational, according to Israel, and none the less so because Modiin was itself a city without Haredim. Israel is right that the vote in Modiin reflected strong anti-Haredi sentiment throughout the country, but this did not explain why this sentiment was still stronger in Modiin than in other cities. "Oh, well, that's obvious," Israel replied when I put this to her. "It's because more than a quarter of Modiin's residents come from Jerusalem." I had heard this explanation before, and dozens of people that I spoke with in Modiin described themselves as "refugees" from Jerusalem, one even calling himself a "displaced person, a victim of the Haredi takeover" of the capital city. "Everyone who came [to Modiin] from Jerusalem," Israel told me, "has seen neighborhood after neighborhood in Jerusalem conquered. Their consciousness of the problem is especially high." Of the Jerusalem expatriates I met, more than half volunteered that escaping Haredim was high on their list of reasons for leaving the city. "Seeing Haredim on a daily basis in Jerusalem and paying property taxes while they didn't definitely has made me anti-Haredi," Debbie Taylor-Zimelman e-mailed me, explaining why she left Jerusalem for Modiin. "I am quite pleased that there are no Haredim here and hope there won't be." Another Modiin resident, Jay Abramoff, explained that taxes were the least of the problems Haredim caused Jerusalem, problems that led him to flee the city in favor of Modiin. In the capital, Abramoff felt that his rights were constantly being trampled, by "religion-based restrictions" on what he could do on Shabbat and by the constant proselytizing that had cost him several friends. Haredim had made life for him in Jerusalem impossible, he said, and if they moved to Modiin, he would move out.

Israel, who also moved to Modiin to escape the "Haredization" of Jerusalem, believes that the experience of living in Jerusalem educated many Modiin residents about the damage the ultra-Orthodox can do to a neighborhood and a community. In fact, the population that left Jerusalem for Modiin is more radical than the secular Jews they left behind in the city. Of course, there are many reasons why people might have chosen to move from one city to the next. Modiin is cheaper, cleaner, more homogeneously middle class than Jerusalem, embodying all the appeal of suburbs everywhere. But a surprising number of those who made the move cite escaping Haredim as their principal motivation, indicating that as a group they found the large Haredi presence in the capital especially difficult to bear. The Jerusalem expatriates in Modiin comprise a sort of vanguard of anti-Haredism. And this, according to Israel, is because as a group they more accurately perceive the Haredi threat than their more quietist neighbors who chose to remain in Jerusalem. In particular, Israel said, they came to understand the dangers of the Haredi "system of incursion."

"People who live in Jerusalem observe firsthand the Haredi 'system.' It works like this: Some sort of religious institution for Haredim is established in a secular or mixed neighborhood, and this serves as an anchor. Around this anchor, a Haredi community grows, and it slowly forces out the secular community. Eventually it reaches a point where we found ourselves having to rescue the last remaining secular families in a given neighborhood. Literally rescue them, because in many cases the last secular Jews living in what used to be a secular neighborhood are actually beaten until they convert or leave."

I asked Israel whether it isn't simply a fact of urban life that neighborhoods change hands, with one ethnic or religious or racial group at first joining those that are already there and, sometimes, eventually replacing them. Is there anything one can do about Haredim who move into a neighborhood, other than living with them and hoping that enough secular Jews remain so that the character of the neighborhood doesn't change entirely? After all, don't Haredim have the right to live anywhere, just like anyone else?

"The problem isn't living together with Haredim, and the problem isn't the natural, evolutionary change in urban neighborhood," Israel replied. "The problem is that this is their plan, their system, their goal. Their goal is clear, and they don't try to hide it, and that is to 'Judaize' a targeted secular neighborhood. They pick a neighborhood on the map and then systematically set about taking it over. This is different from what naturally happens in cities. So they start a *kollel* and bring students, and then they start to proselytize, through classes, and saying, 'Come give a listen, what do you have to lose?' Then a little later they start to say, 'It's not nice, why are you wearing a tank top, it's insensitive to our feelings, and why are you playing your music on Shabbat?' and so forth. It's a long process, it takes years, but it's a clear, highly planned process. Their goal is not to live their lives alongside us, their goal is to bring us to the Truth, which only they know. . . . This goal, in my opinion, is well meaning, according to their way of seeing things. They want to help us to see the light. What they will never take into account, though, is that we don't want to see the light. We don't want to be proselytized, and we don't want our neighborhoods Judaized. We lost the battle in Jerusalem, but we are not going to lose it in Modiin."

Haredim, Israel believes, take advantage of civil society, while refusing to act civilly. She insists that Haredim are free to settle wherever they want, just like anyone else. The problem is that they don't respect the crucial, unspoken codicil of the liberal social contract, which is, live and let live. They willfully commandeer secular neighborhoods with forethought, if not malice, and this makes their activities unseemly and illegitimate, even if there is nothing illegal about them in the strict sense of the word. This strategy, according to Israel, is the secret to their success. Haredim have devised a method of taking over secular neighborhoods that is effective but not illegal—for the law-abiding secular, there is nothing to do but pack.

Israel's feeling that Jerusalem has fallen to Haredim, that the city *was* a major battleground between Haredim and secular Israelis, and that the Haredim won, was shared to one degree or another by every Modiin resident I met who moved to the city from Jerusalem. When they call themselves refugees and displaced persons, they don't seem to be speaking metaphorically. Many of them seem to mean it quite literally when they say that they escaped a war zone after it became clear that their side was doomed. Even among Modiin residents who never lived in Jerusalem, the capital city remains ground zero for their fears of the ultra-Orthodox, the prototype of a place run by Haredim and ruined by Haredim, the model of what they wish Modiin never to become. When Modiin voters slipped anti-Haredi ballots into the box in their first election, most of them were likely thinking more about Jerusalem, the source of their fears, than they were about Modiin itself, the source of their hopes for a new life in a new home.

To find out more about why Jerusalem has left so many secular Jews traumatized, I spoke to Leah Zomer, the Jerusalem chairperson of Shinui. The root of the problem, Zomer told me, lay in its demographics. "Jerusalem is an anomaly. It's the capital city, yet most of its residents do not accept the government it houses, wishing instead to change the very nature of the state they live in. The Arabs want to replace it with some sort of binational state. The Haredim want a state based on Halakha. We Zionist Jews amount to only a third of the population, and we have no voice at all. Our interests are not looked after. We are second-class citizens."

I asked Zomer what practical impact this situation had on secular Jews, and she laughed at my ignorance. "It affects *everything*. I'll give you a small example, close to home. My building is a two-family home, and there was a bidding process on the downstairs unit, which we wanted to buy. We submitted the highest bid, but because it went via the Department of Interior [which is controlled by ultra-Orthodox politicos], instead of letting me buy the apartment next to my own so my family could expand our space, they gave it to an ultra-Orthodox family. Here's how they did it: They claimed that our check wasn't written clearly; one of the zeros was ambiguous, they said, and a comma was missing, so instead of having us rewrite the check, we were disqualified. They gave it to a Haredi family, instead, for much less money."

According to Zomer, ask any secular Jew in Jerusalem, and he or she will produce a story illustrating how they've been screwed by the ultra-Orthodox. After speaking to residents and ex-residents, I don't doubt that she is right. Dozens of women told me about being harassed and berated for

dressing "immodestly," wearing halters or tank tops and shorts in neighborhoods where doing so, until recently, was safe. Parents told me about sending their kids to kindergartens with too few teachers and toys, while the
ultra-Orthodox kids enjoyed the luxury of small classes and limitless supplies. The level of day-to-day friction between secular and ultra-Orthodox
Jews is exquisitely high, and 90 percent of secular Jerusalemites, when asked,
said that their relations with Haredim were either "not so good" or "awful"
(only 43 percent of the ultra-Orthodox felt the same way, with the majority
reporting that relations were "good" or "very good").

Though most secular Jerusalemites have a stash of anecdotes about run-
ins with Haredim and small indignities and deprivations that followed, the
most spectacular frictions take place on a bigger scale, often exploding into
large-scale conflict. The biggest conflict of the 1990s concerned Bar Ilan
Street, and whether it would remain open for traffic on Shabbat.

Bar Ilan is a wide and bustling road that cuts across much of Jerusalem. It is
lined by apartment blocks, and in most stretches the bottom floors of these
buildings house shops and businesses. Bar Ilan Street is secular on either end,
but in the middle it bisects ultra-Orthodox neighborhoods, not far from Meah
Shearim. And that is the cause of the problem. For secular Jerusalem residents,
the road is an important thoroughfare providing access to other secular neighborhoods. For Haredi Jerusalem residents, the road noisily cuts through the
heart of their neighborhood. An entry about the street in the 1997 *Israel Year-
book and Almanac* explained the Haredi attitude toward the road: "They want
it closed [on Shabbat] for three reasons: (1) so they can enjoy the benefits of a
pedestrian mall on their major day of rest and leisure, (2) so that their Sabbath
peace is not disturbed, and (3) so that their religious sensibilities are not offended by blatant Sabbath desecration in their own neighborhood."

For years, Bar Ilan was the site of sporadic ultra-Orthodox demonstrations. These demonstrations were quixotic and largely symbolic, as few
Haredi leaders expected the street to be closed under the administration of
Jerusalem's charismatic and proudly secular mayor, Teddy Kollek. Kollek,
who served as the city's mayor throughout most of the 1960s, 1970s, and
1980s, is the leader credited with transforming Jerusalem from a divided
and parochial backwater into a world-class city. His attitude toward the
ultra-Orthodox was proper but suspicious, and though he carefully enforced all previous agreements granting Jerusalem Haredim the autonomy
to prohibit traffic within their own neighborhoods, and though he recommended the closing of some sparsely traveled streets in Haredi neighborhoods, he steadfastly opposed prohibiting traffic on major streets well
traveled by secular Jews. And few people believed that Bar Ilan could be

closed under any administration. The road was far more significant—both practically and symbolically—to Jerusalem's secular residents than any of the roads that were regularly closed on Shabbat. Closing Bar Ilan adds long sidewise loops to normally simple trips within the city, doubling and trebling their duration. And for the same reason, closing Bar Ilan effectively put a wedge in the city, cordoning off the northern half of the city from the southern. Owing in part to the fact that, until 1967, Jerusalem was a divided city, the notion of splitting the city—even for only one day a week—carried powerfully negative associations for many of Jerusalem's residents.

In 1992, however, Jerusalem politics changed dramatically. Right-wing Likud mayoral candidate, Ehud Olmert, defeated the octogenarian Kollek after making a last-minute deal with the Haredi mayoral candidate, Meir Porush. Olmert promised Porush that in exchange for dropping out of the race on the day before the election, Haredim would enjoy unprecedented powers in Olmert's administration. Porush agreed, calling on his supporters to vote for Olmert, effectively handing the election to the Likud candidate. Part of the quid pro quo expected by his ultra-Orthodox constituents was the closure of Bar Ilan on Shabbat, and Olmert told Haredi leaders in private meetings that he would see to it. Three weeks after the elections, Haredim resumed demonstrations at Bar Ilan Street, and during the first rally after Olmert's election, stones were thrown at passing cars for the first time. Not long thereafter, Olmert appointed a committee to investigate and bring recommendations that would allow the street to be closed on the Sabbath, for at least part of the day.

As it turned out, Olmert had made a promise that he was not authorized to deliver. Most streets in the city fall under the mayor's jurisdiction, but Bar Ilan Street widens in places to six lanes, making it a "major artery," an administrative category that put the city under national government administration. As Olmert and Jerusalem Haredim discovered, this classification meant a decision to close the road could be made only by the national supervisor of road transport, a political appointee in the Ministry of Transportation. At the end of 1994, Olmert received a letter from the supervisor, an old Labor Party man named Alex Langer, stating that "we will not agree to the closure of Bar Ilan Street on Shabbat, holidays, or any other days." This position reflected the prevailing view in the left-leaning coalition that Yizhak Rabin captained—the transportation minister, long-time union boss Yisrael Keissar, was quoted insisting that the road would remain open as long as he was on watch—and it looked at the time as if there was little chance that his situation would change in the immediate future. During the three years after Olmert was elected, Haredi frustrations with the situation on Bar Ilan grew, and the sporadic protests on the street grew more common, ratcheting louder and more violent. In June 1994, the stridency seemed finally to pay off. Moshe Teitelbaum, the Satmar rebbe, announced that he was coming to spend the Sabbath near Bar Ilan Street, in order to dedicate a new yeshiva in the neighborhood. His entourage was expected to reach tens of thousands. The Jerusalem Police met hastily, after which the department's spokesman, Shmuel Ben-Ruby, announced that the street would be closed: "A hundred thousand people will be going to the rebbe's house near the street," he explained. "Once in a dozen years it's acceptable to close the street."

For Haredim who had lobbied for years to close the street, this "once-in-a-dozen-years" decision amounted to a precedent. A Haredi activist named Yehuda Meshi-Zahav told reporters that "the argument against closing the street has always been that there is nowhere to divert traffic. This makes it clear that traffic can be diverted, and no tragedy will ensue." A new era of Haredi militancy had begun, at least as far as Bar Ilan Street was concerned. With growing frequency, secular motorists driving through ultra-Orthodox neighborhoods on Bar Ilan reported being pelted with stones by boys in *peyes* yelling "Shabbes! Shabbes!" (Stoning is an adolescent pastime, for the most part discouraged by adults in much the same way adults discourage teenage subway graffiti: Obviously it is criminal, but perhaps it is crime in the service

Ultra-Orthodox youth hurling a stone at Israeli police on Bar Ilan Street, while others shout insults, in July 1996. © Reuters.

of a higher good.) In 1995, a child who was riding in the backseat of his parents' Subaru was hospitalized after a stone struck him as they drove on Bar Ilan Street on Saturday. Meretz organized "drive-ins"—convoys of several dozen cars that slowly drove up and down Bar Ilan on Saturday, taunting the Haredim, who loudly jeered at them from the sidewalk. The party's city councilman, Ornan Yekutieli, counseled secular drivers that if they found themselves surrounded on the street by "Haredi mobs," they "should put their foot on the gas and flee, even if people are standing in front of them."

Around this time, Yekutieli, who headed the Jerusalem Am Hofshi chapter, founded a local political coalition called Yerushalayim Akhshav—"Jerusalem Now"—and was the charismatic leader of the city's various anti-Haredi groups, began a vigorous verbal assault on the ultra-Orthodox, comparing their rabbis to "ayatollahs" drawing Israel "back to the Dark Ages" and "a step toward Tehran." In the mid-1990s, there seemed to be no municipal problem for which Yekutieli did not hold the ultra-Orthodox accountable. Commenting upon declining enrollment in the city's vaunted, but moribund Hebrew University, Yekutieli explained that "the steady rise in Jerusalem's ultra-Orthodox Jewish population and the religious regulations that its political representatives have succeeded in imposing on the city are making Jerusalem unattractive to students," a statement that likely is true, as far as it goes, but hardly a complete explanation of the university's troubles. Yekutieli distilled the ultra-Orthodox aspect out of whatever complicated cocktail he encountered, tossing the rest of the mix away. What his analysis of Jerusalem politics lacked in balance, it compensated for in *purity*. His political appeal lay in his simple certainty that Haredim were destroying the city he loved. It was for this reason that many Jerusalemites were surprised when, after a congenital heart defect began to threaten his life at the age of forty, Yekutieli turned to a Haredi charity named Kav la-Hayyim—"Lifeline" for help. Kav la-Hayyim referred Yekutieli to Columbia-Presbyterian Hospital in New York, haggled with his insurance company, raised money for the trip and operation, and rented an apartment nearby in New Jersey for Yekutieli and his family. Yekutieli died in New York in April 2001.

The steady geometric growth in tension that marked the first years of the Olmert administration was replaced by steep logarithmic increases soon after Rabin's assassination, when Netanyahu came to power and appointed as his transportation minister Rabbi Yitzhak Levy, head of the modern-Orthodox National Religious Party. Though Levy's views were often at odds with those of ultra-Orthodox leaders, he was sympathetic to their desire to keep their streets free from the heresy of cars on Shabbat, and mindful of the tit-for-tat that characterized the Haredi place in the Knesset, especially in the new Netanyahu administration. By late spring 1996, just two years after it seemed politically impossible, the partial sealing of Bar Ilan on the Sabbath had come to seem like a sure thing.

But as in badly plotted paperback mysteries, in Israeli politics surprise twists of fate are common. That summer, everything changed again. Meretz petitioned the Supreme Court to be allowed to march down the street. When the petition was granted, President Ezer Weizman appealed to the party to postpone its demonstration, which he feared would degenerate into violent clashes with the ultra-Orthodox. Meretz agreed, and though the party did not show up, a Haredi counterrally of 3,000 was staged on July 6, during the course of which stones, bottles, soiled diapers, and rotten vegetables were hurled at police officers, who responded by turning water cannons on the protesters. Knots of Haredim chanted "Nazis, Nazis" at the police. Four days later, on July 10, Yitzhak Levy informed the Knesset that he was ordering the street closed during the times of Sabbath prayers (for an hour and a half each Friday night, all of Saturday morning, and a couple of hours late Saturday afternoon).

The atmosphere was charged. The Supreme Court hastily issued a temporary injunction against the closure. With each passing week, the demonstrations grew bigger and uglier, and on July 27, according to police estimates, 150,000 Haredim gathered. Aware that the situation was explosive and that little fuse was left, Olmert tried desperately to find a compromise. "We must find a solution," he announced, "that will provide an answer to the [ultra-Orthodox] residents, and those who are unwilling to give up their right to drive in the area on Shabbat. There is no other solution than a road that will not disturb the Haredim and will not infringe on the right of the secular population to travel—and that means digging a tunnel." Olmert's thinking borrowed from the prevailing view about how West Bank settlers could be protected from Palestinian stone throwers; a huge chunk of the government's infrastructure budget throughout the 1990s was spent on elevated roads and tunnels separating Jewish traffic from Palestinian. In Olmert's view, the simple strategy of enforcing mechanical separation was the best way to keep the peace between secular and ultra-Orthodox Jews. Of course, building such a tunnel would take years, and tens of millions of dollars.

In the meantime, the Supreme Court ruled that the road must remain open and that a public commission be established to study traffic arrangements in Jerusalem on Shabbat. Levy appointed a handful of prominent professors and rabbis to the commission, which after several months of discussion, recommended that the street be closed during prayer time, and that when a highway that provided a convenient alternate route (which was already under construction) was completed, Bar Ilan be closed altogether on Shabbat. The first part of the recommendation was implemented, though the latter part of the recommendation never was, creating a status quo that leaves both sides feeling cheated. Haredim and secular Jews show up to protest the situation every so often, and to taunt and spit at each other, and the road remains a powerful symbol to all. To the secular, it is a wedge splitting, cracking, the city they loved. To the ultra-Orthodox, it remains a symbol of secular strong-armed hypocrisy. "This is not a religion issue," a telegenic Haredi journalist, Yisrael Eichler, said recently. "It is a quality-of-life issue." It is also, he added, a question of how much autonomy ought to be awarded to local communities. Secular Jews demand that bars be open in their neighborhoods on Shabbat, and the courts have determined that this demand is just, because local communities have the right to define their own character, Eichler explained. But Haredim who want to do the same thing are treated like criminals.

The future of Bar Ilan Street is uncertain, and the road has become a symbol for hundreds of similar, less-publicized disputes. As a symbol, it is evocative. A mainstay of Israeli education is an institution called the *moreshet krav*, literally, "battle legacy." At sites around the country, schoolchildren on field trips, tourists, day-trippers, soldiers, and backpackers learn of significant military battles in great detail. The names of soldiers and commanders are recounted, along with the details of their strategy meetings, and the hour-by-hour progress of their campaigns. Visiting the Old City of Jerusalem, one might learn exactly when each alley was captured, by whom, and under what circumstances. The precise place where soldiers died is soberly marked so that Israelis might know the terrible price paid for each street. A somewhat similar feeling accompanies discussions of the battles for Bar Ilan Street, which, for secular Jews and Haredim alike, are seen as a struggle of liberation and an heroic effort to hold onto a piece of the homeland.

Bar Ilan is important as a symbol, because in the minds of many the dispute there is taking place on a smaller scale throughout Israel. I asked Yossi, the young ex-Haredi leader of Da'at Emet, about the extent of the dispute, and he unfolded a napkin and drew a rudimentary map of the country. He added a small circle to indicate the cities in which the ultra-Orthodox had confiscated public buildings and roads for their own purposes, beginning with the big cities—Jerusalem, Tel Aviv, Haifa, and Beer Sheva—but then continuing to smaller municipalities—Safed, Ashdod, Kiryat Shemona, Beit Shemesh, Beitar, Modiin Elite, Ramat Aviv, Ramat Gan, Petach Tikvah, Raanana. With each circle, Yossi, who retains something of the fastidious genius of a mathematician or the Talmud scholar that he was, recounts names of embattled roads and kindergartens and community centers. By the time he finished, the napkin had an impressive splotch of ink, ranging from the very top of the country to the Negev Desert in the south. Wherever there is population, there is some sort of ultra-Orthodox incursion. This global fact, Yossi complained, is overlooked, because each individual circle represents a local fight. In Kiryat Shalom, the ultra-Orthodox incursion is seen as a problem for Kiryat Shalom. So too in Ramat Aviv, in Modiin, in Jerusalem, and everywhere else. We fail to see the forest for the trees, Yossi said, and soon it will be too late.

Yossi may be right, but then the forest is difficult to apprehend with certainty. His map is not inaccurate, but it is hard to know just what it portrays. The imagery of even a hand-drawn map becoming black, bit by bit, is affecting. It recalls fearful images of Communist red covering the globe, and of maps from the 1930s illustrating the *Anschluss* and the rapid expansion of Germany. The map bespeaks not simply expansion, but willful domination.

Haredi expansion is a fact. Ultra-Orthodox Jews are moving to towns and neighborhoods where they were formerly absent. They are moving to new towns, like Kiryat Sefer and Elad and Beitar, planned and built for Haredim. They are moving to well-established towns, like Zikhron Yaakov, Netanya, and Ashdod, which in the past had very few Haredim, and sometimes none at all. And they are moving to secular neighborhoods in cities, like Jerusalem and Safed, that have long had clearly delineated ultra-Orthodox neighborhoods across town.

This ultra-Orthodox expansion has many causes. Those who mistrust Haredim tend to attribute it to the growing ambitions of Haredi proselytizers, and they have a point. When Yossi finished inking his napkin, I asked him whether he imagined a command center somewhere with a large map on the wall on which ultra-Orthodox functionaries marked with pushpins the progress of their conversion campaigns. He told me that he thought there were many such Haredi situation rooms, and at the time I took this as the feverish paranoia of a conspiracy theorist. Months later, however, when I put the same question to a former Belz Hasid who for a time administered the sect's proselytizing efforts, he said that he himself had such a map. Among the Lubavitch, young couples are frequently sent to bring *Yiddishkayt* to Jewish neighborhoods that lack it, in Israel as in the rest of the world. Most significant of all, Shas activists make no secret of their plans to persuade residents of poor, Sephardi neighborhoods, whom Shas takes as its natural constituency, to send their children to ultra-Orthodox schools and to embrace religion themselves. There are grounds, then, for the complaint that ultra-Orthodox proselytizers target secular towns and neighborhoods, and move to them with the premeditated expectation of Judaizing them and, what is worse, their residents. The notion of a Haredi Comintern hatching five-year plans aiming to turn secular neighborhoods ultra-Orthodox exaggerates the monolithic nature of ultra-Orthodox planning, as well as its efficacy, but it is not without basis.

Still, only a small percentage of Haredim who move to a predominantly secular neighborhood or town do so to subvert the secular. It takes a person of great dedication to devote his life to converting others, sacrificing the comfort of his family to advance the spiritual hygiene of strangers. Such dedication is rare, and it is rarely the motivation of ultra-Orthodox moving into new neighborhoods. The great majority of ultra-Orthodox who move into secular areas do so, not out of commitment to religious ideals, but out of financial necessity. Like most secular Jews, most Haredim wish to live peaceably among their own. Most Haredim regret exposing their children to the mores of secular Jews. Most would rather live in Meah Shearim or Bnei Brak, if only they could afford it.

They cannot. Prices vary, but according to the real estate appraiser Levi Yizhak, an apartment of 1,000 square feet on a good street in Meah Shearim can cost well over $300,000. On a less tony street, the same apartment may cost $200,000. In Bnei Brak, prices are somewhat lower, but the modest apartment that my grandparents owned would now cost almost $200,000. A 1999 report commissioned by the Housing Ministry from the research firm Geocartographia found that Haredim were both the poorest sector of Israel's Jewish population and the fastest growing, and that their housing needs were expanding at a rate of roughly 5,000 units each year. The traditional centers of Haredi population of Meah Shearim and Bnei Brak are overpopulated beyond the saturation point. As demand has grown, housing prices in these neighborhoods have greatly swelled, even though the average wealth of the ultra-Orthodox has steadily shrunk. Both trends—swelling prices and shrinking bank accounts—have been amplified by the increase in the past generation of the ultra-Orthodox birthrate. More Haredim means greater demand for housing, ergo higher prices. More Haredim means more expenses per family, ergo fewer savings. In past generations, it was customary for Haredi parents who could afford to do so to purchase an apartment for each child when they wed. With more kids to buy for, far greater expense for each kid, and less disposable income, many ultra-Orthodox parents must go deep into debt if they are to provide housing for their children at all.

It is not lost on Haredim that few places in Israel are as expensive as Meah Shearim and Bnei Brak. In the past two decades, savvy developers have acquired relatively inexpensive lands from the government (often in the occupied territories), and built entire cities catering to the ultra-Orthodox, in which a new 1,000-square-foot apartment, designed with Haredi amenities like a porch that converts to a sukkah and matching milk and meat sinks, may cost only $90,000. An ultra-Orthodox employee of the Housing Ministry told an interviewer recently that he estimates that apartments in these new Haredi cities are the preferred destination of 80 percent of those squeezed out of the housing market in Bnei Brak and Meah Shearim.

Most of the remaining 20 percent manage to find similar economic relief elsewhere in Israel, in established secular towns. The apartment that costs $250,000 in Meah Shearim sells for perhaps a $90,000 in Ashdod and $65,000 in Beer Sheva. A $200,000 place in Bnei Brak might go for half the price in Holon. These economic facts, far more than an impulse to convert the secular, account for the recent exodus of Haredim from their traditional neighborhoods into secular towns and neighborhoods.

The black-splotched napkin denoting Haredi domination is misleading, not so much because it exaggerates ultra-Orthodox incursions into Haredi areas, but because it implies that these incursions are willful attempts to challenge secularism. They are something less sinister, yet more immutable than that: The incursions are for the most part just families regretfully moving to what is for them a cultural wilderness because they cannot afford to live where they really want to live, among their own.

To those who oppose Haredi infiltration into secular neighborhoods, the economics of the situation may understandably seem irrelevant. A pamphlet produced by the anti-Haredi group Hofesh describes the stages of ultra-Orthodox hegemony:

It is a gradual process, and its characteristic stages are

- Purchase or rental of one or several apartments by Haredim.
- Torah study in these apartments, involving the importation of students from far away, including other cities and towns, and creating a nuisance for the neighbors and residents of the neighborhood. This leads to erosion of housing prices.
- Purchase of additional apartments from the neighbors at significantly lower prices.
- Transformation of apartments into a *kollel* or Talmud academy.
- Leaving the apartments to begin missionary activity: encouraging men to put on tefillin, handing out Shabbat candles and other ritual objects on Fridays at shopping centers.

• Setting up stands proselytizing others to become religious or Haredi, especially near secular schools.

• Transformation of an apartment into a synagogue. Usurpation of a class in an existing school to turn it into a synagogue on Shabbat at first, and then later expansion of religious activity, building a *kollel* near the synagogue, building a ritual bath, a yeshiva, and eventually, closing a street or part of a neighborhood on Shabbat.

• Infiltration of religious and Haredi residents onto the neighborhood association, numerical domination of the association, and exploitation of the democratic process to make decisions to the detriment of the freedom of the neighborhood.

This schematic description is largely accurate in its detail, though the process it describes may well be less menacing than it seems. To the pamphlet's authors, the steps they described add up to a cynical attempt to wrest control of a neighborhood from its peaceable and unsuspecting residents. But these same steps might more reasonably be seen as what ethnic and cultural minorities *do* when they come to live in a new, foreign and unfriendly locale. They recreate, as best they can, the world they came from. They establish churches, mosques, synagogues; they build schools. Then they try to persuade more of their own, their *landslayt*, "compatriots," to join them. They try to build a community and to grow it until it is large enough to sustain itself. The same pattern followed by Haredim in Ashkelon is the pattern followed by Mexicans moving to Los Angeles, Turks moving to Heidelberg, Afghans moving to Islamabad, Pakistanis moving to Birmingham. A generation or two ago, it was the pattern followed by Jews moving to Great Neck. It is a sad fact of modern life that immigrants, wherever they end up, are disparaged for lowering housing prices, for acting unseemly and strange, for taking over schools, churches, and neighborhoods. Haredim may then be the greenhorns of secular Israelis.

The thousands of ultra-Orthodox families spilling out of Meah Shearim and Bnei Brak each year seek what all of us seek: a place they can afford to live, and a place where they can live as they see fit. This desire sounds unobjectionable enough, but in practice, the places they can afford are often not places where they can live as they want. That means that they often try to change those places they *can* afford into the sorts of places they can live as they wish. This change too would be unobjectionable, were it not for the fact that people already live in these places, and they do not wish to see them changed. From the point of view of the longer-term inhabitants, which is no less reasonable that that of the ultra-Orthodox, Haredi immigrants are strong arming their way into places they don't belong and forcing others to live as the Haredim see fit. From this perspective, every new Haredi institution is an affront.

Secular Jews often complain about an asymmetry between their civic attitudes and those of the ultra-Orthodox. "We believe in 'live and let live,'" an anti-Haredi activist in Ramat Aviv told me, "while they try to force everyone to be like them." This complaint captures the reality that secular Israelis for the most part don't care what goes on within someone else's apartment or on the street, so long as it doesn't impose on them. The same cannot be said of Haredim, many of whom care whether cars are being driven down their block on Saturday. But the complaint misses a deeper symmetry between secular and ultra-Orthodox residents. Just as Haredim may wish to outlaw motor traffic on Shabbat, secular Jews often wish to prevent Haredim from building those institutions—kollel, mikve (ritual bath), heder, and so on— that would allow them to live as they wish. This is in part because the secular Jews fear being proselytized, in part because they dislike the institutions themselves, which they regard as primitive and unseemly, and in part because they don't wish to make the place inviting enough that more ultra-Orthodox will come, which is of course exactly what the ultra-Orthodox wish. When secular Israelis embrace the principle of "live and let live," they do so in a limited way, one that excludes the kollel and the mikve and the proselytizer.

Asked by a journalist if he would design mixed neighborhoods, an ultra-Orthodox building developer (who wished not to be identified) said: "It's unhealthy to put a secular Jew into an ultra-Orthodox neighborhood, or an ultra-Orthodox Jew into a secular one. It's like selling an apartment with a defect." The idea is that identity does not stop at the threshold of an apartment, and what one does in the living room is inseparable from how one acts on the street. It may be that what bothers secular Jews the most about the influx of ultra-Orthodox in their towns and neighborhoods is not so much that Haredim will force secular Jews to act like Haredim, but rather that Haredim themselves obstinately refuse to act like decent, civilized, secular Jews.

4

Shylock
at the Mall

In 1999, a controversy broke out over Tarzan. It was followed closely by all the newspapers and on the television news, and many people I've spoken to told me that even though they know it was no big deal—it was, after all, about *Tarzan*—the controversy bothered them at the time and continues to, because of the principle.

The disagreement concerned posters advertising Disney's animated feature, showing the figure of Tarzan, flapping coils of hair and ribbons of bulging muscle, surfing down the mossy limb of a tree. The problem was that Tarzan wore only a loincloth, which did not meet the standards of "modesty" set by a shady and powerful Haredi watchdog group that goes by the name of the "National Committee for the Prevention of Obscene Advertising in the Holy Land." The same day that 300 back-lighted posters advertising the movie were hung in bus shelters and street-side displays around the country, the committee sent a fax to Avi Lent, the director of Maxi-Media (one of the two companies that make up Israel's back-lighted-sign cartel) demanding he either take down the posters or dress up Tarzan.

Forum Films, which distributes Disney in Israel, rejected the demand outright, issuing a statement that the hunky figure in the loincloth was no more than "an innocent image from an animated film," and not at all immodest or sexually provocative. The bravado may have been easy to summon, as the ultra-Orthodox constitute only a fraction of a percent of film audiences. Avi Lent of Maxi-Media was more circumspect, issuing the statement: "We'd like to come to an understanding and find a way to please everyone. I guess we can put sweat pants on Tarzan." Then he added as a joke, "Hey, maybe we should put Nike sport shoes on him, too." Later Tarzan ads showed the Man of the Apes from his chest up. The capitulation to ultra-Orthodox demands—perhaps especially to such silly demands—annoyed many people who did not immediately understand how a Disney cartoon could offend. Linda Lovelace might offend, and perhaps Fritz the Cat could as well, but Tarzan?

It aggravated matters that Tarzan was only the latest in a long string of censored advertisements. A decade before, one of the two large dairies in Israel had launched a line of insulin-shock-sweet yogurt for kids, and the coordinated advertising "concept" it adopted to push it used a dinosaur motif. Everything had dinosaurs. Each flavor yogurt was associated with a dinosaur, the print ads showed dinosaurs, the radio spots aired reptilian growls in the background. Haredim were quick to complain that the lizards were causing their kids to ask uncomfortable questions, including about how dinosaurs fit into the traditional Jewish dating of the world as just over five and three-quarter millennia old. Haredi MK Avraham Ravitz explained that dinosaurs present no real theological challenge to traditional belief, as there are any number of ways to harmonize fossils and scriptures. The problem with the yogurt was twofold. First, not all God-fearing parents were educated enough in religious hermeneutics to explain away the apparent contradiction between the ancient provenance of dinosaurs according to carbon dating and the relative freshness of all creation according to the Torah. For their children, the dinosaurs might actually undermine both their naïve faith and their respect for their parents. But second, even for people who knew how to explain the matter to their children, who wanted to get into complicated theological explanations over breakfast? Who needed the headache? So Haredim demanded that the dinosaurs disappear, and by the next week there was not a trace of them to be found on supermarket shelves or billboards.

Not long after, Pepsi unveiled an ad depicting the "ascent of man" through the secession of a chimp, an ape, a Neanderthal, a man in a hat with a briefcase, and finally a hunch-shouldered kid with a skateboard guzzling Pepsi, and a rabbi from the Eda Haredit (Ultra-Orthodox Community), an anti-Zionist group in Jerusalem, announced a boycott of Pepsi and threatened to pull its *hekhsher*, or certification of kashrut, from all drinks produced by

Tempo, the local distributor of
Pepsi. The ad was unacceptable,
the rabbi explained, because
it assumed human evolution,
which contravened the account
in Genesis of the origins of
man, but the Haredi brief with
Pepsi went beyond that. During
the same summer, Pepsi sponsored two rock concerts—Guns
N' Roses and Michael Jackson.
As between those two, Michael
Jackson was more irksome because his concert took place on
Shabbat. The ads were pulled,
and Pepsi withdrew its sponsorship of the concerts.

מלצר !
יש חרדי
בקולה
שלי...

Ultra-Orthodox pressure on Pepsi satirized.
Customer says, "Waiter! There's a Haredi in
my cola." Cartoon by Moshik Lin, reprinted
with permission of *Shpitz,* journal of the
Israel Cartoonists Union.

Stories of ads disappearing following Haredi boycott threats are perennials here; in 2001, the health and fitness magazine *Menta* was forced to pull
its poster advertisements because they depicted an ivory-soap-wholesome
couple in workout clothes, arm in arm. A message peeled off Maxi-Media's
fax machine complaining that the Committee for the Prevention of Obscene Advertising would not cotton to physical contact between a man and
a woman in a publicly displayed ad. *Menta*'s editor in chief, Liora Boneh-
Azulai, faxed back that the couple—Shelly Gafni and Ofek Kairi—are actually married and thus they are not prohibited from touching each other
even by the most stringent of standards. She swore that she would not be
blackmailed, but two days later the ads were pulled. Boneh-Azulai remained
bitter. "I am distressed that a company that big does not consider itself
strong enough to stand by its clients, and immediately surrenders to religious pressure. We're in the twenty-first century, and it's hard to believe that
a healthy and loving husband and wife are taken to be an abomination."

Such stories raise two questions. Why do mammoth multinational corporations like Disney and Pepsico cave in to Haredi demands, often re-
canting their initial refusal to be bullied? And if the Haredim have the
power to dictate the advertisements of multinational corporations, why
do the offending posters keep appearing at all? What are the mechanics of
this conflict, in which Haredim manage time after time to quash secular
commercial images that they judge offensive, only to have new offensive
images arise in their wake?

The answers to both questions, it turns out, involve the back-lighted-sign cartel—Maxi-Media and Postermedia. These two companies control a large portion of the total advertising space in Israel's cities, and no serious advertising campaign can get off the ground without contracting with one or the other company, or both. That is an unusual situation, one that the Committee for the Prevention of Obscene Advertising has turned to its advantage. Executives from the sign companies were skittish about being interviewed for this book—those I spoke with asked not to be quoted, and in any case offered up platitudes about the importance of sensitivity to the special concerns of all the communities that make up their viewing public—but I spoke with Hillel Wachs, who sold advertising space for Postermedia in the mid-1990s and now heads the marketing department of a high-tech start-up. Wachs explained that the direct pressure on the company with the ostensibly offensive advertisements was rarely what caused the advertisements to be pulled. A company like Disney that runs the numbers will conclude that not many Haredim are going to see their films anyway, and they're likely to gain rather than lose customers by refusing to kowtow to ultra-Orthodox pressure. The same goes for a magazine like *Menta* or a bathing suit company or, frankly, most of the companies that advertise in Israel. After all, aside from food, beverages, tobacco, transportation, and a few other categories tracked by the Ministry of Finance, Haredim spend disproportionately little on consumer goods.

What makes the threat of boycott effective, then, is the pressure it places on the poster and billboard companies themselves, via the producers of those few products that Haredim do consume in bulk. Wachs explains it like this:

> It got to the point where the purchasing power of the Haredi community and those who go by the Haredi *hashgahot* ["oversight," which affords a rabbinic imprimatur that food is kosher] when it comes to food is somewhere along the line of 15–20 percent of the population. If you're talking about a huge dairy that is doing a turnover of maybe 600 million shekels a year, when you say to the CEO, listen, you have a choice, you can either sell 100 million shekels of milk and yogurt, or you can stand up for your values, but you can't do both, what do you choose? The thought process was not very long. So what happened was that every week the Committee [for the Prevention of Obscene Advertising] would say to my boss, if you advertise certain things, we will not only boycott Postermedia, because that's the small part, we will also boycott *all* other clients who advertise through Postermedia, including those whose advertisements are not in themselves offensive. In other words, they were going to punish us and all the advertisers.

Ultra-Orthodox licentiousness and hypocrisy in banning advertising posters
(frames begin at upper right). Cartoon by Michel Kishka, reprinted with
permission of *Shpitz,* journal of the Israel Cartoonists Union.

Although many advertisers wouldn't be bullied by a boycott, Wachs sup-posed, the biggest advertisers would pull their ads, and for good reason. "It was very clear to the parties involved that even if this committee did not represent all the Haredi community, they still represented a lot of people, and it was not worth taking a chance antagonizing them. People were afraid, and they'd say to themselves, 'I don't want to play games with hundreds of millions of shekels. We'd have to shut down production lines, we'd have to fire people.' There was a clear feeling that this was a viable threat." This reaction was rea-sonable, really the only reasonable reaction from a business point of view, es-pecially given the fact that there was another poster company that would be all too happy to run the ads pulled from its boycotted competitor. The Commit-tee for the Prevention of Obscene Advertising has managed to set in motion a perfect "prisoners' dilemma." This is the name game theorists give to a situa-tion in which two parties benefit from cooperating and lose if both fail to co-operate, but in which the greatest gain comes to a party who fails to cooperate when the other does cooperate. (The name comes from the scenario repeated nightly on cop shows, in which partners in crime can either both deny wrong-doing, both snitch on each other, or one of them can turn state's evidence against the other, gaining immunity for himself and leaving his partner to do hard time.) If both companies were to stand up to the committee, big clients would probably have to risk boycott, in order for their goods to be advertised at all. However, if only one of the sign companies defied the committee, the other would stand to gain lucrative clients like Strauss looking to spend money on back-lit posters while at the same time looking to avoid alienating any customers. This dynamic keeps both companies jittery and responsive to the demands of the committee. Wachs explained that as a result:

It got to the point where every week someone came from this committee and looked at the ads that were slated to be printed. At some point we just faxed every ad to them—that's what it got to. It was a pretty big crisis, because there were some pretty provocative ads by European or American standards at the time and of course the Haredim didn't like it. Eventually, there was some sort of reeducation process, and maybe even a formal approach to the advertising agencies that if they wanted the media to exist at all and they didn't want their clients to incur the wrath of the Haredim, that they'd have to tone down their messages and their visuals. And so they did.

Wachs's complaint is that Haredim leverage their influence in a way that is both savvy and unfair. "On the one hand, you can say that it's a totally legitimate use of economic power. The question is, where do you draw the line? . . . There is something infuriating in the fact that all public images in advertising have to conform to 10 percent of the population's wishes and criteria." What galls Wachs and many others is not that Haredim have economic clout—interest groups exerting pressure is a fundamental element of market capitalism. What galls him about Haredim is how they expand their clout beyond its natural ken. In a sense, Haredim lack market *civility*.

Controlling What We Eat

The same complaint unifies a protest group called the "Free Buyers." Free Buyers incorporated in fall 2000 to combat ultra-Orthodox economic power, and in its first year enlisted 2,000 households, an impressive feat at a time when the Palestinian uprising—at once so absorbing and enervating— jammed the wavelengths for almost all political action. The group's analysis of Haredi influence on commerce and advertising is remarkably sophisticated, a fact that owes much to the background of its founder, who asked to be identified only as Tuvia. I first reached Tuvia by writing to an anonymous P.O. box, a procedure that allowed me to be vetted before I was contacted to schedule an interview. I was by now accustomed to this spy-versus-spy protocol, though in this case it seemed perfunctory and ineffective, if only because Tuvia's full identity can hardly be secret. As he told me, until the mid-1990s, Tuvia presided over the "Badatz," an acronym for the Beit Din Zedek (or Tribunal of Justice), which is the most influential of many rabbinic organizations that offer kashrut authorization for pay. Among most ultra-Orthodox, only a Badatz imprimatur confers kashrut—without it, food or cleanser or paper goods are considered an abomination. It is for this reason, Tuvia explained, that Badatz commands 4 percent of the gross income of whatever factories it certifies—a usurious sum, which accounts for an annual income of hundreds of millions of shekels for the organization. Tuvia always had qualms about what amounts to a stiff Haredi tax on all foodstuff, as well as other qualms of a more theological nature, and six years ago he left the ultra-Orthodox community and ceased to practice religion. Several years after that, he became an anti-Haredi activist. In this he followed in the path of his old Talmud study partner, Raffi, who founded Da'at Emet, and whom I had found so winning and persuasive months earlier, on my fortieth birthday, in Ramat Aviv.

"Free Buyers" first came to the attention of the public in a series of advertisements in *Ha'aretz*. "Warning!" the ads read, "You pay, and they benefit. . . .

Emblem of the Free Buyers, depicting a spray-painted
Badatz kashrut certification symbol.

Don't fund another Haredi entity—Join the Free Buyers organization." Once
the group's rolls reached a critical mass, Free Buyers, together with the Meretz
political party and several anti-Haredi organizations, organized a boycott. As a
first step, they sent letters to dozens of food producers who used the Badatz to
certify their kashrut, warning that if the manufacturers did not immediately
cease using the ultra-Orthodox certification, their products would be included
on the boycott list. Expensive Badatz certification, the letters explained, inflate
food prices, amounting to an unjust tax on secular buyers, for whom the certification means nothing. Among the signatories was a Meretz member of
Knesset named Ilan Ghilon, a fact that lent gravitas to the letter's threat. Several weeks later, in September 2000, secular activists started to spend long days
in supermarket aisles in front of Badatz-certified products, persuading customers not to buy them.

The ultra-Orthodox newspaper *Ha-Modia* picked up the story immediately, illustrated its report with an archive photograph of an SS soldier standing in front of a placard he had affixed to the plate-glass window on a Jewish
store. The sign read, "Kauft nicht bie Juden!" (Don't buy from Jews!) A box
insert told the story of a Holocaust survivor experiencing flashbacks of the
Nazis ever since he had been roughly advised in his supermarket not to buy
any products bearing the Badatz seal. The identification of the boycott with
Nazis was an ugly exaggeration, but it took on a certain poignancy because
several years earlier the Anti-Defamation League (ADL) in the United States
had published a much discussed report entitled, "The 'Kosher Tax' Hoax:
Anti-Semitic Recipe for Hate." The report cited KKK and neo-Nazi pamphlets
attacking kosher certification in America, using language remarkably similar
to that of the Free Buyers: "American families are paying tribute to Jews every
time they sit down at the table to eat and in many instances, polish their
shoes, silver or wrap the leftover Thanksgiving turkey. Why? Because Jews
have discovered a way to coerce business to pay taxes directly to Jewish organizations and pass the cost on to the consumer." The ADL dismissed claims
like this as a ruse used by Nazis and other bigots to "exploit legitimate public
concerns (e.g., taxes, the economy, etc.) as vehicles for anti-Semitism." Mutatis
mutandis, the Haredi press said the same of Free Buyers' claims.

It was not only the ultra-Orthodox who took offense at the boycott. The
manufacturers whose products were targeted immediately pressed Oded

Tirah, the president of the Israel Association of Industrialists, to lodge a formal protest. Nissim Weiss, the CEO of a cleaning-supply company named
St. Moritz, faxed Tirah a letter complaining that the boycott was

> an anti-democratic step that damages freedom of commerce and threatens the
> income of hundreds and thousands of workers. It saddens me that those who
> are standard bearers for religious freedom and civil rights are using blackmail
> to create anti-religious coercion and delimit freedom of religion. . . . I hope
> that no organization in the near future will demand that I declare whether or
> not I eat pork, in order to keep my company from falling prey to one or an-
> other boycott.

Arieh Caspi, the economic analyst for *Ha'aretz*, where the first announcements of the boycott appeared, drove to a supermarket to compare six
products bearing the Badatz certification symbol to similar products without it, and found that the Badatz products were most often cheaper. The
claim that the certification made products more expensive, he concluded,
"is interesting; but the only problem with it is, it's wrong. . . . A pluralist
worldview accepts the right of Haredim to purchase products with whatever
certification they see fit, just as seculars have the right to purchase unkosher
products, as their heart desires."

Tuvia, the leader of Free Buyers, finds these criticisms valid. He told me
that the official reasons behind the boycott were for the most part simple
demagoguery, at best half-truths, and many times simply factually wrong.
To attract publicity and members, Free Buyers exploits the fears and frustrations of secular Jews who somehow believe that Badatz is ripping them off.
This strategy works, Tuvia admitted, and many people joined "Free Buyers"
because they feel they're being unfairly taxed—forced to pay for certification that means nothing to them—a feeling that Free Buyers felt could serve
their purposes as well. The truth, Tuvia told me, is more complicated than
what the bumper stickers claim. In some cases, the cost of the *hekhsher* in-
flates prices to consumers, but in an equal number of cases, it does not. As
Free Buyers' critics claimed, by opening large additional markets for certain
products, the *hekhsher* actually affords producers economies of scale that in
some instances allow them to reduce the price. The buying power of Bnei
Brak and Meah Shearim is great enough for some products that the cost of
kashrut certification cannot be seen as linear—sometimes it is passed onto
consumers, and sometimes it reduces prices to consumers. In any instance,
as long as producers are free to do their own cost-benefit analyses, the question of whether to spend money on an expensive *hekhsher* is no different

from the question of whether to spend money on expensive advertising. Ultimately, the market decides.

This view is consonant with the findings of an August 2001 survey of buying patterns, which found that roughly one-third of all shoppers not only checked to make sure that the purchases were certified kosher, but also preferred some certifications over others. Badatz, Tuvia's old employer, was the most widely accepted, as it was viewed by 98 percent of all consumers as authoritative, compared with 50 percent acceptance for the seal of some local rabbinates. As Arieh Frankel, director of public relations for BSD, an ad agency specializing in products aimed at a religious clientele, put it, "If a product doesn't bear a certification symbol the customer finds acceptable, he won't purchase it. If it's got a fancy certification, only then does the game revert to typical marketing considerations of product, quality, price." Because in many instances the kashrut certification is the first consideration affecting purchase decisions, it can greatly affect sales. Thus, buying a premium certification, even at a premium price, can increase a manufacturer's sales and profits. The Badatz is to yogurt what Michael Jordan is to athletic shoes.

Controlling Whom We Can Hire

Tuvia recognized the economic logic behind this analysis, and freely admitted that the real issue had nothing to do with prices. "The more important thing," he told me, "is the vast power of the Badatz that stems from the very fact that it grants *hekhsher*s, and transcends it. This would be a problem even if it gave certifications for free." The problem with Badatz is that it makes demands "that have nothing to do with whether the food they oversee is kosher. For instance, it won't certify a hotel as kosher if it hosts New Year's Eve celebrations. For example, there's a hotel in Tiberias that agreed to host a convention of a group that does meditation. The rabbis threatened the hotel that if it hosted the convention, it would lose its certification. Naturally, there's no connection between this particular convention and the kashrut of the food served in the hotel. And it succeeded in forcing a big corporation to fire one of their managers because he was a Jehovah's Witness. All of this is religious coercion, pure and simple."

The last case Tuvia referred to, that of the Jehovah's Witness, had been a cause celebre in the last months of 1999. At its center was Eduardo Campos, a human resources manager for the large food producer Vita, and a fervent Jehovah's Witness, who, true to his faith, saw it as a personal responsibility to missionize. Campos is a youthful sixty-two, with soft gray-green eyes and a quick smile, and if it's true what they say that by fifty everyone has the face he or she deserves, then he must have been doing something right all this time. His life has followed an unusual path. He was born in Mercedes, Uruguay, a town of 40,000 on the banks of the Rio Negro. His father was vigorously atheist, but his mother was a Catholic who was persuaded to join Jehovah's Witnesses while Eduardo was still a boy. He himself joined the faith when he was fourteen. By seventeen he was married; by eighteen he was a father. He worked various jobs, but viewed proselytizing as his calling. Twenty years later, in 1979, in the process of divorce, Campos decided to take a "sabbatical" in Israel, bringing along his twenty-year-old son. During that year he met and married an Israeli Jewish Jehovah's Witness, and though he returned to South America, from then on both he and his son were drawn back to Israel, eventually settling there permanently. Campos's son found a job driving a truck for a food-processing plant in the run-down southern city of Ashdod, and later hooked his father up to a job in the personnel department. Campos rose through the ranks, and after the plant was purchased by Vita, one of Israel's largest food concerns, Campos stayed on to become personnel director. Throughout the whole period, Campos was an active Witness, spending afternoons and weekends knocking on doors, trying to spread the word. He did not missionize at work, but he never hid his religion either, and his beliefs were well known by his bosses and by those he hired.

It is hard to pinpoint when Campos's ultra-Orthodox troubles began. From about 1995, he said, Haredim sporadically followed him about town, taunting and threatening. Some years after that, several ultra-Orthodox thugs beat his mother-in-law, who had followed her daughter into the Witnesses. By 1999, ultra-Orthodox Jews were regularly monitoring the activities of the small Witness community in Ashdod (which numbered about seventy, perhaps half of whom were new immigrants from the former Soviet Union), often videotaping the groups activities. A group based in Bnei Brak called Yad le-Achim (which is a bit of a pun, meaning "a hand to our brothers," presumably a helping hand to Jews being proselytized, and also "a memorial to our brothers," presumably to Jews whose proselytization succeeded) organized the harassment, posting placards with the photographs of group members, organizing rallies against Jehovah's Witnesses, and screening videotapes of local Jews being baptized.

Yad le-Achim was well practiced at stirring up fear and anger against Christian missionary groups working in Israel, especially Jehovah's Witnesses. Its mission, or calling, is to identify and halt proselytizing of Jews (aside from proselytizing by more religious Jews). It tries to do this in several ways. Yad le-Achim representatives lobby the Knesset to enact a law forbidding proselytizing, which is at present permitted under the general rubric of "freedom of worship." The organization also maintains a database of missionaries and their activities, most of the data for which comes via a toll-free hotline they run for people alarmed that missionaries visited them in their homes. This information is also funneled to the public through warning posters and emergency meetings organizing in neighborhoods worked by missionaries.

Alongside these activities, and off the record, Yad le-Achim's modus operandi is significantly more aggressive. Mark Einstein, Jehovah's Witnesses' spokesperson in Israel, believes that the group was responsible for the trashing of the sect's Kingdom Hall in the town of Lod in 1997. A group of ultra-Orthodox men broke into the hall, hastily heaving Bibles and religious pamphlets into the courtyard and setting them ablaze. As the holy texts burned, they danced around the fire singing songs in praise of the Lubavitcher rebbe. In Bat Yam, a Jehovah's Witness was beaten with sticks while his wife and kids stood by helplessly, and in Tel Aviv, a Witness was doused with a bucket of yellow paint while leaving that city's Kingdom Hall. In nearby Holon, goons broke into an a apartment shared by two Jehovah's Witnesses, gutted their sofa, ransacked their library, and spray-painted swastikas and death threats on the walls. The thugs were never caught in any of these cases, but Witnesses believe that they were sent by Yad le-Achim.

Yad le-Achim also tries to harm Witnesses in less direct ways. In the case of Campos, representatives of Yad le-Achim, working with local rabbis, threatened to organize a boycott against Vita unless the corporation fired him, and to persuade Badatz to pull its certification of Vita's products. As Campos recalled, late in 1999 his boss showed him a copy of a threatening letter the company had received from Yad le-Achim rabbis and suggested that Campos take paid leave until the troubles blew over. When Campos refused, his boss offered him an early retirement package that included full pension. When he refused that too, his boss told him that Vita would have to let him go. In despair, Campos contacted Ilan Ghilon, the Meretz MK who not long before had been assistant mayor of Ashdod. Ghilon arranged for journalist Akiva Eldar to write a long exposé in Ha'aretz, which made it nearly impossible for Vita to fire Campos without seeming to have capitulated to the ultra-Orthodox. Vita proved particularly inept at damage control, at first issuing a statement that Vita steadfastly refused to punish employees for what they did and thought after working hours, but almost immediately issuing another statement implying that the company had evidence suggesting that Campos had proselytized workers that he had hired. These statements were meant to mollify secular and Haredi consumers in turn, but instead they angered each group. Campos kept his job, Vita kept its Badatz certification, and both secular and ultra-Orthodox activists launched boycotts of Vita products, the precise cost of which has never been made public by the company.

Just as Campos was being pressured to leave Vita, another scandal—this one involving an assistant chef named Ronit Penso—became a cause celebre. Penso worked at the Jerusalem Hilton, and at forty was seen by her colleagues and hotel management as a rising star. When Bill and Hillary Clinton arrived for their final presidential visit, Penso was chosen to travel with them to the zealot ruins at Masada, in the Judaean desert, to prepare their dinner there. On September 3, 1999, Penso was summoned to the hotel personnel manager, who told her, to her astonishment, that she was fired. The rabbinate had issued an ultimatum to Ashley Spencer, the Hilton's manager: Either Penso goes, or the hotel loses its kosher certification. Spencer concluded that the Hilton could not be run profitably without certification and decided to fire Penso. The rabbis' brief against Penso was that she was belligerent toward the *mashgiah*, or rabbinic supervisor, and that she did not fastidiously adhere to kashrut regulations. They cited an instance in which Penso used a pot dedicated to milk products to cook rice that would be served with meat (traditionally rabbis have taken the biblical injunction against cooking a kid in the milk of its mother to require that milk and meat products be cooked and served in different vessels, and consumed separately, with intervals of several hours), and that when the supervisor asked her to dispose of the rice, which was no longer kosher, she refused.

Penso denies that this event, or any like it, ever took place. She remembers that once after painstakingly cleaning a vat of artichokes, the supervisor summarily demanded that they be thrown out because the vegetables might contain insects too small to be seen by the human eye. In another instance, Penso remembered being told to toss parsley and lettuce because it had been chopped on Shabbat in the same way that Penso chopped during the week; on Shabbat, the supervisor told her, one has to chop differently. When Penso refused, he told her that she didn't know the rules, so she should shut up and obey. "Your job is to give me instructions about kashrut," she remembered telling the rabbi, "not to shut my mouth." Later, she reflected about why the rabbis disliked her: "I think that this is a matter of my sex. The supervisors called me a 'liar' . . . and a 'Lillith.' . . . The fact that a secular woman reached such a senior position, and in the kitchen of all places, made their blood boil."

Penso's case was taken up by the Association for Civil Rights in Israel, which unsuccessfully sued the Hilton for discriminatory firing, arguing that

Penso would not have been disparaged and dismissed were she a man. For Penso herself, the experience was radicalizing:

> I am completely secular, I don't eat matzos on Passover, I don't fast on Yom Kippur, and I don't do any religious rituals. But even I, what did I do all these years? I sat and complained [about the ultra-Orthodox], but I ignored them and didn't do anything. . . . Now I think that it's impossible to get along with them. To them, we are just trash. The *mashgihim* would tell me that for them, secular Jews are . . . empty, they have no culture, nothing. And we secular Jews fund people like that from our pockets. . . . I think that the time has come for secular Jews to declare war.

As the Free Buyers see it, the ultra-Orthodox are running a protection racket, one that is particularly effective when it comes to hotels, restaurants, food corporations, and others for which rabbinic certification is a business necessity. For these businesses, a few rabbis have wide influence, far beyond the realm of food preparation itself, influencing advertising, hiring, and client relations. It's as if a Haredi is always tapping menacingly against their plate-glass display windows saying, "Nice business you got here; it'd be a shame if anything were to happen to it."

Tuvia and Free Buyers are right about this, to a degree. *Mashgihim* have the power to harm the businesses they oversee, and whoever oversees the overseers is not particularly effective. There are abuses. MK Tommy Lapid told me that he has a thick file documenting crass abuses of this power—extorted hotel rooms, contract fixing, and that sort of thing—and I don't doubt that he does. Still, some apparent abuses result from the fundamentally different ways that secular and religious Jews understand what it means for food to be kosher. Ronit Penso, for example, maintains that the only factor that influences kashrut is the state of the food itself at any given moment. Anything else—the piety or probity of the chef, for instance—is irrelevant. It was precisely such a view that led Israel's Supreme Court to rule at the beginning of 2002 that it was unlawful for rabbis to withhold kosher certification from a slaughterhouse in Hadera that, alongside its trade in kosher meat, sold *treyf* leftovers to an unkosher butcher shop in Tel Aviv. The court's reasoning was that since the slaughterhouse "keeps kosher" and didn't transgress religious injunctions concerning the meat it markets as kosher, the rabbis ought not punish its owners for purveying unkosher meat on the side. Haredim that I spoke with had a broader understanding of what it means to be kosher. Many cited the centuries-old rabbinic judgment that food prepared by someone who does not observe the prohibitions of the Sabbath is unkosher, regardless of the treatment of the food itself. In this view, the rabbis are not mere technocrats, limited to the narrow confines of the treatment of this or that meal. They are responsible for ensuring that establishments certified kosher also have a certain *character* that is consonant with religious sensibilities. It was with this in mind that MK Rahamim Melloul, of the ultra-Orthodox Shas Party, recently proposed a law expanding the discretion of rabbis to refuse to certify as kosher establishments that might treat their meat according to the letter of religious law, but that at the same time undermine religious law in other ways.

For many secular Israelis, this effort to control the "atmosphere" of establishments is most upsetting of all. Few dispute the rights of Haredim to produce food that meets whatever standards they choose, no matter how exacting or how ridiculous. But this does not mean that they have the right to remold the stores, restaurants, and hotels in the image that they wish. That is going too far. The principle behind this view is the one summed up in the old adage, "your right to swing your fist ends at my nose."

Controlling What We Buy

In the view of many secular Israelis, Haredim are ever rapping them on the nose, insisting that they alter their private lives in ways that ought not matter at all to the ultra-Orthodox. Perhaps the best example is pornography.

No reliable statistics have been compiled for the pornography trade in Israel, yet it is unquestionably a part of Israeli life. At the kiosk down the block where I buy my Haredi newspapers, it is possible to buy the latest issue of *Juggs, Cum, Legs, Barely Legal, Teenz, Amateur Porno,* and *Over 40,* as well as a bewildering assortment of hard-core German skin sheets. By conservative estimate, more than fifty different titles are available each month. On Allenby Street in Tel Aviv, not far away, several dilapidated porn theaters operate in close proximity to strip clubs and low-rent brothels staffed principally by Eastern European women, some of whom are bought and sold by entrepreneurial sleaze-meister slave masters. Pornographic cassettes account, in many areas, for the greatest share of video stores rentals and sales. And roughly half the display space on the many video vending machines nearly as common as ATMs in Israel's cities is filled with sex films. In my affluent Tel Aviv neighborhood, there are three triple-X sex shops within a three-block radius. In all these things, Israel is roughly like most Western democracies.

The laissez-faire attitudes that prevail toward most of the sex industry are not shared by everyone. There was opposition when a company named *Yes* included a porn package as an option in the satellite television service it introduced in 2000. The package was modest, including two channels, the soft-core Playboy Channel and a somewhat more explicit channel called Blue. Broadcasts begin at 10 P.M. and are activated when a secret code is entered into the satellite descrambler. The cable channels immediately followed with their own porn packages. Prices varied slightly, but most television subscribers could add porn to their nightly fare for roughly $7.00 a month. Almost half of all subscribers paid the seven bucks.

The first attempt to limit home access to porn took the form of a petition submitted to the Supreme Court by former Education Minister Shulamit Aloni and sitting Knesset Education Committee Chairman Zevulun Orlev. This collaboration shocked pundits and Knesset veterans. Aloni, a secular feminist who founded the strongly antireligious "Ratz," Citizens' Rights Party (which has since merged with other liberal left parties to form Meretz), made a career of fighting what she took to be religious efforts to limit personal freedoms and choice. As a student I saw her speak stirringly at Tel Aviv University against the ultra-Orthodox: "They're in your plates, they're in your wallets, they're in your bedrooms!" she said to a standing ovation in an overflow auditorium. Orlev represents the National Religious Party, a modern-Orthodox party that, while not Haredi, takes seriously religious injunctions that Aloni considers primitive and damaging to women. Orlev explained the cooperation: "It has nothing to do with being religious or secular. We wanted to prevent hard-core pornography that will hurt youth and breed violence against women. These are *universal* concepts that need to be addressed." Aloni described the dangers of porn more vividly, capturing the gravity of the issue that justified making common cause with religious politicians. She told journalists, "If we have pornography on television, this will incite rape and violence against women and children. . . . Fathers will willingly permit their sons to view these stations, and then these young boys will go out and mimic what they saw on television and rape girls." The Supreme Court rejected the petition.

Not long after, ultra-Orthodox politicians joined the fray, and they were more successful. Yizhak Vaknin, of the Shas Party, working within a growing coalition of feminists and religious Jews, made his party's support of a comprehensive telecommunications bill—perhaps the most cautiously crafted and economically significant bill to arise in that parliamentary session—contingent on eliminating cable and satellite porn. Vaknin asserted that pornography ought to be banned on the humanitarian grounds that to do so would save lives: "People watch porno movies all night, then wake up tired and

unfocused, and this causes serious automobile accidents." The chairman of
the Knesset Finance Committee, Avraham Poraz of Shinui, objected vigorously to ultra-Orthodox interference with the telecommunication bill, interference that he characterized as just another example of ultra-Orthodox
blackmail. In the end, over the objections of Poraz and many others, pornography was eliminated from cable. This victory of the odd coalition of
Haredim and feminists was widely seen as the latest instance of ultra-
Orthodox interference in the economics of the country and the private lives
of its citizens. Israel's answer to *TV Guide*, an anemic weekly named *Rating*,
covered the decision in a feature called "Welcome to Afghanistan." It began by
pressing the comparison between the ultra-Orthodox and the Taliban:

> Every so often we see on news magazines . . . pieces about the extremist
> Moslem Taliban rule in Afghanistan. We watch and we're shocked, at least
> that's what we tend to think, though apparently not everyone is shocked.
> There are more than a few members of Knesset . . . for whom Taliban rule—
> veiled women, no Internet, no movies, no mention of any other culture or re-
> ligion—has appeal. They are not Moslems, they are Jews, but they like the
> format. A closed, isolated state, which controls almost completely the private
> lives of every citizen. Democracy? Forget it, that's for the goyim. . . .

A Gallup poll indicated that a large majority (more than two to one) of affluent, secular Israelis believed that porn should be broadcast. Echoing and exaggerating this sentiment, the Shinui Party published a cartoon near the
banner of *Ha'aretz*, with the party mascot, a baby, uttering the words: "The
Haredim screw us already, even without porno." Another cartoon in the satiric
page of the weekend *Ma'ariv* showed two Haredim talking: "We really fucked
the seculars with the porno channels, eh?" "Yes. We got our satisfaction."

Among those who criticized the ultra-Orthodox, few had a kind word for
porn. *Rating* magazine interviewed politicians, athletes, and entertainers
about pornography, and no one admitted to watching it ever, a fact that, if
true, suggests that celebrities maintain a higher moral standard than rank-
and-file satellite and cable subscribers. The basis of the criticism of Haredim
was not that they were wrong to disdain porn, but rather that they ought not
interfere with the consumer preferences of others. "I was not against [this
bill] because I am for porn," Shinui's Poraz told journalists, "but because [it]
contradicted freedom of speech." Or as columnist Ron Miberg wrote in
Ma'ariv, "This is simply another battle for individual rights," in this case, the
right to buy and watch what you want, when you want to.

Mock-up of imaginary Haredi porn magazine cover. Collage by artist Moshe Halevi (Halemo).

Skimming from the Top

The wish to preserve individual rights also fueled, though in an entirely different way, protests over new, ultra-Orthodox lines that the state-backed busing duopoly, Egged and Dan, launched at the end of 2001. "The Transportation Ministry Egged and Dan surrendered to Haredi pressures," reporter Rami Hazzut wrote in *Yediot Aharonot.* "They will operate a "*glatt* kosher" bus line, Number 402, between Jerusalem and Bnei Brak, with total segregation of men and women." This segregation drew sharp criticism. "From now on, Egged and Dan will have Taliban lines," Shinui MK Yossi Paritsky announced: "I suppose that the next stage will be having secular Jews sit in the luggage compartment underneath the bus, and the Arabs will be tied to the luggage racks. This is ugly coercion, without parallel, especially [bad] coming from Egged, which receives a billion shekels in government subsidies each year." Avinoam Reches, a neurologist at Hadassah Medical Center who heads the Israel Neurological Association and chairs the ethics committee of the Israel Medical Association, as a "guest interviewer" on a popular morning-drive-time radio show asked: "Are we going to build banks with separate entrances for men and women, which charge smaller transaction fees? Are we going to build supermarkets that will be open to men on Sundays, Tuesdays, and Thursdays and to women on Mondays, Wednesdays, and Fridays?" The allusion to transaction fees referred to the decision of the two bus companies to lower fares on the 402 line from eighteen to fifteen shekels, making it more than 15 percent cheaper for Haredim to travel from Tel Aviv to Jerusalem than for anyone else. In the view of Reches and many others, preferential pricing for segregated buses adds insult to outrage. Worse still, Egged and Dan agreed to ban airing the radio over the bus loudspeakers during the forty-five-minute voyage. Ron Ratner, the spokesperson for the Egged Cooperative, explained in a press conference that the ban reflected the bus company's awareness of "the great sensitivity that the Haredi public has about radio."

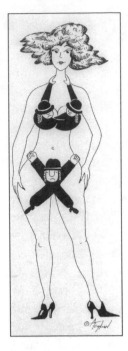

Ultra-Orthodox opposition to pornography. Cartoon by Arcadi Zyskun, originally published in Russian-language newspaper; reprinted with permission of *Shpitz,* journal of the Israel Cartoonists Union.

Ultra-Orthodox segregation on buses. From the top down, the levels read, "Men," "Women," "Arabs," "Blacks." Cartoon by Nissim Hezkiyahu, reprinted with permission of *Shpitz,* journal of the Israel Cartoonists Union.

MK Paritsky led the unsuccessful fight to prevent the Number 402 bus line from operating, going so far as to file suit against it in the Israeli Supreme Court. In Paritsky's view, at stake is fundamental principle, in fact, the bedrock principle of democracy itself:

> A democratic country must reject every form of separation on the basis of sex, race, or creed. It's surely unacceptable for Egged, a public transportation concern that received monopoly status from the government and that receives more than a billion shekels from the public coffers, to create such separations. There's a tough moral problem here. I have no doubt that there is in Israel a sector that does not wish to travel with Arabs because they are afraid that one of them might have a concealed bomb. There isn't true democratic thought in the State of Israel.

Ha'aretz sent a reporter to take a trip undercover on the bus line, and the story she filed portrays a stark, pre–Rosa Parks picture of quotidian back-of-the-bus discrimination. An Egged manager told her on condition of strict anonymity that the new bus line "is disgusting. No one likes to feel second-class. A couple of days ago, I saw a woman sit by mistake in the front, and one of the men screamed at her and sent her to sit in the back.

Those women are terribly unfortunate." The women themselves interviewed for the article claimed not to mind their relegation. "If women sat in the front, then men would have to see us, and that wouldn't work," said one woman named Haya. "It's the woman's responsibility to take pains not to arouse the man." To some readers, such statements impeached both Haredi men and women; men because they are inveterate lechers, and woman because they have—as encounter-group feminists used to say—"internalized their oppression."

To the bus companies, the regulatory agencies that sanctioned the new line, and Haredim themselves, such criticisms are misguided. Itzik Kagen, the spokesperson of the Dan Bus Cooperative, explained their decision to run segregated lines as follows: "All the passengers on this line are Haredim. We provide them with a service, and therefore we try to take their special needs into account. In the same way, we take the needs of seculars into account when, in certain areas, we run our bus lines before Shabbat ends." Avner Ovadia, the spokesman of the Transportation Ministry, which approved the Number 402 line, made much the same point: "Since the Ministry operates transportation routes according to the needs of the population, we thought it was right to fulfil their request. We are talking about a population that uses almost exclusively public transportation, and there was no reason not to accommodate them." One might say that Kagen and Ovadia have a different notion of democracy than Paritsky. If in Paritsky's view, democracy demands unyielding mechanical equality, in the views of Kagen and Ovadia, democracy allows small communities to set their own standards, including standards that are strictly speaking discriminatory. Of course, the issue is hardly as high-minded as this abstract analysis suggests. The real issue, according to Ron Ratner, the Egged spokesperson, is that market forces too great to be ignored are at work: "In an age of free competition, we must consider the special needs of the Haredi population, which accounts for a sizable portion of the business of Egged and Dan. . . . We are not in the morals business." Per capita, fewer Haredim own cars than any other sector of Israel's population save kibbutz members; they are highly dependant upon public transportation. Egged research demonstrated that recently a great portion of the lucrative Haredi market was being siphoned off by pirate minibuses illegally culling customers from the bus lines, charging less, and allowing segregation by sex. The big bus companies did what big concerns always do when challenged by unorthodox competition—they co-opted their competitors' innovations in order to crush them.

Even if the new bus line *was* born purely of economic exigency, it may be that what annoys secular Israelis most of all is precisely the Haredi economic clout that created this exigency. Rabbi Yaakov Hesse, the chairman of the

Haredi Advisory Board to Egged, gleefully thanked the bus company in the press conference announcing the new route: "The degree of attentiveness and responsiveness [on the part of the bus companies] is as great as can be, especially concerning anything to do with improving public transportation services for Haredim." Such a statement is highly unusual in Israel, where the notion that companies ought to foster customer satisfaction is by no means a part of corporate culture. And bus companies are not the only concerns that treat Haredim preferentially. In May 2002, the mobile phone company Cellcom announced that it was launching a new area code exclusively for Haredim. Calls within this area code would be the cheapest form of telecommunications in the country. Customers can also dial "star-613" to be connected to the "daily commandment" line, whereon they will hear a learned dissertation on one of the 613 biblical commandments. Should the customers wish, the phone company will also contact them at the start and finish of prayer time, or inform them when it's time to light candles at the start of Shabbat, operating essentially as a miniature ritual valet. Pelephone, a competitor of Cellcom, offers a free service before the High Holidays in which customers can phone to receive advice from a rabbi about effective repentance.

Haredim receive special attention—typically extra services for lower prices—in almost all sectors of the economy they patronize. Clal Insurance offers a Haredi mutual fund that promises to invest in bonds and securities from companies that observe Shabbat. The manager has promised to consult the "greatest rabbis of the generation" before deciding if a concern is kosher for investment. Though the fund is not large by mutual fund standards, in the intimate, investment-starved business community of Israel, it creates incentives for companies to refashion themselves as Haredi-friendly. One such company is the national airline, which advertises:

> Only on El Al are there flights that are especially appropriate for the religious public. [They are scheduled so that] you can pray as you should, confidently and comfortably, in your regular minyan in your synagogue, make the flight on time without rushing, and avoid having to pray in rough conditions during the flight. This is in addition to our uncompromising commitment that there be only *glatt* kosher food, a movie-free area, and extreme consideration for the religious traveler.

This feeling of being preferred customers has created in some a sense of entitlement. In November 2001, ultra-Orthodox passengers noted that the typical flight path from Ben Gurion International Airport took them over a large graveyard in the Tel Aviv suburb of Holon. *Cohanim*, descendants of the biblical priestly class, are not permitted to enter a cemetery (intimate contact with death is taken to defile the purity needed for them to carry out their holy duties), and the question was brought to Rabbi Yosef Shalom Al-ishiv of whether flying *over* a cemetery constituted entering a cemetery. His ruling was, yes, flying thousands of feet above a cemetery served to defile *co-hanim* and was hence prohibited, which created a problem for the hundreds of ultra-Orthodox *cohanim* who wished to exit Israel by air each day. Haredi leaders demanded that El Al change its flight path, a suggestion that was at first judged infeasible by aviation experts. In a technical solution that wafted of macabre street theater, rabbis instructed *cohanim* wishing to fly to zip themselves inside body bags upon takeoff, which for obscure reasons would keep them from being defiled by the graves far below. Haredi leaders demanded that El Al at least provide free body bags for its passengers, a request that was denied on the grounds that having tens of men zip themselves upon takeoff into bags that, in Israel, have close association with casualties of war and terror, would be unnerving to other passengers. For several weeks there was a standoff, during which time a prominent Jerusalem rabbi chartered a private plane to take him and his entourage to Cyprus, avoiding the Holon cemetery, from whence they continued to New York on commercial airliner. The growing threat that the airline would lose Haredi business and goodwill, added to growing political pressure on the government-owned concern, led El Al to bypass the evaluation of the aviation experts and to reroute their flights to avoid the controversial cemetery.

If Haredi pressure is so potent against a quasi-monopoly like El Al (there are other airlines that service Israel, but as the national carrier, El Al flies most often to the most destinations), then it is more potent still when competition is a factor, as it is in health care. Save a very small market for private doctors made up of the wealthy and the desperate, on the one hand, and a small number of government-owned and operated hospitals on the other, health care in Israel is provided through "Patient Cooperatives" roughly equivalent to health maintenance organizations (HMOs). The oldest patient cooperative was started in the 1920s by Israel's omnipresent labor union, the Histadrut, and dozens of others came into being and disappeared over the years since. There are now three large HMOs and about a dozen small ones operating in Israel. In the mid-1990s, the Knesset finally ratified a national health bill that had been debated, in one form or another, since 1948, when Israel was established. The bill guaranteed universal nearly free access to health care, funded by a newly levied health tax. The care itself is provided by existing HMOs, which receive budget allocations based on their membership rolls. Each citizen is free to choose any provider and to move from provider to provider.

The dynamics established by the new law create, in theory at any case, powerful and unending competition among the providers to snag and maintain membership. Studies have shown that few patients actually switch providers (in fact, approximately 90 percent of Israelis continue to use the provider that they used before the law was passed almost a decade ago). Still, since the law came into effect, providers have paid much greater attention to both customer satisfaction and to advertising. The four big HMOs have each launched new services—free alternative medicine, for instance, or exercise classes or Internet access to personal health records and test results—and whenever one HMO has innovated, the other three have quickly copied the initiative. The result is that the quality of care has risen steadily; in short, a consumer revolution in health care has occurred.

One of the unanticipated results of new market forces is that the HMOs now compete most vigorously for entire sectors of the population. If a provider can create a reputation of being particularly convivial to, say, the Arabic-speaking population, then it stands to gain hundreds of thousands of new members. If a provider can demonstrate that it provides better services to women than the others, then it can attract millions of new members. And if a provider can convince ultra-Orthodox community leaders that it best provides services suited for Haredim, it stands to attract hundreds of thousands. Of all the sectors targeted, industry market analysis has suggested that the last—that of the ultra-Orthodox—is the most cost-effective to woo, a conclusion based on the judgments that ultra-Orthodox have less brand loyalty to their present provider than other sectors of the population, and that their consumer decisions are more decidedly influenced by the instruction and example of a few Haredi opinion makers. Get a blessing from the right rabbis, and you've persuaded thou-

Cover of ultra-Orthodox health magazine published by Maccabi HMO.

sands of their followers. It was for this reason that soon after one HMO managed to persuade the spiritual leader of the Shas Party, Rabbi Ovadiah Yosef, that it offered the best services, it was rewarded with a lucrative agreement to provide its services to thousands of members of health organizations affiliated with Shas. It was for the same reason that a competing HMO soon thereafter issued a press release announcing that the centenarian kabbalist mystic Rabbi Yizhak Kaduri had just transferred to its care. Never has a client so old and frail been embraced by a health-care provider with such enthusiasm.

The recognition that Haredim are a huge market that can be swayed has led HMOs to offer a variety of services to the ultra-Orthodox that are not available to secular Jews or to Christians and Moslems. In the Haredi town of Elad, the United Patient Cooperative offered a "Shabbat Clinic, run by a senior, non-Jewish doctor, beginning two hours before the onset of the Sabbath and continuing straight until 11:00 P.M. on Saturday night." No such clinics exist in most secular towns, and if a child is sick late Friday night, parents often have to travel a long way to find care. The General Patient Cooperative in Elad, to keep from hemorrhaging patients to United, offered to pick up patients and drive them to their appointments, for free. The National Patient Cooperative organized for the children of their insured day camps that provide meals, trips, and supplies for about $15 a week. It also delivers prescribed drugs to the patient's home, for free. No parallel services are available to those living in secular neighborhoods and towns, a fact that infuriates many secular observers.

It is a fact that may also be, strictly speaking, illegal. According to Michal Abadi, the assistant director of the Ministry of Health, the health-care providers are barred from using funds they receive from the government in such discriminatory fashion. When Abadi turned to the attorney general, Elyakim Rubinstein, to ask his opinion of the matter, he concluded that the HMOs were breaking the law. "Health services . . . must be provided according to the principles of justice, equality, and mutual aid," Rubinstein concluded. "Creating meaningful gaps in the level of services given to different groups of insured is not consistent with the principle of equality. A service provider is permitted to improve its services . . . only if all of the insured are eligible to enjoy these services. Service providers may not provide free transportation to some insured, or medicine delivery services, unless it can offer these same services to all its insured." Rubinstein's judgment carries weight and may lead to future legal action. For the time being, the ultra-Orthodox continue to receive service that the rest of Israel's citizens do not.

Modern-Day Shylocks?

Add up the various Haredi influences on the economy—censuring advertising, coercing kashrut and then leveraging this coercion into influence on how hotels, restaurants, and clubs are run, preventing businesses from opening seven days a week, killing cable pornography, parlaying their consumer clout into advantageous deals on what they buy, and so on—and one is left with the feeling that Haredim ruthlessly exercise vast economic control practically everywhere. Markets in Israel seem anything but free. Commerce is seemingly manipulated on the sly by a group of self-serving seekers, experts at devising ways to twist everything to their benefit.

The ultra-Orthodox are commonly referred to as a mafia, the invocation of the Costa Nostra serving, not just as a slur, but also as a precise metaphor. Just as the Mafia operates as a sort of invisible tax on the whole economic system, in the view of many here, so too Haredim extract their tribute from the economy in countless unseen ways. Mafiosi insinuate themselves as silent partners to thriving businesses, siphoning off a steady levy, and so do Haredim, for instance, when they leech their kashrut supervisors onto hotels and restaurants. The price of these unofficial taxes by both the Mafia and the Haredim is borne unwittingly by regular consumers and taxpayers. And the price isn't economic alone. Both the Mafia and the Haredim have a way of manipulating economic activity so that it best meets their ends. The result is that normal citizens have less control over their financial lives than they should. We are all patsies, and we all pay the price in cash, freedom, and dignity.

But is this perception accurate? To a certain degree, in certain realms, it is. When it comes to kosher food, most Israelis who neither know nor care about the Jewish dietary laws pay both in money and in delimited freedom. Citizens of Jerusalem hoping to greet the third millennium sloshed in the company of dozens of sloshed strangers had a hard time finding a place to do it; New Year's Eve 2000 fell on Shabbat, and Badatz threatened to pull its kosher certification of any establishment holding a party to mark it. People like Eduardo Campos live in fear of losing their jobs because a bunch of rabbis have the economic force to fire workers they don't even employ. Haredim have power, and they don't hesitate to leverage that power whenever and wherever they can.

Considered analytically, the complaint against Haredim seems to be double. First, they are artificially strong, because their unity gives them more clout than any other sector of the population of similar size. It is unfair, in a sense, that HMOs pander to the ultra-Orthodox when, by dint of raw numbers, they ought to be pandering first to Arab Israelis. The second complaint is that Haredim are shameless about imposing their standards on others who do not share them. They lack economic civility.

Both these complaints are accurate, in their way, but it is questionable how large an impact Haredi consumer power has and whether their exercise of this power is illegitimate in a pluralist society. Organizing in order to maximize economic power has a long and esteemed tradition. Groups have long organized in order to advance altruistic aims; I grew up demonstrating for divestment from South Africa to weaken apartheid and boycotting Nestlé to protest exploitation of indigenous Africans. But people everywhere organize to advance their own selfish aims as well. Buying clubs, credit unions, mutual funds, group pensions and insurance plans, trade unions, collective bargaining: All of these are examples of individuals banding together in order to create economic power, which is then used to promote the interests of the individuals. If there is a difference between this and Haredim lobbying Egged to provide bus service more to their liking, it's not obvious.

In other words, though Haredim may not comport with the standards of capitalism set by Milton Friedman, they are a seamless part of contemporary corporate capitalism, as it is practiced in Israel and elsewhere by secular citizens. It is often said of the ultra-Orthodox that they do not play by the rules. But on reflection, the problem seems to be that Haredim play the game all too well, using the rules cleverly to their advantage.

If this analysis is correct, the commonplace image of the Haredi in the mall, a Shylock scheming to control commerce, to skim profits for his own, to force others to buy only when and what he judges permissible, is oddly overwrought. Whatever economic clout Haredim have, significant though it may be, the irreducible fact is that, should I want, on any given Shabbat, I can eat a ham sandwich while reading kiddy porn while gambling the slots, and then buy groceries, a gift for the wife and kids, and a pipe wrench all without leaving the neighborhood. If my freedom has been severely curtailed, I too must have internalized my oppression, for I fail to see how.

Perhaps Israel's ultra-Orthodox are like Shylock, after all. Like Shakespeare's famous Jew, Haredim are seen as more menacing and malevolent, and far more powerful, than they actually turn out to be. Haredim may have cost Penso her job, but in the end Campos kept his. In fact, it may be that Penso is the only employee in Israel fired because of Haredi pressure. The meaning of this fact is open to interpretation: Does it mean that Haredim have too much power, or not much at all? Probably both at once. If Penso hadn't angered her ultra-Orthodox *mashgiah*, or if she were a man, then she'd still be a sous-chef at a major hotel. It is sad and despicable that she lost her job, but is a single unfair firing a sign of strength or a token of weakness? The latter seems more likely. And while I cannot watch *Behind the Green Door* on my cable TV without placing a special pay-per-view order, I can see Kim Catrall naked in *Sex and the City* during prime time on broadcast TV. Haredim that I have spoken to evince gloom at their own lack of influence more often than a recognition of their own power. They display more my-daughter-my-ducats despair than I-shall-have-my-pound-of-flesh assurance.

Some anti-Haredi activists agree. The problem, they say, is not that Haredim use the system to their own economic and political advantage. Everyone is self-interested. The problem is that the secular government of Israel does nothing to delimit the natural rapaciousness of the ultra-Orthodox. If there is a root problem it is not that the ultra-Orthodox have taken over the economy, but that they have taken over Israel's government.

Rabbis
and Ayatollahs

The Protocols of
the Elders of Bnei Brak

I first heard of ultra-Orthodox concentration camps for secular Jews in a sitting room at MIT, in front of a floor-to-ceiling window overlooking the Charles River, a setting about as far from barbed wire and barking dogs as one can imagine. The woman who introduced me to the notion—a mild and kind-hearted forty-year-old art historian named Rita Amorai (I have changed details to mask her identity)—is not someone given to flights of fancy or paranoia, and she seemed really to believe that these camps would be constructed.

Amorai chairs her small department at Tel Aviv University, and she has written a lovely book tracing how changes in science in the fourteenth century altered the painting of the same period. Her classes provide a panorama of Western culture, moving lightly but surely from Aristotle to Leonardo da Vinci to Galileo to Bach. She earned her doctorate at a leading

American university, and along with her husband, who is a highly educated
and successful authority in his field, and her two kids, she lives in an elegant
house in a bedroom suburb of Tel Aviv. Her students (of whom I was one)
find her easy to approach and cheerfully accommodating, the sort of
teacher you might seek out if you were breaking up with your girlfriend and
needed someone to talk to. She is a model of cultured gentility, and she
rarely has a bad word to say about anybody.

The only time I ever heard her raise her voice was that day at MIT. I had
turned down a job in Massachusetts in favor of one in Tel Aviv and Amorai
thought this was a mistake. In her view I was selfishly ignoring the welfare
of my family. She itemized America's advantages: high salaries, no army service for the kids when they grow up, peace with neighboring countries, religious freedom, and so on. I replied by listing Israel's advantages: vitality, a
life-is-with-people *gemeinschaft*-iness, scattered traces of European sophistication, and so forth. Amorai grew frustrated with my line of argument and
then angry. She said that the future would show that I was making a mistake, a tragic mistake, and it was then that she mentioned the camps: She
told me that one morning I will wake up to find my daughter was deported
to a concentration camp, and then I'll remember her advice, but it will be
too late. I asked who would build and run these concentration camps, and
she answered that the Haredim would. She shrugged when I asked if she really believed that: "Why not? What's so hard to believe?"

We were arguing, which led each of us to ratchet our rhetoric tauter than
had we been in a calmer frame of mind. Amorai was alarmed by my stub-
born naïveté and annoyed by my vanity (and after returning to Israel I soon
came to appreciate her criticisms of the country, and her description of the
difficulties of living there). Concentration camps are perhaps a more extreme forecast than Amorai would warrant in other circumstances. Or she
may believe, literally, that such camps will be constructed. I have met others,
of less temperate natures, who do. (The notion that the ultra-Orthodox hope
to establish prison work camps for the secular is something of a commonplace.) What's important is that behind this apocalyptic scenario lie real fears
that Amorai and many others feel all the time: that ultra-Orthodox have
great control over secular Jews in Israel, that this control will grow in the
years to come, and that it will be exercised with malevolence. In short,
Haredim are taking over, stealthily and steadily, and the rest of us will suffer.

Such fear has two elements, broadly speaking. The first is what I described
in the previous two chapters: a feeling that Haredim are growing in numbers
and in influence. They are overrunning the rest of us. They are taking over
our neighborhoods, and they are taking over our malls. The second element

is that the ultra-Orthodox image of the good society is at odds with that of the rest of the country, more Taliban than Tel Aviv, and that, owing to their growth, owing to their true-believer certainty that their vision alone is sanctioned by God, and especially owing to their savvy at manipulating the government to do their bidding, one day they will control us, even if doing so requires great brutality.

שחור בעיניים

Secular Jews depicted as Gulliver, bound by tiny Haredim, a common theme in caricatures, showing ultra-Orthodox control over secular Israelis. February 1994 cover of *Shpitz*. Drawing by Moshik Lin, reprinted with permission of *Shpitz,* journal of the Israel Cartoonists Union.

The fear that Haredim will wrest control of Israel's government and then subdue and enslave the rest of us is vivid for many Israelis, and it finds frequent expression. In December 2001, I went to the premier of a play called *Atom: A Political Fantasy*, finding myself shoehorned between my companion and a heavyset asthmatic in Tel Aviv's Cameri Theater, filled to standing room. I paged absentmindedly past the cosmetics ads in the playbill, until my eyes settled on the playwright's introduction:

> Fear of ultra-Orthodox Jews is like the weather: Everyone thinks and talks about it, but no one actually does anything about it. Many view the ultra-Orthodox takeover as a great danger to the existence of the state as we know it, yet the secular majority continues to provide the ultra-Orthodox with the means and power to grow, spread, and eventually even dominate. In fact, the secular majority behaves much like an ostrich, stubbornly and persistently refusing to face reality.

Atom was written by Matti Golan, who was in the audience on opening night to head a panel discussion after the curtain fell. Golan is among Israel's leading journalists, the host of popular radio and television shows, onetime managing editor of *Ha'aretz*, Israel's paper of record, and by turns editor in chief of the leading financial dailies, *Globes* and (now defunct)

Telegraph. In the years following the Camp David agreements, Golan served as director of information in Israel's embassy in Canada. Among Golan's friends are former prime ministers, countless Knesset members, diplomats, and other politicos (*Atom* includes a cameo on video by Samuel Lewis, one-time U.S. ambassador to Israel), industrialists, and literati; he is royalty in Israel's fifth estate. He wrote the play as a call to arms, a bleak vision of what will happen "if Israel's secular Jews continue to bury their heads in the sand and ignore reality, instead of facing up to it and taking steps to change it." This is the "imaginary scenario" he created to dramatize this danger, as Golan himself describes it:

> It is 2025, only weeks before the general election in Israel. Meir Peleg is the Left's candidate for prime minister. Peleg was born into an ultra-Orthodox family and was a yeshiva student until he lost his faith at the age of seventeen and went into politics. His platform includes far-reaching concessions to the Palestinians, dividing Jerusalem and surrendering Temple Mount and the Jewish settlements in the occupied territories. He is in favor of separating religion from state and abolishing religious political parties. He explains to the public that the ultra-Orthodox believe in the coming of the Messiah by the end of the sixth millennium according to the Hebrew calendar, and since we are fast approaching the end of this period, preparations need to be made now for his coming. According to Jewish religious belief, the Messiah will only come after the world has been purified, in other words, following an apocalypse, or in the language of ultra-Orthodox tradition, the battle of Gog and Magog at Armageddon, after which only believing and observant Jews will remain in Israel.

Peleg wins in a landslide, his campaign facilitated by his sleazy womanizing aide de camp, Shaul Levy, and clinched when the CIA provides compromising photos of the incumbent's son debauching himself in New York (just how is left to the viewers' imagination). Once elected, Peleg begins to act erratically. He appoints a minor officer to be the army's chief of staff. He delays conceding land to the Palestinians. He confronts the American ambassador with CIA photos ostensibly demonstrating that Iran has nuclear warheads trained on Tel Aviv and despite her protestations that the photos are fake, he sets in motion the deployment of Israel's nuclear arsenal. With nuclear war now unavoidable, Peleg and Levy disclose that they are ultra-Orthodox moles, sent thirty years earlier by a powerful rabbi to pose as secular Jews, gain control of the country, and spark a worldwide nuclear war, to accomplish the mass destruction that must precede the arrival of the Messiah. The photos that precipitated the nuclear war were provided by another ultra-Orthodox mole, planted in the CIA thirty years earlier to serve this purpose. The Israeli army is also infiltrated by crypto-Hasidim. By the finale, the world is in flames, and what is left of Israel is ruled by black-coated Jews with Uzis slung over their shoulders. A chilling scenario, but still, in Golan's view, "a situation that could occur in the not-too-distant future."

In the panel discussion that followed the play, Golan explained why he wrote the play:

> I wrote this play not so much as a statement about the ultra-Orthodox, as about secular Jews, who allow the ultra-Orthodox to multiply, to spread, to get whatever they want and do whatever they want. We are still the majority in this country, as far as I know, but we act like a minority because we are divided, while they are united. . . . There can be no common language between a believer and a nonbeliever. So what have all the democratic countries of the world done? They have separated religion from state. For us, everything is mixed, a fact that is exploited by religious circles that are undemocratic, anti-Zionist, very monolithic, highly unified. They exploit the divisions within the secular populace. More than anything, this play is meant to open our eyes, to warn: Gentlemen, we are the majority in this country, let us begin to act like a majority. [Thunderous applause.] I want the public, when it comes time to vote, to vote in such a way that forces the secular parties to form a coalition without the religious, and to enact laws separating religion from state.

Golan believes that his cautionary tale warns us to join forces to defeat the ultra-Orthodox at the ballot box. In the play, however, the secular public does precisely that, voting for the ostensibly antireligious candidate, and in so doing unwittingly facilitates a holocaust. In *Atom*, the ultra-Orthodox weasel their way into power by lying, cheating, manipulating, slandering, and murdering. They do so by exploiting their extraordinary covert control of a variety of institutions—in politics, in the military, in the police, in the CIA. They are diabolical and omnipresent. The implicit point is that no political action will stop the ultra-Orthodox conspiracy.

To create this image of the ultra-Orthodox, Golan borrows prefabricated themes from a variety of sources. The insane eschatology driving *Atom*'s plot is borrowed from American Pentecostalist theology, incorporating elements of *The Rapture* that have no analogue in any Jewish tradition. The notion that all secular Jews must die for the pious to be saved is a montage of esoteric Protestant ephemera, themselves caricatured, and reflects no possible ultra-Orthodox view.

But more significant, to construct his parable, Golan borrowed liberally from the dusty warehouses of anti-Semitism. When Peleg and Levy divulged their ultra-Orthodox identity, my companion whispered in my ear: *The Protocols of the Elders of Bnei Brak* (after the notorious forgery documenting Jewish world domination, relocated to the largest ultra-Orthodox city in Israel), and the comment captured something of the familiarity of the scenario Golan created. Ultra-Orthodox Jews controlling the CIA? Jews scheming for a generation to topple governments? Jews leading to total world destruction? On the surface, these things are reminiscent of the stock images popularized in nineteenth-century Europe (and tragically empowered by the Nazis) of Jewish fat-cat capitalist degenerates controlling banks, newspapers, and parliaments and the armies they command. But Golan himself is not an anti-Semite, a point he takes pains to emphasize. Why is Haredi world domination Golan's dystopic "*Political Fantasy*"?

Part of the answer is that the political power of the ultra-Orthodox has grown greatly during the past twenty-five years, and if it continues to grow at the same pace, then in another generation, Haredim will have more power than the rest of us. This conclusion is natural enough, though its assumption may well be faulty. If Starbucks continues to open new franchises at its present rate, then sometime in this century, every storefront in the world will be a coffee shop. Mechanically extending growth curves rarely predicts what will actually happen in the future. Still, most secular Israelis are unnerved by the recent increase in ultra-Orthodox influence within the government, and their dismay is not unfounded.

No one has followed this increase with greater attention than Shahar Ilan, the young journalist who covered the Haredi beat for *Ha'aretz* through most of the 1990s (he has since become an editor at the paper). Ilan is a great, hulking bear of a man, now in his early forties, with a thick mop of dark hair. He has the presence of a charismatic front man for a hardworking rhythm and blues band. Perhaps for this reason, one instinctually expects him to rasp when he speaks, so it comes as a surprise that his voice is soft and mild. But despite his tranquil voice, when Ilan speaks about the ultra-Orthodox, he does so with passion and intensity. Animating what Ilan says is a great reserve of outrage for the ultra-Orthodox, whom he regards as cynical scoundrels who never get the comeuppance they deserve.

In articles, lectures, and ultimately in a much-discussed book, *Haredim Ltd: The Budgets, Draft-Dodging, and Trampling of the Law*, Ilan has described what he sees as "a well-oiled machine for channeling budget allocations and benefits from the state's coffers" to Haredim. This machine ruthlessly manipulates the political system—with remarkable success—to see that Haredim get more than their share. Secular Israelis, Ilan wrote in the introduction to his book, are like lambs among ultra-Orthodox wolves, a metaphor that at once emphasizes the artlessness of secular naïvité and the cunning of Haredi duplicity.

The most crass form of Haredi political machinations described by Ilan may be election fraud. Broadly, the ultra-Orthodox cheat at elections in two ways, which can be characterized as "soft" and "hard" fraud. Soft fraud includes voting en bloc, which is not illegal but, in the view of many Israelis, is at odds with the spirit of democracy. Voting en bloc has two principal elements, each of which magnifies the impact of the other: an extravagantly high voter-turnout rate, and extraordinary homogeneity among the votes cast. Labor MK and former speaker of the Knesset Shevah Weiss checked the ballot boxes in Haredi neighborhoods after the 1996 elections (in which Benjamin Netanyahu won the premiership by the narrowest margin in Israel history), and found that eighty-two Haredi polling places in Jerusalem had a voting rate of 89 percent, and certain polling places in Bnei Brak showed a rate of 93 percent. In the Haredi town of Kiryat Sefer, the rate reached 95 percent. By way of comparison, the nationwide voter-turnout rate in that year was 79.3 percent.

Considered in isolation, high voting rates are commendable. As Ilan and others see it, however, the legitimacy of the near-perfect voting rates of Haredim is compromised by the fact that the ultra-Orthodox tend to vote as their religious and communal leaders instruct them. This putative fact of Israeli politics has a great impact on the way that politicians campaign, encouraging candidates publicly to supplicate themselves to exotic rabbis. In the 1999 election, Yizhak Mordechai, the then-popular leader of the centrist party who since quit politics after multiple sexual-harassment convictions, kissed the long white beard of Ovadiah Yosef, the ex-chief rabbi of Israel, who is considered the "spiritual leader" of Shas. The kiss eventually was remembered in a series of off-color jokes (of the sleazy "what's Mordechai kissing now?" variety), but at the time it most notably inspired Shinui's MK Avraham Poraz to announce that his party would not join any coalition with "beard-kissers." Poraz was referring directly to Mordechai, but indirectly he was referring to all the other major candidates, each of which fastened a yarmulke uncomfortably on his head and made repeated trips to ultra-Orthodox Talmudists, mystics, and jurists esteemed by their congregations, in hopes of winning endorsements. In the 1999 campaign, Netanyahu received the support of the Council of Torah Sages of Agudat Yisrael, and the parallel body of the Degel ha-Torah Party, along with the specific endorsement of other prominent rabbis, including Yosef Shalom

Eliashiv and Chaim Kaneivsky. On election day, Netanyahu received 99 percent of the Haredi vote, with Barak picking up the remaining 1 percent.
Such election results—with higher voter agreement than that registered in
most presidential elections in Iraq or Syria—suggest to many secular observers that ultra-Orthodox voters are zombies mindlessly fulfilling the instructions of their masters, and that such a state of affairs is an insult to the
very notion of democratic franchise.

The notion that the Haredi electorate is effectively a massive proxy vote
for a small cadre of rabbis can be disputed. In 1999, Ehud Barak launched
his campaign with the populist pledge to force the ultra-Orthodox to enlist
and serve in the IDF (a promise about which he later prevaricated), and for
many weeks he cultivated the image of an anti-Haredi crusader, presumably to increase his appeal to the secular electorate. Against this backdrop,
one need not hypothesize mind control to explain why Barak received only
one in a hundred ultra-Orthodox votes at the same time that he received
almost six of every ten secular votes. In fact, it sometimes seems that the
rabbis are controlled by their constituents more than they control them.
Ovadiah Yosef advocated negotiations and territorial compromise in the
years immediately prior to and following the Oslo Peace Accords, ruling
that transfer of lands to the Palestinians in exchange for peace was permissible by Jewish law. He convinced few of his followers to adopt this position, and some political analysts explained his steady drift rightward over
the past decade as an effort to close the ideological gap between himself
and those who view him as their spiritual leader. In the case of Rabbi Yosef,
it seems that the rank and file have dictated politics to their rabbi, more
than the reverse.

One might also argue that the partisan politics of influence, in which
charismatic leaders promise and deliver the votes of large constituencies, are
a legitimate part of democratic process. They are certainly a common form
of politics: Al Sharpton promised neighborhoods to Mark Green, labor
leaders promised industrialized states to Al Gore, and the Christian Coalition promised the Bible Belt to George Bush, and with varying degrees of
success they all delivered. The notion that bundling votes into ethnic, class,
or religious voting blocks somehow contravenes the democratic process
probably rests on an overly idealized notion of democratic society as an ag-
gregate of individuals with no loyalties beside to self and state. It may be
that group voting does not constitute any sort of fraud at all, not even "soft"
fraud, and that it constitutes no insult to democracy at all.

Another perhaps more pernicious form of "soft" fraud is the distribution
of free amulets and blessings in exchange for votes. It might be easy to dis-

miss this practice as absurd and ineffective, but in Ilan's analysis, in certain elections it produced as many as two or three extra Knesset seats for ultra-Orthodox parties, enough to shift the balance of power between the Left and the Right. The exchange of amulets for votes was also seen as effective by Israel's lawmakers, who passed legislation as early as 1991 outlawing the practice. ("Anyone encouraging another to vote for a particular list of candidates using oaths, curses, excommunication, vows, or promises of blessings" became eligible for up to five years imprisonment, a bizarre piece of legislation in a modern democracy.) Ilan recounted that use of amulets and blessings as electoral assets was pioneered in 1988 by representatives of the Lubavitcher rebbe, Menachem Schneerson, working to enlist votes for Israel's Agudat Yisrael party. Aryeh Deri, the former leader of Shas who was imprisoned for financial irregularities and breach of trust (which I will soon describe), explained the modus operandi of the Lubavitchers, from which he would learn important lessons for the elections that followed:

> They would have a person sign a letter to the Lubavitcher rebbe, in which they committed to voting for the Agudah. The next day, someone would call the same person, presenting himself as a pollster for a public opinion research center, asking how the person planned to vote. If he answered with some other party, they would later call him again, this time in the name of the Lubavitchers, and say, "We sent your name by fax to the Rebbe in New York, and we received a reply that you're unreliable."

This tactic combined spiritual carrot and stick: blessings for compliance, and the Rebbe's omniscient wrath for noncompliance. For people who care about this sort of thing, it was powerful incentive to vote the way the Rebbe (or, at least, his representatives) wished. In the 1992 election, immediately after passage of the law banning such practices, the traffic in prayers, blessings, and amulets was greatly curtailed, but they have reappeared *samizdat*-style, in every election since. On my desk is a small vial of water blessed by Rabbi Ovadiah Yosef, which was distributed as a token during the 1999 elections. Such tokens, in Ilan's view, amount to further "soft" election fraud. Especially when accompanied by the sort of telephone pressures pioneered by the Lubavitchers, this form of campaigning amalgamates harassment, blackmail, and bribery—a mix inconsistent with the spirit of democratic politics.

There are different ways to interpret the issue, however. Democracy vigilantly protects the right to vote of the beguiled and gullible, the dupes and the kooks, and it may be that promising a blessing to those who take such a promise seriously is not really so different from promising to end poverty or build roads to those who take such promises seriously. The question is, is offering an amulet more like a bribe or a political pledge, and the answer to this question is not obvious. Those who cast their vote in order to afford the talismanic protections of an amulet for their family may not be less entitled to their electoral calculus than those who cast their vote in order to afford the more practical protections of, say, beefed-up military spending. In other words, this form of soft fraud may not be fraud at all, but rather a legitimate appeal to closely held beliefs and values of many voters that just happen to seem nutty to the rest of us. The extent of this difference in beliefs and values became crudely obvious when Shas lodged a complaint to the 1999 Central Elections Committee that the leftist Meretz Party was violating the law by handing out *hamsa* keychains (a *hamsa* is a popular good luck charm in the shape of a hand that in the mind of secular Israelis has roughly the efficacy of a rabbit's foot) embossed with the party logo. Shas's representatives apparently did not realize that the joke was on them— Meretz chose the charm as a gimmick poking fun at the ultra-Orthodox, indirectly reminding voters that Meretz is the antithesis of superstitious religion. To representatives of Shas, for whom good luck charms are serious business and often powerful, the *hamsa*s were no joke. But the point is that the case can be made that if secular parties offer visions of secular improvement and redemption to their voters, perhaps religious parties are within their rights to offer visions of religious improvement and redemption, as reified in amulets, charms, and blessings.

Still another form of soft fraud is the ultra-Orthodox willingness to enlist people and resources from outside Israel to influence internal politics. In the view of some political analysts, Netanyahu's victory over Peres in 1996 was the product of the meddling of Australian and American Haredim, who used great stores of money and the influence it bought to manipulate the Israeli electorate. The manipulation was engineered by an Australian businessman named Rabbi Joseph "Diamond Joe" Gutnick. When the markets in gems and precious metals are bullish, Gutnick is perhaps the richest man in Australia, and he made his fortune twice. While still in his twenties, during the first years of the great bull market of the 1980s, he made tens of millions of dollars speculating in the stock market, primarily on mining stocks. When the stock market crashed in October 1987, Gutnick was highly leveraged, and he found himself with dwindled assets and $200 million in debt.

Here the story gets interesting. Gutnick's father was a disciple of Menachem Schneerson, the Lubavitcher rebbe, and Gutnick matured to similar devotion. During the buoyant years before the crash, Gutnick gave generous sums to support the Rebbe's causes, explaining that the only reason he wished to be rich in the first place is so that he might become a *gvir* (wealthy patron) of Lubavitch. The Rebbe offered Gutnick business and investing advice, which Gutnick implemented with the same rigor with which he followed the Rebbe's ritual instructions. After the crash, Schneerson gave a *droshe*, or sermon, about Wall Street in which he optimistically (and accurately, as the following decade would show) characterized the crash a *yeridah le-tzorech aliyah*, a "descent for the sake of [later] ascent." Privately, the Rebbe told Gutnick that the speech was intended as a personal message for him, as a sign that the market would recover, and that Gutnick would rebuild his fortune. Later, after Gutnick bet what remained of his fortune on gold and diamond mines that for months proved barren, the Rebbe met with his chief geologist, studied maps of the quarries, and concluded that both gold and diamonds would be found on those sites. Gutnick contemplated cutting his losses in the mines and selling off before they drove him bankrupt, but the Rebbe determined that he should not give up. In an interview broadcast on ABC in 1993, Gutnick expressed unquestioning faith in the prediction: "We *will* find a diamond mine because I am confident the Rebbe's prophesy will come true. There won't be a stone unturned." Only months later, both gold and diamonds were found, as the Rebbe predicted, and Gutnick was soon the wealthiest man in Australia and one of the wealthiest men in the world. In early 1990, with his fortune again intact, the Rebbe appointed Gutnick as his "Special Emissary for the Integrity of the Land of Israel." As Gutnick described it in 1999, the job description was the following: "I have been entrusted with a clear mission: That there will be a right-wing government, and that this right-wing government will stand firm and will not give away land."

To achieve this mission, Gutnick insinuated himself into Israeli politics in many ways. He befriended Benjamin Netanyahu, who was then heir apparent to Yizhak Shamir, the aging leader of the Likud. He broadened the scope of his philanthropy in Israel, giving millions to benefit Jews arriving from the deteriorating Soviet Union. He made trips to Israel with growing frequency, taking care to meet with crucial politicians in right-wing parties. Of Prime Minister Shamir, for example, Gutnick remembered: "I had absolute access to him. I'd pass on a lot of messages to the Rebbe from him." After Rabin defeated Shamir, Gutnick began organizing for the next election, which came eventually in 1996, after Rabin's assassination. Gutnick, who believed that the Oslo Peace Accords were a disaster for Israel, worked tirelessly in support of Netanyahu,

getting out the message that he was the Rebbe's personal choice, a claim that was not discredited by the inconvenient fact that the Rebbe had died more than a year and a half earlier. Gutnick campaigned hard in the Russian community, using groups and individuals to whom he had donated millions as a conduit to the broader community. As a *gvir* of the Russian community, Gutnick had free access to the sympathetic Russian-language Israeli press. Polls taken during the campaign showed that his efforts produced results, and that Russians were shifting support from the Labor Party to the Likud, a state of affairs that led Shimon Peres, Labor's candidate, to invite Gutnick to meet face to face in the Jerusalem Holiday Inn. Peres began the meeting with stern

Benjamin Netanyahu beneath a large poster of the late Lubavitcher rebbe, Menachem Schneerson, at a mass bar mitzvah ceremony at the Western Wall, sponsored by Habad (Lubavitch) Hasidim. © Reuters.

moralism, warning Gutnick, "Don't bribe people!" and adding the weakly masked threat that doing so was against the law, and the law would be enforced. Gutnick, unmoved, continued. He funded a famous and notorious ad campaign employing the slogan, "Bibi [Netanyahu] is good for the Jews." The slogan resonated with voters who felt that Peres was too conciliatory toward the Palestinians, capitalizing on a potent mix of Jewish patriotism and anti-Arab sentiment. Perhaps the single most effective part of Gutnick's campaigning was organizing thousands of Lubavitch volunteers to campaign and get out the vote. As Gutnick described it:

> Helping Chabad in Israel . . . get thousands of Lubavitchers out on the streets was worth more than $10 million. The Likudniks paid $30–40 an hour to guys working for them. We had 5,000 Lubavitchers on every corner and street in the

country, who voluntarily put in 72 hours' work—5,000 X 72 X 40 is many millions. The voluntary army of Chabad was worth a fortune.

Though it is impossible to determine precise causes for Netanyahu's victory (and there were dozens of important causes), Gutnick's efforts may have paid off. In 1992, Russians supported the Labor Party against the Likud by a margin of 60 percent to 40. In 1996, these proportions were almost reversed, with the Likud polling 58 percent and Labor 42. And there was record turnout at ultra-Orthodox voting places throughout the country. As critics saw it, a foreigner shilling the endorsement of a dead American rabbi had bought off tens of thousands of votes through masterfully crafted "philanthropy." Illegitimate interference in a foreign election, bribery, and burlesque abuse of superstitious devotion to a dead religious huckster had changed the course of Israeli history. Though no one could find criminal offenses in what Gutnick had done, for critics his role in the election contravened the spirit of democracy, effectively using loopholes in the democratic process to subvert the process itself. It is another form of soft fraud.

Even if Haredi "soft" fraud never levitates above the realm of the distasteful into the realm of the criminal, Shahar Ilan's investigations demonstrate that Haredim are also guilty of "hard" election fraud, of the Tammany Hall, Huey Long, Daley Machine variety. Anecdotal evidence of such fraud is commonplace, and though its true extent cannot be known, there are indications that in some elections it has been extensive. Before the 1999 elections, an eighteen-year-old named Eli Pelles disclosed that in the election three years earlier, he had voted three times at three different polls. Pelles, who fled the ultra-Orthodox at sixteen and soon joined the anti-Haredi Meretz Party, described how he was coached and provided with false identity cards by party hacks who had recruited a small army of multiple voters. "In the morning they sorted us according to the color of our beard, its length, our glasses, the pallor of our skin." The operation that ran him as a child was only one out of dozens, according to Pelles. They traffic the identity cards of the newly dead and overseas travelers or residents (there is no absentee balloting in Israel, for fear that the million Israelis residing permanently abroad would swing elections and thereby determine policy for a country they do not call home), and in rare cases forge ID cards. Reporters from *Yediot Aharonot* cited an anonymous Haredi informant in New York who alleged that rabbis ordered overseas Haredim to send their ID cards to Israel, where they could be used by imposters: "It wasn't a matter of choice. There is no such thing as not handing over your ID card." A similar exposé in *Ma'ariv* quoted another anonymous Haredi informant who described smuggling parcels of ID cards from New York into Ben Gurion Airport in the weeks before the election. The picture that emerges is of an impressively regimented international conspiracy.

An equally impressive conspiracy allowed Haredim to exploit the votes of hundreds or perhaps thousands of dead people. Raffi Tatarka, who served in the past as the deputy director of the General Security Services (Israel's highly regarded analogue to the FBI, known as the "Shin Bet" to Americans, "Shabak" to Israelis, and "Muchabarat" to Palestinians), was hired by Barak's One Israel coalition in 1999 to ferret out voter fraud. He reviewed voter rolls and found that they contained more than 30,000 eligible voters over ninety, a demographic anomaly that piqued his suspicions. Statisticians hired by Tatarka consulted actuarial tables and tabulated that the real number ought to be closer to 5,000. Twenty-five thousand extra eligible voters, Tatarka concluded, were actually dead, their votes fraudulently cast by others. In principle, this fraud is impossible to perpetrate. By law, before anyone can be buried in Israel, the person's ID card must be submitted to the Ministry of the Interior, which produces a death certificate and updates its computer files, automatically deleting the deceased from the voting rolls. Unscrupulous members of ultra-Orthodox burial societies, however, are willing to bury dead without informing the Ministry of Interior. This allows family members to continue receiving government pensions and other cash benefits that normally cease with death, a portion of which may be funneled back to the burial society as a kickback. An added benefit of this financial scam is that, come elections, the dead not only cash their checks, they also cast their votes.

Using the ID cards of others, living and dead, requires planning, luck, and strong nerves on the part of the fraudulent voter. Fraud is easier to carry out when the polling committee includes a confederate who does not insist that the ID card of the voter match the name on the voter roll. In the 1998 municipal elections in Jerusalem, for example, a twenty-eight-year-old yeshiva student named Sharyahu Finkel served on the polling committee and allowed Haredim to vote in the name of others. The transcript of his trial verdict described his modus operandi:

> At 1:00 P.M. a man whose identity remains unknown arrived at the voting place and gave to the defendant an identification card belonging to Israel Guttman, in which there was a small note. On one side of the note was written the number 506 and on the other side was written "Poll 18." Voter number 506 on the voter registry is Nahum Friedman, who did not show up to vote, and the defendant announced that voter 506 had arrived, even though he had full

knowledge that the man who had arrived was not Friedman. . . . An observer from the One Jerusalem Party asked to check the identification card, and while the chairman of the polling committee was giving it to her, the other man fled the building, leaving the identity card that he submitted.

It was later discovered that Finkel had successfully facilitated fraud in the same fashion at least four times earlier in the day. He was tried, convicted, and sentenced to five months in prison, though his father, who heads the powerful Mir Yeshiva in Jerusalem, summoned the support of ultra-Orthodox politicians who persuaded Israel's president, Moshe Katzav, to pardon Finkel after he had served just over a month.

No one knows how many votes such conspiracies add to Haredi columns at election time. Estimates range from several hundred to tens of thousands, and the numbers vary greatly by election. These highly structured scams may account for a minority of the total fraudulent Haredi vote. Probably the most effective vote swindle is the simplest. Israeli polls employ no technology more complicated than a Magic Marker. Voters line up in front of card tables manned by election officials with long, alphabetical computer printouts of all the eligible voters in a given polling place. When you reach the front of the line, the official holding the printout crosses off your name with a heavy marking pen and gives you an envelope that you take to a counter demarcated by curtains, upon which are slips of paper with the election call letters of all the competing political parties. In the general elections in 1996 and 1999, you were given an additional envelope for your choice of prime minister. You put the proper scraps of paper in the envelopes, put the envelopes in a big box, and walk away. The votes are later counted by hand.

In short, the election is run pretty much like the student council election in any midsized high school. This system allows corrupt election officials, at the end of the day, to sneak into the box dozens or hundreds of envelopes with slips for the party or candidate of their choice, taking care to strike out an identical number of names of no-show voters. Through most of the 1980s and the 1990s, Shahar Ilan suggested, this practice might well have been common among the ultra-Orthodox. Its precise extent is imponderable. Some believe that this fraud provided the very narrow margin by which Benjamin Netanyahu defeated Shimon Peres in 1996, soon after Rabin's assassination. Most estimates of its extent exceed the difference in votes polled by the two candidates, and no one doubts that Netanyahu was the candidate strongly preferred by most Haredim, especially Haredi party operatives, suggesting that whatever votes were illegally cast were cast for

Netanyahu. It does not take a conspiratorial frame of mind to conclude then that Haredi fraud may account for Israel's shift from left to right at an exquisitely sensitive moment in the continuing negotiations mandated by the Oslo Peace Accords, eventually leading to the deterioration of the peace and the annihilation of the fragile détente between Israel and the Palestinian Authority.

The belief that Haredi fraud had cost them the 1996 election left a powerful imprint on the Israeli Left, and it led to an extraordinary political innovation in the next election. For the 1999 elections, the election committee of the left-leaning United Kibbutz Movement organized a massive effort to oversee ultra-Orthodox polling places and practices. Normally, each voting station is overseen by a three-member poll committee, including a representative of the ruling coalition, the opposition, and any third party that has in the past had delegates elected to the Knesset. By law, additional political parties may send representatives to polls as observers, though in the past most party organizers have preferred using their election-day volunteers to ferry potential voters and to display hand-held signs at well-traveled intersections. The strategy adopted by the kibbutzniks was to exploit the observer positions allotted to the various left-wing political parties, filling them with volunteers who might or might not have been members of the party they represented, but who were committed to preventing ultra-Orthodox fraud. To execute this strategy, the kibbutzniks attained permission of Barak's One Israel coalition, Tommy Lapid's liberal Shinui Party, and the leftist Meretz Party to use their allocations of party representatives. Through a variety of statistical and demographic analyses, they identified 532 polling places most likely to host ultra-Orthodox election fraud. They then recruited, through newspaper advertisements, direct mail, and word-of-mouth, a battalion of thousands of volunteers, for whom they ran half-day seminars to train them to spot potential fraud and successfully prevent its perpetration. Ilan reported that 1,500 of these volunteers came from kibbutzim and another 1,300 from the rest of the country.

These figures do not reflect the fact that many thousands of potential volunteers were turned away, unneeded; the supply of volunteers would likely have been great enough to meet a demand ten times as great as the organizers identified. The secretary-general of the Labor Party reported that 40,000 activists from his party alone had been recruited, should the need arise. Meretz reported that 22,000 volunteers attended its training seminars. Having gathered and trained these volunteers, the organizers had to assign pairs or trios of volunteers, in shifts, to targeted polling places, and arrange transportation for them at the appointed times to the appointed place. In addition, they recruited an "intervention force" of 900 graduates of crack IDF combat units. These reserve soldiers traveled in small units from polling place to polling place in Haredi areas, ready to aid the volunteers should the ultra-Orthodox attempt to harm them or prevent their election oversight. The presence—or constant threat of—beefy commandos was meant to keep the ultra-Orthodox in line, protecting the safety of the observers and ensuring the success of their mission. The entire operation was efficiently executed and, by most reports, a great success.

The observers performed several functions. At the most basic level, they tried to verify that voters were who they claimed to be, and not imposters voting with imported or fabricated identification cards or IDs of the newly dead. This task was more difficult than might at first be imagined, because to secular eyes, the ultra-Orthodox (especially men, with their long beards, homogeneous dress, and large hats) look remarkably alike. In their training sessions, volunteers were advised to instruct voters to remove their hats and glasses, which made comparison to ID card photos easier. Volunteers also asked voters to repeat their ID number several times, checking to see if they stumbled, which would likely indicate fraud. (Since ID numbers are a ubiquitous standard of identification, they are as firmly fixed in an individual's memory as a telephone number or address.) According to Ilan, Haredi sources reported that some overzealous volunteers pulled on voters' earlocks to verify their authenticity or demanded that women remove their wigs (ultra-Orthodox women are required by Halakha to shave their hair close, to reduce their seductiveness, a state of affairs that they typically negate by wearing stylish wigs), practices that were perceived by Haredim as harassment. Weeks before the elections, a popular satiric front page called *Davar Aher*, printed weekly in *Yediot*, had run the headline, "A New Proposal to Prevent Election Fraud: Anyone Who Votes Has His Beard and Earlocks Removed," and enthusiastic volunteers perhaps took the logic behind the joke in earnest. These things may have happened in a few isolated cases, but they were not widespread, and the volunteers with whom I spoke reported genial surprise at the generally positive atmosphere they encountered.

At the same time, none of the volunteers that I interviewed felt confident that they had prevented imposters from voting. Tal Littman, a computer analyst from a village in the north of Israel, described manning the polls as a patriotic duty, as "doing something good for the country," but still felt that imposters may well have slipped through on his watch. Littman believes that "cheating is an ideology" for the ultra-Orthodox, and that their talents for defrauding are exquisitely developed: "It's a whole population with nothing else to do, so this is what it does with its time. It's the same with

everything: the elections, child allowances, taxes; it's a conspiracy that includes everything, every imaginable area. Defrauding the state is an ideology for them. They're terribly destructive." Given the high motivation of
Haredim to cheat, and given the objective difficulty of uncovering the fraud,
in Littman's view, it is likely that individuals voted twice, even at the polling
place that he observed. "Look," he told me, "a person comes in, and it's hard
to tell if he matches the picture on the ID card. There's time pressure at the
polls, and crowds, so you really cannot check everyone the way you might
want to. Plus, there were a lot of people at the polls, observers from this and
that religious party, and it's hard to keep track of everything that's going on
at one time." Anyone highly motivated to slip by with a false ID could do it.
Still, Littman said, if it was impossible to prevent the small-scale fraud,

> the greatest frauds take place when the votes are being counted. I took the voting
> box with several representatives from other parties, we went to the place where
> the votes are counted and where they submit the vote counts. This was the most
> important thing that I did, verifying that the votes were properly counted. We
> prevented the sort of wholesale fraud that had taken place in the past.

This "wholesale fraud," as Littman put it, included mass voting in the name
of no-shows at precincts after the polls closed and fraudulent vote counting
or reporting after the count. As Littman and many others saw it, preventing
these wholesale frauds may have kept thousands of unlawful votes from being
added to official tallies. In Ilan's reckoning, the police reported sixty-nine
cases of voter fraud (including fifteen forged voter registrations and fifty-two
cases of "unlawful voting"). Thirty-five criminal investigations were initiated,
and the Jerusalem police recommended bringing charges against eight
Haredim. According to Ilan, the police statistics underrepresented the true extent of voter fraud, as the volunteers observed greater numbers of attempted
fraud (one of which, at least, the police handled by removing an imposter
from the polling place, rather than booking him). Ilan also reported the case
of a ballot box from Bnei Brak in which there were dozens more votes cast
than there were voters whose names were marked off on the rolls. This suggests that half a fraud was perpetrated—extra votes were slipped into the box,
but through the incompetence of the offenders or the vigilance of the observers, the matching number of names was not erased from the list. Ilan reasonably concluded that if this fraud was uncovered, one might well think that
other, similar frauds were brought to their successful completion.

In response to the kibbutz movement's monitoring of ultra-Orthodox
polls, Haredi politicians predictably complained that vote stealing is more

common on kibbutzim than it is in Meah Shearim or Bnei Brak. An election-day coordinator for the Agudah, Yizhak Pendruc, organized a mirror operation to monitor the voting on leftist communal settlements. "We took all the places that had an extraordinarily high voter turnout and will staff them first." Pendruc claimed that the 1996 records revealed voter turnout of as high as 97 percent in some kibbutzim, a rate that would be unlikely unless some residents cast votes for others who were abroad, in the hospital, or otherwise indisposed. Before the election, Pendruc claimed to have recruited about 2,000 volunteers to observe voting on various kibbutzim. In the end, the number of ultra-Orthodox observers was much lower, and those that did spend the day at sleepy kibbutz polling places did not report any voter irregularity to the police.

It is easy to believe that voting irregularities take place on some kibbutzim, where it may seem harmless enough for one member to cast a vote for another member who, say, went into labor hours before the polls opened and whose political sympathies were well known. Perhaps there is also voting fraud on a larger scale, for less forgivable, party machine reasons. But Pendruc's claim that there is some symmetry between kibbutz and ultra-Orthodox voting fraud is hollow. That is not only because there is likely much more fraud in ultra-Orthodox communities. To many, the extent of Haredi voter fraud, which is ultimately unknown and probably unknowable, is less disturbing than what Littman called the "ideology" of political fraud. In Ilan's analysis, Haredim cheat because deep down they reject the very notion of democracy. Just as kids cheat because school "sucks," Haredim defraud elections because, to their way of seeing things, democracy is a flawed and evil system. Their calculus factors, not what is right or wrong, but rather what they can or cannot get away with.

It is this fundamental rejection of democratic values that makes Haredim dangerous, in Ilan's view. Ilan described a eulogy delivered in 1993 by Rabbi Eliezer Shach for Rabbi Shraga Grossbard, who had served as the director of the ultra-Orthodox Agudat Yisrael school system. In the eulogy, Shach likened democracy to cancer: "Just as this evil was visited upon us, and this terrible disease came into the world, so too was an inoperable evil visited upon the world in the form of democracy. This is a terrible disease that is spreading and destroys spirit and flesh." Eliezer Shach has since died, but at the time he made those remarks he was the most powerful, widely respected ultra-Orthodox authority in Israel. And he was not alone in his diminished view of liberal society. Ilan cited studies finding that two of every three ultra-Orthodox Jews favor dismantling Israel's democracy in favor of a theocracy, basically rule by a junta of rabbis, with the Torah as a constitution and the Talmud and rabbinic Halakha as the legal code. He contrasted this find with that of another survey indicating that one of every three secular Jews wishes to radically separate religion from state, and he reasonably concluded that "the percentage of Haredim wishing to impose their views on the general public is double the percentage of secular Israelis wishing to do the same." Ilan cited numerous other findings, all supporting the same conclusions: Only 31 percent of the ultra-Orthodox surveyed object to the installation of a strong leader who need not stand for regular elections; more than 60 percent of Haredi youth agree with the statement, "a few strong leaders could repair the ills of the country more than all the laws and discussions combined"; 90 percent of Haredim display support for "antidemocratic positions"; and roughly two-thirds of Haredim do not trust the institutions at the heart of Israel's democracy, including the courts, Knesset, political parties, and the army. And so forth. Ilan's conclusion is so well supported by data as to be what social scientists call "overdetermined." Democracy—as a concept, as an institution, as a *value*—is held in low esteem by Israel's ultra-Orthodox. This fact is crucial to understanding Haredi political behavior, and the disquiet with which it is typically regarded by many secular Israelis.

The late Ernest Gellner, one of the twentieth century's great polymaths, memorably observed that durable democracy depends upon civil society: "No civil society, no democracy." In the case of Israel's ultra-Orthodox, the opposite can be said to be true as well. Without deep commitment to the ethos of democracy, Haredim display little social or political civility. Tocqueville wrote of nineteenth-century American citizens: "Enlightened regard for themselves constantly prompts them to assist one another and inclines them willingly to sacrifice a portion of their time and property to the welfare of the state." What disturbs many secular Israelis most deeply about Haredim is that, in their politics, they display no such willingness to sacrifice for the greater welfare. Haredim are seen as singlemindedly pursuing a politics of self-interest, wherein the only criterion by which ministerial or legislative machinations are judged is the benefit they produce for Haredim alone. This perception is not fully accurate, but it is abundantly justified. For many secular Israelis, it makes sense of what they take to be widespread ultra-Orthodox corruption and cronyism, as well as the performance of Haredim in coalition politics, ministerial politics, and legislative politics.

When tallying political deceit among the ultra-Orthodox, it is best not to begin with preconceived notions of what counts as corruption. While Haredi politicians have had their share of bribery, influence peddling, and graft scandals, these garden-variety offenses are only part of the story. When my grandmother died in Bnei Brak, the chief of the burial society asked my father, who flew from America to handle the arrangements, to pay a fee of several hundred dollars to compensate society members for their labors. My father told the rabbi that my grandmother had paid for these services some years in advance, a fact that she related to me repeatedly in the final months of her life, and from which she drew comfort; she worried about being a burden to her family in life and was gratified to think that, in death, she would not be. The rabbi told my father that he had no memory of being paid and knew of no record of such a transaction. Perhaps receipts could be produced in time, but in the meanwhile, tradition demanded that my grandmother be buried immediately, and this could only be done if my father would issue payment in cash. There can be no doubt that my grandmother had paid; she was fastidious about such matters. Nor can there be any doubt that record of the prepayment can be found in the files of the burial society. Put simply, my father was shaken down by a rabbi exploiting the occasion of his mother's death. Because by law, funerals must be administered by local burial societies, which receive government funding and whose employees receive government paychecks and pensions, my father's experience is properly considered low-level political corruption.

This experience is not unique. In November 1999, Hadas Regulesky, a journalist for *Yediot*, pretended to be a bereaved daughter looking for a burial plot in the Holon cemetery, which had recently been declared full. Her investigations turned up the phone number of a *"macher,"* a person who claimed to have useful connections with the local burial society. "Bring four or five thousand shekels as a down payment," the man told her on the phone, and the plot would be hers. "But how?" she asked. "The cemetery is full." "I control the whole burial society. Tomorrow alone I have four funerals planned." In the old cemetery in the center of Tel Aviv where the poet Hayim Nahman Bialik and many other early luminaries of the city are buried, plots can be purchased directly from the burial society for upwards of 50,000 shekels, a handsome sum especially in light of the fact that almost no money is spent on upkeep. On a recent visit, I saw smashed tombs and littered bones that had been gnawed by dogs. Motti Yeshoviov, the assistant personnel manager of the society, explained to reporters that the poor repair of the cemetery owed to its miniscule revenues. Though burial plots are the most expensive in the country, there are very few left, and the cemetery sells a plot only every several months. The income this generates pays for only elementary security needs, and very little janitorial services. This explanation is reasonable, though to many secular observers, the decision to treat each cemetery as its own profit center is a bookkeeping trick to allow

Haredi managers to pocket huge profits in active cemeteries without dilut-
ing them in less-active ones. This criticism is reasonable as well.

About the same time the Holon plot-gouging scandal was first reported,
attorney Aviad Hacohen issued a government oversight report criticizing
mismanagement and corruption in the Tel Aviv Burial Society, including a
recommendation to shut down the society immediately. "Negligent, ama-
teurish management allowed those wishing to take advantage of loopholes
to do so in style. The near-total silence of the oversight committee, the im-
potence of board members, the blind eye of society members who knew
[about the corruption] and kept silent, created circumstances in which
whoever wanted to take, took."

The troubles of the Tel Aviv Burial Society are not new. Rabbi Israel Er-
lich, who managed the society through most of the 1980s and 1990s, was indicted for stealing up to a million shekels of society funds. Several years ago,
tax officials reached a quiet settlement wherein the society agreed to pay 3.9
million shekels in back taxes. The society neglected to submit annual financial reports, as required by law. Moneys donated to charity boxes near the
gates of cemeteries are divided up between the ultra-Orthodox political
parties. In 1997, ex-Shas Knesset member Raphael Pinhasi was selected to
serve as the chairman of the finance committee of the society, despite the
fact that he had been convicted of financial corruption. The Movement for
Quality of Government brought suit to the Supreme Court, asking that Pinhasi be removed from his post owing to his prior felony conviction, and
prevailed. Before he left the chairmanship of the finance committee, however, Pinhasi arranged a job for his daughter Yehudit as a secretary of the
Burial Society, and a job for his brother Shmuel as a functionary at the large
Yarkon cemetery. Pinhasi himself continued to serve as a member, though
not chairman, of the finance committee. Among the employees of the society was the manager of the car pool (which counted six vehicles), who, with
benefits, received roughly $100,000 a year, and an office worker who re-
ceived roughly $125,000. The average income in Israel, with benefits, is
somewhat under $25,000.

The scandals of the burial societies took their place alongside a number of
similar scandals that also became large media events. In 2002 a prime-time,
Sixty Minutes sort of investigative journalism show named *Hasifa* (Disclosure) reported on unscrupulous Haredim who persuaded lonely retirees to
transfer title to their homes to yeshivot and other ultra-Orthodox institutions. According to the report, though the donors were led to believe that
they had bequeathed the property, they in fact had signed over ownership
immediately. In some cases, according to the show, the Haredim evicted the

now-prior owners. Donors who regretted their generosity found that they had no legal recourse; they had legally given their most valuable possession away, and it was unrecoverable. The show interviewed embittered middle-aged daughters and sons convinced that their father had been bamboozled out of their inheritance. In the final scene of the show, a homeless octogenarian sat on a public bench in front of what had once been his home but was now an improvised yeshiva, rueful and confused about how he lost everything he had owned.

Some years earlier, in 1997, a similar television show, *Uvdah* (Fact), used a hidden camera to film Rabbi Michael Dushinsky, then the kashrut supervisor at the Ministry of Labor and Social Affairs, taking $15,000 in cash to facilitate a fast-track religious conversion. A Jerusalem journalist and a kibbutz volunteer from Peru came to Dushinsky pretending to be a couple wishing to marry because they were soon expecting to have a child. Dushinsky told the couple on film that in normal channels, conversions take at least a year, but that for a fee he would provide them with false witnesses that would allow them to complete the conversion immediately. Immediately after the show aired, the police arrested Dushinsky and an accomplice, Rabbi Binyamin Bar-Zohar. Investigation revealed that Dushinsky had fast-tracked many conversions in exchange for cash (evidence turned up for ten such conversions), typically between $7,000 and $15,000. Two-thirds of the money was passed on to Bar-Zohar, who used connections with the rabbinic court to ensure that the conversion was approved. According to Rabbi Einat Ramon, who was then the spokeswoman of the Masorti (Conservative) Movement in Israel, roughly half of those who sought Conservative conversion in Israel did so after being shaken down for bribes by ultra-Orthodox rabbis.

This sort of one-on-one corruption—bribery to get a prime funeral spot or a quickie conversion (or marriage or divorce or adoption or any of the "domestic" government services that are controlled by the ultra-Orthodox establishment) or scamming the naïve out of their inheritance—is a perennial story in papers and on television, and each new case magnifies the already ample perception among secular Israelis that they are being bilked by the ultra-Orthodox. This perception has been still further amplified by revelations of cronyism and corruption among ultra-Orthodox politicians. Like Americans, most Israelis evince weary cynicism about elected officials, seeing them as unscrupulous and self-serving (a 2003 poll found that 83 percent of Israelis believe that their elected representatives "tend to be corrupt"), but no group is regarded with the same contempt as ultra-Orthodox politicians.

The 1990s were not a good decade for ultra-Orthodox politicians, who increasingly found themselves under police investigation. The first to be arrested was the assistant chairman of Shas and one of the party's representatives in the Knesset, Yair Levi. Levi's rise in politics had been quick, and it was distinguished by his savvy—he had a knack for being in the right place at the right time—and his affability—he had a talent for making friends among the party powerful. His career began when Shas Party leaders decided in 1985 to run a slate for the powerful Histadrut labor union in addition to the Knesset. This was a sensible strategy, as the Histadrut controlled a vast network of properties and local political organizations, and it was a traditional stronghold of the sort of populist eat-the-rich ideology that appealed to Shas's largely disenfranchised working-class electorate. The party faced an immediate technical problem implementing its plan: finding party activists who were already members of the leftist labor union and thereby eligible to run for office. Someone remembered that a young, marginal Bnei Brak political activist named Yair Levi had a red Histadrut membership card (the color symbolizing workers' unity), and Levi was drafted from obscurity to head the ticket. Weeks later, Shas leaders cut a deal with Yisrael Keissar, the Labor Party chairman of the labor union, and abandoned their plans to campaign independently in the Histadrut, but by that time, Levi had already impressed the Shas Party leader, Aryeh Deri, and Levi's national political career was launched. Deri asked Levi to replace him as party chairman, and Levi replied with the politic suggestion that Deri retain the title, while Levi did the grunt work with the title of assistant chairman of the party. The mix of ambition and sycophancy struck perfect pitch, and Levi took hold of the party, becoming one of the most powerful men in Israeli politics. He was barely thirty.

The precise reasons for Levi's rise in politics are difficult to reconstruct in retrospect. He is a short man, round as a muffin, and his broad, easy smile lends him a jovial but half-witted demeanor. He looks like a gnome on his way to a bar mitzvah. But in the mid-1980s he had a reputation as a political bulldozer, carelessly brushing aside opponents and other obstacles to advance the agenda of his party. Levi's political career collapsed as rapidly as it had grown. While Levi was on a Knesset junket to the U.S. State Department, Israeli police announced that they would detain him upon his return for questioning concerning financial irregularities in the school system he ran. Levi panicked and disappeared, going underground in the United States. Local newspapers hypothesized his whereabouts with great relish—Levi's disappearance was one of those rare "Lady Di" occasions that erase the line between respectable and yellow journalism, between the op-ed and the gossip column. After three days, Levi resurfaced, sending by fax a doctor's note explaining that he was sick and would need to undergo surgery, a ham-handed effort to spin his disappearance that was generally received with bemused scorn.

When Levi returned and was questioned, it emerged that he had stolen money from the school system he ran with the same incompetence that marked his crude doctor's note attempt at PR. Shmuel Erez, the lead detective of the investigation team, said of Levi's ineptitude as a crook, "It's impossible, no one steals this way." Levi had drawn checks to suppliers and employees (including, quaintly, several fortune-tellers) to pay for fictitious goods and services, and then endorsed the checks to himself, in his own hand. His lawyers reached a plea bargain with prosecutors resulting in three years and four months of prison and a fine of 275,000 shekels, ostensibly to cover the sum Levi embezzled. The presiding judge, Arieh Seligman, rejected the agreement, finding Levi guilty of stealing 311,791 shekels, and sentenced him to five years, in addition to the original fine (which was later paid by donors from abroad). Levi claimed not to have benefited personally from the embezzlement, maintaining that he gave the money to needy yeshiva students who were unfairly ineligible for proper government aid. This claim was neither verified nor refuted, though it is generally regarded with considerable skepticism.

Levi's incarceration did not go well. After only eleven months, he petitioned his parole board for medical release. Prison life did not suit him, he claimed, and he repeatedly fainted in his cell. At times, he found himself too weak to get out of bed. The request was rejected, but Levi persisted and eventually he was granted a special work furlough arrangement that allowed him to spend days and weekends out of prison, in a more convivial environment, his home. When a journalist disclosed this unusually lax arrangement, prison officials quickly rescinded it, and Levi found himself back behind bars, a circumstance about which he complained vigorously to friends and journalists. When he was finally released, Levi was a broken man. He accepted a Shas sinecure as one of the directors of a girls' school in Bnei Brak and disappeared from public view.

If Levi's rise and fall are a made-for-TV special, the trajectory and tragedy of the career of his benefactor, Aryeh Deri, is opera, alive with grandeur and pathos. Deri's career and his criminal case were the backdrop of the turbulent 1990s in Israeli politics. The decade of the Madrid conference, the Gulf War, the Oslo Peace Accords, the assassination of Yizhak Rabin, the rise to power and collapse of Benjamin Netanyahu and Ehud Barak, and the second intifada was framed by the corruption trial of Aryeh Deri: The investigation

began in June 1990, and he finally went to prison in August 2000. Deri's incarceration was a significant event; among recent events it is surpassed in
emotional impact only by Rabin's murder. It is often compared to the Drey-
fus Affair, an exaggeration that reflects the importance with which it is regarded. Something in Deri's story made him a symbol of conflicting things:
of Haredi insatiability, of Sephardi talent, of the danger of challenging
Israel's traditional elites, and of the country's deep ethnic resentments, easily
manipulated by cynics and scoundrels. It is a complicated story that reflects
the tremors and aftershocks that have dazed Israeli society in the past thirty
years. It is a story that has been told and retold thousands of times, in articles, books, and television and film documentaries.

Deri was born in Meknes, Morocco, an accident of geography that later
had a great impact on his political career. His father, Eliahu, was an expert
tailor, who over the course of Deri's first decade built a profitable business
producing high-end suits made-to-order from imported fabric, eventually
employing five other tailors. As a toddler, Deri bumped around a two-room
walk-up in the old Jewish section of town, but by the time he was ten, his
family had moved into an exclusive apartment in a luxury hotel, a part of
the Jewish upper crust. Postcards depicting the eleventh-century Almohade
citadel and the seventeenth-century Sultan's palace that are Meknes's greatest attractions refer to the city as the "Versailles of Northern Africa." This
comparison exaggerates the beauty of the city to a great degree, but it is
charming, mixing French colonial influences with the traditional Moslem
architecture of the Old City. The city has two Jewish quarters, an old "Mel-
lah" and a new one constructed in the 1920 under French rule. When Deri
grew up, the Jewish community of Meknes numbered about 40,000, many
of them successful in business and trade. The Jewish community supported
dozens of synagogues and many schools combining a progressive European
curriculum with traditional Jewish study. Aryeh Deri was identified as an
"*illui*," or prodigy, when he entered school, and by the time he was ten, he
had completed the entire preparatory curriculum and was boosted ahead to
high school.

It was at this moment, just after the Six-Day War, that Deri's father, like
many other Jews in Meknes, decided to immigrate to Israel. The war had
been an unnerving interlude for Moroccan Jews. Official radio broadcasts
wishfully reported that Israel had been conquered by the Egyptian, Syrian,
Jordanian, Lebanese, and Iraqi armies. Deri's family knew that this was not
true—as did most Jews in Morocco—and they received a more accurate
portrayal of the war via short-wave radio tuned to broadcasts from
Monaco. But attitudes toward Jews became less cordial during the war

(Deri's father remembers a former customer calling him a "dirty Jew" from across the boulevard) and remained so for a long interval afterward. The haberdashery lost clients in significant enough numbers that Deri's father decided to liquidate his assets and move to Israel, joining his two brothers who had done so years earlier. He sold his store and apartment, arranging for the money to be transferred to France, and then applied for exit visas to France for his family. By the end of 1967, the Deris were in a holding facility in Marseilles. They soon boarded a boat to Haifa, where Deri's uncle Yosef was waiting to welcome them.

Like many immigrants before and since, the Deris did not find Israel welcoming. Yosef Deri was the chairman of the postal workers' union, a position that conferred on him some influence, but he was unable to persuade the Jewish Agency functionary who greeted the Deri family that they should be settled in the Tel Aviv suburb of Holon, where Yosef and another brother lived. Instead, the Deri's were sent to a run-down neighborhood in Rishon le-Zion, where addicts were desperate enough for a hit that residents installed double latches on their doors, at a time where in most of the country it was not necessary to lock the door at all. The Deris were used to a level of wealth and cultivation that could not be found in their new backwater home, and they reacted with shock that later fermented into despair. When the kids were taken to register for school, Department of Education bureaucrats refused to credit the certification that both boys had completed elementary and middle school in Meknes and were ready for high school. With condescension characteristic of the treatment of most immigrants since Israel's establishment, and especially immigrants from places other than Europe or North America, Aryeh was assigned to third grade, a demotion of five grade levels.

I first visited Meknes in 1983, a decade and a half after the Deris had left the city. Much had changed in the Jewish community. Most Jews had left; of 40,000 only 1,000 remained when I visited. The rest had gone to France or Israel. The Jewish community of Meknes remained highly cultured. The children I spoke with (and I was not that much older than a child myself on my first visit at the end of college) spoke three languages—French, Arabic, and Hebrew—and many were fluent in English as well. They were sophisticated about world politics and culture, and were the products of effective religious training as well, capable of quoting stretches of Bible and Talmud. When I visited Meknes Jews in their homes, I was served a combination of traditional Moroccan and French haute cuisine. Over dinner, I learned that many Jews in Meknes resented the way in which they and their relatives were treated and regarded in Israel. One woman, upon hearing my plans to live in that country, recounted the difficulties that she and her family had faced when they themselves immigrated there in the 1950s, and were shipped off to the small barren desert town of Mitzpeh Ramon against their will. She recalled being doused with DDT upon their arrival from Paris ("as though Haifa is more hygienic than Paris!" she laughed), and begging the clerk who processed her papers to send her to Jerusalem or Tel Aviv, anywhere with culture. She described how her aging mother died in a dirty, understaffed medical clinic, waiting for a doctor. The prejudice against Moroccan Jews current at the time was that they were all thieves, and she recalled people locking up their handbags at work when she was around. It was too much to take. After less than a year, she gathered her belongings and moved back to Meknes, a city of greater civility than any found in Israel. "A horrible place, a horrible place," she said of her disappointing months in the Holy Land. Thirty years divided her experiences in Israel from our dinner together in Meknes, but the shock of her ill-treatment in the Jewish State remained raw and painful.

Deri's family experienced similar shock. Eliahu Deri, only months before a highly successful businessman, was for a time unemployed. When he was finally sent to work as an assistant tailor in Tel Aviv, he was dismayed by his new customers' lack of flair and taste in clothing. Work had been a source of great satisfaction for Eliahu Deri in Morocco; in Israel it was a trial and humiliation. Meknes is a lovely city, and the Deris had lived large there. Rishon le-Zion in 1968 was not lovely, and the family lived in a slum. Yehudah and Aryeh Deri had been recognized as brilliant children throughout their lives, and now they were faceless immigrants whose native intelligence and great academic potential were unappreciated by their fellow students, teachers, and principals, in short, by everyone who mattered.

By everyone, that is, except recruiters for ultra-Orthodox boarding schools. A member of the Bnei Brak group Yad le-Achim knocked on the Deris' door offering to find young Aryeh a place in the famous Ponevezh Yeshiva, run by Rabbi Eliezer Shach. Ponevezh is considered by cognoscenti to be the Oxford of Ashkenazi ultra-Orthodox academies. Deri accepted the invitation, but his tenure at the yeshiva was not a success. He did not fit in well there, in large part because its Eastern European traditions of study were foreign to a boy raised at the foot of the Atlas Mountains. Deri then passed through a number of Ashkenazi boarding yeshivot of some renown, finally settling with his brother in a small start-up yeshiva named Mesivta, in Hadera. Soon after his bar mitzvah, three years later, the school folded and on its rabbis' recommendation, the Deri brothers enrolled in the Porat Yosef Yeshiva in Jerusalem, a school that was the Cambridge of the Sephardim, and the place where, for better or for worse, Aryeh Deri became Aryeh Deri.

Relations in Israel between Sephardim (the term means "Spaniards," but refers to Jews of North Africa and the Middle East whose ancestors were expelled from Spain by Ferdinand and Isabella in 1492) and Ashkenazim (the term means "Germans," but refers to Jews of Europe and North America whose ancestors lived in Central Europe while the Sephardim were being expelled) were troubled from the start. Jerusalem, Safed, Jaffa, and several other cities had had small populations of Sephardi Jews before the rise of modern Zionism. To this day, descendants of these Jews have a Brahmin self-image, calling themselves "*pure* Sephardim," and keeping tally of through how many generations they can trace their lineage in the Holy Land, in contrast to the mongrel latecomers of the twentieth century. However, the colonization of Palestine through the first half of that century was a European, Ashkenazi affair. The founders of modern Zionism as a viable political and social movement—Theodor Herzl, Max Nordau, Asher Ginzburg, and many others—were Europeans, who expected that the Jewish state they planned would be a liberal, European-style democracy. Although most held some romantic affection for what they took to be the "authenticity" of oriental culture (an enthusiastic fringe going so far as to reject "degenerate" European culture in favor of primitive "Palestinianism"), this affection was alloyed by what Edward Said long ago condemned as "orientalism," a toxic form of colonial condescension that sees natives of the Middle East as simpletons of such understated civility as to be more animal than human. To the political leaders of the *yishuv*, the "pre-state settlement," who were immigrants from Europe striving to create a highly technological social democracy, the native Palestinians were quaint reminders of how far there was to go. "A land without a people, for a people without a land," was one early Zionist slogan that reflects how easily the Arab Palestinians faded into the landscape of early-twentieth-century Palestine. (Though not for everyone; Asher Ginzburg, who went by the pen name "Ahad ha-Am" [One of the People], decried the dismissive attitude toward the native Palestinians, as did Vladimir Jabotinsky and many others.)

Early Zionist condescension toward Palestinians applied, though with less force, to oriental Jews, or Sephardim. Relatively few of these Jews joined the Ashkenazi pioneers, and in contrast to the upheavals in Europe, most of the Jewish communities in North Africa and the Middle East were stable during the first half of the twentieth century. As the establishment of a Jewish homeland in Palestine became increasingly inevitable, and then in 1948 a political fact, conditions in most Sephardi communities quickly eroded. The new Jewish State became officially an enemy of every country in which Sephardim resided in large numbers, and the Jewish residents of these countries—whose position had never been that of equal citizens—were viewed with growing suspicion. Deterioration at home, together with the promise and romance of the new Jewish State in Palestine, persuaded many Sephardim to emigrate. After each of the first three Israel-Arab wars in 1948, 1956, and 1967, the numbers of emigrants spiked, owing to the same push and pull—worry that home was growing inhospitable and proud hope that Israel offered better prospects. After graduating from college in 1982, I got a grant to spend a year traveling North Africa with a backpack, a portable Royal typewriter, and a Canon AE-1, documenting what was left of these communities, and what I found in most places was the skeleton of once-grand communities (Casablanca and Djerba were two exceptions). Cairo, Alexandria, Tunis, Algiers, Fez: All these cities had magnificent synagogues that could no longer be maintained by the dozens of hobbled, poor, suspicious Jews who were the last remnant of communities with histories reaching back hundreds of years, but with no future. Entire communities, entire heritages, had resettled themselves, en masse, in Israel. There, absorbing new immigrants from Arab lands (as well as refugees and survivors from Europe) took priority in policy and budget decisions, and diplomats negotiated secret deals with enemy states—Yemen and Morocco, for instance—that allowed the fledgling state to transport tens of thousands of Jews to within its embattled borders.

How well or poorly these new citizens were treated upon their arrival is a matter of continuing debate in Israel, though there is agreement about certain basic facts. The conditions that most of the new immigrants found, especially the first of them, were harsh. For a period, Jews arriving from Arab lands were "disinfected" with DDT, a rude practice that was widely taken to reflect skepticism concerning the hygiene of Sephardim. Many were sent to *ma'abarot* (transit camps), where they lived in tents for periods of several months to several years. These camps provided poor nutrition, unsanitary conditions, inadequate medical care, and little opportunity for employment. When permanent housing was provided, it was generally assigned with no regard for the preferences of the immigrants. Most were sent to "development towns" in far-flung places, the locations of which were selected according to "national priorities"—typically defense reasons—rather than native conviviality. Thus, many immigrants found themselves in desolate towns with fierce and forbidding climates and no economic infrastructure. Most difficult of all, certain immigrant families were divided by the authorities, who strongly encouraged, and in some cases forced, children to leave their parents in favor of boarding schools, sometimes at kibbutzim. Dozens of couples from Yemen believe that their babies were kidnapped by government authorities; women were told after giving birth that their babies had died, though despite their protests and tears, they were not allowed to view the dead child. Rumors arose that the babies were being transferred to Ashkenazi parents, often to kibbutzniks, where they would be raised as modern, secular Israelis. In 2002, a third blue-ribbon panel of inquiry completed its investigation of these claims, finding no unambiguous support for the claims, but no definitive contravening evidence either. Recently, a bill was proposed in the Knesset to fund a massive DNA information bank that would allow the issue to be decided once and for all.

The idea that Yemenite babies would be purloined and shipped off to antireligious, Ashkenazi kibbutzim gains what plausibility it has from the general ill-regard with which Sephardi culture was held during the first years of the state. David Ben-Gurion, the founding prime minister of Israel, whose influence on the nascent state was unparalleled, called the new immigrants "the dust of humanity" and advocated remolding them in the Zionist "melting pot." The image of the ideal Israeli—the *Tzabar* (Sabra)—was drawn from the pages of romantic, German youth movement pamphlets: a blond, muscular, Nietzschean, who could pull a plow and play guitar. Sephardi kids were raised to revere European Zionists and, to a degree, European culture. In early textbooks, novels, films, and so on, Sephardim were portrayed as simple and good-hearted fodder for the new state, raw material to be remolded in a stronger, more sophisticated, more cultured image. Sephardi kids were raised to disparage their parents.

This condescension toward Sephardi culture had a parallel among the ultra-Orthodox. Ultra-Orthodoxy is itself a European, that is to say, Ashkenazi, phenomenon. As philosopher David Hartman told me, religious fanaticism has no roots in Sephardi culture; it thrived only among the more brutal and schismatic Europeans. The Jewish cultures in Arab lands, for reasons that sociologists debate, were far more flexible in their attitudes toward observance. For example, the Deris spent Saturday afternoons in Meknes attending soccer matches, and no one thought this cause to doubt their piety. The majority of Sephardim in Israel today define themselves as neither secular nor religious, but rather, "traditional," a term that describes families that on a typical Friday night might light candles, bless the wine and the challah, eat a festive meal, and then hunker down together on the sofa to watch Van Damme on DVD.

This fundamental difference between the religious sensibilities of Sephardim and Ashkenazim created a dilemma for Sephardim seeking serious religious training in Israel. For the first decades of the state, religious institutions, including yeshivot, were for the most part controlled by the

Ashkenazi rabbinic establishment. The curriculum of religious public schools was largely controlled by the Ashkenazi National Religious Party, and the curriculum of the independent Haredi schools was largely determined by European rabbis in Meah Shearim and Bnei Brak. There were exceptions (each system included a small number of Sephardi schools), but most kids received a primarily Ashkenazi education. Unusually talented children like Deri were typically enrolled in highly regarded Ashkenazi schools, as Deri himself had, when he was sent to the Ponevezh Yeshiva. To succeed in these institutions, clever Sephardi youths found themselves adopting an Ashkenazi cultural idiom: dressing in the heavy black overcoats of seventeenth-century Poland, speaking Hebrew with Yiddish inflections, and citing mostly European rabbinic sources in their disputation. Very pious Sephardim increasingly had the look and feel of the European ultra-Orthodox. The European cultural hegemony that stained secular culture left no less a mark on religious life in Israel.

But at about the time Deri began to distinguish himself at Porat Yosef, Sephardim started to chafe against this hegemony. Borrowing their name from militant African Americans, a group of young activists calling themselves Black Panthers staged demonstrations protesting the rough conditions in which most Sephardim found themselves: poorer, less educated, and less healthy than their Ashkenazi neighbors. Golda Meir, an Ashkenazi prime minister who grew up in Milwaukee, failed to understand how young men whom Israel had gone to such trouble to absorb could be so ungrateful. In a famous meeting with Black Panther leaders, she lectured like a stern aunt, cluelessly chiding the agitators for their lack of civility and poor grooming. While Deri studied Talmud in Jerusalem, Sephardi dissatisfaction with Israel's "establishment" simmered and increased in volatility. The mid-1970s—the period between the Yom Kippur War and the election of Menachem Begin—was a time of malaise and dissatisfaction, and against this backdrop, Sephardim grew ever more disenchanted. This disenchantment became an electoral asset for Begin, who came to power in 1977 by campaigning against the traditional Ashkenazi elites, who had run the country through the Labor Party without interruption since Israel's establishment (and for the generation before, as well). Begin promised to appoint Sephardim to crucial ministerial positions, and after his election, he did. Begin's opponents accused him of cynically manipulating Sephardi discontent for his own political benefit, but twenty-five years later, there is ample evidence that although Begin appreciated the electoral value of Sephardi rage, he was also himself outraged by the dismissive disregard Sephardim had suffered from the Ashkenazi Left.

The Sephardi challenge to secular Ashkenazi elites had a parallel within religious circles, crystallizing around a single, extraordinary personality, Rabbi Ovadiah Yosef. Yosef was born in Baghdad in 1920 and moved with his parents to Jerusalem when he was four. His intellectual talents were recognized immediately, and he was accepted for study at the same Porat Yosef Yeshiva in which Deri began to study almost half a century later. He demonstrated a prodigious memory, as a child committing whole books of Jewish law to memory. As an adult, his talent for Torah study funded a rabbinic career almost unparalleled in its success. By the age of twenty-four he was appointed a judge in the Sephardi Rabbinical Court of Jerusalem. Two years later, he was elected to head the Cairo Rabbinical Court, and at the same time to serve as deputy chief rabbi of Egypt. Yosef returned after Israel was established, serving on the rabbinical courts of Petach Tikvah and then Jerusalem. In 1965 he was appointed to the Supreme Rabbinical Court of Appeals in Jerusalem, and in 1968 he became the Sephardi chief rabbi of Tel Aviv–Jaffa. In 1970 he was awarded the Israel Prize, the local equivalent of the Nobel Prize, for the corpus of religious books he had written throughout his career (he published his first when he was only eighteen, and by the time he received the prize, his corpus numbered more than thirty volumes, the collective influence of which is unparalleled by a Sephardi rabbi since Yosef Karo wrote the *Shulhan Arukh* in the mid-sixteenth century). In 1973, Yosef became the Sephardi chief rabbi of Israel.

Yosef is widely regarded as the greatest Torah scholar of our age. "No one alive today knows as much [about] rabbinic responsa as he does," said Zvi Zohar, a scholar who follows Yosef's career and its impact. "His knowledge is awesome." This erudition has always had a political agenda, which he described in the introduction to his book *Yabia Omer*: "It is known that the Sephardi chief rabbis before me were subordinated to their colleagues, the Ashkenazi rabbis. And for the sake of peace, they said nothing, but I, who am not subordinate, praise God, will uphold my mission to restore the crown to its old glory."

Throughout his career, Yosef has issued bold rabbinic rulings. In the 1970s, for instance, he ruled that the "Falashas" of Ethiopia ought to be considered fully legitimate Jews, despite the fact that their community had lost contract with the rest of world Jewry before the Talmud was written. His rulings generally share two characteristics. They tend to be more lenient than those of his Ashkenazi ultra-Orthodox colleagues. And they tend to be anchored in centuries-old Sephardi rabbinic precedents. Yosef seeks single-handedly to bring Sephardi traditions front and center, after they had for decades been shunted aside by European rabbis and their Israeli descendants.

Along the way, Yosef met resistance from Ashkenazi rabbis and their disciples, resistance that often translated into slights and humiliations. Yosef's books were ignored in the important Ashkenazi yeshivot of Bnei Brak and Meah Shearim. His erudition was derided as the brilliance of an idiot savant; no one doubted his prodigious memory, but it was dismissed as a parlor trick, unaided by the sort of probing intelligence that would allow Yosef to exploit his miraculous mind. A quip common in the study halls of Bnei Brak described Yosef as "a donkey hauling books." Another had Yosef taking to bed owing to a "computer virus." "The Ashkenazim didn't give him the honor he deserved," said Menachem Friedman, the world's leading authority on the ultra-Orthodox. Even as chief rabbi, Yosef found himself constantly at odds with his Ashkenazi counterpart, Shlomo Goren. The spectacle of the two rabbis bickering embarrassed leaders of the National Religious Party, whose Knesset representatives sponsored a bill that limited the service of both chief rabbis to a single ten-year term. Yosef, who had expected to continue serving as chief rabbi until he was well into his seventies, was angered by the slight, which he took as another instance of Ashkenazi hegemony. Now, more than twenty years later, he is still angry.

Yosef's term as chief rabbi ended in 1983, and when it did, he was anxious to find new ways to challenge entrenched Ashkenazi authority. To do so, he enlisted the help of Aryeh Deri. Early in his tenure as chief rabbi, word had come to Yosef of a brilliant student studying at his alma mater, Porat Yosef, and Yosef hired Deri to tutor his own youngest child in rabbinics. Deri made a powerful impression on the rabbi, who developed paternal affection for the young tutor. Deri also became fast friends with Yosef's eldest son, Rabbi David Yosef. So it was when a group of politicians sought Yosef's help in founding a new Sephardi political party, Deri was among its leaders. The initiative to start a new party had its own proximate causes, reflecting the frustrations of a group of Sephardi activists within the Ashkenazi ultra-Orthodox Agudat Yisrael Party, who found themselves continually marginalized, facing a political glass ceiling, which would prevent them from ever reaching the Knesset. For complicated reasons, the party also had the imprimatur of the most powerful Ashkenazi rabbi, Eliezer Shach, widely recognized as who, like Yosef, saw in Aryeh Deri a competent and, above all, loyal disciple. Yosef correctly saw in the initiative a chance to exact some revenge against the Agudah, the party of his nemesis Shlomo Goren, and also a chance to advance politically the same agenda that he had promoted through his religious rulings. It is no surprise that the new party—Shas—memorialized in its campaign slogan Yosef's goal of "restoring the crown to its old glory."

Deri and Shas were successful. They polled over 63,000 votes in 1984, giving them over 3 percent of the vote and four seats in the Knesset. In the next election, in 1988, they tallied 107,000 votes, for 4.5 percent of the vote and six seats. In 1992 they received 130,000 votes, or 5 percent, retaining their six seats. In 1996, they doubled their vote, receiving 260,000, for almost 9 percent of the vote and ten seats. And in the 1999 parliamentary election, they polled 460,000, which was more than one of every eight votes cast, earning seventeen Knesset seats.* For the first decade and a half of the party's existence, Deri was its undisputed leader, earning himself a reputation as a brilliant political tactician and an administrator of talent unparalleled in Israel. With the exception of brief interludes, Shas has joined the ruling coalition in every government since its founding, a circumstance that allowed Deri to rise through a series of ministerial positions of steadily increasing influence. At first Deri served as the director-general of the Interior Ministry, a subministerial executive appointment, and he squeezed more influence and power than any of his predecessors had. The Interior Ministry controls enormous budgets—all municipal funds pass through the office, for example—and important issues of domestic policy, such as which marriages, divorces, and conversions are recognized by the state. As director-general, Deri increasingly molded Ministry policy. After the 1988 election, Deri was appointed minister of the interior, and his influence, now unchecked, grew geometrically. It was his ability to exploit the powers of his office that ultimately led to Deri's arrest and imprisonment.

Before the arrest occurred, Deri accrued power and influence beyond the well-tended lawns surrounding the Ministry of Interior. The founding of Shas came at an opportune time, as the mid-1980s was a period of political stalemate in Israel. For the first twenty-nine years of the state, the Labor Party was elected and reelected by large margins, as a matter of course. In 1977, Menachem Begin and his Likud Party won a handsome victory, drawing voters disgruntled for various reasons: angry Sephardim, as I've described, and others dismayed by Labor's inept failure to foresee the 1973 war, or by the deep recession that followed the war, or by a series of political scandals involving central Labor Party politicians (including Prime Minister Rabin, whose wife, Leah, was found to have kept foreign currency in a U.S. bank account, which was illegal at the time). Begin's popularity reached its apogee with the signing of the Camp David Peace Accords with Egypt, but in the years that followed, the economy slipped and skirmishes within the ruling coalition grew more frequent and more violent, creating a feeling

---

*In the 2003 parliamentary election, Shas won only eleven seats.

among many voters that government policy had become ad hoc and volatile. Begin's support waned, and ever since, at least until the beginning of the second intifada in September 2000, the strengths of the Left and Right in Israel have been preternaturally balanced. In the past twenty years, the Likud has formed the government four times, Labor twice, and the two have entered a coalition involving rotation of leadership once. The last six elected prime ministers have been Shimon Peres (Labor), Yizhak Shamir (Likud), Yizhak Rabin (Labor), Benjamin Netanyahu (Likud), Ehud Barak (Labor), and Ariel Sharon (Likud); the checkerboard pattern of party affiliations and the fact that no man was elected twice in succession reflect both the volatility of recent Israeli politics and the parity between the parties over the years. This created an opportunity for Shas, which, as it grew in power over the two decades of its existence, increasingly played the role of kingmaker, effectively deciding which of the two large parties would be able to form the coalition.

Shas played this role in part because it conferred enormous political leverage, which it used to advance its own pork-barrel projects. But Shas played this role also because its own answer to the question that divided Labor and Likud—should lands on the West Bank and Gaza Strip be ceded to Palestinians, and if so, which lands and under what circumstances?—is uncertain. Polls show that most of Shas's voters share the Likud's skepticism about whether Palestinian leaders can be trusted to honor political agreements, and the Likud's reticence to relinquish occupied territories. Ovadiah Yosef, however, may be of a more conciliatory nature, more consistent with Labor than Likud views. In 1989, he told friends of a dream he'd had: dozens of missiles raining down on Israel, some with chemical warheads, some nuclear, until the land churned like Sodom and Gomorrah. Not long thereafter, he spoke at a Jerusalem symposium alongside Yizhak Rabin, giving what seemed to be a Halakhic ruling in favor of ceding territories: "To hold or conquer territories in the Land of Israel by force, in our time, against the will of the nations of the world, is a sin. If we can give back the territories and thereby avoid war and bloodshed, we are obligated to do so under [the religious injunction of] saving life."

Yosef later told reporters that he meant this ruling hypothetically. As matters stand now, he said, returning territories would not avoid war or bloodshed. Given the unreliable nature of Yassir Arafat and his colleagues, ceding territory would most likely accelerate war, thereby increasing bloodshed. This clarification still left no doubt that when the conditions *were* right, Yosef could earnestly instruct Shas to join a Labor coalition. This fact gave Shas the bona fides to be what might be called "authentically opportunistic" during coalition negotiations—ingenuously telling each side that if the conditions of Shas were not met, the party could comfortably join forces with the other camp. This trait was never more evident than in 1990, when Shimon Peres tried to topple Yizhak Shamir in a sort of bloodless parliamentary coup.

In the 1988 election, the Likud won forty seats to Labor's thirty-nine. A plurality of smaller parties supported the Likud, so it was possible for Yizhak Shamir to form a narrow, right-wing coalition. Shamir believed that such a coalition would give too much power to small parties, allowing their influence on policy and budgets to be far greater than their size justified. To diminish the influence of these small parties, Shamir invited the Labor Party to join in a coalition of national unity. Such a coalition would have the further advantage of dampening criticism within Israel of uncompromising repression of Palestinian demonstrators in the first intifada. By including Labor in the coalition, Shamir could reappoint Yizhak Rabin to be defense minister, an arrangement that deflected from Shamir and the Likud criticism concerning the brutality of the IDF in the occupied territories. (Rabin had issued orders that soldiers "break the arms and legs" of Palestinians caught throwing stones at soldiers, an edict Shamir supported, surely relieved that it did not originate within his party.) Peres tried to persuade Shamir that a feature of the coalition should be rotation of prime ministers at midterm, as Peres and Shamir had done during the prior term; Shamir, knowing that he had the seats to form a narrow coalition and that Peres did not, rejected Peres's proposal. The Likud would be the senior partner in the coalition, and Shamir would remain prime minister throughout the term. Labor took the deal, but Peres felt that he and his party had been slighted.

This fact was not lost on Deri, and in 1989 when Peres's closest confidant, Yossi Beilin, asked Deri what he thought of the national unity government, his reply was: "I don't understand you in Labor. Why don't you topple the government? You could form your own narrow government." Deri figured that if Labor could persuade the Ashkenazi ultra-Orthodox parties and the nonrejectionist Arab parties to support them, then they could create a coalition of sixty-two even without Shas. Shas would then join the coalition, giving it a comfortable majority of sixty-eight, again with fifty-two seats in the opposition. Deri told Beilin that Shas would not take part in toppling the government, but assured him that it would join the new government once it was formed. The idea appealed to Peres (who had formulated a similar plan himself) and to the young Turks in the Labor Party, and secret negotiations began. Several months of palace intrigue ensued, culminating in agreements between Peres and the Ashkenazi Haredim, the Arab parties, and the small liberal and leftist parties. A vote of no confidence toppled the Shamir government, and Peres was given thirty days to present his new coalition.

Almost as soon as the government fell, doubts arose about whether the ultra-Orthodox would honor the agreements hammered out with Labor. Posters appeared announcing a crucial speech by Eliezer Shach at Tel Aviv's Yad Eliahu Stadium. On the evening of March 28, 1990, the stadium filled to overflowing; the sea of black overcoats and black hats creating an odd spectacle. Shach swallowed his words and drifted from Hebrew to Yiddish, masking the lucidity of his speech. To most secular Israelis who watched the speech broadcast live, broadcast during prime time on television, the aged sage sounded unintelligible, perhaps senile. Only later, when the speech was rebroadcast with Hebrew subtitles, did it make its full impression. Shach said, among other things:

> We live in a terrible, awful time. Each day is more cursed than the last. All the wars and upheavals did not begin today. It began before World War I, and to this day calm has not been restored, and only the Holy One, Blessed be He, knows what is next. All of the nations are getting stronger, each with weapons in hand, and the weaponry grows more and more sophisticated. . . .
>
> The Jew, though, cannot be destroyed. They'll kill him, but his sons will remain loyal to the Torah. As long as Jews do not cut themselves off from their heritage . . . they will live. . . .
>
> What is special about a Jew who learns secular subjects and foreign languages? Don't the gentiles know these things as well? . . . There are kibbutzim that don't know what Yom Kippur is, or the Sabbath, or the ritual bath. They know nothing, and they raise [unkosher] rabbits and pigs. Do they have any tie to their forefathers? How will this generation survive, [with sons] seeing their father eat on Yom Kipper?
>
> We need to cut our ties with parties that have no tie to Judaism. . . . They cut themselves off from their forefathers, and what is the pedigree of someone with no past?

Shach's broad condemnation of secular culture was greeted with a thunderous standing ovation in the basketball stadium, and with rage by many secular viewers in their living rooms. Some weeks later, at the end of his thirty-day negotiation period, Peres announced that he had signed agreements in hand, and that he was ready to present his new government of sixty-one seats. One of the Agudat Yisrael Knesset members, Avraham Vertiger, did not arrive. Earlier he had threatened to resign from the Knesset rather than support a Peres government; had he done so, he would have been replaced by another representative who doubtless would have voted for the new coalition. But he did not resign; he disappeared. Without his vote, Peres could not form the government, and no one could find Vertiger. He was later located at a rest home, where he issued a statement that he had decided to neither resign nor support the government, a position that scuttled Peres's hopes of becoming prime minister. Vertiger reported that while he was wavering, he had received phone calls from both Shach and the Lubavitcher rebbe in Brooklyn, who together persuaded him to destroy the Peres initiative.

Peres tried to persuade Deri to add Shas support to his fledgling coalition, but failed. Rabin disparaged Peres's efforts as a *"targil masriah,"* literally, a "stinking stratagem," by which he meant a loathsome bit of political manipulation. The epithet stuck, and Peres's career never fully recovered. It may be that Deri's career too was destroyed by his part in this bizarre political sideshow. For only weeks later, after Shamir reconstituted his coalition, the police began to investigate Deri on charges of corruption. Deri insists that the investigation, trial, and imprisonment are all retribution for his part in Peres's stratagem. There is some support for this version of events, according to journalist Yoel Nir, author of *Aryeh Deri: The Rise, the Crisis, the Pain.*

Nir reported that more than six months before the collapse of Peres's stratagem, on September 14, 1989, David Bar-Yehudah, one of the intelligence officers for the northern branch of the National Fraud Investigation Unit, filed paperwork concerning a conversation he had had a week and a half earlier. In the "concerning" space, he wrote "A Government Minister—Suspicion of Fraud and Foreign Currency Crimes." He elaborated in the report:

> Minister of the Interior Aryeh Deri stole moneys estimated in the millions of shekels from the Shas movement and from contributions solicited abroad for the benefit of Shas. He deposits the moneys in Swiss accounts, using a courier who was a Shas operative during the last election, a resident of Atlit named Yakov Shmuelevitz. . . . Shmuelevitz even said that in his possession are many tapes on which he recorded the minister issuing directions for depositing the moneys in Switzerland, which he is saving for when a need arises, and which he will then publicize in the press.

It was only in April, after the failed coalition stratagem, and after Shamir appointed as minister of police Ronni Miloh, a long-standing enemy of Deri, that the police followed up on this dramatic report, a fact that supports suspicions that the investigation had political motivations. When detectives visited Shmuelevitz in April, he refused to cooperate. At roughly the

same time, police received reports of alleged unlawful transfers of funds
from the Ministry of the Interior to religious institutions in Hadera, transfers via the city's municipal coffers. Reports of similar transfers to Shas institutions in Zikhron Yaakov soon followed. These allegations would
multiply, but the basic structure of the case against Deri was already becoming clear. It had two elements, private embezzlement and public misalloca-
tion of funds.

From this moment, events unfolded with the insistence of Greek tragedy.
In June 1990, the criminal investigation of Aryeh Deri was officially opened.
The investigation focused on several alleged crimes. Police suspected that
Deri had accepted bribes and kickbacks, funneling government funds to a
nonprofit association named Lev Banim, and receiving a portion of the
funds back in payments masked as fees for fictitious services. Police also suspected that Deri unlawfully diverted Ministry of Interior funds to a great
number of institutions affiliated with Shas. One year after the investigation
was formally launched, Comptroller Miriam Ben Porat, issued a report detailing these illegal transfers and describing the method by which these funds
were laundered through municipal budgets provided by the ministry. The
report alleged that Deri strong-armed mayors into providing extra cash to
Shas institutions, sometimes threatening to withhold other crucial budgets if
the mayors refused. Two years later, in June 1993, Yosef Harish, Israel's attorney general, issued a draft indictment; in August, the Supreme Court ruled
that Prime Minister Rabin was obliged to sack Deri as interior minister.

In December 1993, a trial finally began in a Jerusalem district court, limited in scope to the personal corruption charges of taking bribes and peddling influence in connection with Lev Banim. For more than two years the
prosecution laid out its case, in the process calling 117 witnesses, of whom a
now-cooperative Shmuelevitz was the most valuable. Deri's attorneys argued that he had never taken bribes, and that the large sums of money in his
bank accounts and his luxury duplex (with a Jacuzzi and $30,000 in im-
ported plumbing fixtures alone), had been given to him by Isser and Esther
Werderber, the adoptive American parents of his wife, Yaffa, who were
Holocaust survivors. Isser, a leather cutter by profession, died before Deri's
investigation, but at the start of the trial, Esther Werderber was alive in New
York. (She was stuck by an automobile and killed in June 1991, and some
idly speculated that she was murdered by Deri's goons.) Before she died,
one of Deri's codefendants, Shmuel Weinberg, traveled to New York and
surreptitiously taped a conversation in Yiddish that he hoped would support Deri's version of events, thereby exonerating Deri and Weinberg both.
But on the tape, which Deri—who does not understand Yiddish—supplied

to the police, Werderber complained that Deri pressured her to sign a false affidavit. "They want me to go to jail for Aryeh . . . but he did it, and he'll pay for it."

Finally, in April 1999, a three-judge panel found Deri guilty of most of the charges against him, arguing in their decision that Deri's crimes represented "not a single failure of a young man new to the gratifications of government, but rather an individual who insistently pursued a lifestyle grounded in graft." He was sentenced to four years of prison and ordered to pay a fine of $155,000. Upon appeal, the Supreme Court reduced Deri's sentence to three years, and the fine to $60,000, while confirming most of the guilty findings of the lower court. A council of rabbis that considered his case reached a different conclusion, finding Deri innocent according to Halakha. That symbolic ruling notwithstanding, on September 3, 2000, Deri entered the religious wing of the Maasiyahu Prison in Ramle to begin serving his sentence, the first minister in Israel's history to be sent to prison.

On the day of Deri's incarceration, I joined 50,000 ultra-Orthodox Jews baking in the 100-degree Mediterranean sun in the prison parking lot. The scene was like Altamont: festive with a worrying edge of simmering violence. A band played crackling rock 'n' roll between speeches by rabbis. During one slapping bass solo, the crowd raised its arms and swayed back and forth. In the crowd were ultra-Orthodox Jews with Walkmen and Discmen. While jostling to see the stage, I overheard two teens with earlocks engaged in learned disputation about how to maximize the efficiency of Windows 2000. A billboard on the side of a truck at the entrance to the prison read: "They hate us. They hate us in the Knesset. They hate us in the Universities. They hate us in museums. They hate us in the street." Protesters pinned yellow stars to their black coats, likening themselves to Holocaust victims. Others wore stickers showing Deri's face, with the slogan, "We Won't Forget, We Won't Forgive." Another had the slogan, "Aryeh Deri: Prisoner of Zion," what the Jews imprisoned by the Soviets for applying for an exit visa to Israel were called. Rabbi David Yosef, the son of Ovadiah Yosef, took to the dais to lead the crowd in chanting, "Police state! Police state!" Another rabbi likened the day's rally to "an ultra-Orthodox Bastille Day." Popular singer Benny Elbas sang the song he had written about Deri's case, which had become a hit on pirate radio stations: "He's Innocent."

Overhead, a man with an oversized motorized fan strapped to his back piloted a paraglider in wide circles over the crowd. On his parachute in huge black letters were the words, *"Ganav Mispar Ehad"* (Number-One Thief). People in the crowd booed loudly when he first passed, and at the edge of the crowd young boys ineffectively threw stones. My mind wandered and I found myself worrying, vaguely, that if the pilot encountered technical problems and was forced to land, he would be mauled by the mob. I imagined the sputtering of the lawn-mower engine, the stuttering of the fan, and the panicked recognition on the pilot's face as he frantically looked for an open spot to land his contraption. Many years ago, I saw such a crash, and I recalled it vividly. I had gone to see the Blue Angels perform in a Washington air show. During a vertical ascent one of the jets tumbled out of formation. At first I thought it was part of the show, but as the plane tumbled end over end, it became clear that the machine had failed. The crowd stood strangely silent. The jet fell out of sight on the horizon, and it was replaced by a small mound of fire, and then a coil of smoke. For a time, no one spoke. I imagined a similar scene, with the paraglider spiraling toward the ground, crumbling into a lump on contact. I imagined someone shouting, "He's over there," and then the angry crowd rushing toward him. From the stage, Rabbi Uri Zohar tried to divert the crowd's attention from the paraglider, saying that it didn't matter what the man in the contraption thought, millions of people knew that Deri was innocent. "Let him be," Zohar told the crowd, "let him be."

Dozens fainted in the heat before Ovadiah Yosef and Aryeh Deri showed up. When Deri finally took the stage, the applause continued for long minutes. Deri cried as he described taking his daughter to first grade that morning on the way to prison. But he was not regretful. "These bars will not keep us apart. My heart will be with you and your hearts with me." I heard sobs in the tightly packed crowd. When he was finished, Aryeh Deri picked up a Torah scroll and walked toward the gates of the prison, where the warden met him with a phalanx of guards and showed him in. It was a strange, affecting moment.

Aryeh Deri is, for many people, an embodiment of what is wrong with ultra-Orthodox politics and politicians. He is personally corrupt, in their view, taking kickbacks and bribes. He is a gifted practitioner of ministerial corruption, illegally diverting government money to party institutions. And he dabbles in electoral corruption, toppling governments to advance career and party. Even critics realize that these forms of corruption are not unique to Haredim. They recur in every democracy. Each of Deri's putative crimes has precedents in Israeli politics, as Deri's supporters often point out, though there may be no prior cases of anyone as *comprehensively* corrupt as Deri. What makes ultra-Orthodox corruption of the Deri sort so infuriating, according to critics, and so dangerous, is that among the ultra-Orthodox it goes unrecognized as crime. David Yosef, quaking with emotion at the dais in front of Maasiyahu, pointed to a police helicopter hovering above and shouted into the microphone, "Just one of these helicopters, just one, costs

Rabbi Aryeh Deri addressing crowd outside the Maasiyahu Prison on September 3, 2000, immediately before entering to begin his sentence. On the left is his mentor, Rabbi Ovadiah Yosef. © Reuters.

more than all that Aryeh Deri *didn't* take." The strained sentence structure captured two ideas at once. Deri is innocent. And even if he is guilty, his crime is negligible. This second idea, that even if he did it, he should be forgiven, is what most infuriates some secular Israelis. The ultra-Orthodox do not seem to understand that crimes like those attributed to Deri *matter*.

Critics break down this failure to appreciate the gravity of corruption into two more-primitive emotions. The first is contempt for secular laws. Jerusalem rabbi and yeshiva rector Eliyahu Bar-Shalom captured a popular sentiment when he spoke to a reporter just after Deri was sentenced:

God in Heaven! Where did he funnel the money? Into his own pocket? Stupid fools! He funneled it to the Torah world, and it is only thanks to him that we now have 270 ritual baths and 84,000 yeshiva students.

You should know that the people hate judges and hate the media and have no faith in them, because they draw from a world of gentile values that has no correlation to the values of Judaism. . . . How can we believe in a true justice that is based on the teachings of gentile judges and not our own sources?

Bar-Shalom is a community leader and, in his circles, something of a public intellectual, so it is worth pondering why he thinks so little of the laws of the State of Israel. His sympathy for Deri's diverting government funds to Shas institutions suggests, first, a rejection of the bureaucratic formalism that characterizes the rule of law. Laws are made to be broken, Bar-Shalom seemed to be saying, at least when breaking the law will produce a compelling good, like increasing the annual index of Talmud pages studied or mitzvot performed. There are values more important than rigid adherence to law and, as Bar-Shalom seemed to see it, laws must be judged on a case-by-case basis according to these higher values. But Bar-Shalom went further, associating legal formalism with "the teachings of gentile judges," which are inferior to the teachings of "our own [Jewish] sources." It may or may not be an overinterpretation to conclude that, for Bar-Shalom, secular laws are a continuation of gentile hegemony and oppression. Secular law, to Bar-Shalom, is anti-Semitism carried out by other means. This view explains why Deri is a hero, not despite breaking the law, but *because* he broke the law.

Given their dim view of the law, it is perhaps inevitable that many Haredim disparage the courts that enforce it, especially Israel's High Court of Justice, or Supreme Court. Perhaps the biggest public demonstration ever held in Israel—by some estimates 20 percent larger than the Tel Aviv rally protesting the massacres in Sabra and Shatilla—was an ultra-Orthodox protest against

Rabbi Ovadiah Yosef beheading Supreme Court Chief Justice Aharon Barak on the tablets of the Ten Commandments. "The Rule of Law" is written above Barak's back. Cartoon by Yakov Shiloh, first appeared in *Ma'ariv;* reprinted with permission of *Shpitz,* journal of the Israel Cartoonists Union.

the Supreme Court. On Sunday, February 14, 1999, between a quarter million (police estimate) and a half million (organizers' estimate) Haredim gathered in the quad dividing Jerusalem's old bus station from the convention center. Film taken from helicopters showed an impressive sight: a great stain of black eclipsing the huge white concourse of Jerusalem stone. A two-story high banner hung on a building overlooking the quad, reading "Massive Prayer Gathering in the Face of Judicial Assaults on the Jewish Faith." Hundreds of buses, from dozens of towns around the country, clotted the shoulders of streets for miles around.

The immediate cause for the rally was a ruling handed down by the Supreme Court two weeks earlier, on January 28, ordering Yizhak Ralbag to convene the Jerusalem Religious Council, which he chairs. Conservative and Reform Jews had won council seats during the past election and Ralbag, who believes that the stringently observant should alone determine religious policy in the city, swore to fight their installation. At first he continued to convene the council without inviting the Conservative and Reform representatives, but their attorneys petitioned the Supreme Court, which instructed Ralbag to invite them to all meetings. In response, Ralbag decided that he would no longer call council meetings at all, instead controlling religious affairs through administrative orders issued after informal consultation with his ultra-Orthodox colleagues, thereby neutralizing the Conservative and Reform representatives. The new Supreme Court ruling, however, made this impossible. It also levied a fine of 30,000 shekels on Ralbag for having failed to comply with the spirit of the court's earlier ruling.

Ralbag's run-in with the courts sparked Haredi protests, but the anger behind them had been building for some time. In the three years prior to the ruling, the courts had issued many rulings viewed as hostile by Haredim. Two months before the rally, on December 9, 1998, eleven Supreme Court justices decided unanimously that the traditional draft deferral granted to yeshiva students was illegal. One month before that, on November 3, 1998, the Supreme Court ordered the minister of religious affairs to install a woman who had been elected to the Petach Tikvah religious council. Two months earlier, the Supreme Court overturned the decision of a rabbinic court ordering a secular woman to honor her ex-husband's wish to send their son to religious schools. Days earlier, the Supreme Court rescinded a decision by the mayor of Modiin to turn a secular nursery school over to Shas. Some months before that, the Supreme Court had overturned the appointment of several Shas volunteers to local councils in Bedouin settlements in the Negev Desert. Before that, the Supreme Court had ordered the Jerusalem police to allow secular protesters to march on the embattled Bar Ilan Street on Saturday, to protest Haredi efforts to close the street on the Sabbath. Not long before that, the Supreme Court had stripped rabbinic courts of the right to excommunicate or ostracize.

The Supreme Court's rulings did not always go against the wishes of the rabbis. In its final ruling in 1996, the court rejected a petition to overturn a law newly passed in the Knesset banning importation of unkosher frozen meat. Secular activists turned to the Supreme Court in efforts to sanction the deputy mayor of Jerusalem, Hayim Miller, when he called the Israeli flag "a stick attached to a blue and white rag," but the justices refused. There are other examples as well. Still, as Haredim see it, the Supreme Court frustrates their wishes far more often than it facilitates them. If one tallies the score-card, one sees that on a purely numerical basis, this perception is correct.

The cumulative disappointment with the rulings of the courts was a large part of ultra-Orthodox anger at the courts, but there was more to it as well. Some Haredim view the judicial system as a club that won't have them, and where they are viewed as primitives and pariahs. In 1998, Beer Sheva Magistrate's Court Judge Oded Al-Yagon, who, while making a toast at a retire-ment party for another judge, called Haredim "mutated lice [who] are huge, as big as human creatures, whose greed knows no bounds and . . . look like a cross between a poisonous snake and a tiger with long claws and sharp jaws . . . for whom the court represents a barrier to their tyrannical takeover of all the government's systems and indeed of the entire public."

Though it is difficult to overlook the ugliness of Al-Yagon's imagery, the remarks themselves may not be worthy of great attention. Al-Yagon is an equal-opportunity offender. His toast lambasted a sampling of "parasites"; not just the ultra-Orthodox but also "the classic criminal public, and the big organizations that regularly need the services of the Courts," by which he meant lawyers. A year after labeling these groups and the ultra-Orthodox "lice," he offended the disabled by suggesting that when a lawyer with a bum leg did not show up to a trial moved to a third-floor hearing room with no elevator access, he was "using his disability" to weasel a con-tinuance. Moreover, although some of his colleagues defended Al-Yagon's remarks, most registered disapproval. But Al-Yagon's remarks were re-ported repeatedly in the ultra-Orthodox press, and to this day they turn up in editorials about the courts. In part, that is because the remarks are ex-treme and dramatically, if somewhat speciously, illustrate the point that courts may be biased against the ultra-Orthodox. But the remarks resur-face frequently, I think, also because they reflect what many Haredim take to be a fundamental truth about the legal system in Israel, that it is run by people with an immoderate and irrational dislike for the ultra-Orthodox, and that this sentiment influences rulings. As they see it, the difference be-tween Al-Yagon and, say, Aharon Barak, the chief justice of the Supreme Court, is only that Al-Yagon in an unguarded moment said what both men, and most of their colleagues, believe all the time: that the ultra-Orthodox are an enemy, and that the courts must fight them energetically and resourcefully. And it was this feeling, that the courts had declared war on their way of life, that brought hundreds of thousands of ultra-Orthodox to the concourse near the old bus station in protest.

"Mass Prayer Rally," February 14, 1999, the largest demonstration ever staged in Jerusalem. The protestors claimed ill-treatment of the ultra-Orthodox by the Supreme Court. The signs read, "End the Destruction of Judaism." © Reuters.

The rally was a call to arms. Menachem Porush, the Haredi Knesset member who organized it, said as much from the dais: "If after this demonstration, the High Court is not convinced to cease involvement in church-state issues, there will be war. The people who were here are ready to invade any space." Dudi Silberschlag, the official spokesman for the event, told journalists that they were witnessing the beginning of a battle between the ultra-Orthodox and the courts, and in the end only one combatant would be standing. Silberschlag was confident that the ultra-Orthodox would prevail: "We *will* undermine the legitimacy of the Supreme Court." David Yosef said that, in general, secular "judges are wicked and because of them all suffering comes into the world," and that, in particular, Aharon Barak is an "enemy of the Jews." (This echoed the sentiments of David's father, Ovadiah Yosef, who said in a sermon before the rally that Supreme Court justices were "slaves, who now rule us" and that they were "worse than a tribunal of gentiles.") At the end of the rally a shofar was sounded slowly and mournfully, seven times; the wail of the ram's horn, seven times, being the biblical symbol for a declaration of war, deployed by Joshua before he conquered Jericho.

For secular Israelis watching the rally simulcast on TV, the symbol was clear; many of them also saw in the Haredi rally a declaration of war. Five hundred yards away, in Sacher Park, fifty thousand secular Jews gathered for their own counterprotest. Yossi Sarid, the head of the leftist Meretz Party, described the significance of the day much as Rabbi Porush did some blocks away: "This is a war! You must understand, this is a war, a war over the character of our beloved country. This is the most important demonstration in the history of the state." Then Justice Minister Tzahi Hanegbi said from the podium, "There is no way that the majority of the citizens of Israel will let the Haredim destroy the High Court of Justice. No way." Posters juxtaposed photographs of Deri and Ayatollah Khomeini, with the legend, "Can you spot the difference?" Joseph Edrey, the dean of Haifa University's Law School, told reporters that evening that the country now faced "a national emergency, . . . an attack by an anti-Zionist entity that opposes the existence of a democratic state. This is . . . a threat to the existence of the state of Israel."

Edrey's alarm is understandable. As a law school dean, he has made the rule of law his profession and his calling, and to see the rule of law dispar-

Secular counterrally, February 14, 1999, protesting ultra-Orthodox demonstration against the Supreme Court. One of the signs reads, "Eating Pork Enhances Intelligence." © Reuters.

aged proudly and publicly by so many people must certainly be unnerving. Edrey's alarm is not simply that of a law school dean, however; it is just as much the alarm of a citizen who sees in the courts the glue that holds together a fractious society. The attack on the courts amounts to a threat to Israel's existence, because if a very large minority stopped obeying court rulings, it is easy to imagine that Israel's fragile civil society would disintegrate. Ralbag's refusing to convene the Jerusalem Religious Council may be a rarefied case of civil disobedience; if the council never met again, it would not have much impact on most Israelis' lives. But what if Haredim brushed off more important laws?

This question highlights both the strengths and weaknesses of Edrey's line of reasoning. Its strength lies principally in pointing out the crucial role that courts play in creating social stability. Haredi attacks on the courts and on judges (including the dozens of credible death threats that Chief Justice Barak received at the time of the rally from ultra-Orthodox thugs) are an expression of more than dissatisfaction with a single government institution. Attacks on the courts amount to an attack of the very notion of government. When Silberschlag threatened to "undermine the legitimacy of the Supreme Court," he was really threatening to undermine the legitimacy of democratic rule in toto. The scope of the threat is breathtakingly broad, as Edrey implied.

At the same time, this line of reasoning overlooks two important facts. One is the great power of the courts. Silberschlag blusters about undermining their legitimacy, but in the context of modern Israel it is hard to imagine just how this might be accomplished. Some Haredi leaders threaten to use well-worn civil disobedience strategies—tax strikes and the like—and others encourage their constituents to use only the alternative rabbinic legal system. Neither of these strategies threaten the hegemony of the civil courts, however. The courts have at their disposal a variety of techniques for ensuring that their judgments are honored: police enforcement, for example, and the ability to delay or curtail the disbursement of government funds. Though Haredim may delegitimate the courts in their own minds and in their communities' public opinion, that is a far cry from diminishing the clout of the courts.

The second fact missing from Edrey's analysis is that Haredim, after all, do seem to heed the courts. For all their bravado, the organizers of the rally collected in small coins the sum Ralbag was ordered to pay in fines for his noncompliance to the earlier court ruling. Filling bag after bag with pounds of coins was an act of political theatrics so elegant that many pundits seemed to miss the fact that the organizers had publicly accepted the verdict of the court. The same has been true of almost every ruling that went against the ultra-Orthodox (save isolated bits of civil disobedience like Ral-bag's refusal to convene his council). While ultra-Orthodox leaders regularly bluster against the courts, they comply with the courts rulings. Even more telling, they regularly turn to the courts when they think that doing so will protect their interests. The ultra-Orthodox oppose the courts de jure, but they do not de facto.

It is possible, then, to interpret the rally against the courts as a complicated bit of theater: at once a sign of alienation from the courts and of commitment to them. To understand this ambivalent attitude, it helps to take seriously the comparison drawn by Ovadiah Yosef and many other ultra-Orthodox leaders between secular Israel courts and gentile courts. Canvass Jewish history, and one will find many examples of Jewish frustration with non-Jewish courts, of attempts to avoid non-Jewish courts, and especially of anguish at the unfairness of non-Jewish courts. One will find few, if any, examples of Jews circumventing non-Jewish courts. A Talmudic dictum states that *dina de-malkhuta dina* (the law of the land is the law). This dictum, by and large, describes ultra-Orthodox relations to Israel's courts, just as it described traditional Jewish relations to Christian and secular courts in Europe through much of the last millennium. Viewed from a helicopter hovering near the old bus station on February 14, 1999, the ultra-Orthodox seemed like a mob ready to storm the courts. (The threat was taken seriously by the police, which posted hundreds of officers, armed with batons, around the entire perimeter of the new Supreme Court building on the day of the rally to protect it, while sharpshooters lay waiting on the rooftops and helicopters circled above. Only a dozen or so protestors arrived, and these were noisy but not violent.) However, what is most remarkable about this group is not their volatility, but their fealty to an institution that they find is at odds with much of what they believe, and that they see as a threat to their way of life.

Uri Regev, a gifted and winning Reform rabbi and lawyer, founder and head of the Israel Religious Action Center, told me the following story about Haredim and the courts:

Professor Joyce Brenner was the Reform candidate to join the Netanya Religious Council. The Supreme Court instructed that she be appointed, and the minister of religion then was Eli Suissa of Shas. Eli Suissa was interviewed, and he said with candor, "I have a dilemma. On the one hand, the court tells me to appoint her, and on the other hand, my rabbi tells me not to appoint her." Then he said, "In this dilemma, it's obvious to me whom I'm going to obey." What happened was, the court got tired of waiting, and issued an order that by such and such date, Brenner had to be appointed. The date grows closer, but he doesn't appoint her. Now this was near the end of Netanyahu's term as prime minister, and finally, if you check the records, you'll find this unprecedented anomaly. A few days before the court's deadline, Netanyahu officially assumed the position of minister of religion. And in those few days that he is minister of religion, *he* issues the appointment. After that he hands the authority on. . . . A government minister refusing to obey a judicial ruling, and no one is shocked. He doesn't accept the law, or at least does not accept that he, as a government minister, must obey it. Now, his worldview isn't one that I identify with, but it's a plausible worldview, it's got its rationale, its logic. But not in the government. Not in the Knesset. But this is a reality that has so twisted the rule of law that nobody even notices that something is wrong.

But this anecdote can properly be interpreted two ways. It can be seen, as Regev sees it, as a token of the alarming fact that for many Haredim, rabbis trump even Supreme Court justices. But it can also be seen as a token of the reassuring fact that Haredim find formalisms allowing the justices' instructions to be followed, without the rabbi's instructions being ignored. At the end of the day, the will of the courts was done, and with a nod and wink, it was Eli Suissa who saw to it. Rebellion against the rule of law? Hardly.

The fealty of the ultra-Orthodox to the secular courts is more impressive still, given that their criticisms of the courts are not entirely without foundation. Recently, these criticisms have been given their most articulate expression by an unlikely ally, Ruth Gavison. Gavison defies easy characterization, though her bona fides are easy to list. She was born in 1945, and by the time she was twenty-five she had completed at the Hebrew University a joint degree in philosophy and economics, alongside a law degree (which she finished first in her class), whereupon she clerked for Israeli Supreme Court Justice B. Halevi. At thirty she received her doctorate from Oxford. Ever since, she has taught law at the Hebrew University, spending sabbaticals at such institutions as Yale, University of Southern California, and Princeton. Until 1999 she served as the president of the Association for Civil Rights in Israel, and she now serves as a senior fellow of the Israel Democracy Institute. She appears frequently on television and radio and is perhaps the country's most famous legal gadfly. If her opinions have anything in common, it is that they are in equal measure brilliant and unconventional. But what sets her apart from other local pundits is her insistent decency. Now in her late fifties, her pinched demeanor has begun to grow grandmotherly, she speaks calmly and quietly, and even when she criticizes, she does so with a this-is-for-your-own-good earnestness that is disarming and eccentric in Israel's generally aggressive culture of public debate.

In recent lectures and interviews, Gavison has said that the ultra-Orthodox have three important, and substantially correct, criticisms of the courts. Haredim are right, in her view, when they criticize the Supreme Court as too activist. Chief Justice Barak once said in a lecture that, in his view, "everything is judgeable," meaning that there are no issues that are a priori beyond the jurisdiction of the courts. Gavison rejects this expansive description of the court's jurisdiction, telling journalist Ari Shavit of *Ha'aretz:*

> I think it is proper for the court to give expression to our common values, such as the basic human rights. But I do not think it is right for the court to make use of its power to give priority to the values of one group in society at the expense of the values held by other groups. I do not think it is right for the court to decide in favor of Westernism and against traditionalism; or in favor of modernity and individualism and against communitarianism. I find that very problematic.
>
> I also do not think that it is the court's role to be the supreme moral arbiter of society. That was not why it was appointed, and it is also unclear that it has the necessary skills for that. . . . There is nothing in [judges'] training that affords them the right, the authority, or the ability to determine moral norms, to be the teachers of the generation. . . . There are many people in this country for whom Ovadiah Yosef is the supreme moral authority and for whom the Halakha is the appropriate supralegal authority. The court should not ignore them. The court should not compete with Rabbi Yosef for their hearts.

Gavison also believes that the courts create the impression that they selectively enforce the law, even though this impression is not fully accurate:

> Here the feeling is that the [legal] system is not blind, and that it is protecting itself. After all, it is unconscionable that on the one hand [judges] will condemn conflicts of interest in the political system, but on the other hand will say that it is perfectly all right to have police officers investigate their [own] friends or enemies. It cannot be that they should tell us that when someone wants to appoint an attorney general and talks it over with his friends, that constitutes corruption of the system, whereas when someone wants to investigate an enemy of his and tells a friend about it, that is fine. That is a double standard which is intolerable.

Haredim are exquisitely sensitive to this sort of double standard. As Gavison sees it, the great success of Shas in the 1999 election was the result, more than anything else, of a feeling among voters that Deri was being shafted by the courts. It resulted, in Gavison's view, "from the feeling that at the same time as resources were being allocated to investigate the Deri affair, an indulgence that is difficult to explain is shown toward information which, prima facie, incriminates people who hold positions of equal importance regarding actions that are no less serious, and perhaps more so."

Gavison may have been referring to Israel's former president, Ezer Weizman. Weizman had been a public figure since his uncle, Chaim Weizmann, became the nation's first president in 1948. After serving in the Royal Air Force during World War II, Weizman returned to Palestine to help found the "Air Service" of the Haganah fighting brigade. He commanded a fighter squadron during the War of Independence, ten years later becoming the commanding officer of the air force. By the time of the Six-Day War, he had become the chief of operations of the general staff, and soon thereafter, deputy chief of staff. In 1969, he left the army a major-general, turning to politics. In 1977, he managed the campaign that brought Begin to power; Begin, repaying the favor, appointed him defense minister. He helped negotiate the Camp David Peace Accords with Egypt, where he remains highly regarded, alone among Israelis, to this day.

After a break of some years, Weizman returned to politics in the mid-1980s, assuming various cabinet posts. In 1993, he was elected the seventh president of Israel. Throughout his career, Weizman built a reputation for unreflective honesty; he seemed to say whatever came into his head, a trait that gave him an appealing air of guilelessness. As president, he seemed to glide like Mr. Magoo from faux pas to faux pas, all the time comically unaware. (While touring a shelter for battered women, he admitted that now and then he has an urge to give his wife a slap, but prided himself on not surrendering to these urges.)

In January 2000, just as Deri's appeals were being heard by the courts, Channel Two television news reported that Weizman had in 1983 and 1984 received $50,000 payments from a reclusive French businessman, Edoard Saroussi, ostensibly for serving as an adviser to the latter's textile company. Saroussi also gave Weizman cash gifts amounting to $313,000 between 1987 and 1993, as well as a car. Saroussi also gave $100,000 and a car to Weizman's daughter. Weizman admitted receiving the money, but characterized it as a "gift from an old friend." Police, however, found evidence that during the years Saroussi gave the gifts, he also sought Weizman's help in advancing Saroussi's business interests in Israel. Not long before Deri started serving his sentence, police recommended that no criminal charges be brought against Weizman. There was evidence that Weizman had committed fraud and breach of trust, police sources said, but the statute of limitations on these crimes had already lapsed. The police further said that Weizman had apparently evaded paying taxes on the gifts, but this may have resulted from a failure to understand the tax code, rather than an effort to defraud the tax authority. Weizman resigned in shame, a sad end to a charmed career. But as Deri followers were quick to note, he got to return to his villa in the seaside resort of Caesarea at the same time that Deri, accused of having pocketed a smaller sum, was on his way to jail. To most ultra-Orthodox Jews (and to most Sephardim) this represented a clear double standard.

And Weizman was not alone. During the long years of Deri's trial, almost a dozen secular politicians were indicted for corruption and betrayal of public trust, but almost none were convicted. The list includes Jerusalem Mayor Ehud Olmert (cleared of having run fictitious books in his Likud campaign), MK Meir Shitrit (cleared of using Jewish Agency money for personal benefit when he served as that organization's treasurer), ex-mayor of Herzlia Eli Landau (cleared of taking bribes), ex-MK and ambassador to the United States Simha Dinitz (cleared of using Jewish Agency money for his own benefit when he ran that organization), ex-mayor of Petach Tikva Giora Lev (cleared of taking kickbacks from contractors), ex-mayor of Haifa Aryeh Goral (cleared of fraud), and more. Each of these cases is a prime-time miniseries unto itself, and though the decent thing to do is to assume that each man is innocent, not having been proved guilty, there is enough evidence in each of these cases for skeptical Haredim to suspect that secular politicians are held to less rigorous standards of probity than ultra-Orthodox politicians.

This double standard, in the view of many Haredim, is the result of the clannish homogeneity of judges in Israel, most of whom are what ultra-Orthodox newspapers typically call "the secular elites." Here too Gavison finds grounds for this complaint, as she told Shavit: "There is a problem regarding the appointment of judges. Nowhere else in the world is there a situation in which judges have control over the process of appointing judges. It is very good that judges have input in the process, but it is very bad when they have control over it. It gives those who head the system too much power, and turns the system into a kind of closed caste, which is too uniform and which effectively perpetuates itself."

Some years earlier, in a 1995 symposium on "the philosophy of the Supreme Court," Gavison put it more succinctly: "Supreme Court Justices represent a subculture in Israel—male, Ashkenazi, secular—and it is unclear why Israeli society ought to live according to its dictates." To many ultra-Orthodox, Israel's judges are a protectionist sort of secular vanguard, diligently promoting the interests of their caste.

Distrust of the courts and of judges and of police, suspicion that they are innately hostile, are as commonplace among Haredim as they are among American blacks, and are founded on the same potent mixture of fact and paranoia. Aryeh Deri may be Israel's O. J. Simpson, and that accounts for the disparity between ultra-Orthodox and secular views of these institutions. Lacking faith in the law, some ultra-Orthodox politicians and intellectuals look to the Knesset, hoping to achieve through legislation what they believe they can never achieve through litigation. This ultra-Orthodox hope, naturally enough, translates into fear for many secular Israelis, who worry that Haredim are growing ever more adept at manhandling the Knesset, and that they are now in the process of transforming Israel into a theocracy, law by law. They worry, as one friend put it, that "the Haredim have the Knesset by the balls."

It is taken as an article of faith by many that the ultra-Orthodox aspire to theocracy. Look in the Congressional Quarterly's *Encyclopedia of Politics and Religion*, for example, under the entry "Theocracy" and there, right after Khomeini and the Taliban, you will read that "in Israel as well there are political pressures to move in the direction of restoring the theocracy of ancient times. Several ultra-Orthodox parties advocate such a return." Gore Vidal, in his introduction to the late Israel Shahak's book, *Jewish History, Jewish Religion*, praised the author's analysis of "not only the dismal politics of Israel today but the Talmud itself, and the effect of the entire rabbinical tradition on a small state that the right-wing rabbinate means to turn into a theocracy for Jews only." Typing the words "Haredim" and "theocracy" into "Google" produces hundreds of hits, each illuminating in its own fashion how the former wish to bring about the latter. Among liberal and leftist politicians in Israel, the notion that the ultra-Orthodox are angling for a theocracy is barely questioned. Ornon Yekutieli, the Jerusalem Meretz activist who led the fight against the Shabbat closure of Bar Ilan Street, went as far as to define the ultra-Orthodox in terms of this aspiration. At a "town meeting" in Arad publicized as "A Jewish State: Mission Impossible," Yekutieli opened by setting out his working typology of the religious, in order to distinguish between modern religious Jews, with whom he has no beef, and the ultra-Orthodox: "Religious nationalists worked with us to build this country," he said. "The Haredim are those who want to turn Israel into a theocracy."

In contrast to the United States, Israel does not abide the principle of separation of church and state, and it never did. In the protocols of the meetings of the first Knesset one finds among the foundational principles of the new government the assurance that "the State shall provide for the public religious needs of its residents," putting the country in the synagogue, mosque, and church business from the start. Just why this is so is open to interpretation, but it is very likely linked to the vague and poorly conceived notion of many of Israel's founders that it was to be a "Jewish State" and at the same time a democracy. Shai Horowitz, the young director of the Haredi anti-defamation league Manof, showed me an eccentric little note that Ben-Gurion had written in 1954 to Moshe Sharett, who succeeded him as prime minister:

DEAR MOSHE,

We oughtn't separate religion from the state. The State of Israel and the Jewish People share a common destiny. This State will not endure without the People, and the People will not endure without the State, and therefore three things are intertwined: love of homeland, national loyalty, and loyalty to the Jewish people. This is a triple thread, which should not be disentangled, but should remain connected and intertwined.

SINCERELY,

DAVID BEN-GURION

Lenny Bruce used to perform a sketch in which he admitted that the Jews killed Christ: "I'll clear the air once and for all, and confess. Yes, we did it. I did it, my family. I found a note in my basement. It said: 'We killed him.' Signed, 'Morty.'" Ben-Gurion's note has the same bizarrely bald directness as Uncle Morty's. But figuring out just how to harmonize the "Jewishness" of the state with the pluralism and secularism typically associated with democracy has been at the heart of the intellectual agenda for many Israelis ever since. It is not an easy task, and after generations one cannot be faulted for concluding that it may be impossible, a fool's errand. In any circumstance, the notion that the state funds religious institutions and that religious institutions administer state services remains imbedded deeply in the structure of Israeli politics. The principle of "providing for religious needs" has been variously interpreted over the years, and it has given rise to mountains of complicated legislation, much of it the outcome of byzantine compromises delicately crafted to resolve political exigencies now long forgotten. In broad terms, though, it is possible to list succinctly the issues that have fallen, in whole or part, into the realm of religious legislation. They are marriage, divorce, circumcision, burial, conversion, adoption, abortion, ordination of rabbis, public Sabbath and religious holiday observance, kosher certification, and provision of religious services, in addition to legislation of budgets, including stipends for religious studies, subsidies for religious institutions, and differential assessment of taxes and entitlements to religious and nonreligious populations.

The Knesset approves the budgets and entitlements presented to it by the Treasury Ministry, jimmying the numbers a great deal in the process, and polls consistently show that the amount that ends up going to Haredim and their schools and centers and associations is perhaps what most infuriates secular Israelis. But it is not these allocations that create the impression that Israel is creeping toward theocracy. Funneling cash to yeshivot may make secular Jews less flush, but it does not, by itself, make them less free. What spawns fears of theocracy is the legislation that impinges on the freedoms of secular Jews.

Benjamin Netanyahu's initiation to the politics of ultra-Orthodox power. Illustration from now-defunct daily, *Hadashot*.

Not all legislation that impinges, impinges equally. The laws pertaining to kashrut—ensuring that government buildings maintain a kosher kitchen, giving the rabbinate exclusive rights to issue kashrut certification, limiting the importation of unkosher meat and the local husbandry of pigs, preventing the sale of bread on Passover, and so forth—impinge relatively little. In a growing number of cities, nonkosher restaurants outnumber kosher ones (in Tel Aviv, where I live, probably by a factor of ten to one). And there is practically nowhere in the country where you cannot buy great cuts of *treyf* beast and mollusks and crustaceans by the salty bucketful. An upscale coffee shop and bakery in my neighborhood has its highest take of the year on Passover, when it runs its traditional "bread fest," churning out pumpkin seed baguettes and marble ryes as fast as its stone hearth allows (in open violation of the law, which is infrequently enforced). The kosher laws have symbolic weight, but they don't really impinge.

Shabbat legislation is more troublesome to many. Commerce is squelched, although the number of stores open on Saturday (and their variety) is increasing rapidly. For those who use buses and trains, however, the agreements that prevent the bus cooperatives from operating most lines (save in Haifa and Eilat) is a true hardship.

The extent to which religious legislation interferes with personal freedom is greater still when it comes to what rabbis and psychologists call
"life-cycle events," and what Israeli law calls "matters of personal status":
marriage, divorce, birth and circumcision, burial, conversion, and adoption. As a matter of law, all of these issues are governed by the recognized
authorities of whichever religion the citizen was born into. This state of affairs harks back to Ottoman rule in Palestine and was preserved through
the British Mandate, and it allows mullahs, bishops, priests, and rabbis to
determine the terms and conditions of their flocks' "status" from cradle to
grave. In 1953, the State of Israel recognized this legal state of affairs, an-
choring it in legislation detailing the expansive authority of rabbinic courts
over such matters. For Jews, this law gave a coterie of rabbis the exclusive
power of a cartel to determine just how they'll be married and divorced,
born and buried.

Marriage and divorce may be the worst of it. I remembered that this is an
issue that exercised Reform Rabbi Uri Regev, and I traveled to his office in
Jerusalem to discuss it with him. Regev is a darling of the press, and it is easy
to understand why. His is an unusual biography, at least for Israel. He grew
up secular in Tel Aviv in the 1950s and 1960s, attending socialist schools. At
sixteen he went as an exchange student to America, where he saw for the
first time a Judaism that wasn't dark and primitive, and at that moment his
life careered off at an unexpected angle. "The very existence of a liberal, dynamic, egalitarian alternative, sensitive to questions of social justice, all this
attracted me a lot, and since then my involvement in the movement grew
and one thing led to another until I decided to devote my time to rabbinical
studies," which was just about the last thing his parents might have expected. Regev was given an army deferment to study law, which he then
practiced for five years in the IDF, after which he studied for the rabbinate at
the Jerusalem campus of Hebrew Union College. Upon graduation, he combined this training in law and rabbinics by establishing a center for civil
rights, especially civil rights for non-Orthodox Jews, the Israel Religious Action Center (IRAC). Regev is passionate, articulate, and evinces decency. I
asked him why he objected to Israel's marriage laws.

> I object because literally hundreds of thousands of Israeli citizens cannot ex-
> ercise their rights to marry because of religious compulsion. [This marriage]
> law has no parallels in any democratic country on earth. The only countries
> with parallel approaches are in fundamentalist Moslem states: Iran, Saudi
> Arabia, Afghanistan, Somalia—these are the only places you'll find laws like
> that of Israel, that outlaw or limit alternatives to religious marriages.

Just like marriage, divorce in Israel is governed by Halakha, and Halakha, just as it keeps some people from getting married, keeps others from getting divorced. A key feature of rabbinic divorce is the fact that it must be granted willingly by the husband, a feature much in the spirit of the passage in Deuteronomy (24:1–2) that first described divorce: "When a man has taken a wife, and married her, and it comes to pass that she finds no favor in his eyes, because he has found some unseemliness in her: then let him write her a bill of divorce, and give it in her hand, and send her out of his house. And when she is departed out of his house, she may go and be another man's wife."

As long as a husband willingly gives a *get*, or bill of divorce, to his wife, then divorce is simple and, insofar as divorce can be, painless. When the husband cannot give a *get*, or won't, the wife enters a sort of legal purgatory. She cannot remarry. She does not receive child support or alimony. This state of affairs fosters blackmail, and it is not rare for a husband to offer a *get* on the condition that the wife renounce all claim to child support or joint property. Women are likely to agree to such terms because the alternative is worse: being legally linked to a man who is distasteful or violent or dangerous to her children.

Even if one assumes that most of the rabbi-jurists are men of probity and integrity, and in my experience they are, the legal system in which they practice (and, as a result, the legal system by which all Israelis live) is doubly unfair to woman seeking divorce. First, the laws themselves are not just by any modern definition: They discriminate by sex. They legislate women to be helplessly dependant upon the goodwill of their soon-to-be-ex-husbands, goodwill that is often lost in the acrimony of separation. And second, the application of these laws, even by rabbis with the best intentions, is condescending and insensitive. It is common, for instance, for rabbinic courts to try to negotiate a reconciliation between a woman and man seeking divorce, and it is not unusual for rabbinic courts to insist, as a prerequisite to granting divorce, that a petitioning woman return home for a trial reconciliation period of two weeks or a month or six months, even to a husband who beats her. I briefly volunteered in a shelter for battered women in Jerusalem some years ago, and several residents told me that they came to the shelter only after the rabbis from whom they sought a divorce sent them back to the husbands who beat them, twice, three times, or four, until the women finally concluded that running away was their only option.

Rabbis ordering women to return to men who slap and punch them: This for some secular Israelis is an emblem of religious legal intervention into the personal lives of citizens. Rabbis have installed themselves, by law, as gatekeepers and toll collectors at important junctions and junctures. You marry only at their pleasure; you divorce only at their pleasure. Roughly the same pattern holds for burial (where rabbis decide who may be buried in a Jewish cemetery and who may not), for adoption (where rabbis decide which children must be ritually converted before they may be adopted), and abortion (where a panel of doctors and rabbis must grant its approval before the operation can be performed). In most cases, there are sneaky ways to circumvent the rabbis. A woman can download from the Internet, for example, instructions about what to tell abortion panels to ensure approval of an abortion. The panels typically approve abortions for unmarried woman, but are more reticent to do so for married woman (who, in the view of the rabbis, should not squander the opportunity to bring more Jews into the world). Telling the panel, however, that the pregnancy is the product of an extramarital affair (better yet, an affair with a gentile) typically secures approval. Still, just the fact that by law one must genuflect to rabbis about a matter as personal as abortion, or lie to them, is seen by many as an unacceptable intrusion.

Rabbis are gatekeepers not just when it comes to very personal matters, affecting one person or couple at a time. They are also, in a way, gatekeepers for the whole country, at least when it comes to what counts as authentically Jewish, seeking to pass laws weakening what is known here as "alternative Judaism," a blanket term covering both Conservative and Reform Judaism. The name "alternative Judaism" is misleading. Viewed from a global perspective, Conservative and Reform Jews outnumber the ultra-Orthodox by a wide margin. What makes them "alternative" in Israel is that they offer religious services that parallel those offered by the religious establishment. The Reform and Conservative movements each have its own seminaries in Israel that ordain rabbis. These rabbis perform weddings (though the resulting marriages are not recognized by the state). They perform conversions (though, at the moment, those who undergo these conversions are recognized as Jews only sporadically, under certain circumstances). For some years, Reform and Conservative rabbis have lobbied and sued to have these parallel services recognized by the state, enjoying some small successes and meeting with many large failures. In response, ultra-Orthodox politicians have lobbied to pass a law popularly known as "Who is a Jew?" that give Orthodox rabbis, and only Orthodox rabbis, absolute authority on all matters of personal status. Passing the "Who is a Jew" law has been the most enduring and elusive ultra-Orthodox political aspiration for almost two decades.

The question of who counts as a Jew in Israel is complicated, owing to an odd set of ideological and political circumstances. In 1950, the Knesset passed the Law of Return, stipulating that "every Jew has a right to come to this country as an immigrant" and be granted citizenship immediately and automatically. The law did not, however, define "Jew." There was a tendency, at the time, to view this term broadly. The Nazi definition of Jew, for the purposes of selection for deportation to work and death camps, had been very liberal, ultimately including those who had a single Jewish great-grandparent. This definition was much more inclusive than the traditional Jewish religious definition, by which one is Jewish only if one's mother is Jewish. Just five years after the concentration camps had been liberated, Israeli authorities were reluctant to classify as a gentile anyone seeking citizenship who had been (or would have been) classified by the Nazis as a Jew. In any case, in the first years of the state, with many immigrants arriving from Europe and from North Africa without proper or complete documents, government clerks tended to accept as a Jew anyone who identified him- or herself as such.

This informal approach proved inadequate when, in 1962, a Pole named Osward Rufeisen sought citizenship as a Jew. Rufeisen had converted to Catholicism during World War II, and eventually had become a Carmelite monk, taking the name Brother Daniel. He remained, he claimed, "Jewish by nationality," even though he was Catholic by profession. The case was compelling. By traditional Jewish law, which does not recognize conversion *from* Judaism, Brother Daniel was unquestionably Jewish. He also could demonstrate his commitment to "the Jewish people"; witnesses testified that he had concealed Jews from the Nazis, an act for which he would have been killed had he been caught. Still, the Ministry of Interior officials who considered his application concluded that there was something implausible, even illogical, about considering a Catholic monk a Jew. Rufeisen appealed to the Supreme Court, which ruled that, while "Jew" did not imply religious observance, it was not a term that applied to one practicing another faith. His petition was denied.

The legal definition of Jew was further tested several years later by Benjamin Shalit. Shalit, an officer in the navy, married a Scottish woman abroad. The couple moved to Israel and had two children. As Shalit was an Israeli citizen, the children were automatically citizens themselves. However, as Shalit's wife was Christian, the children were not Jewish. Shalit asked that the children's identity card designate "Jew" under "nationality," but nothing at all under "religion." When the Interior Ministry refused, Shalit took his request to the Supreme Court, which supported him (in a 5 to 4 decision). The court's decision was a technical side step of the real issue—it questioned the right of the clerk to question Shalit's application. The ruling also advised the Knesset to clarify the definition of "Jew" legislatively.

Responding to the court, the Knesset amended the Law of Return in 1970 to read that a Jew is any "person who was born of a Jewish mother or has become converted to Judaism," adding (in deference to the Brother Daniel ruling) that "a person who has been a Jew and has voluntarily changed his religion" is not covered by the law. Golda Meir, who was then prime minister, met with a group of visiting Conservative rabbis on the day the amendment became law and presented it as a great step toward "liberalizing" Israel's attitudes toward religion. The fact that the law did not stipulate that conversion must be according to Orthodox rules, Meir explained, was a compromise that recognized, de facto if not de jure, the validity of Conservative and Reform conversions, at least of those performed abroad.

Meir overstated the case. Rather than a recognition of the validity of Conservative and Reform conversions, the effect of the law was to initiate a debate about them that has continued ever since. In 1985, Shoshana Miller, who had converted to Judaism in the United States, immigrated to Israel and became a citizen automatically under the Law of Return. When she applied for her identity card, she was informed that she would be designated a Jew only if she could prove her Jewish birth or present an *Orthodox* certificate of conversion. As the case would have it, Miller had been converted by a Reform rabbi. With lawyers paid by the Reform Movement, Miller petitioned the Supreme Court to force Yitzhak Peretz, the ultra-Orthodox minister of the interior, to register her as a Jew. Peretz offered as a compromise designating Miller as a "convert" on her identity card. This the court rejected on the grounds that it would divide Israel "into two peoples," instead ruling unanimously that Peretz had to register Miller as a Jew. Days after winning her case, Miller, who found it dispiriting to be a cause celebre and whose affection for Israel had dissipated during her troubled year in the country, went back to America before her identity card was ever issued. The precedent was on the books, however, and Conservative and Reform conversions performed abroad were now recognized within Israel.

Four years later, in 1990, a woman named Elaine Goldstein immigrated to Israel, and one year after that she underwent a Reform conversion in Israel, in preparation for marrying a Jewish, Brazilian-born Israeli. Goldstein applied for citizenship under the Law of Return, and for an identity card designating her a Jew. When the Ministry of Interior refused to honor her certificate of conversion, she too petitioned the Supreme Court, which ruled that the Interior Ministry had no authority to demand a conversion certificate from the Orthodox rabbinate. The verdict meant that, de facto at least, Reform and Conservative conversions performed in Israel were legally recognized. In their decision, however, the Supreme Court justices directed the

Knesset to formulate laws that would clarify the status of these conversions in Israel.

The religious parties set out immediately to do so. After his May 1996 victory, Benjamin Netanyahu agreed, in exchange for Shas and the National Religious Party joining his coalition, that "the law of conversion shall be changed so that conversions to Judaism in Israel will be recognized only if authorized by the Chief Rabbinate." Five months later, Shas proposed a bill to the Knesset that exceeded the coalition agreement with Netanyahu, withdrawing recognition of Conservative and Reform conversions performed *abroad* as well: "There shall be no legal validity whatsoever to a conversion unless it receives the approval of the highest religious court in Israel of the religion to which the aforementioned wishes to join." This language gave the Orthodox rabbinate veto power over any and all Jewish conversions throughout the world. American Jewish leaders condemned the proposed law, threatening Netanyahu with withholding both financial and political support for his administration, at a time when Warren Christopher was pressuring Netanyahu to make political concessions to the Palestinians. In March 1997, the cabinet approved a more modest bill that delegitmated Conservative and Reform conversions carried out in Israel, but not those carried out in America.

Hoping to find a way to satisfy all the parties to the dispute, Netanyahu created a committee on conversion, and appointed Ya'akov Ne'eman to chair it. Ne'eman is a religious attorney with a reputation for fastidiousness and integrity that Netanyahu hoped would allow him to negotiate a settlement. (Two months later, Netanyahu appointed Ne'eman as his finance minister.) In fifty meetings over the next half year, the Ne'eman Committee developed a plan to create multidenominational "conversion institutes." These institutes would be sponsored by the Jewish Agency and run jointly by Orthodox, Conservative, and Reform representatives. They would work according to traditional, Orthodox guidelines governing the requirements of conversions. The proposal had supporters in all camps, but the progress toward establishing such institutes has been fitful. Fearing that the compromise would not successfully be implemented, Avraham Burg, then Jewish Agency chairman and later speaker of the Knesset, suggested a different sort of compromise, involving a technical solution to the problem. Burg suggested that instead of using the word "Jew" to designate religion on identity cards, the Ministry of Interior could use the first letter of the word in Hebrew, the letter "yud." The ultra-Orthodox need not see this as a confirmation of the Judaism of those whose religious identity they doubt, as it nowhere would say that someone is "Jewish." Conservative and Reform Jews, however, could derive satisfaction from the fact that their conversions conferred the same status—the status "yud"—as being born ultra-Orthodox did.

Burg is a politician seeking an elegant solution to an intractable political problem, and perhaps his suggestion is a good one. Even if it is, it is at the same time farcical: a solution less Solomon than Monty Python. And the fact that it could have been proposed as a possible solution to a problem that has occupied lawmakers and judges for over fifty years highlights the through-the-looking-glass nature of Haredi power in the Knesset. The problems that arise from religious legislation can be as serious as a heart attack. The poor Russian couple in Ashdod who wish to marry but cannot find a way around the rabbis are suffering a personal tragedy. The woman in Jerusalem who petitions for divorce only to be sent back to the husband who slaps her when his coffee is cold is suffering a personal tragedy. These circumstances, which ultimately can be traced back to ultra-Orthodox lawmakers, are grave, but that does not alter the fact that there is something ludicrous about the exercise of ultra-Orthodox power in the Knesset, and something even more absurd about the way this exercise of power is perceived by the rest of us.

In summer 2002, a fight broke out in the Knesset about daylight saving time. Economists have estimated that shifting the clocks an hour ahead each spring, and then back again in the fall, saves the country several hundred million dollars. This calculus combines the results of longer working hours, power savings on lights and appliances, longer shopping days, and so forth. Researchers in the United States and Britain have also found that daylight saving time decreases roadside pedestrian deaths, owing perhaps to the increased visibility during evening drive time. Despite these benefits, ultra-Orthodox politicians in Israel object to changing the clocks, for two principal reasons. Doing so interferes with the early morning *Selikhot*, or penitential prayers, that religious Jews recite during the month of Elul, just before Rosh Hashanah. Daylight saving time is also a hardship for those who do not eat on the traditional fast days of Tisha be-Av and Yom Kippur, as shifting the clock puts the end of the fast very late in the evening. Throughout the 1990s, lawmakers wrangled each year about whether and when to shift the clocks, and each year a new ad hoc conclusion was reached. Finally, in July 2000, the Knesset passed a law establishing the dates of daylight saving time for the four subsequent years. The bill, hammered out in rare cooperation between Shas MK David Azoulai and Shinui MK Avraham Poraz, called for the clock to be turned ahead in April of each year and turned back again just before Yom Kippur. This represented a compromise for each side, as Shas had earlier insisted that the clock be turned back weeks before Rosh Hashanah to accommodate *Selikhot* prayers, while Shinui had earlier insisted that it be turned back only at the end of October, as is the practice in the European Union. Calendars were consulted, and the law stipulated that the clock would be turned back on October 6, 2000, on September 24, 2001, and on October 7, 2002.

It was not until the summer of 2002 that anyone realized that there had been some sort of clerical error, and that Yom Kippur fell in that year on September 15. Knesset members from Shas drafted a bill to shift the clocks back three weeks earlier than the date appearing in the 2000 legislation, persuaded that this correction reflected the spirit of the original agreement. The new bill was not well-received within the Knesset or beyond it. Avraham Poraz, who had negotiated the original agreement, rejected the change out of hand: "It will only complicate things for the economy and cause harm, and all to appease the ultra-Orthodox. So what if they have to suffer another hour of fasting?" *Ha'aretz* columnist Yoel Marcus wrote:

> Sadly, the prediction of the founders of the state that Israel would be a "light unto the nations" has not come true in too many spheres. But in one department, at least, we've shown the world what we're made of. When it's summer in Europe, Israel ushers in winter time. . . . This invention screws up the airline schedules at High Holiday time and makes us miss our connections. . . . And we haven't even mentioned the loss of millions of shekels in electricity consumption and traffic accidents.
>
> But none of this—nor anything else that the general public or the state might need—interests Shas. Shas doesn't give a hoot that God Almighty set the date for Yom Kippur at the end of the summer, or that the length of the fast (25 hours) is exactly the same everywhere in the world, rain or shine, light or dark. The main thing is that Shasniks get another hour of sleep and an easier fast. "Ye shall afflict you souls" deluxe. . . .
>
> We don't have to turn the clock to see the darkness.

Surprised by the irate reaction, the Shas minister of the interior, Eli Yishai, and the Likud minister of justice, Meir Shitrit, embraced a compromise solution. Someone had suggested turning back the clocks on the day before Yom Kippur and then moving them forward again after the holiday, until the date stipulated in the original 2000 bill. This idea met with derision, becoming the butt of jokes in late-night television monologues and political cartoons (one showing an ultra-Orthodox cuckoo dressed for winter whispering furtively to the female cuckoo out the window in the blazing summer sun, "it's just for two days"), and an op-ed piece in *Ha'aretz* by Uzi

Benziman calling the proposal "pathetic." Matters became worse still, though by only a small increment, when *Ha'aretz* published a letter several days later by Amiram Carmon, a physician and researcher at Hadassah Hospital, who was also the founding director of the National Institute for Psychobiology in Israel. Carmon wrote:

> In his article . . . Uzi Benziman attacked Minister Meir Shitrit for "supporting Shas's pathetic idea to suspend daylight saving time for two days to make it easier for those who fast on Yom Kippur." This is wrong. . . . The "pathetic" idea of suspending daylight saving time on Yom Kippur eve and on Yom Kippur, and reinstating it until October 7, the original date, is the mischievous response of the undersigned, which I sent to MK Avraham Poraz. . . . Ministers Meir Shitrit and Eli Yishai jumped at the idea, without understanding that it was just a joke, the purpose of which was to show just how pathetic our politicians are.

No longer in a mood to compromise, Shas threatened to bolt the government if it did not support the party's position, and the cabinet met and decided to officially sponsor the bill and send it to the Knesset for a vote. In the banter between news presenters following the report of the bill's passage on the Channel Two news, the square-jawed anchor, Gadi Sukenick, said that, once again, the ultra-Orthodox had passed a law without concern for the millions of shekels and tens of lives it would cost the rest of us. In general, the bill's imminent passage was taken as the latest example of Haredi muscle and *machtpolitik*.

This assessment seems plausible at first, but upon further reflection, it does not match the facts. Eli Yishai is a deputy prime minister, the head of an important ministry, and the chairman of Israel's third-largest political party, Shas. In the fight over daylight saving time, he was ridiculed in papers, on TV, on the floor of the Knesset, and in coffeehouses from Eilat to Metulah, and for what? To amend a law in order to bring it in line with what he understood to be the compromise negotiated two years earlier. In the end, Yishai attained government sponsorship only after threatening to withdraw his party's support from the coalition. The cabinet reluctantly backed his bill, which is an indication—as if another were needed—that he and his party can make their coalition partners kowtow to them even when a bill is at odds with what most Israelis want. In the end, however, summer time did not end early. The bill sent by the cabinet to the Knesset was waylaid by House Committee Chairman Yossi Katz of the Labor Party, who exploited a procedural loophole and refused to transfer the bill to a committee for discussion. The bill languished and expired when the Knesset adjourned for its

High Holiday recess. Whatever he might wish, Yishai is no Il Duce. There is some *mot-juste* in Benziman's and Carmon's description: In the controversy over daylight saving time, Yishai and Shas were *pathetic*, at least in the Webster's sense of being miserably inadequate.

The ultra-Orthodox are the "Great Oz" of Israeli politics. They bluster and they seem omnipotent, able to ignore the courts of the land and remold the laws of the land. If one looks behind the curtain, though, one finds figures that are far from forbidding. At that moment, it is the limits of Haredi power that make the greatest impression.

The booming-voiced, all-powerful Great Oz image of Haredim can be said to have a static element and a dynamic element. The static element is the control that religious authorities wield over important aspects of the private lives of Israelis—weddings, divorces, and so forth—and that they have wielded basically since Israel came into existence. The dynamic element is the perception that realms of life over which the rabbis have control are growing and will continue to grow until they include all aspects of life.

It is with respect to this dynamic element—the view that new, more restrictive religious regulations regularly become law—that public perceptions diverge most sharply from reality. The legal status of religious regulations has deteriorated over the past decade, at precisely the time that Haredi electoral power grew most rapidly. In 1992 and 1994, the Knesset passed two new Basic Laws, one covering "Human Dignity and Liberty" and the other, "Freedom of Occupation." Israel, like England, has no written constitution. Instead, certain bedrock principles are expressed in a small number of Basic Laws, which have privileged legislative status (they can be amended only by vote of at least sixty-one members of Knesset), and privileged judicial status (in that, when there is a conflict between a regular law and a Basic Law, the Supreme Court gives priority to the latter). The first of the new laws, "Human Dignity and Liberty," defines fundamental individual freedoms: freedoms from search and seizure, freedom of property, freedom of self-defense, freedom to enter and leave the country, freedom of privacy, freedom of expression. The ultra-Orthodox parties opposed such a Basic Law for decades, which they felt—quite correctly, as it turns out—would provide a basis for legal challenges to religious laws. Chief Justice Aharon Barak said as much several years after the law was enacted: "In the past, freedom of worship and religion did not enjoy a supralegal constitutional status. With the passage of the Basic Law: Human Dignity and Liberty, it is included [as part of the] implied recognition of human dignity."

In a passage added as a concession to the ultra-Orthodox, the law reads "This Basic Law does not diminish the validity of any law preexisting the

framing of the Basic Law," a clause that protects the religious laws already
on the books from legal challenge. This concession has ambivalent meaning. On the one hand, it further entrenches Haredi authority over the things
they now legally control. On the other hand, as jurist and MK Shimon
Shetreet has written, it "reduces the ability of religious factions in the coalition to push through laws bypassing the High Court of Justice."

As a general rule, most Haredi efforts over the past years have been to preserve the religious laws already on the books, not to add to them. When
Ariel Sharon negotiated with the Shas and Yahadut ha-Torah, the two ultra-
Orthodox parties with seats in the Knesset he inherited from Ehud Barak, to
join his coalition, each party demanded that the government allocate funds
to its yeshivot and schools and other institutions. Shas added the demand
that several pirate radio stations run by its supporters be granted legal rights
to use the airwaves. But both parties had identical demands concerning legislation: "The status quo concerning matters of religion and state will be
preserved."

It is a good rule of thumb that the truly powerful do not fight to preserve
what they have. The converse is no less true. The fact that the ultra-
Orthodox are militant to preserve the "status quo" indicates, not strength,
but weakness. This would be true even if their success in protecting existing
religious norms was total and indisputable, but this is hardly the case. The
"status quo" has deteriorated steadily over the past years and will most likely
weaken in the future. There is more commerce on Saturdays and holidays,
unkosher food is everywhere, numbers of marriages between Jews and
Christians—owing to the Russian immigration—are multiplying, pornography can be had on almost any street corner, and so on. Haredim describe
the trend with resignation. I asked Uri Regev whether the ultra-Orthodox
had good reasons for feeling that they are losing the battle to pass and enforce religious legislation, and he readily agreed that they did.

Of course they're right, but so what? . . . They say, there have never been as
many movie theaters, restaurants, discotheques, coffee shops, and so on open
on Shabbat as there are now, and they're right. But in my view, they've decided
to choose their battles. The battles are today focused on money, . . . lands, jobs,
and less on a struggle that they think will enrage the public. I suppose they did
their own calculations. But this is not what I'm talking about. I agree that in
most things, the status quo has retreated in favor of secular Jews. It's not relevant. I'm talking about foundational issues . . . The contradiction here is existential. It is impossible for there to be a democratic state that supports
institutions that reject democracy.

Regev has a point, but matters are more complicated than he implies. Many secular Israelis understand Haredi politics as a small minority cynically manipulating the political system to advance their partisan preferences at the expense of the majority, and doing so with great success. This way of viewing things is not so much wrong as poorly conceived. The problem is rather, Regev said, that Haredim bring to politics a profoundly different conception of the common good than the liberal one to which we are accustomed. In his famous analysis of liberal politics, philosopher John Rawls proposed that just laws are those that might be legislated by rational individuals *unaware* of their own circumstances—their religion, race, class, sex, and so forth. Haredim in Israel do not abide by this definition of justice. They never relinquish the certainty that they are, in a sense, God's representatives in the Knesset. And they never relinquish the dream that, one day, God will set the workings of the Knesset a completely new foundation, that of the Torah. At the height of ultra-Orthodox discontent with the courts, an editorial appeared in the Haredi daily, *Yated Ne'eman*:

> We accept the de facto existence of the institutions of government in the State of Israel, but this loyalty is limited [to when] it does not conflict with observing the Torah and Halakha. . . . This system was forced upon us by circumstances, and we must accept its decisions, as long as they do not collide with Halakha. . . . Parliamentary democracy is, as we see it, the lesser of evils, which allows us to survive in a secular state, until the Just Redeemer will arrive, when the Creator of the World will eliminate the unjust government from the land.

Shinui MK Yosef Paritzky included this editorial in an anthology he published of ultra-Orthodox press clippings. In his introduction, Paritzky wrote that the excerpts

> reflect strong hatred for the state of Israel today, deep loathing for liberal and democratic ideals, demonization of anyone who is not Haredi, total obedience to the anti-Zionist Rabbinic leadership, and dismissal of all liberal and humanistic values. In the state of Israel there is a growing block of citizens that wishes, simply, to destroy, obliterate, and demolish Zionism and democracy. If we do not internalize the profound danger . . . we will find ourselves, in a few years, in a dark theocracy, in a Halakhic state that is anti-Zionist and antidemocratic.

This interpretation misses a fact of great importance in understanding Haredi attitudes toward politics. In the editorial Paritzky quoted, as in all ultra-Orthodox writing about the issue that I have come across, the theocracy that Paritzky fears is consigned to a distant, messianic future. Certainly, Haredim wish for a Halakhic state, in the way that college anarchists wish for the state to wither or socialist-leaning union organizers pine for a socialist state. They know it will never come to pass. Moreover, many of them probably would not really wish it into actual existence if they could. A poll found recently that roughly 60 percent of Haredim surveyed hope to live to see the establishment of a theocracy in Israel. This result caused a stir, but no one noted that roughly 40 percent of Haredim had said that they do *not* wish to live in a state governed by Jewish law. The real numbers may be much higher, as it is a well-known phenomenon that people tend to tell pollsters what the pollsters expect to hear.

It may be that for some ultra-Orthodox, a theocracy is not a real aspiration but a psychological and philosophical tool for defining their values. On my dorm room wall, I hung a poster of Che Guevera, and I mugged around campus with a green Mao cap with a red star that my girlfriend brought back for me from a trip to the People's Republic. My late-night radio show was called "Sounds of the Revolution," and it started at midnight every Saturday night with George Harrison's raging guitar intro to the White Album's "Revolution." I subscribed to the *Weekly Worker,* and on one occasion railed into Philadelphia to attend a meeting of the Trotskyite Sparticus Society. But I didn't *really* hope for the overthrow of American liberal government. I could adopt the pose of a Communist precisely because real communism was so distant, so inconceivable, that my faux affiliation was a statement about me, a statement of my aspirations for perfection, and a statement of my dissatisfaction with the imperfect present.

It may be that something like that holds true for the ultra-Orthodox, for whom the abstract mythology of a state run by rabbis has great appeal precisely because it is so distant as to be messianic. This is a question that only thoughtful empirical research can answer. What can be said with certainty is that the trajectory of Haredi politics can be mapped in very different ways. It can be depicted, as in Paritzky's portrayal, as a growing realization of an overriding aspiration to turn Israel into a theocracy. But it can also be depicted, far more reasonably, as the growing enfranchisement of the ultra-Orthodox and absorption of them into the messy culture of Israeli democracy.

With all our scrutiny of the ways Haredim bend the rules of the game in Israeli politics, we tend to overlook the great degree to which they also play by these rules. To date, Haredim heed the dictates of the courts. They leverage their electoral power to drain cash from the government and support for laws that matter most to them, but this too they do according to the norms and standards that characterize Israel's fractious system of coalition politics. They limit their realms of involvement in legislation for the most part to a small number of (admittedly important and intrusive) laws pertaining to "personal status." They compromise even on matters that are of great importance to them, as when they grudgingly accepted the Basic Law on Human Dignity and Liberty that will surely stymie their ability to pass and uphold religious laws in the future. The more I examined the evidence, the less it seemed to point to the political power of, and the more it seemed to indicate the weakness of, the ultra-Orthodox.

On a hot day late in October 2002, I invited MK Yuval Steinitz out to lunch on the dock of Tel Aviv's defunct port, to hear what he made of the evidence. I had met Steinitz in graduate school, and I translated his precocious philosophical manifesto, *In Defense of Metaphysics*, into English for American publication. A decade ago we might argue until early in the morning about Descartes's proof of God's existence, but the years since have taken us in different ways. At the university, Steinitz was a Peace Now leftist, but his views have drifted rightward since the signing of the Oslo Peace Accords. In 1998, he wrote several op-eds that caught the eye of then–Prime Minister Benjamin Netanyahu, who invited Steinitz to his office, where he pressed him run as a Likud representative from Haifa. To his own surprise and that of his friends and family, Steinitz found that he could accept Netanyahu's offer. The complicated party ranking system placed him as the twentieth candidate on the Likud list. The Likud's showing was unexpectedly poor, and when the numbers were tabulated, the party won only nineteen seats. Several days later, in acknowledgement of his defeat, Benjamin Netanyahu resigned his seat in the Knesset, and Steinitz was sworn in.

When we were students, Steinitz had been highly critical of the ultra-Orthodox, whom he saw as lazy freeloaders. Now, over salad, I asked whether his years in the Knesset had affected his views. "People have always hated Haredim, and I remember that I certainly did," he told me. He now sees this hatred as misplaced, part of a regrettable cultural tendency to "demonize the ultra-Orthodox and see in them a threat where there is none."

I asked Steinitz if he thought his ultra-Orthodox colleagues in the Knesset had more influence, head for head, and he shrugged and said no.

In the past twenty years, the status quo has moved only to the detriment of the Haredim, with a few, small exceptions. . . . The trend is very clear: secularization, secularization, secularization. This is true of religious restrictions on economic activity, and it is true too of the laws concerning marriage, divorce, etc. People speak about Haredi domination in Israel, but there is something totally irrational behind such talk.

Steinitz insists that the ultra-Orthodox are constantly losing ground in the Knesset, and if this is so, one may wonder what all the fuss is about. There is no plausible scenario leading from religious legislation today to *Der Shtrayml*–style concentration camps tomorrow. Steinitz may be right that the reasoning that leads some Israelis to envision the ultra-Orthodox enslaving the rest of us is irrational, but it is not *totally* irrational. People of great sensitivity and goodwill can continue to believe that this is where Israel is headed because they accurately, rationally, perceive that the political power of Haredim has *grown*, and at the same time greatly exaggerate, irrationally, the scope of this power.

There is something self-contained and circular about this mix of rational concern and irrational apprehension. People fear that Haredim will behave like Nazis because they perceive that Haredim are ruthless totalitarians whose power is growing geometrically. But at the same time, people perceive that Haredim are ruthless totalitarians whose power is growing geometrically in large part because they fear that they are like Nazis. The circularity is dizzying and leaves unanswered the question that has troubled me since my argument with Amorai at MIT: Why does the gentlest Israeli I know believe that my baby girl will one day curse me from behind ultrareligious barbed wire?

Conclusion

Tartuffe and the

Ultra-Orthodox Parallax

Israelis experience, to an extreme degree, a problem found in all democracies. As in France, England, Germany, and the United States, among Israel's citizens are true believers of many varieties—Orthodox Jews, Moslems, Catholics, Protestants, enthusiasts of New Age, Marxists, and on and on—as well as a majority who have no clear credo, save that all people should be allowed to believe whatever they wish. The views of different true believers typically clash: Seat a Southern Baptist alongside a cosmopolitan Marxist at a dinner party, and they'll be indignant before the appetizer plates are cleared. But the more elemental divide may be between true believers as a group and those liberal live-and-let-live types who proudly have no "true belief." Political scientists sometimes call this state of affairs "the paradox of liberalism," because liberalism as an ideology makes the paradoxical demand that citizens tolerate those who, if *they* called the shots, would never tolerate them back. It is this paradox that found the ACLU defending the rights of Nazis to march in Skokie, a Jewish suburb of Chicago. Contemplate the image of the lawyers who fought Jim Crow and marched in Selma defending with equal passion dozens of goose-stepping thugs, and you begin to feel the frustration that the paradox of liberalism can engender. Why should Nazi Neanderthals benefit from the freedom of expression that they would ban? Tune into late-night talk radio, and you'll hear irate callers opining that it is precisely this pathetic American softness that will one day allow Marxists, Nazis, Al Qaeda (or any other group whose members have more conviction than decency) to overrun the damn country, and what will the elite, effete ACLUers say then?

This same paradox of liberalism gnaws at secular Jews in Israel, and on a scale much greater than that engendered by the numerically insignificant Nazis in America. Perhaps one in ten Israelis is ultra-Orthodox, and this fraction may be growing. Haredim benefit greatly from Israeli democracy, which grants them rights, political influence, financial support, military protection, and more, but it's easy to believe that given the chance, they would gleefully dismantle democracy. In this light, the notion that Israel is being overrun by Haredim is the neat result of a syllogism of seemingly undeniable logical force:

Haredim do not appreciate democracy, and would do away with it if they could.

Democracy is exceedingly good to Haredim, who thrive under it, growing in numbers, wealth, and power.

Ergo, under democracy, the ultra-Orthodox will grow and grow until they are numerous, rich, and powerful enough to dismantle democracy itself.

It was with such a syllogism in mind, I think, that MK Tommy Lapid (who, as an avid chess player, seeks in his politics the inexorable logic of game theory) told me that he has no beef with the ultra-Orthodox themselves, who are simply doing what comes naturally. His complaint is against secular liberals, who, like Otto Braun, Alexander Dubček, or other weak, ineffective leaders, let their own democratic values be exploited by people who didn't give a fig for democracy.

But it is exactly in its mathematical precision that this syllogism is flawed. Matters are too messy to be captured in generalizations of such elegant economy. While many ultra-Orthodox dream of messianic times in which the law of the land (or, more properly, *the* Law of *the* Land) is legislated flat out by God, it is a mistake to conclude that they don't appreciate the democracy that allows them, in the interval prior to the Messiah's arrival, to live pretty much as they please. And while Haredim do benefit from their unique position in Israel's fractious body politic, whether they are gaining or losing numbers, cash, or power is a matter of debate.

All of these factors make for a situation that graduate students and French intellectuals call "dialectical." It is at once the case that the syllogism I described above *explains* secular anger toward Haredim and, paradoxically, that secular anger toward Haredim *explains* the power and plausibility of the syllogism itself. It explains secular anger toward Haredim by illustrating why, to many secular Israelis, ultra-Orthodox domination is inevitable. During the Cold War, politicians spoke about the "logic" of communism, which made Soviet hegemony inexorable, almost a law of nature. A similar belief is widely held in Israel, that the "logic" of ultra-Orthodoxy makes Haredi hegemony inexorable.

But the belief that ultra-Orthodoxy has a "logic" at all comes to seem plausible (and, in fact, comes to seem self-evident) because Haredim are ill regarded in the first place. It gains its seeming facticity from a potent mixture of data and prejudice. The legislative achievements of the Haredim are mixed, yet according to some polls, Haredim are perceived as having more power than any other sector of Israel's population. For most of us Israelis, the ultra-Orthodox have no influence on our day-to-day life (with the crucial, though fleeting, exceptions of the days we marry, divorce, and die), and yet we feel as if we are constantly under the Haredi thumb. There are innumerable good, objective reasons to fight ultra-Orthodox political initiatives, begrudge the money they get from the government, and resent the fact that they don't serve in the army. Yet, when it comes to the ultra-Orthodox, secular Israelis regularly overestimate the threat posed by Haredim, and the injustice perpetrated by them. Fact is augmented by fantasy, and in this way, Haredim come to seem more potent and malevolent than they really are. The systematic overestimation of Haredi power might be called the "ultra-Orthodox parallax," a distortion of our perception of ultra-Orthodox behavior that makes it appear more debauched, despicable, and dangerous than it in fact is. Traits that seem normal in secular Jews come to seem sinister in Haredim; shortcomings accepted with a shrug among secular Jews come to seem monstrous among the ultra-Orthodox.

These curious warps in perception create inconsistencies in the way Haredim are viewed, inconsistencies that are all the stranger because they are rarely recognized. For example, Haredim are often said to be insatiably greedy, a trait that explains their willingness to fleece the Treasury to support extravagances from which they alone benefit. They are at the same time disparaged for living of their own free will in borderline poverty, incomprehensibly sacrificing vacations, VCRs, and automobiles in order to spend their days studying. To be sure, these two accusations can be harmonized—social studies textbooks teach that the French nobility collapsed because the dukes and duchesses were rapacious and lazy in equal measure. But often the two beliefs about Haredim—that they care too much, and too little, about money—coexist comfortably, one alongside the other, each invoked in its proper context. So too, another odd couplet of beliefs: that Haredim are Machiavellian geniuses who control Israeli politics, and are at the same time haughty in their refusal to participate in democratic process.

Haredim are also regularly blamed for almost every social problem. I kept a tally during a recent episode of *Good Morning, Israel;* in the course of an hour, the budget cuts in secular schools and universities were attributed to ultra-Orthodox extortion, as was the inadequate budget to improve defenses against suicide bombers, cuts in support for the arts, and shortfalls in hospital funding. In addition, the army's inability to squelch the intifada was attributed (though only in part) to the failure of ultra-Orthodox men to enlist. Over breakfast, Haredim had been held to explain deteriorating education, bloody and indiscriminate murder, bad theater, medical malpractice, *and* the Palestinian conflict. Although it is true that if funds allocated to yeshivot were slashed, the money saved could probably reduce the size of my daughter's classes and buy lots of books for my university library; it could not do that and dramatically upgrade the IDF and build new museums and theatres and add the hospital beds and supplies that hospitals lack. Like a gambler who hits the trifecta after a cold streak, secular Israelis tend to overspend the windfall they imagine would result if Haredim were put in their place. The winnings may pay the mortgage, retire the loan, buy that new refrigerator, or fix the transmission on the Ford, but it won't do them all.

Another result of the ultra-Orthodox parallax is that Haredim are often regarded crassly and without nuance. The sorts of statements one hears about Haredim—that they are leeches, for example, and so beyond reform that it would be best if they were all gassed—are unsubtle. It is doubtful such immoderate descriptions could accurately portray any group, anywhere, ever. And yet, somehow, when applied to Haredim, they seem to sensitive and discriminating people not only plausible, but true. Perhaps this is to be expected of politicians with careers to advance. The lack of nuance is more surprising, though, among novelists and screenwriters and directors and painters and sculptors and scholars. After all, for these literati and cognoscenti, nuance is their stock in trade. And yet the way that the ultra-Orthodox are portrayed in literature, on the serious stage, in film, or on cable is hardly more textured than the way they are portrayed in a political caucus of the anti-Haredi Shinui Party.

"Tartuffe," Dan Urian told me. "The Haredi is always portrayed as Tartuffe." Urian is a renowned professor of theater studies at Tel Aviv University, and though his office is only ten minutes through the park on bicycle, I caught up with him by telephone in Oxford, where he is a sometime fellow at a center for Judaic studies.

Why? Molière put it like this: "Although I am a pious man, I am not the less a man." In other words, the Haredi may be religious, but he is motivated mostly by his appetites. All those dark clothes are just a costume hiding the real person underneath, who is a hypocrite, self-aggrandizing, holier-than-thou, fanatic. That is how Molière sees Tartuffe, and that is how many Israelis see the ultra-Orthodox.

The invocation of Tartuffe is not entirely metaphoric. As Urian describes in his extraordinary book, *The Judaic Nature of Israeli Theatre*, Molière's satire of religious hypocrisy may be the play that has been translated into Hebrew more than any other, and is among the most often performed plays in the history of Israeli theater. It was first translated into Hebrew in 1862 by Adam ha-Cohen Levinsohn, and later translated by Abraham Shlonsky, Nathan Alterman, Edna Shavit, and Joshua Sobol. Shlonsky and Alterman were giants of twentieth-century Hebrew letters, and Sobol is one of the most productive and important playwrights of this generation. Molière's skewer of the sanctimonious and unscrupulous religious has appealed to Hebrew-speaking audiences because of resentment against the rabbis and their Orthodox followers. Viewers of the play in Jaffa and Jerusalem and Tel Aviv had no trouble applying Molière's roast of Catholic hypocrisy to their own local variants of the same. Joshua Sobol made the parallel explicit in his translation of the play, in which Tartuffe unmistakably speaks the idiom of pious Judaism. Whereas Molière's Elmire tells Tartuffe, "C'est pousser bien avant la charité chrétienne. Et je vous dois beaucoup pour toutes ces bontés" ("That's pushing Christian charity too far; I owe you many thanks for so much kindness," in the Harvard Classics translation), Sobol has her say, "Don't exaggerate the mitzvah of 'love thy neighbor as thyself'—it only says *as* thyself, not *more*." In Sobol's hands, Tartuffe becomes an overgrown *yeshive bukher*, an exercise of artistic license that won immediate approval from Israeli audiences. Sobol's *Tartuffe* was first staged more than fifteen years ago, and today it remains one of the most popular plays performed regularly by the acclaimed Russian ha-Gesher repertory troupe in Jaffa. And as Urian described in his book,

Tartuffe is only one of dozens of plays in which Haredim are portrayed as hypocrites and manipulators.

This same image turns up in novels. In 1990, Yehoshua Bar-Yosef published *A Heretic Despite Himself*, a rehash of Abraham Cahan's "Rise and Fall of David Levinsky," tracing the degradation of a brilliant and promising Haredi scholar, Akivah Youngman. Everyone expects great things from "Kiva," and he does not disappoint, steadily rising in the ultra-Orthodox yeshiva hierarchy. But as he becomes more powerful and respected, his spirit implodes. He forces his wife to perform strange sexual acts. He seduces the nanny. He cheats the yeshiva. On the outside, he is a pillar of ultra-Orthodox society, but on the inside he's a libertine, a manipulator, a swindler, and a hypocrite. A note on the cover of my copy describes the author as: "The son of a well-known Haredi family. Many of his stories were written against the backdrop of Meah Shearim, and they are distinguished by their sensual-erotic tone and their exposure of the lusty side of the old *yishuv* and their concern with the heresies of ultra-Orthodox Jews." Bar-Yosef's books are light fare, bodice rippers with suitable morals, and they sell briskly.

But just as "true crime" books have cut a large swath into the sales of airport novels, recently, nonfiction accounts of Haredi debauchery have captured a growing market share. In 1999, a thirty-six-year-old man named Shaya Brizel wrote a memoir, *The Silence of the Haredim*, describing his father's serial seductions of young boys. Brizel's book belongs to a genre that might be called the "ultra-Orthodox confessional." A few months after Brizel's book came out, another odd little volume appeared: *Black on White: A Peak into the Intimate Lives of Haredim—Part I. Black on White* is an anthropological study of the ultra-Orthodox with special attention to their sexual habits, intended "to liberate the secular Jew from his ignorance about all matters related to Haredim." The author, an ex-Haredi, chose to publish under a baroque pseudonym—Hayyim ben Tzirel Applebaum—for fear that should his identity become known, his family would be beaten and excommunicated.

Not long after Applebaum published his book, Tzvia Greenfield published *They're Scared: How the Religious and Ultra-Orthodox Right Became a Leading Force in Israel*. The book—which bore an epigraph by W. B. Yeats: "The best lack all conviction, while the worst / Are full of passionate intensity"—analyzed religious radicalism in Israel, focusing as much on the modern Orthodox settlers' movement as on the ultra-Orthodox, but it became a sensation largely because Greenfield herself "lives in the Haredi world in Jerusalem, from whence she comes," as the book jacket puts it. Everything about Greenfield is extraordinary—she is finishing her Ph.D. in political philosophy ("Democracy as a Value System") at fifty-five, she heads an institute promoting education for tolerance, she is on the board of the human-rights watchdog group Be-Tzelem, she is a feminist, she lived for over a decade in the United States with her newly religious American physician husband from Hollywood, and she so much looks like central casting's notion of a Jewish mother that one rather expects to hear Al Jolson crooning every time she appears—but she is everywhere introduced first and foremost as "an ultra-Orthodox Jewess." *They're Scared* remained on the best-seller list for over half a year, during which time it was difficult to turn on the television or open a magazine without being confronted with Greenfield's wry smile. Greenfield's view of religion in Israel is nuanced, but one often got the impression that her success resulted less from the sensitivity of her analysis than from her audience's ability to overlook it.

Yoram Bronowsky, the revered *Ha'aretz* critic, described an exchange that took place in one of Greenfield's television appearances with uncharacteristic approval:

> "There is no limit to your nerve," Tzvia Greenfield says with proper emphasis, indicating that she means just what she says, and she turns to the arrogant yeshiva student sitting with her in the studio, and adds that he and Haredim like him should not interfere with political matters concerning war or peace so long as they are not willing to die for the country, and instead let others die for them.

When Elliot Jager interviewed her for the *Jerusalem Post*, he asked Greenfield long leading questions, prodding her to discredit the ultra-Orthodox:

> *You make the case that the Haredi world's long-standing goal is the destruction of the Zionist enterprise from within. To that end, Haredi leaders have aligned with the bellicose Zionist Right, which is less likely to lead the nation toward conflict resolution. The resultant war weakens the state. Is this a fair summary of your viewpoint.*
>
> No. It is a very superficial description. . . .
>
> *You devote a chapter to what daily life in the Haredi world is like. You present a subculture that is parasitic and superstitious; obsessed with the minutia of ritual to the point of absurdity. Essentially, you're describing a sick counterreformation—a relentless battle against modernity. Why stay in such a world?*
>
> That's an insulting question, and I disagree with the description.

Greenfield's popularity owes largely to the perception—which has grown no weaker despite her own protest to the contrary—that she has broken

ranks and is willing to confirm with authority what the rest of us already
know about the ultra-Orthodox.

Several years before Greenfield, it was a decidedly secular Jew, Seffi Rachlevsky, who published the best-selling book about the ultra-Orthodox. *Messiah's Donkey* remained on the best-seller list for the better part of a year and
was reviewed and discussed *everywhere*, an unusual distinction for a 500-
page book dense with analyses of arcane Jewish texts. Still, Rachlevsky
thinks big, and though the book is filled with esoterica, his basic arguments
are straightforward and bold. It is no coincidence, he wrote, that Rabin was
murdered, and that he was murdered by a religious Jew. For generations, religious Jews accepted secular Jews in Israel on the grounds that they were
handmaidens preparing for the End of Days or, in one famous rabbi's for-
mulation, the donkeys of the Messiah. Secular Jews were tolerated in Israel
as beasts of burden, draining swamps, fighting wars, building hospitals, and
so forth. But now, in Rachlevsky's view, the religious have grown enraptured
by their own messianic propaganda and think that the day will come when
then can rid themselves of their tired, aging, secular asses. Rachlevsky reviewed dozens of books by Jewish luminaries from Maimonides in the
twelfth century to Rabbi Kook in the twentieth, discovering throughout a
tradition of viewing secular Jews as patsies and expendable servants of the
Orthodox. Though Rachlevsky's thesis and scholarship were criticized almost unanimously by professors of Jewish philosophy, that did nothing to
diminish the popularity of the book among almost everyone else.

A freelance editor told me recently that it is a rule of Israeli publishing
that the market for books about Haredim is never saturated. Between Brizel,
Greenfield, Rachlevsky, and Shahar Ilan, for years, the best-seller list included one or another book highly critical of the ultra-Orthodox. The publishing phenomenon began in 1990, when a journalist named Amnon Levy
wrote a best-seller, *The Haredim*, which opened with a dramatic description
of ultra-Orthodox thugs trashing the synagogue of a rival ultra-Orthodox
clique, beating their opponents to a pulp and sending their octogenarian
rabbi to the hospital. The book was a great success, establishing Levy as a
major figure in Israeli media; he is now the popular host of a prime-time
television variety and interview show.

It is no coincidence that Ilan and Levy are journalists, each of whom worked
the Haredi beat (Ilan for *Ha'aretz* and Levy for the now-defunct *Hadashot*), because even more than from plays, movies, and books, it is from the daily paper
that most Israelis derive their information about the ultra-Orthodox. Journalists write frequently about the ultra-Orthodox, so frequently that in the ten

years since I developed my particular interest in Haredim, I have never come across a daily paper, any daily paper, that did not carry at least one piece about them. Most of these have concerned political matters of the day, which is not surprising in light of the near-constant coalition jockeying and budget battles in which the ultra-Orthodox have taken part during this period.

It is when one leaves the realm of political reporting that newspaper portrayals of the ultra-Orthodox become especially revealing. There are several sorts of stories about Haredim that appear over and over, though the details change from day to day. The most common of these stock stories concerns ultra-Orthodox sex crimes. In January 2001, the local weekly *Tel Aviv* ran a story called "A Rare Glimpse," with a series of surveillance stills and a large-type caption: "Scene One: A Haredi Hones in on a Woman in a Store at the New Central Bus Station / Scene Two: He Kneels to Check Out His Object / Scene Three: His Sex Organ Is Pulled out / Scene Four: He Is Caught and Confesses." In the same week, *Yediot* carried a fuzzed photo of an ultra-Orthodox man (his large black hat and beard the only clear features) with the headline, "The Haredi Courts 'Punished' a Rabbi Suspected of Sodomy: Expulsion from the Yeshiva." In honor of Yom Kippur, 2002, *Ha'aretz* ran a feature called, "In the Place Where Sex Criminals Pray," which began like this:

> The Holy Congregation of the religious wing of Ayalon prison includes as members the rabbinic sage convicted of raping his niece, the bride rapist of Bnei Brak, and also a rapist nicknamed "Bin Laden" because of the physical resemblance. Three of every four inmates in the wing are sex criminals. It's not just repentance that draws them to the wing; rather, it is the fact that in the other wings of the prison they could expect serious abuse.

The "bride rapist" mentioned is a man that *Zman Tel Aviv* called "The Devil in Bnei Brak." His name is Yizhak Feder, and he is a twenty-six-year-old ultra-Orthodox man who confessed to having persuaded perhaps as many as eight Haredi women engaged to be married that he was an official "bride's guide," sent by the rabbi to teach proper wedding-night behavior. He then raped these woman, under the guise of conducting a seminar. "In past years Bnei Brak has known many cases of juvenile rape, sexual abuse of children, and serious sex crimes within the family," the *Zman Tel Aviv* article reported. "But this time one of the victims is the daughter of one of the world's greatest rabbinic leaders." The story made banner headlines in all the papers and occasioned thoughtful features, as, for example, one by Anat Segalman in *Ha'aretz* about how the cloistered nature of ultra-Orthodox society, and especially the taboo against providing any sexual education to women, made crimes like Feder's easy to perpetrate.

Feder's crime was hideous and deserved to be reported. It was also unusual and piquant, and it is overly high-minded to expect people not to want to read about it or to expect newspapers not to pander to readers' natural voyeurism. When dog bites man, it's not news; when dog persuades woman that God Himself wants her to have sex with him, well, that is news. Reporters made much of Feder's ultra-Orthodoxy, which they reasonably saw as an integral part of the story itself, which could only have taken place in the ultra-Orthodox community. Reporting Feder's atrocities as an *ultra-Orthodox* story is justified, as when Catholic priests are identified as Catholic priests—the fact that these men represent the Church, and the fact that parents trusted them in particular, is relevant. This is also true for a percentage of the stories about ultra-Orthodox rape, incest, and sexual harassment (as when these take place in the yeshiva or the rabbinate, as they sometimes have).

But only for a percentage. Haredim are *always* identified as such—explicitly, or through telling photographs, or through inclusion of the hometown of the criminal (Meah Shearim or Bnei Brak)—in stories of sexual misconduct and sex crimes. But in almost all the cases, the fact that the perp is ultra-Orthodox is irrelevant. Yet this fact inevitably appears, more often than the identity of other ethnic or religious subgroups within Israel, except Israeli Arabs or Palestinians.

Papers always note when rapists and pedophiles are ultra-Orthodox, I think, because this identification, while perhaps legally irrelevant, matters to readers. Stories about ultra-Orthodox sex offenders are appealing, in part, because they demonstrate that Haredim, who are taken as haughty and holier-than-thou, are in fact capable of great debasement. The message behind each story, which usually remains unstated, is that Haredim believe themselves to be morally superior to the rest of us, but here, look, all their Talmud study and prayer doesn't keep them from fondling schoolkids or raping their own daughters. The *Ha'aretz* feature about the religious prison wing makes the point that sex offenders, who would be ostracized by secular prisoners, are blithely accepted by the religious. It is difficult to judge whether this assessment is accurate. It is certainly powerfully affecting, largely because it is at odds with the view that Haredi society is somehow more principled than secular Israeli society. As the reporter told it, even secular crooks are more decent than ultra-Orthodox ones.

The constant stream of articles about debased Haredim creates, in net effect, the impression that they are not only *capable* of debauchery, but that they gravitate toward it. No statistics are kept on the numbers of sex crimes com-mitted by the ultra-Orthodox, but a police officer I spoke with, who asked not to be identified, told me that there was no evidence that the rate per capita was greater than in any other population. It is hard to estimate, because such crimes are probably less likely to be reported among the ultra-Orthodox, but his hunch was that they are somewhat rarer among Haredim than among the general population. It may be that the impression that the ultra-Orthodox are especially likely to rape and sexually abuse results from the emphasis in the media on those rapes and abuses perpetrated by the ultra-Orthodox, and by the media emphasis on the *ultra-Orthodoxy* of the perpetrator. Perhaps the opposite is true, and press coverage reflects, rather than causes, a widespread presumption that Haredim are perverts. In either case, it is noteworthy, but hardly surprising, that when on two recent occasions Haredim performed acts of heroism—in one case, a young *yeshive bukher* saved the lives of a drowning mother and daughter before being swept to his death at sea, and in another a fifteen-year-old boy dragged his seven brothers and sister from their burning apartment—their deeds were reported everywhere, but none of the articles in the secular press reported that the heroes were ultra-Orthodox. Ultra-Orthodoxy is newsworthy when linked to vice, but not when linked to virtue.

This rule applies as well to reports of nonsexual crimes as well (which typically involve thievery, drugs, and fraud, as Haredim very rarely commit violent crime other than rape). "A Haredi who scratched off tens of lottery tickets in a lottery stall in Haifa tried to escape without paying for the tick-ets," began one article in *Hadashot* by a reporter named Yigal Kotzer, who nicely illustrated the way that emphasizing the ultra-Orthodoxy of a crimi-nal can punch up an otherwise pedestrian story. "A passerby who saw what happened pulled out his wallet and paid the Haredi's bill, 185 shekels. 'I thought I would win the big prize,' the Haredi explained and disappeared without thanking his benefactor." The religious identity of the passerby is not noted, in contrast to the criminal, and the reader is left to assume that he was not ultra-Orthodox. The story, then, which is as beautifully compact as a parable, is about the thievery, greed, and ingratitude of a Haredi, set against the generosity and forbearance of someone who is not. Significantly, in the end no laws were broken. It may not be too much to conclude that the subject of the story is not so much a petty crime, as the more timeless theme of Haredi thievery, greed, and ingratitude.

Experts at parsing media representations might reach the same conclu-sion about much of the reporting of ultra-Orthodox crime. One banner headline in *Yediot*, Israel's tabloid, largest-circulation daily, read, "Suspicion:

The Drug Deals Were Carried Out with the Knowledge of the Rabbinic Master." Another read, "Suspicion: The Rabbi Was Caught Stealing, and Cancelled the Kosher Certification." Another: "Five Israeli Haredim Are Accused of the Great Judaica Heist: According to Suspicions, in Two Years They Went to 60 Synagogues, Libraries, and Museums Around the World, Pretended to be Innocent People Praying, and Ripped Off Items Worth About 50 Million Dollars." In each of these cases, and the many other examples that can be found almost each day in the papers, the story is not so much the crime itself as the fact that it was committed by a Haredi. This general truth about coverage of the ultra-Orthodox is most clearly evident in the short item that appeared (alongside a photograph of two well-dressed men in a moving car) in the Tel Aviv local, *Zman Tel Aviv*, in August 2000:

THE VERSACE GANG
MAKES A MOCKERY OF THE LAW

"Don" [Eli] Yishai, one of the gang bosses, makes his way this weekend to a meeting with Prime Minister Barak. He doesn't fasten his seat belt because he is above the law and God will protect him. His driver doesn't fasten his belt, and in one hand holds a mobile phone and in the other is fingering the door of the car. No hands on the wheel. Count how many traffic crimes there are here. But what do they care, they belong to a group that the prime minister is scared of, and the police is scared of. Does anyone have the balls to give them a ticket for moving violations?

There is no groundswell of popular concern about moving violations in Israel. The story behind this story was not the crime, which everyone would agree is negligible, but rather the criminals—ultra-Orthodox politicians.

Alongside stories about political greed, licentiousness, and disdain for the law, Haredim are also often portrayed in the press as primitives and naïfs. In 1999, a seven-year-old boy, Amiel Feldman, living with his mother in Safed, died of pneumonia, because his ultra-Orthodox mother, Yoheved Feldman, refused to allow him to be treated in a hospital. This story became a sensation, and talk-show producers hastily organized segments about the problem of ultra-Orthodox refusal to use modern medicine. What emerged only later was that Feldman—an American ecstatic fundamentalist Protestant who converted to Judaism and made her home in a community of American ecstatic, New Age, Hasidic kabbalists living in Safed—was judged no less critically by ultra-Orthodox leaders and pundits, who maintain it is a religious duty to seek out the most effective medical treatment one can find, than she was by secular television hosts. The tenor of the reports in secular media—that the ultra-Orthodox are primitives who would rather see their children die than use antibiotics—was inaccurate. According to Ministry of Health statistics, residents of Bnei Brak have a longer life expectancy than residents of any other city in Israel (81.1 years for women and 77.4 years for men), and while these statistics owe something to the fact that Haredim do not die in wars, they probably reflect more than anything the vigorous use made in ultra-Orthodox circles of the health-care system.

Ambivalence toward technology and progress among Haredim is a popular theme in the press. "Rabbis Decided: Cellular Telephones—Not in Yeshivot." "Fearful of Innovation: A New Start-Up Claims to Have Invented a Program That Will Allow Haredim to Surf the Internet Without Sinning." "Belz Hasidim: The Computer Turns Haredi Children into Predatory Animals." "Rabbis: No Mobile Phones in Lavatories." Such headlines are perennials. As a group, they create the impression that the ultra-Orthodox reject technology and perhaps more generally reject all modern things.

These items stand in odd relation to another recurrent theme in newspaper coverage of Haredim; their use of cutting-edge technologies to serve primitive ends. *Yediot* published a large photograph of a Haredi pushing a miniature compact disc into a crack in the Wailing Wall. For centuries, Jews have written prayers on small slips of papers and slid them between the stones of the last remaining vestige of the ancient Temple in Jerusalem, and the photo was a contemporary variant of this traditional practice. The caption read, "A modern replacement for the traditional placement of notes in the Wailing Wall: An Internet site receives supplications and prayers, which are sent to the site by electronic mail. Once a week, all the requests are saved to a CD-ROM, which is placed between the stones of the Wall." Around the same time, the paper published a story headlined: "The Kabbalists' Start-Up—An Internet Site for Rabbi Kaduri." "At the site it will be possible to find pearls of wisdom of the rabbi about Arabs, such as, 'It is necessary to crush the heads of snakes, and [especially] the head of the leader himself.'" The appeal of these stories, and their humor, lie in the jolt of seeing the primitive incongruously juxtaposed with the advanced. The image of, say, an ultra-Orthodox fighter pilot offers a pleasant shock and a chuckle to readers, in much the same way that the image of a child in the cockpit would.

There is another sort of story about the ultra-Orthodox that is also popular because it is amusing: reports of rabbinic rulings. Two recent *Yediot* headlines are good illustrations: "Rabbi Ovadiah: Ice Cream Is Not Part of the Meal." "Rabbi Ovadiah: A Woman Who Doesn't Know How to Cook—

Is Disabled." The first headline concerned a ruling by Rabbi Ovadiah Yosef that one need not repeat the blessing after the meal if one subsequently consumes ice cream for dessert. The second reported Yosef's instruction that mothers ought to teach their daughters to cook. Such rulings are deeply embedded in a system of religious requirements that can reasonably be criticized as overly legalistic (in the first case) and repressively sexist (in the second). The short articles (thousands of similar items have appeared over the past decade) do not so much criticize as lampoon. A weekly satiric magazine has taken to publishing regular comic exaggerations of these rulings, alongside a photo of Rabbi Yosef with his index finger deep in his nostril, a visual flourish that captures the tenor of the nonsatirical articles as well. Each offers the thrill of Josef von Sternberg's *Der Blaue Engel*, in which the self-serious, self-righteous, and pedantic Professor Rath is shown, after all, to be a clown. Yosef is *Yediot*'s Rath.

To all these press portrayals must be added the images of the ultra-Orthodox in caricature and political cartoons. Shai Horowitz, the young executive at Manof, the ultra-Orthodox anti-defamation league, has collected these for over a decade, and when I visited him he showed me a thick file of them, and a small volume he published in which he reprinted some outstanding samples. In them, Haredim are drawn as ugly hook-nosed creatures, chasing women to rape them, tossing bombs and firing machine guns at unsuspecting secular Jews, drinking secular blood, reclining peacefully on the backs of exhausted secular laborers, and most often, joyfully fingering piles and piles of bills and coins. None of these images is new to the reader of Israeli daily newspapers; I felt dizzy, however, when confronted with hundreds of these images at once, and my heart was pounding when I closed the file, before I had seen even half the images.

Months later, I spoke about this to Dan Kerman, a prolific illustrator and cartoonist who has produced several dozen newspaper caricatures of Haredim and who collaborated on a book of cartoons about the ultra-Orthodox, *Who Is a Jew,* which was publicly censured in the Knesset. Kerman said that people like me tend to overlook the fact that it is the nature of political cartoons to exaggerate, and that the genre renders everyone monstrous. "Take one of my drawings of, say, a secular kibbutznik, add a beard and earlocks, and what you get is *Der Stürmer.*" Interpreting the ugliness of Haredim in political cartoons as anti-Semitism, Kerman continued, is a simple confusion of form and content. Kerman is steamed at being compared to a Nazi, as he often is, and his anger is understandable. I spent a morning discussing art and politics with Kerman at his modest Tel Aviv apartment, and I left with no doubt about his extraordinary decency; he is no hate-monger. It may be, however, that the delineation between the genre of the caricature and the message of Haredi caricatures is less stable than he takes it to be. What makes the caricatures so hard to look at is the tight intertwine between their uglifying visual syntax, and the specific criticisms that the syntax portrays: Haredim are leeches, bloodsuckers, pariahs, power hungry, and the rest. It is this confluence of form and content, I suspect, that brings jackboots and yellow stars to the minds of critics.

One cannot properly speak of a single monolithic image of Haredim in Israeli popular culture, which is too anarchic to present a single monolithic image of anything. Still, some traits do stand out as common stereotypes of Haredim. On stage and screen, in newspapers and magazines, the ultra-Orthodox are most often portrayed as lazy, oversexed, greedy, manipulating, debauched, self-righteous, clannish, self-serving, crass, primitive buffoons. They are Tartuffe, Shylock, Falstaff, and Rath.

All of this has a familiar ring. The image of the Haredim in Israel's popular culture bears a striking resemblance to European anti-Semitic stereotypes of the Jew, which have maintained currency over the past two centuries. It is well known that many Enlightenment intellectuals—and, no less, several generations of European literati that followed—disliked Jews, feared them, and distrusted them. Scholars disagree about where to squeeze this "Enlightened" anti-Semitism (or anti-Semitism of the Enlightened) into a typology of Jew-hating. Because post-Enlightenment intellectuals were by and large enchanted by reason and ostensibly guided by it, their brand of anti-Semitism rarely rested explicitly on a foundation of rank fabrication or fantasy (Jews killing for blood, raping young woman out of ritualistic obligation, and so forth). And because their own ties to the Church were often attenuated, their dislike of Jews rarely had a dogmatic foundation (Jews killed Christ). The new "Enlightened" Jew hatred was, in keeping with its Enlightenment lineage, more a "science" of anti-Semitism than the more visceral varieties that preceded it. It rested—so the literati seemed to have believed—on disinterested observation of the Jews.

Voltaire, perhaps the archetype of the "Enlightened" anti-Semite, conceded wryly that "we ought not to burn them." At the same time, it was crucial in his view to recognize that Jews fashion themselves "to be the enemies of all men." Further: "We find in them only an ignorant and barbarous people, who have long united the most sordid avarice with the most detestable superstition and the most invincible hatred for every people by whom they are tolerated and enriched." Given these basic anthropological facts, Europeans must ever beware the Jews, even as they tolerate them.

Post-Enlightenment literature is filled with statements that echo Voltaire. Johann Fichte saw in the Jews "a powerful, hostilely disposed nation . . . infiltrating almost every country in Europe." Jakob Friedrich Fries observed that Jews "shy away from industrious occupations, not because they are hindered from pursuing them, but simply because they do not want to." Hartwig Von Hunt-Radowsky characterized the Jews as "a class of morally and spiritually degenerate people, whom we shelter and who have benefited from the state but never benefit it at all." Richard Wagner, whose distaste for Jews was great, remarked on the "disagreeably foreign" appearance of Jews. Wilhelm Marr lamented that "there is no stopping . . . Jewry's control of society and politics." None of these comments is extraordinary, and for each one there are, in libraries around Europe, reserves of many thousands of similar quotations. A life's work awaits the scholar who sets out to compile the authoritative anthology of the anti-Semitic bons mots of the post-Enlightenment, European intelligentsia.

Despite the vastness of this body of literature, the image of the Jew that emerges is relatively simple. It is the image of powerful, predatory, Machiavellians, interested in advancing only their own odd, insular, licentious, money-mad clan. It is Tartuffe, Shylock, Falstaff, and Rath. It is, in short, the same as the image that many Israelis hold of Haredim.

Perhaps this should come as no surprise: The image that many of us carry today may be patterned, in part and indirectly, after the Enlightenment version of anti-Semitism. "Creating a *new* Jew" was a popular desideratum of early Zionists of many different stripes; it was at times the only slogan that could be uttered ingenuously by factions of all sides of the byzantine ideological schisms of the early days of the Zionist movement. This desideratum was itself not entirely new. It had earlier been formulated by *maskilim*, the advocates of Jewish Enlightenment, who hoped to modernize Jews and Judaism. To many Zionists, like many *maskilim*, a *new* Jew was necessary because the *old* Jew was pathetic and lamentable. This old Jew—a figure to be left behind, transcended, superseded—was, as often as not, drawn directly from a stock bestiary of social types. The image of the pitiful and degraded Jew, the lazy and debauched Jew, the Jew with neither honesty nor honor, served as a counterweight essential to rhetoric of early Zionist polemic, which argued that the new national movement would produce Jews that were none of these things, Jews of probity and accomplishment and virtue. This image was in large part borrowed, occasionally plagiarized intact, from post-Enlightenment European intellectuals. In the hands of Zionist publicists—as in the hands of *haskalah* publicists before them—the image of the *Altjude* was refined (Voltaire's *Juif* and Fichte's *Jude* vested increasingly in the garb of the *Ostjude*—that crass, ne'er-do-well relative suffered by the Jews of the West with self-conscious embarrassment), but it did not change fundamentally.

One need not search hard to find denigrating images of the *Altjude* in Zionist rhetoric and pamphletry. Herzl had already noted in 1894 that Jews had "taken on a number of anti-social characteristics" in the ghettos of Europe, and that Jewish character was "damaged." David Frischmann wrote that traditional "Jewish life is a dog's life that evokes disgust." Chaim Brenner likened Jews to "filthy dogs, inhuman, wounded dogs." A. D. Gordon wrote that European Jews were parasites. M. J. Berdyczewski called traditional Jews "spiritual slaves, men whose natural forces had dried up and whose relation to the world was no longer normal," and elsewhere, "a non-people, a non-nation—non-men, indeed."

In some instances, Zionist criticism was aimed against all *galut* (diaspora) Jews—religious and atheist alike, ghetto and assimilated alike, Western Jews and *Ostjuden* alike. But the most violent rhetoric was often reserved for the religious. Berdyczewski fashioned the slogan, "Yavneh and Jerusalem are enemies" to capture the fundamental antagonism between the old religious Jews and the new national Jews. The former "led us into exile," and their culture "cannot live together with the national culture which wants to break the thread of exile and plant within us new values and a totally new will." When Heinrich von Treitschke launched his famous attack on Heine's writing, which he saw as degraded in a particularly Jewish sort of way, placing it at odds with the true German spirit, he was attacked with vigor by Jewish intellectuals around the world. It was Berdyczewski who distinguished himself by writing that though Treitschke exaggerated his case against the Jews, he was in essence right.

Other Zionists, less thoughtful than Berdyczewski, were more vindictive. Samuel Joseph Ish-Horowitz wrote, "The Jew must negate his Judaism before he can be redeemed." Judaism, seen as traditional observance, was considered to be standing in the way of human redemption. Marcus Ehrenpreis was less charitable still to traditional Judaism:

> We have liberated ourselves from the shackles of a sickly, rotten, and dying tradition! A tradition that cannot live and does not want to die; a tradition that manacled our hands, blinded our eyes, and confounded our hearts, that darkened our heavens and banished light and beauty and tenderness and pleasantness from our lives, that turned our youth into old men and our elders into shadows. We have liberated ourselves from the excessive spirituality of the Exile. . . . We have liberated ourselves from the rabbinic culture, which confined us in a cage of laws and restrictions.

Such displays of rationalist scorn were commonplace in Zionist circles. A leitmotif of much Zionist prose is a yearning for *normalcy*. Normal, of course, is in the eye of the beholder; to most early Zionists, normalcy meant achieving a close match to one or another of the leading European social theories of the day. Thus, the distaste that these Zionists felt for the "old" Jew overlaps with the post-Enlightenment antipathy for Jews, precisely because the Zionists' worldviews overlapped with so much of post-Enlightenment European thought. That Herzl—whose vision of the Jewish state described in his utopian *Altneuland* bears more than a passing resemblance to European parlor society—adopted a rather standard bourgeois critique of European Jewry is no surprise. Neither is it that A. D. Gordon, whose own worldview was deeply influenced by Tolstoy, should develop a romantic critique of *"luftmentshlekh,"* urban Jewish sensibilities.

Just what one ought to make of all this is not self-evident. Anita Shapira, a historian of Zionism of extraordinary sensitivity and insight, and, until recently the dean of humanities at Tel Aviv University, warned in a recent essay called "Anti-Semitism and Zionism" against drawing reckless conclusions from the apparent anti-Semitism of Zionist ideologues. There are, she wrote, "several methodological problems that demand attention." One of these problems "concerns the question of sources."

> The Jewish nationalist movement drew its ideas and measures of what is exalted and what is debased, what is honorable and abominable, admirable and loathsome, from the conceptual world of European social and national movements. This rich reservoir also served the anti-Semitic movements. Does the existence of images, stereotypes, and myths shared by Zionists and anti-Semites indicate mutual interactions between the two streams, or does it indicate common sources?

Another sort of methodological problem, in Shapira's view, "concerns the question of the line between anti-Semitism and legitimate criticism." Surely not every criticism of the sociology of fin de siècle European Judaism is anti-Semitic—to lump Jewish intellectuals' pained self-scrutiny together with the casual defamation by Christian intellectuals, schooled from an early age in distaste for Jews, is surely to miss something important. "To my taste," Shapira wrote:

> the line distinguishing pathological signs of self-loathing from the shards of anti-Semitic ideas, images, and stereotypes that seeped into Zionist thought and mythology is the line of demonization of the Jews. . . . The moment that

one . . . attributes to Jews imaginary traits, like fanatical belief in the power of Jewish money, or a world-wide Jewish conspiracy, and adds to these the element of biological determinism, which makes self-improvement impossible, then criticism turns to the perversion of self-hatred.

Shapira's point, that Zionists might have come to some of the same conclusions as anti-Semites without themselves *being* anti-Semites, is of great importance. It means that one must be careful before applying so charged an adjective as "anti-Semitic" to so charged a noun as "Zionism." It does *not* mean, however, that the close intertwine of the intellectual roots of European anti-Semitism and Zionism ought be denied or overlooked. Shapira herself concludes:

> It appears that anti-Semitic stereotypes and tropes did nourish, to a certain degree, the thought of Zionist public-opinion makers, especially those . . . hoping to affect a deep revolution in the lifestyles [of Jews in the Holy Land]. . . . These people absorbed more than a little of the anti-Semitic analysis concerning the Jewish past during years in diaspora, and the present in the diaspora.

And the story did not end after Israel was established in 1948 as a sovereign state. In fact, the "anti-Semitic stereotypes and tropes" that funded early Zionist thought and produced the caricature of the "old" Jew are alive in present-day attitudes toward Haredim. Haredim are "old" Jews par excellence, and it seems to me that the way they are popularly portrayed still draws freely from the genre of Jew-hating. If early Zionists drew their image of the degraded diaspora Jew from the dusty warehouses of anti-Semitism, then many contemporary Israelis draw their image of the degraded ultra-Orthodox Jew from the dusty warehouses of Zionism.

It would be a mistake to conclude from this insight that the modern view of the ultra-Orthodox was passively inherited by modern Israelis. Images of the ultra-Orthodox as debased parasites retains currency not simply because they are *there* and freely available. The images retain their currency because they remain useful. In Shapira's view, such images were useful to Zionists from the beginning, by providing a model of what *not* to be. "What was the 'anti,' against which the Jewish nationalist movement sharpened its identity?" Shapira asked. "Who was the 'other,' who provided a negative example, the object of attack and hostility? Against whom did the Zionist movement educate, against whom did it preach, in whom did it see its polar opposite? . . . The 'other' against whom the new national identity was formed was what was called the 'diaspora Jew.'"

Even today, the "other" remains a crucial element of Israeli identity, and
for many Israelis the most salient "other" is the Haredi. The popular image
of the ultra-Orthodox is, in many senses, the photo negative of the image of
the *tzabar*, the mythical native-born Israeli. The Haredi is pasty and sallow,
but the *tzabar* is tanned. The Haredi spends his days among dusty old
books, while the *tzabar* works the fields. The Haredi is scrawny, and the
tzabar is what Max Nordau called a *Muskeljude*. The Haredi weasels out of
the army, and the *tzabar* leads troops to the battlefield with the cry,
"*aharai!*" (after me). The Haredi takes and takes, while the *tzabar* produces.
The Haredi manipulates, while the *tzabar* is earnestly direct. The Haredi is
hunched, hook-nosed, dark, and deformed, but the *tzabar* is blond, beautiful, and robust.

It is easy to see why the negative image of the ultra-Orthodox is important to many of us secular Israelis. When comparing ourselves to Haredim,
Israelis feel heroic, and this in part explains the success that anti-Haredi political parties and organizations enjoy when recruiting, especially among the
young. Opposing the ultra-Orthodox can be a form of self-congratulation
(as distaste for Jews has sometimes been in the parlors of Europe). A curl of
the lip or a roll of the eyes when the topic of Haredim arises over espresso in
a café on Dizengoff may be a densely packed signal that we are progressive,
liberal, modern, and decent. Disliking Haredim is attractive, in part, because it allows malice to serve as a mark of virtue.

In 1990, when Rabbi Eliezer Shach attacked secular Israelis on national
television, one of his complaints was that they know only brute strength,
and nothing else. There were hundreds of angry secular responses (including hastily organized protests), among them an op-ed piece by journalist
Kobi Nir in the now-defunct socialist daily *Al ha-Mishmar*, in which he
wrote that Shach was mistaken to say that secular Jews had no values: the
value of secularism lay in the fact that it was *not* ultra-Orthodox. Shach and
his ilk, he wrote, represented "the dark ages, misanthropy, oppression of the
spirit, oppression of women, oppression of humanity, narrow-mindedness,
narrow horizons, the past." To have transcended this legacy, Nir implied,
was itself an accomplishment of some moment. This is essentially the message that attracted one in twenty Israelis to vote for the Shinui Party. Nir's
message was, simply being anti-Haredi is a position of moral worth, of
gravity. To oppose ultra-Orthodoxy is itself the basis of a positive identity.

Naomi Hazan, just months after she was elected to represent the Meretz
Party in the Knesset (in the elections that brought Rabin to power), warned
the audience of "Jewish humanists" that antipathy for Haredim had displaced their other ethical commitments. Hazan has sponsored legislation to

expand the rights and benefits of homosexuals, women, foreign laborers, and Palestinians. I met her at a working group of an environmental caucus. Her credentials as secular humanist are above reproach, and as a result, her warning made an impact:

> For so many years we have convinced ourselves that only if we manage to get rid of the black hobgoblins will we be able to advance what is good in this country. . . . Our focus on the fight against religious coercion has taken us to places that are in utter contrast to the basic values of humanism. There is no secular culture in Israel. The crux of secular culture today is hatred for religious coercion. We know so well what we don't want that we don't have a shadow of a notion of what we do want. . . . What is our secularism apart from hatred for religious coercion?

The late Yehosafat Harkabi, who was chief of military intelligence before retiring, and whose leftist credentials were also beyond reproach, replied to Hazan, "What is wrong with defining the positive by demarcating the negative? Sometimes the only way to define who you are, is to say what you are not." It may be that the greatest value of the Haredim lies in the fact that we are not them.

It should be said that the Haredi is not the only "other" in contrast to which Israelis may formulate their identities. The Palestinian, too, is the "other." In the first years of Zionism, Shapira observed, Palestinians did not serve this function. "It turns out that, at least until the establishment of the state, the Arab didn't fulfill the role of the 'other.' To a certain degree, he was even taken to be a positive and romantic archetype, worthy of emulation. In any case, he was not the focus of hostility for the emerging Zionist identity." The same cannot be said today. Israeli pundits and intellectuals labor to explain, for instance, how Palestinian mothers can, as they sometimes do, tell interviewers immediately upon learning that their teen detonated himself in a crowded café, that they are happy and proud. This phenomenon mystifies many Israelis (I am one of them), and because the issue is electric and important, its fascination is not hard to grasp. But we Israelis are not just fascinated by this question, we are haunted by it. The near-obsessional interest we have in the question of how mothers feel about their sons' murderous martyrdom suggests that perhaps this question has some value or serves some purpose that is not immediately obvious. That purpose, I think, is that it draws a bright line separating us from the Palestinians. The comparison is often made explicit, on television interview shows, in the newspapers, and in thousands of conversations repeated around dinner tables all over Israel: We weep and mourn for every one of our dead, while they, their own mothers, celebrate their dismemberment.

There was a similar reaction to the horrifying lynching in Ramallah, in 2001, when two pathetic reservists lost their way as they tried to reach their base, were picked up at a Palestinian checkpoint and brought in to the Ramallah police station, where an ecstatic mob tore them limb from limb, and while an Italian television crew was filming them, the murderers held up their bloody hands to the hysterically cheering crowd. I watched the films on the nine o'clock news, and heard that the wife of one of the soldiers had phoned his mobile while he was being killed, and one of the mob answered and held the phone up so that the woman could hear her husband's last scream. My reaction was, "The people that do such things are not human in any sense that I recognize." Friends told me that they reacted in the same way. The Palestinian is the "other," and increasingly he is the "other" by whom Israelis define themselves. After the long standoff at the Church of the Nativity in Bethlehem finally drew to a bloodless conclusion in 2002, a fellow teacher at my university offered, "This is the difference between us and them. We negotiate, they lynch."

It is in this way, I think, that hatred of the ultra-Orthodox and hatred of Palestinians is linked. They serve similar functions. Dedi Zucker, once a Knesset member from the left-wing Meretz Party, wrote not long ago that Shas is the PLO of the Israeli Left, providing an "ultimate enemy by virtue of which they define their political identity," and I believe this is true. "In the past twenty years," he wrote further, "no two entities in Israel have been more rejected, hated, and disparaged than the PLO and Shas." This point was nicely illustrated by a political cartoon that ran some time ago in *Yediot*, showing a Palestinian and a Haredi, each poised to throw a firebomb. The caption read: "After you." . . . "No, after you." It is not surprising, then, to find that hatred of Haredim and hatred of Palestinians oddly, *dialectically* linked. It was after the Oslo Peace Accords were signed, when it briefly seemed to many Israelis that the long conflict with the Palestinians was drawing to a close, that anti-Haredi sentiment grew to dimensions greater than at any time in Israel's history. That anger with the ultra-Orthodox grew after the peace agreements does not mean, of course, that this anger grew *because* of the peace agreements. It was also during this period that the Knesset representation of ultra-Orthodox parties ballooned, and with it the government funds they commanded. But it is still possible, and it seems to me likely, that fear of Haredim grew at precisely the moment when fear of Palestinians ebbed, because hating and fearing the ultra-Orthodox took on greater importance at precisely that moment.

When the Palestinian becomes a less viable "other," the Haredi is pushed into more demanding service as the "other."

This surmise can be dismissed as curbside psychology, and I would not take it seriously myself were it not for the odd empirical relationship between Palestinian terror and attitudes toward the ultra-Orthodox. Since the collapse of the Oslo Peace Accords, and the beginning of the second intifada and the suicide bombings, the force of anti-Haredi feeling has diminished no-

Palestinian and Haredi violence. Caption reads, "After you." "No, after you." Cartoon by "Mike," reprinted with permission of *Shpitz*, journal of the Israel Cartoonists Union.

ticeably. One rough, unscientific indication of this trend is newspaper reporting. For some years, I have made of point of reading the Friday (weekend) edition of all the national newspapers, clipping items about the ultra-Orthodox and obsessively stacking them in small piles. Before the collapse of the peace process, I rarely harvested fewer than seventy-five clippings in a weekend. After the intifada began, the number dropped by roughly half. During especially violent periods, the number drops to half again. And on the few occasions when suicide bombers attacked Meah Shearim, leaving Haredim dead on the sidewalk, no pejorative articles about the ultra-Orthodox appeared. There are many possible explanations for this. Wholesale violent death will tend to push everything else out of the headlines, and though I haven't checked, I would be surprised if the number of movie reviews didn't decline in the wake of suicide bombs as well. Suicide bombings, as news stories, are naturally hegemonic, and that goes part of the way toward explaining the diminishing negative coverage of the ultra-Orthodox over the past two years. But only part. Another part of the explanation, I think, is that when Palestinians assume so comprehensively the role of national enemy, of "other," then most Israelis feel less compelled to view the ultra-Orthodox as enemy and "other."

This is the dialectic of the "other." We need "others"—the *shahid* flashing a demonic smile before detonating the explosives wrapped to his chest in a crowded café; his mother, telling CNN that she only hopes that her other children will someday do the same; and the Haredi, wan, pale, weak, and pathetic. These others show us that if the world is to be divided in binary moralism—into good versus evil, civilized versus primitive, gentle versus violent, productive versus parasitic—then for all our faults, we remain on the side of the good, the civilized, the gentle, and the productive. When for a time, our nightmares are fully populated by Palestinians, then we may feel more generosity of spirit to Haredim. But should Palestinians come again to seem more benign, I expect that this generosity will evaporate. At that moment, hating Haredim will again be as important as it ever was.

It is my opinion—or guess, I suppose—that hating Haredim, despite its recent setback, is a growth industry because Haredi-hating is a defining element of Israeli identity and is perhaps on the way to becoming *the* defining element of Israeli identity. Palestinian suicide bombers pose a more bloody threat to the safety of Israelis than the ultra-Orthodox ever would, but ultimately it is still the ultra-Orthodox who provides the most useful foil for Israelis seeking to understand ourselves. In the end, the Haredi is the better "other."

This is because, as the Zionist enterprise tires, as it projects a less and less positive vision of society, the counterweight of the Haredim as a justification for Zionism becomes more important. Rabbi Shach was not right in charging that secular Zionism has produced little as a culture aside from a powerful army and the resolve to use it, but he was perhaps not as wrong as many of us who live in Israel, and love Israel, would have hoped. Early Zionists expected that they would be vindicated, that the value and truth of the ideology they embraced would be confirmed by the society they built. After Zionists produced the Good Society, they reasoned, no one could doubt that Zionism itself is a social good. And for some time, it seemed that this formula had proved itself. Israel has existed as an independent state for roughly two generations. During the first of these generations, it was taken by many, not least by Israelis ourselves, as a model of state building. Israel was the only country in the world in which volunteerist socialist communities—kibbutzim—thrived, producing not only a plurality of the country's food, but providing in extraordinary numbers charismatic leaders in government and the army.

Even beyond the green lawns and gates of the kibbutzim (which accounted, after all, for only a bit over 3 percent of the country's population), economists determined that Israel was the nation with the smallest "socioeconomic gap" in the world, that is, the difference in income between the richest decile and poorest decile was smaller than anywhere else. Israel had undertaken and succeeded in massive development projects. The country had absorbed several times its population in immigrants, many poor, and many refugees arriving from dreadful circumstances. Israel reversed the regional trend toward desertification, reclaiming tens of thousands of acres of arid land for productive agriculture. By virtue of these local successes, Israelis became agricultural advisers through much of Africa, helping to spark a short-lived but significant increase in African agricultural production. And of course, Israel had assembled an army and air force recognized for its effectiveness and creativity. Generals like Moshe Dayan and Yizhak Rabin became international celebrities and found themselves dining at the tables of princes and starlets.

Looking back from a more sober perspective, it is now possible to see that the image of Israel that arose from aggregating these early successes was in good measure mythological. It is not so much that these successes were not accomplished as that each particular one was more ambivalent than it was at first taken to be. Kibbutzim, it now emerges, were often experienced by their members as rigid and unfulfilling; recently a man raised in a communal children's house sued his kibbutz for abuse and causing mental anguish. The ostensible economic justice of the early days was, in part, an artifact of widespread poverty; once the economy became productive, equality quickly disappeared. The absorption of new immigrants was accomplished in a fashion that led Jews from North Africa into lives harsher than those of immigrants from Europe, and so on. But the fact remains that it was possible in the mid-1960s, in fact, almost inevitable, to see Israel as a small country of near-miraculous achievements, that deserved the attention and admiration of people everywhere. I grew up near Washington, D.C., in the early 1970s, and now and then a local synagogue or Jewish community center would host a lecture by an Israeli functionary like Abba Eban or Moshe Dayan. These men attracted great crowds—everyone I knew was there, and many others—and they were occasions of significance. I had other childhood heroes (by the age of ten I had already read *two* books by Joe Namath), but Moshe Dayan was a god to me.

Such gods are now dead. No one holds a heroic view of Israel anymore, not abroad and not here. In the past five years, dozens of kibbutzim have become "privatized," dividing up what was common property. I recently visited a friend on Kibbutz Neot Mordechai in the Galil; she told me that somehow when assets were split up, the old had been given next to nothing. She herself had come to the kibbutz after the Nazis had confiscated her parents' properties in Germany, and she had worked there for almost sixty years. Eventually, when her monthly German reparation checks began to arrive in the 1960s, she transferred them to the kibbutz as well. Now in her late seventies, she was forced to survive on several hundred dollars a month. Recently, the Supreme Court ruled that it is unlawful for kibbutzim to sell off to developers valuable government-owned lands that had been lent to them for agriculture. Today's kibbutzim are not a source of national pride.

Israel's social gap is now considered among the greatest in the developed world. The most recent wave of immigrants, from the former Soviet Union, are largely disgruntled, and surveys suggest that a large percentage of them, in any instance, are not Jews. Several of Israel's large development projects damaged the environment in unforeseen and irreparable ways. Today Israelis are largely unwelcome in African capitals. They are largely unwelcome anywhere. A recent survey of hotel owners in Europe found that Israelis are the least welcome of all guests, a fact that probably owes more to their reputation as boisterous and demanding than it does to politics or prejudice.

Most important of all, Israel's military excellence has been tested in a twenty-year misadventure occupying southern Lebanon, and in laboriously maintaining the peace on the West Bank and in the Gaza Strip. Whatever one's views of the morality of ruling these lands are, the experience of patrolling Palestinian cities nervously clutching an M-16 is enervating and depressing. I enlisted in the Israeli infantry in August 1984 and served—as a regular and reserve soldier—until I was retired in 2000. My service was often trying, and I never excelled at being a soldier. I tended to avoid confrontation. When my jeep was stoned, my impulse was to drive on, as though nothing had happened. This was seen by some of my fellow soldiers as appalling cowardice, and—though I'd like to attribute my behavior to some high-minded recoil from violence—in retrospect I think they were right. But if I did not feel like a hero, neither did those soldiers who found themselves chasing down groups of teens, shooting real or rubber bullets, pummeling those they caught in the stomach or face—and neither could the majority of decent soldiers who fell somewhere in between my military autism and the others' enthusiasm, doing what they had to do to get by to ensure their own safety and that of the rest of us. It is difficult to be viscerally proud while patrolling in the territories (though it *is* possible to feel satisfaction in protecting the lives of people you care about, in your jeep or in distant Tel Aviv), and it was difficult to experience straight up pride in Lebanon either. Even for those who never doubt that such service enhances Israel's security, the dull depression of policing foreign and frightening landscapes tends to make one's patriotism more abstract, less immediate.

The weariness that so many men like me feel has had an important impact on Israeli political culture. During the war in Lebanon, a billboard on the side of the Tel Aviv–Haifa highway kept a running tally of how many Israelis had died north of the border. The message was clear; that these hundreds were victims of government misjudgment and adventurism. Refusing to answer a call to the reserves was almost unthinkable before 1980; now refusal has a certain chic, at least in some circles. Refusing specific orders—an order to evacuate Jews from a settlement, for example, should matters ever come to that—is now advocated by certain prominent rabbis and some members of Knesset. Though only a small minority of Israelis approve of such refusals in principle, many more find informal ways to refuse service. In my unit, dozens of reservists found ways out—medical discharges (some real, some fictions), "hardship" discharges, psychological discharges, whatever. After two decades of dispiriting service, many Israelis—on the right and the left—are disenchanted with the army, with the government, with the whole damned country. Let someone else get pelted with rocks. The recent intifada has reinvigorated Israel's reserves to a significant degree, as it is now quite easy to see how successfully guarding a checkpoint near Jenin in the morning might save your kid's life in Jerusalem in the afternoon. Many Israelis once again see army service as honorable and meaningful. But it is not heroic in the sense that it once was, before army service became almost synonymous with policing the territories.

But the malaise of IDF service is only part of the story. The portrayal of Israel in its own universities is increasingly veined with doubt and self-criticism. For over a decade now, Israeli revisionist historians—we call them the "new historians"—have been feverishly rewriting the hagiographic accounts of all these remarkable achievements that were for generations the standard fare of Zionist history. Hebrew literature and language are now shown to be laden with colonialist ideology and propaganda. The ingathering of Jews is now shown to have been a highly selective affair, and immigration and absorption policies and priorities reflected Eurocentrism, at best, and often downright racism. Israel is now shown to be prosperous by virtue of systemic exploitations of occupied Palestinians, and it is a democracy only if one ignores the millions of disenfranchised Palestinians whose fate it controls. The army is now portrayed as an instrument of murder, vicious repression, and massive confiscation of lands—much of it calmly premeditated—since before the state was declared. And so forth. These accounts are vigorously debated in seminar rooms and public lecture halls, on the pages of newspapers and magazines, and increasingly in the great hall of the Knesset, as Sharon's first minister of education, Limor Livnat, swore to root all vestiges of such revisionist historiography from school curricula.

Whether one ought to see in such academic accounts of Israel's history refreshing honesty or neurotic self-mutilation (or perhaps both) is a matter of considerable debate in my circles. But no matter what one thinks of this sort of scholarship, this much is true: The strong impulse to "demythologize" earlier heroic accounts of Zionist accomplishments is at once an effect and a cause of disenchantment with Israel. It stems from a certain exhaustion, and it results in a certain exhaustion. To be an Israeli in 2003 is a demoralizing affair. We are tired: tired of the Palestinians, tired of Arafat, tired of the bombs, tired of UN and European Union condemnations, tired of having so much of our daily wage taxed to buy guns and missiles, tired of the army reserves, tired of being hated, tired of going to bed and waking up to reports of kids— Jewish kids, Palestinian kids—watching their parents die or dying in their parents' arms. We are tired of our lives and tired of ourselves.

It is for this reason, I think, that the symbolic importance of Haredim is increasing. Now more than before, we need the ultra-Orthodox and now, more than before, we need to hate them. We need Haredim to serve as representatives of the "old" Jew, pathetic and debauched, that the rest of us have superseded. We need Haredim as living proof of Zionist achievements, as a breathing moral missing link that shows just how far we have evolved. Haredim serve as a token of the continued relevance of the secular Zionist program, at a time when this claim to relevance is no longer evident, certainly in Europe and America, but also increasingly within the borders of Israel itself. But unlike the more confident earlier pronouncements on the obsolescence of the "old" Jew, the current, growing fascination with the ugly Haredi—based in part on fact and in part on fantasy—is bleak testimony to the weariness of the Zionist vision, and the shattered confidence of many Israelis in the worth of their own ideals and dreams.

It makes matters worse that the ultra-Orthodox refuse to see themselves as we see them, as fossils from a time when Jews were weak, primitive, and pathetic. They do not recognize their own obsolescence. Nothing illustrates this fact better than the vigorous efforts of some ultra-Orthodox Jews to persuade secular Jews to adopt their way of life. To some ways of looking at it, it is as if thick-browed Cro-Magnons set out card tables on street corners, distributing literature to persuade homo sapiens to *devolve*. The notion of "free" Jews, as members of one of the anti-Haredi organizations designate themselves, opting to return of their own choice to the bondage of primitive religion seems almost to be a crime against *nature*.

And yet, it happens. Among the ultra-Orthodox are many individuals and groups that proselytize, and they meet with some measure of success. Just how much is impossible to determine with confidence. According to Shahar Ilan of *Ha'aretz*, throughout the 1990s, the Ministry of Religion funded the studies of 43,000 people (27,000 men and 16,000 women) in yeshivot meant for proselytes. This number is hard to interpret because, as Ilan pointed out, only a portion of newly religious Jews register to learn in such institutions. At the same time, for a variety of reasons, these institutions attract students who are not newly religious Israelis: Some of their students were in fact raised religious, and a fair portion of them are not Israelis at all, but Americans and Europeans who eventually plan to return home. Also, no reliable longitudinal studies have been done of the durability of newly adopted religious identities. Of these 43,000 who studied in the 1990s, no one knows how many remain religious, much less ultra-Orthodox, today. In 1997, a poll by the Dahaf Institute found that 7 percent of adult Jewish Israelis had recently embraced religion to one degree or another (roughly 200,000 people), and 17 percent reported "moving closer" to religion in some way. The questions asked by the polls were too vaguely formulated to allow any serious analysis; for one thing, religion is a general term that includes ultra-Orthodoxy, Reform Judaism, and New Age spirituality. Still, only a committed contrarian could deny that ultra-Orthodox Judaism in particular has recently demonstrated surprising ability to draw converts from among the secular.

Behind the statistics are sad stories. Every conversion represents tears, sleepless nights, and broken hearts. A university colleague who is herself Orthodox recently told me that her husband never recovered from their daughter's decision a decade and a half ago to marry a Haredi and become one herself. "She won't visit us anymore; she won't eat at our house; and we rarely see our grandchildren. When we do, their parents hover, nervous that we might say or do something forbidden." This case is particularly mild, as both parents are themselves observant Jews, and they understand much about their daughter's new life. Secular Israelis, who have no natural sympathy for religion, especially not for ultra-Orthodoxy, invariably experience greater alienation and, often, greater anger. Sophia and Dan Mahler, the founders of the Organization for the Prevention of Ultra-Orthodox

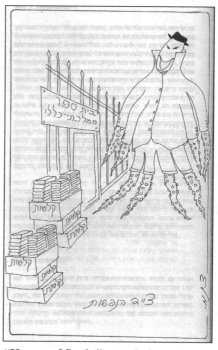

"Hunter of Souls," proselytizer distributing religious videos outside secular public school. Cartoon by Dan Mahler, originally published by Zemora Bitan, reprinted with permission of artist.

Domination, themselves "lost" a son to the ultra-Orthodox, as Dan put it to me when we spoke, and they have for years run a support group for parents who suffered a similar loss.

Recently the Mahlers published *Devils Emerging from the Dark: Stories of Haredization*, a collection of pseudonymous first-person accounts by the group's participants. In one account, a mother named Zafrira described her experiences with her daughter Adva, who in high school graduated from dope to heroin, and left home an emaciated junkie. "One day she appears at home, out of the blue. 'I'm here,' she said, no longer strung out, though still thin and pale. 'I've come home. I'm taking courses in Judaism, and if you don't mind, I'll live at home.' I thought I would faint from joy." As Adva became more and more ultra-Orthodox, however, Zafrira's joy dissipated. Soon Adva married the proselyte son of secular kibbutzniks. "We got the impression that they were growing more extreme, getting 'blacker,' becoming less and less Zionist, and very 'anti'—anti-state, antidemocratic, and anti the surrounding society. That hurt all of us. . . . Adva, what can I say, every year she had another kid. It didn't make her any more healthy. Even without this she was a waif—small and thin as a hatchling." It grew harder and harder to visit and, particularly, to maintain ties to the grandchildren. Adva and her husband and kids would not stay for more than a couple of hours and refused to eat at Zafrira's inadequately kosher apartment. Since Adva would not welcome secular guests, including her parents, on Shabbat and holidays, it was hard to find a time to visit the seven grandchildren. One year, Zafrira and her husband planned to visit on Independence Day, which is a holiday, but one without religious restrictions. They were stunned to learn that their grandchildren would be in school on that day. "They said it's not their holiday! Did you hear? Independence day is not their holiday! It's a normal day for them!" At that moment, more than most, it was obvious to the parents how distant their daughter had become from them and from everything they cared about.

Emotional distance is only part of the problem. Parents whose children have "become black" (ultra-Orthodox) worry about those things that parents often worry about—the health and financial well-being of their children—with an especially great sense of despair and foreboding. Zafrira worried about Adva and her family: "What do they live off? Donations, I think, but they don't tell us. They get a monthly stipend from the *kollel*, and from the government, and mostly from us, their families give them something each time, and especially groceries. . . . You should see how impoverished they are."

I have by now met many mothers and fathers whose children have become ultra-Orthodox, and they commonly expressed worries of these sorts; about their children's poverty, about their lack of education, about their futures. Some were concerned that their children would disappear from their lives completely, and I spoke to parents who had not conversed with their children in years, sometimes decades. This sort of estrangement does not always follow when a son or daughter becomes Haredi. My wife is an obstetrician at a city hospital that serves a large population of newly ultra-Orthodox, and it is not unusual there to see a secular mother feeding ice chips to her ultra-Orthodox daughter in labor. An acclaimed 2001 television miniseries, *To Catch the Heavens,* followed a Tel Aviv family over the course of the father's conversion to ultra-Orthodoxy, as he forces his wife to go to a ritual bath, the *mikve,* after her period, gives away the family dog, and koshers the kitchen. What was most affecting about the broadcasts (the production company created a chat room, and thousands of viewers conversed each week about what they saw) was the great love that the characters had for one another. The man, the woman, the girl, and the boy wished only that their family would remain intact, and each sacrificed so that it would. In the end, the Haredi left his family, in which he could no longer find his place.

Even those relationships that survive are often accompanied by a sense that something important has been lost. Parents feel that they have lost the respect of their children, and that they are viewed as sinners and ruffians by their grandchildren. I have spoken to parents who said that even though they maintain their relationship with their children, it is as if they are simulacra, not really their children at all, the way that some parents report about kids who have become junkies, that they seem like shells, somehow fragile and empty. The chapter in Mahler's book about Zafrira and Adva is entitled, "Maybe Drugs Are Better?"

The comparison is not idle, as fear that their children will become ultra-Orthodox probably exceeds most parents' fear that their children will become junkies. Statistically speaking, the chances are greater. The commonplace fear that missionaries will snatch our children accounts in part for the anxious attention with which the spiritual lives of celebrities are monitored here. In the past months worried features have appeared about actors (Michael Weigel, Sasha Demidov), directors (Yehuda Barkan), beauty queens (Miss Europe, Lilach ben Simon), soccer stars (Ayal ben Ami, Udi Ashash, Gili Landau, Shlomo Kiret, Ophir Shmueli, Yigal Menachem, Avi Hadad), singers (Ehud Banai, Etti Ankori, Ophir Levy, Nissim Menachem), fighter pilots (Rafi Peretz, Baruch Ganot, Tzvi Spiegel), hi-tech entrepreneurs (Shlomo Kalish), secret agents (Avi Sinai), writers (Roy Newberger), and children of celebrities (Binyamin-Sayyar Zeevi, son of the assassinated minister, Rehavam Zeevi, the anonymous son of a supreme court justice), all of whom are reported to have edged toward ultra-Orthodoxy, some in small steps and some in great leaps. Seminal conversions of the 1970s—those of actor-comedians Uri Zohar and Mordechai (Pupik) Arnon, who went from being symbols of Tel Aviv nihilism to proselytes and then on to proselytizers, for example—are still discussed in the hushed tones usually reserved for malignant tumors. And gossip columnists are sensitive to any rumors about the new rich and famous showing an unseemly interest in religion. Recently, the very secular feminist television and radio talk show host Shelly Yahimowitz, was mistakenly outed: "I heard that I was going to appear at the national convention center to publicly accept the Torah, and all sorts of nonsense like this. . . . In the beginning it amused me, but after a while it annoyed me . . . as a believing secular humanist." And alongside celebrity stories are great numbers of human interest stories involving secular Jews becoming ultra-Orthodox, for example, the story of Nuriel Tobias, who became at once both gay and ultra-Orthodox, and the story of the ten members of secular Kibbutz Ayelet ha-Shahar who together became religious, or of Moshe Aaron Ben Ami, who became religious at age 77, and is now 102, or that of Ilan Horowitz, a New Age guru who disappointed followers by becoming a Haredi rabbi, or of the woman who withheld sex until her husband agreed to become religious alongside her.

Taken together with Shahar Ilan's statistics, these stories create an impression that the ultra-Orthodox are adding great numbers to their ranks by persuading secular Jews to join them. The Mahlers wrote another book, *The Soul Hunters*, in which they described the sophisticated brainwashing techniques by which the ultra-Orthodox carry out this persuasion, and Dan Mahler said that while writing it he realized that he is "damn scared of Haredi domination," because Haredim are adept at converting secular Jews one by one, and these single conversions, each a family tragedy, add up to a national tragedy. This is not an eccentric view; among the dozens of anti-Haredi activists I have spoken with, all but a few described proselytizing as the most immediate danger posed by Haredim. If so many secular Israelis have become ultra-Orthodox, how long can it take until they become the majority?

No one can answer this question with confidence, but the argument can be made persuasively that the ultra-Orthodox do not gain numbers from conversion. Just as among the secular, among the Haredim I have spoken with almost each one tells stories of familial tragedies, in which a father, daughter, sister, or cousin left the faith and became secular. In these cases, too, families are torn apart, parents and children break off contact, grandparents are kept apart from their grandchildren. It happens in the best of families—it was recently revealed that one of Rabbi Ovadiah Yosef's sons is no long ultra-Orthodox. Recently, several charitable organizations have formed to give financial and emotional aid to people who leave ultra-Orthodoxy. There are no reliable statistics about the extent of this sort of conversion. One possible indirect indication of its significance, however, is that according to Boston University economist Eli Berman, for almost twenty-five years, rates of child-birth among the ultra-Orthodox have been between two-and-one-half and three-and-one-half times as great as secular birthrates. Yet during this time, the populations of ultra-Orthodox relative to secular have grown far less than childbirth rates alone would suggest. To parse this data accurately would require complicated analysis and the collection of new data (espe-cially, the numbers and religious affiliations of mostly ex-Soviet new immi-grants). Until this work is done, I am left only with an intuition, reinforced time and again by tearful anecdote, that the numbers of ultra-Orthodox re-moving their black coats and yarmulkes may not be less than the number of secular Israelis putting them on for the first time.

If I am right, then the reason why Haredi missionizing leaves some secu-lar Israelis fearful and enraged may have nothing to do with the actuarial threat it poses. The actor or soccer star who ceases to go to clubs and starts instead to go to shul is unnerving for reasons that have nothing to do with any great existential threat. It is unnerving for at least two reasons. First, be-cause each man who grows earlocks and each woman who starts to wear a wig is a man or woman who is in some deep way lost to us. They have be-come "other." This is sad enough when the woman is an adored entertainer; it is unbearable when she is the daughter one taught to ride a two-wheeler. The other reason is related. Each new conversion is an assertion that we have failed. If so many choose to devolve, perhaps we are not as evolved as we think. If we are who we think we are, why are our children leaving? How can they choose *other* over *us*?

Several dozen miles away, as I write these words, laborers are constructing the first sections of a fence outfitted with state-of-the-art motion sensors. If the most ambitious plans are realized, the fence will one day encompass most of Israel's population—surrounding the pre-1967 borders and the set-tlements beyond them that lie close to Jerusalem. Designers of the fence be-lieve that it will keep suicide bombers out of Israeli cities, save the extraordinarily lucky and ingenious few. I hope they are right, of course, and that the fence proves effective. Even if it is, the symbolism of the fence—Jews of their own initiative surrounding themselves with what amount to high-tech ghetto walls—is unsettling.

It is also unsettling to think of what is happening within these walls. Should Israel and the Palestinians ever find the way toward peace, it will take only hours for bulldozers to rip to shreds the quarter-billion-dollar fence now under painstaking construction. The divide between the ultra-Orthodox and the rest of us—each group passionately intent on denying the legitimacy, the probity, the decency of the other—may prove harder to close.

This saddens me. If I were nailing my Ninety-Five Theses to the door, they would say that despite the high price they extract, Haredim—out of uniform, in their yeshivot, not earning hard currency—provide good value, shekel for shekel, to the rest of us. In a country enthusiastically embracing Starbucks and McDonald's, in which entrepreneurs who managed to cash out before their Internet companies became worthless are cultural heroes, and in which consumerist materialism has the cast of historical inevitability, Haredi society offers a bracing vision of how things might be different. The Haredi traits of voluntary poverty, antimacho quietism, pasty-faced bookishness, and learning-*über-alles*, unnerve the rest of us because they stand as a genuine challenge to the *mall-above-all* values that we tend to take for granted. There is much to dislike and reject in the values of the ultra-Orthodox, but there is something sumptuous and virtuous in them as well.

Some may see this as romantic claptrap, and perhaps it is. In a way, this hardly matters. What is important is not so much how Haredim ought to be seen than about how they ought *not* to be seen. Hating the ultra-Orthodox has appeal that is almost irresistible to the rest of us here in Israel. But hating the ultra-Orthodox also has a price. In one of my daughter's storybooks, goblins steal a baby, replacing her with one made of ice, and her parents are oblivious to the change. For a growing number of us here in Israel, raging against the ultra-Orthodox provides us with a durable political and moral identity: a sense of who we are and a feeling of decency and integrity. This identity is an ice baby.

When my grandparents retired to Israel, despite their apparent vigor, they too were weary. They were born at the beginning of the twentieth century, and in the years since they had seen a lot. As kids they saw whole towns ransacked by hooligans in pogroms. They saw Jews die pointlessly in the brutal skirmishes between White Russia and Red, between Mensheviks and Bolsheviks. They heard stories of relatives drafted out of yeshiva into the Soviet army, and never heard from again. They left everything behind to come to America and raise children whom—like America itself—they loved but could not understand. The Great Depression found them with young children to provide for, and they managed by procuring and creating odd jobs. From the safety of New York, they learned that the Nazis had destroyed the world in which they had known as children and everyone they left behind.

Soon, they registered with worry expert predictions that the Jews in Palestine, and later Israel, would be wiped out by the armies of Egypt, Syria, and Iraq. When my grandparents finally moved to Israel themselves after the 1967 victory created the impression that the country was powerful and secure, the place offered retreat from fear and angst.

My grandfather and grandmother died years before I overheard the playful conversation between two students musing that if Saddam Hussein gassed the ultra-Orthodox to death, Israel would be better off. They died years before hatred of the ultra-Orthodox became the trait most widely shared by the rest of us in Israel. They died before the Cameri Theater produced plays about ultra-Orthodox treachery. They died never having been called parasites, bloodsuckers, traitors, lechers, hypocrites, or Nazis.

Had they lived, I think they would have been puzzled by these things. They would not understand how just the sort of hatred that they moved to Israel to escape had somehow reappeared. They would not understand why they, who had devoted their lives to *Yiddishkayt* and raised their children to do the same, came to be considered freeloaders and bad Jews. They would not understand how a century of upheavals, migrations, wars, and death that left nothing in the lives of Jews unchanged, somehow left within the souls of Jews, as a bitter precipitant, precisely the sort of hatred and anger they sought to escape.

And they would not understand why secular Jews in Israel feel so embattled and embittered. To my grandmother, Israel—modern, secular Israel—was a cascade of miracles. On her wall, alongside etchings of great rabbis like Maimonides and the Vilna Gaon, she hung photos of Theodor Herzl and David Ben-Gurion. What these very secular Jews had accomplished, it seemed to her, was no less valuable—indeed no less divine—than anything the great rabbis had ever done. When I told her that I was moving to a kibbutz, she was as proud as if I had gone to a great Talmudic academy, perhaps more. But the sense of shared purpose and grand accomplishment that enchanted my grandmother has now largely evaporated. One of the few values still shared by most secular Jews in Israel is rage aimed at the ultra-Orthodox.

My grandparents did not live to see the self-assurance of secular Israel disintegrate. They did not live to be hated by people whom they loved so deeply, and for this I am relieved. Even in these very troubled times, I sometimes think that this relief saddens me most of all.

Index